THE SOCIAL SUSTAINABILITY OF CITIES: DIVERSITY AND THE MANAGEMENT OF CHANGE

Edited by Mario Polèse and Richard Stren

Cities are a locus of human diversity, where people of varying wealth and status share an association within a particular urban boundary. Despite the common geography, sharp social divisions characterize many cities. High levels of urban violence bear witness to the difficult challenge of creating socially cohesive and inclusive cities. The devastated inner cities of many large American urban centres exemplify the failure of urban development. With an enlightened, democratic approach to policy reform, however, cities can achieve social sustainability.

Some cities have been more successful than others in creating environments conducive to the cohabitation of a diverse population. In this collection of original essays, case studies of ten cities (Montreal and Toronto in Canada, Miami and Baltimore in the United States, Geneva and Rotterdam in Europe, São Paulo and San Salvador in South America, and Nairobi and Cape Town in Africa) are presented and analysed in terms of social sustainability. The volume as a whole looks at the policies, institutions, and planning and social processes that can have the effect of integrating diverse groups and cultural practices in a just and equitable fashion.

The authors conclude that policies conducive to social sustainability should, among other things, seek to promote fiscal equalization, to weave communities within the metropolis into a cohesive whole, and to provide transport systems that ensure equal access to public services and workplaces, all within the framework of an open and democratic local governing structure.

MARIO POLÈSE is a research professor at the Institut National de la Recherche Scientifique–Urbanisation, Université du Québec à Montréal, as well as director of the Montreal Inter-University Group, Cities and Development. He also teaches in urban planning and management programs in Mexico, Central America, and Haiti.

RICHARD STREN is Professor of Political Science at the University of Toronto, and the Director of its Centre for Urban and Community Studies. He has carried out extensive research in Africa, where he also worked as a planner. Most of his current research and teaching involves Latin America.

EDITED BY
MARIO POLÈSE AND RICHARD STREN

The Social Sustainability of Cities

Diversity and the Management of Change

UNIVERSITY OF TORONTO PRESS
Toronto Buffalo London

© University of Toronto Press Incorporated 2000
Toronto Buffalo London
Printed in Canada

ISBN 0-8020-4767-X (cloth)
ISBN 0-8020-8320-X (paper)

Printed on acid-free paper

Canadian Cataloguing in Publication Data

Main entry under title:

The social sustainability of cities : diversity and the management of change

Includes bibliographical references.
ISBN 0-8020-4767-X (bound)   ISBN 0-8020-8320-X (pbk.)

1. Sociology, Urban.   2. Cities and towns – Growth.   I. Polèse, Mario,
1943– .   II. Stren, Richard E.

HT155.S62 2000   307.76   C99-932237-0

University of Toronto Press acknowledges the financial assistance to its
publishing program of the Canada Council for the Arts and the Ontario
Arts Council.

This book was developed with the support and involvement of the
Management of Social Transformations (MOST) Programme of UNESCO.

University of Toronto Press acknowledges the financial support for its publishing activities of the Government of Canada through the Book Publishing
Industry Development Program (BPIDP).

Canadä

Contents

Foreword

HUMANIZING THE CITY:
A VIEW FROM UNESCO'S MOST PROGRAMME

Within its own fields of competence, and especially in the Social and Human Sciences sector, UNESCO's message on urban issues is both moral and intellectual: cities must serve the people who live in them. For UNESCO, the real challenge is to improve the conditions in which urban growth takes place in order to build cities of peace, democracy, and development.

The cities of the twenty-first century must place the citizen at the centre of public policy, reinvent the concept of the city, and realize the many ways of sharing in urban life.

The impact of globalization on urban systems and the strategic role of large cities in the world economy are among the factors now jeopardizing the quality of urban living. There is an urgent need to offset the tendency to subordinate cities to the needs of business and the economy – which are important in their own right – by devising an ethical approach that takes into account the needs of the individual, based on a better balance between men and women, and cities and nature, in which the quality of the environment is primordial and which allows for town-dwellers to make city life a shared experience.

Giving cities a human face is more than a Utopian dream: it can be achieved when the initiatives of the inhabitants, as both users and builders, are encouraged and supported.

Our goal is to implement policies that will awaken the creative capacities of all those – men, women, and young people – who live in cities. We must create the city of the democratic age, in which the ideals of emancipation, equality, freedom, and solidarity can be achieved for everyone.

UNESCO has identified five challenges to be taken up in promoting a city of solidarity and citizenship:

1 To act against intolerance and prevent the development of social apartheid between the 'city of the citizens' and the 'city of the excluded';
2 To affirm solidarity as a fundamental value of democracy and human rights by inventing a city of solidarity, through the encouragement of cultural and social pluralism and the promotion of integration through social policies, particularly employment policies;
3 To promote a culture of peace: democracy was born in cities, and in cities it is most under threat from tensions of all kinds and from the forces of disintegration. It is also in the city that a new social contract must be worked out;
4 Development and peace are intimately linked: with cities increasingly becoming the scene of conflicts, UNESCO is implementing a 'culture of peace' program that includes social-development activities aimed at peace-building, particularly in cities in recovery after a period of conflict;
5 To turn city-dwellers into citizens through education in citizenship: citizens must be given the means to express themselves in public and have an impact on their city. They must be placed at the centre of choices and decisions for the creation of a multifaceted city by measures to promote democratic discussion and participation.

Intellectually, the mission of UNESCO's Social and Human Sciences sector is to contribute to generating and transferring social knowledge to policy-makers and civil society.

For this purpose, the Management of Social Transformations (MOST) Programme was created in 1994 with the goals of (a) improving understanding by generating policy-relevant knowledge on three major issues of our time: managing multi-ethnicity and multiculturalism, city governance, and coping with the impact of globalization; and (b) improving the communication between researchers and decision-makers. The program is overseen by an intergovernmental council and an independent scientific steering committee. A small secretariat coordinates the program from UNESCO Headquarters, and national MOST liaison committees (to date established in thirty-five countries) relate the program to national social-science and policy communities.

The MOST Programme is basically a cooperative framework for the promotion of high-quality, policy-relevant, comparative international social-science research, and national decision making through improved use of social-science knowledge. In a world where many of the social, economic, demographic, environmental, and technological processes have become transnational and global, we believe this to be a useful undertaking.

The particular theme of 'cities as arenas of accelerated social transformations' resulted from various consultations with specialists, as well as regional, thematic, and statutory meetings.[1] The choice of such a theme shows MOST's salient interest in understanding how social transformations affect the city of today and tomorrow.

The research projects selected by MOST have as their goal a comparative and international analysis of some of these changes (such as urban governance, urban social sustainability, and the issues of environment and gender in cities). In the restructuring process of contemporary urban spaces, at stake is not only changes in terms of morphology, terminology, or practices, but also the relationships between such changes and the underlying social, cultural, economic, and political processes.

Understanding social processes that take place in urban centres is a prerequisite for guiding and changing urban development. Based on MOST's goal to produce policy-relevant knowledge and UNESCO's task to cooperate in the implementation of the plan of action of Habitat II, activities in the urban field have focused particularly on social, economic, and political urban governance. This approach is of relevance to decision-makers and stakeholders in the relationships between the state and civil society. It involves the implementation of both 'bottom-up' and 'top-down' strategies to favour active participation of all those concerned in open negotiations, transparent decision-making mechanisms, and the formulation of urban-management policies.

Urban governance and management of urban areas within MOST have branched out into three subareas – namely, scientific research and networking; action-oriented projects on sustainable and integrated urban-development strategies geared towards a participatory approach and the revitalization of inner cities; and training and capacity-building for city professionals.

I am particularly glad that the international project 'Towards Socially Sustainable Cities: Building a Knowledge Base for Urban Management,' which generated this book, has developed within MOST. The project was initially coordinated by Richard Stren, of the Centre for Urban and Community Studies, University of Toronto, and Mario Polèse, of Montreal Inter-University Group (MIG), Cities and Development, and subsequently by Antoine Bailly, of the Faculty of Economic and Social Sciences, University of Geneva. It is one of the best and particularly relevant activities of the MOST Programme. I would like to express my deep gratitude to the above-mentioned coordinators, as well as to all those who participated in the project, and also extend my appreciation to Geneviève Domenach-Chich, Chief of the Cities and Human Habitat Unit, who monitored this project from the MOST side.

Ali Kazancigil
Executive Secretary, MOST Programme
Director, Division of Social Science, Research and Policy, UNESCO

Note

1 Notably the first MOST workshop on the theme 'cities' in Vienna, in 1994, and the 1994 session of the Intergovernmental Committee of MOST. Cf. Céline Sachs-Jeantet 1995.

Reference

Sachs-Jeantet, Céline. 1995. *Managing Social Transformations in Cities: A Challenge to Social Sciences*. MOST Working Document no. 2. Paris: UNESCO.

Acknowledgments

This book is a truly collective endeavour. Numerous institutions and individuals have contributed to its production and to the international research initiative from which it stems. Four consecutive workshops were held during the five-year period separating the birth of the idea in a Viennese coffee house in 1994 and publication by the University of Toronto Press: in Montreal and Toronto, 1995; in Geneva, 1996; in Utrecht, 1997; and in Cape Town, 1998. For their generous help in the organization of these workshops, we are grateful to: the Montreal Inter-University Group (MIG), Cities and Development; the City of Montreal; the Centre for Urban and Community Studies, University of Toronto; the City of Toronto; the Department of Geography, University of Geneva; the University of Utrecht; the Netherlands Graduate School of Housing and Urban Research; and the Cape Metropolitan Council.

The international research project 'Towards Socially Sustainable Cities: Building a Knowledge Base for Urban Management' was made possible by the financial support of many agencies and organizations, among them the MOST Programme of UNESCO, Paris; the Canadian Commission for UNESCO, Ottawa; the Canadian International Development Agency (CIDA); Citizenship and Immigration Canada; le Ministère de l'Immigration et des Communautés Culturelles, Gouvernement du Québec, Montreal; the Social Sciences and Humanities Research Council of Canada (SSHRCC); COST C2, European Cooperation Programme on Large-scale Infrastructure, Urban Form and Quality of Life; DPTE, Canton of Geneva (Department of Public Works); the Swiss Office for Scientific Research (OFES Switzerland); and the Centre for Urban and Community Studies, University of Toronto.

On a more personal level, we wish to thank Elizabeth Barot in

Ottawa, who first opened the door to the UNESCO MOST Programme, and to Ali Kazincigil in Paris for guiding us through. We cannot fail to mention, at UNESCO in Paris, Geneviève Domenach-Chich, who has followed and supported our project through a number of ups and downs. We owe special thanks to two early pioneers of the 'social sustainability' idea: Davinder Lamba, in Nairobi, and Céline Sachs-Jeantet, in Paris.

We wish to thank Philippe Joye, in Geneva, for his warm and enthusiastic support, as well as Richard Anderegg, Antoine Bailly, Philippe Brun, and Pierre Pellegrino. Without Swiss support the project would not have survived. Special thanks go to Frans Dieleman and to Dr B.E. van Vucht Tijssen, in Utrecht. The people in Cape Town to whom we are indebted are too numerous to name; let us simply mention Pierre Uys, Kent Morkel, Stewart Fisher, and François Theunissen, of the Cape Metropolitan Council, and John Abbott, of the University of Cape Town.

Finally, closer to home, we wish to express our gratitude to Claude Chapdelaine and Elena Pou of GIM in Montreal; to Christiane Desmarais of the Service de cartographie, INRS-Urbanisation in Montreal; and last, but definitely not least, to Judith Bell, of the Centre for Urban and Community Studies in Toronto, for her skill, patience, and devotion in the final editing of this volume.

To all of you, and the many we have not named, this book is also yours.

Mario Polèse, Montreal
Richard Stren, Toronto

Notes on Contributors

John Abbott is Professor of Urban Engineering and coordinator of the Urban Management Program at the University of Cape Town, South Africa. In 1984 he was a founder and first chair of Planact, a nongovernmental organization established to support the emerging civic movement in its struggle for urban equality. Since then he has worked on the development of integrated approaches to informal settlement upgrading and community management. He is also closely involved in the development of an urban management framework for Cape Town, and was a member of the commission to determine the powers and duties of the new Metropolitan Authority. His book, *Sharing the City: Community Participation in Urban Management*, was published by Earthscan in 1996.

Antoine S. Bailly is Professor of Geography at the University of Geneva. He has a PhD from Paris Sorbonne (1977) and has taught in universities in Canada, France, and Switzerland. Professor Bailly is the honorary president of the Association de Science Régionale de Langue Française and vice-president of the European Regional Science Association. He is also the president of the Swiss section of the International Geographical Union. He is the author of 30 books and more than 300 papers in economic and urban geography and in regional science.

L.S. Bourne is Professor of Geography and Planning at the University of Toronto, where he has in the past served as the director of the Graduate Planning Program and of the Centre for Urban and Community Studies. For eight years he chaired the Urban Commission of the International Geographical Union. His research interests include comparative analysis of urban systems and policy, new forms of urban development, inner cities, social polarization and spatial inequalities, housing and land markets, migration and immigration, and the monitoring of change in urban Canada. Among his recent publications are *The Changing Social Geography of Canadian Cities* (McGill-Queen's University Press, 1993) and 'Reinventing the Suburbs: New Myths and Old Realities' (*Progress in Planning*, 1996).

Frans M. Dieleman is Professor of Urban and Rural Geography in the Faculty of Geographical Sciences, Utrecht University, The Netherlands. He also serves as the scientific director of the Urban Research Centre, Utrecht (URU). He received his PhD from the Free University of Amsterdam in 1978. His main areas of research interest are residential mobility, housing policy, and Randstad Holland.

Frances Frisken is professor emerita and senior scholar of Urban Studies at York University, Toronto. She has published on metropolitan governance, city and regional planning, urban transit politics and policy-making, the politics of property-tax reform, the role of provincial governments in Canadian urban governance, and Canadian/U.S. differences in urban policy-making. She is also coordinator of the Greater Toronto Area (GTA) Forum, which brings together academics, public officials, urban professionals, and concerned citizens to hear and talk about issues of importance to the development and character of the Toronto metropolitan area.

Gunter Gad is an associate professor of geography at the University of Toronto, at Mississauga. He has long-standing research interests in the development of the inner city, the decentralization of offices, and the geography of employment in large urban areas. His research focuses on Canadian cities, especially Toronto and Montreal. He has PhD degrees from the Universität Erlangen-Nurnberg, in Germany, and the University of Toronto.

Annick Germain is an associate professor at the Institut National de la Recherche Scientifique-Urbanisation, the urban-research institute of the Université du Québec, in Montreal. A sociologist by training, she taught at the University of Montreal before joining the research faculty of INRS. Among her published works are several studies on urban

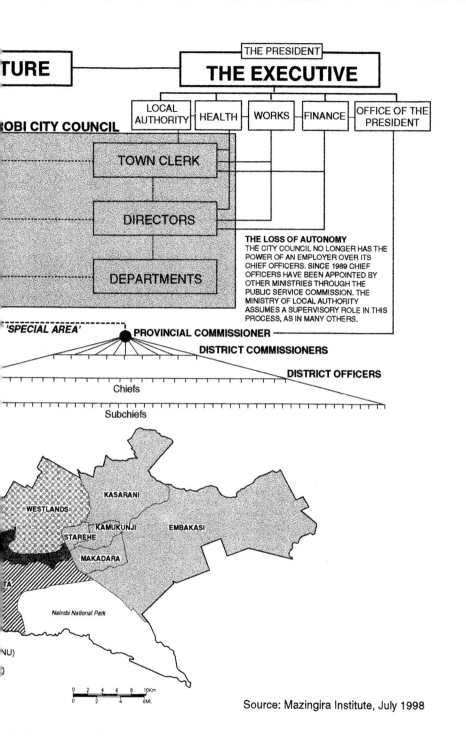

TURE

ROBI CITY COUNCIL

THE PRESIDENT

THE EXECUTIVE

| LOCAL AUTHORITY | HEALTH | WORKS | FINANCE | OFFICE OF THE PRESIDENT |

TOWN CLERK

DIRECTORS

DEPARTMENTS

THE LOSS OF AUTONOMY
THE CITY COUNCIL NO LONGER HAS THE POWER OF AN EMPLOYER OVER ITS CHIEF OFFICERS. SINCE 1989 CHIEF OFFICERS HAVE BEEN APPOINTED BY OTHER MINISTRIES THROUGH THE PUBLIC SERVICE COMMISSION. THE MINISTRY OF LOCAL AUTHORITY ASSUMES A SUPERVISORY ROLE IN THIS PROCESS, AS IN MANY OTHERS.

'SPECIAL AREA'

PROVINCIAL COMMISSIONER

DISTRICT COMMISSIONERS

DISTRICT OFFICERS

Chiefs

Subchiefs

KASARANI

WESTLANDS

KAMUKUNJI   EMBAKASI

STAREHE

MAKADARA

Nairobi National Park

Source: Mazingira Institute, July 1998

al Government Structures?,' on page 270

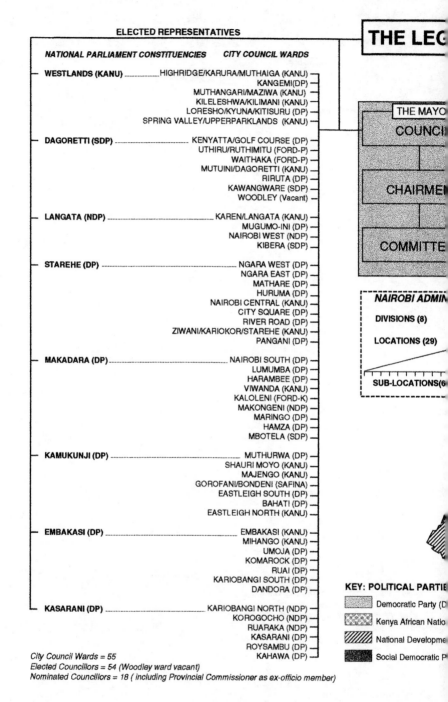

ELECTED REPRESENTATIVES

THE LEG

NATIONAL PARLIAMENT CONSTITUENCIES   *CITY COUNCIL WARDS*

- **WESTLANDS (KANU)** ———— HIGHRIDGE/KARURA/MUTHAIGA (KANU)
  - KANGEMI(DP)
  - MUTHANGARI/MAZIWA (KANU)
  - KILELESHWA/KILIMANI (KANU)
  - LORESHO/KYUNA/KITISURU (DP)
  - SPRING VALLEY/UPPERPARKLANDS (KANU)

- **DAGORETTI (SDP)** ———————— KENYATTA/GOLF COURSE (DP)
  - UTHIRU/RUTHIMITU (FORD-P)
  - WAITHAKA (FORD-P)
  - MUTUINI/DAGORETTI (KANU)
  - RIRUTA (DP)
  - KAWANGWARE (SDP)
  - WOODLEY (Vacant)

- **LANGATA (NDP)** ———————————— KAREN/LANGATA (KANU)
  - MUGUMO-INI (DP)
  - NAIROBI WEST (NDP)
  - KIBERA (SDP)

- **STAREHE (DP)** ———————————— NGARA WEST (DP)
  - NGARA EAST (DP)
  - MATHARE (DP)
  - HURUMA (DP)
  - NAIROBI CENTRAL (KANU)
  - CITY SQUARE (DP)
  - RIVER ROAD (DP)
  - ZIWANI/KARIOKOR/STAREHE (KANU)
  - PANGANI (DP)

- **MAKADARA (DP)** ———————————— NAIROBI SOUTH (DP)
  - LUMUMBA (DP)
  - HARAMBEE (DP)
  - VIWANDA (KANU)
  - KALOLENI (FORD-K)
  - MAKONGENI (NDP)
  - MARINGO (DP)
  - HAMZA (DP)
  - MBOTELA (SDP)

- **KAMUKUNJI (DP)** ———————————— MUTHURWA (DP)
  - SHAURI MOYO (KANU)
  - MAJENGO (KANU)
  - GOROFANI/BONDENI (SAFINA)
  - EASTLEIGH SOUTH (DP)
  - BAHATI (DP)
  - EASTLEIGH NORTH (KANU)

- **EMBAKASI (DP)** ———————————— EMBAKASI (KANU)
  - MIHANGO (KANU)
  - UMOJA (DP)
  - KOMAROCK (DP)
  - RUAI (DP)
  - KARIOBANGI SOUTH (DP)
  - DANDORA (DP)

- **KASARANI (DP)** ———————————— KARIOBANGI NORTH (NDP)
  - KOROGOCHO (NDP)
  - RUARAKA (NDP)
  - KASARANI (DP)
  - ROYSAMBU (DP)
  - KAHAWA (DP)

City Council Wards = 55
Elected Councillors = 54 (Woodley ward vacant)
Nominated Councillors = 18 (including Provincial Commissioner as ex-officio member)

THE MAYO

COUNCI

CHAIRME

COMMITTE

NAIROBI ADMIN

DIVISIONS (8)

LOCATIONS (29)

SUB-LOCATIONS(6

KEY: POLITICAL PARTIE

Democratic Party (D

Kenya African Natio

National Developme

Social Democratic P

Replaces Figure 10.4, 'Who Governs Nairobi: Centr

planning and on Montreal. Her most recent work is on the impact of immigration on the social structure of cities.

Robert C. Kloosterman is Senior Researcher at the OTB Research Institute for Housing, Urban and Mobility Studies at Delft University of Technology in The Netherlands. His research specialization is in the urban economy, urban labour markets, and entrepreneurship. He has published in the *Cambridge Journal of Popular Music, Urban Studies, West European Studies, Regional Studies, New Community, Housing Studies,* the *International Journal of Urban and Regional Research,* and *Area.*

Davinder Lamba is an architect and environmental planner, and the executive director of Mazingira Institute, a Kenyan interdisciplinary research and action non-governmental organization (NGO). A human-rights activist, he is engaged in constitutional and governance reforms in Kenya. He served on the Scientific Steering Committee of UNESCO's MOST Programme and, with Dr Mario Polèse, conceived the Socially Sustainable Cities research initiative. He convened the Training and Research Partners for Habitat Caucus for the Habitat II Conference. He founded the African Research Network on Urban Management (ARNUM) and is the Anglophone Africa representative on the board of Habitat International Coalition (HIC), the global NGO alliance on human settlements.

Diana Lee-Smith is an architect who has lived and worked in Kenya for thirty years. She was one of the founders of Mazingira Institute and also founded Settlements Information Network Africa (SINA) and the Women and Shelter Network of Habitat International Coalition (HIC). Her career spans academic, research, and activist spheres. She has held appointments in five universities in Africa and North America and is a member of the World Conservation Union team, which is developing methods of assessing sustainability. She holds a doctoral degree in Architecture and Development Studies from Lund University in Sweden and has published widely on urban and gender issues.

Marc V. Levine is the founding director of the Center for Economic Development at the University of Wisconsin–Milwaukee, where he teaches in the Department of History and the Urban Studies Program. He is also *professeur invité* at the Université du Québec Institut

National de la Recherche Scientifique–Urbanisation, in Montreal. Levine received his BA, MA, and PhD from the University of Pennsylvania. His research focuses on urban redevelopment, wage polarization and urban labour markets, and tourism as an economic development strategy in the United States and Canada. He has also written extensively on language policy and cultural diversity in cities. Levine is the author or co-author of four books, the most recent of which is *La reconquête de Montréal* (VLB Éditeur, 1997). He is currently completing a book on the history of urban redevelopment, ghetto poverty, and metropolitan restructuring in Baltimore since the 1950s.

Mario Lungo is a Salvadorean urban planner who studied at the Institut d'Urbanisme of the University of Paris. He is now a professor at the Universidad Centroamericana José Simeón Cañas, and the executive director of the Bureau of Planification of the Metropolitan Area of San Salvador. Professor Lungo is in addition a research associate of FLACSO, the Latin American Faculty of Social Sciences, and was the Central America coordinator for the Global Urban Research Initiative, a project coordinated by the Centre for Urban and Community Studies at the University of Toronto.

Robert A. Murdie is Professor of Geography at York University in Toronto. He is also the Housing and Neighbourhood domain leader for the Joint Centre of Excellence for Research on Immigration and Settlement in Toronto. His research interests include the housing experiences of immigrants and refugees in Toronto, the changing social composition of public-sector housing, and housing and immigrant settlement in Swedish metropolitan areas.

Mario Polèse is a research professor at Institut National de la Recherche Scientifique–Urbanisation, Université du Québec, in Montreal, as well as the director of the Montreal Inter-University Group, Cities and Development, designated a Centre of Excellence by the Canadian International Development Agency. He holds a PhD in City and Regional Planning from the University of Pennsylvania. He has published widely in the field of urban and regional development, among his more recent work being *Economie urbaine et régionale* (Economica, 1994), the principal university text in French (also translated into Spanish and Portuguese). He has held many positions as an adviser with the Canadian federal government and the government of Quebec, as well as with international agencies and community groups. Outside Canada he has held teaching and research positions in the United States, Switzerland, and France, and currently teaches in Mexico, Central America, and Haiti.

Anne-Marie Séguin received her PhD in geography from the Université Laval and has been a research professor at Institut National de la Recherche Scientifique–Urbanisation, Université du Québec, in Montreal, since 1990. Her current areas of research interest are poverty and exclusion; employment and housing careers; gentrification; immigrant residential location; and urban policy, particularly housing policy.

Ana Amélia da Silva received her PhD in sociology from the University of São Paulo, Brazil. She teaches at the Catholic University of São Paulo and is a research fellow of the Centre for the Study of Citizenship Rights, an interdisciplinary institution at the University of São Paulo. The centre's research program covers the historical pattern of social and human rights in Brazil, the obstacles to their implementation, and the social spaces in which new democratic innovations emerge. She was, until 1998, a research consultant at Polis Institute, a public-policy NGO in São Paulo.

Jonathan Simon is Professor of Law at the University of Miami. He has also taught at the University of Michigan, New York University, and Yale. Simon received his law degree and a doctoral degree in Jurisprudence and Social Policy from the University of California, at Berkeley. His research deals with the transformation of regulatory and crime-control strategies in advanced liberal societies. He is currently at work on two book projects: one is a study of the explosive growth of the U.S. prison population; the second examines the history of twentieth-century tort law as a window into the changing rationalities behind liberal governance.

Richard Stren is Professor of Political Science at the University of Toronto, and the director of the Centre for Urban and Community Studies. He received his PhD in political science from the University of California, at Berkeley. Over the past thirty years, he has carried out extensive research on African cities, still a major research interest, together with urban politics in the developing world and comparative urban policy and the environment. His major publications include *Housing the*

Urban Poor in Africa; African Cities in Crisis (co-edited with Rodney White) and *Sustainable Cities* (co-edited with Rodney White and Joseph Whitney), and he also edited the four-volume *Urban Research in the Developing World,* the result of the Global Urban Research Initiative, a major international collaborative research project of which he was the coordinator.

THE SOCIAL SUSTAINABILITY OF CITIES

1 Understanding the New Sociocultural Dynamics of Cities: Comparative Urban Policy in a Global Context

RICHARD STREN and MARIO POLÈSE

Of Viennese Coffee Houses, a Bridge in Herzegovina, and the Socio-ethnic Diversity of Cities

The idea of a project dealing with the management of the social and cultural diversity of cities was born in February 1994 in a café in Vienna, following the first Management of Social Transformations (MOST) Programme workshop on the theme of 'cities.' That Vienna should be the birthplace of this project is entirely appropriate, for few cities, certainly few in Europe, better exemplify the essential meaning and challenge of what we call 'social sustainability.' As we shall explain, 'social sustainability' refers to *policies and institutions that have the overall effect of integrating diverse groups and cultural practices in a just and equitable fashion.* This is an important and challenging goal for all cities in the closing days of the twentieth century. Later in this introductory chapter we discuss the more precise meaning of 'social sustainability,' but first we explore some of its historical and analytical antecedents.

The Vienna of the Coffee House

By most measures, *fin de siècle* Vienna was an extraordinary success story; that is, if we define 'success' to mean an urban environment conducive to the compatible cohabitation of culturally and socially diverse groups, while at the same time encouraging social integration. Few cities were more culturally diverse than the old Habsburg capital. Peoples from all corners of the Austro-Hungarian Empire flocked to Vienna: Germans, Czechs, Hungarians, Croats, Italians, Slovenes, Slovaks, Serbs, Poles, not forgetting Jews, Ruthenians, and Romanians from the far-flung eastern provinces of Galicia, Bukovina, and Transylvania. Count Metternich, a powerful Habsburg diplomat of the nineteenth century, is reputed to have once said that 'the Orient begins at the Landstrasse' (a street in eastern Vienna), referring to the traditional role of Vienna as the point of juncture between Catholic (and Protestant) Western Europe, and the Greek Orthodox and Ottoman Muslim East.

Despite this diversity and clash of cultures, or perhaps because of it, Vienna succeeded in developing a definite sense of common identity, of which the extraordinary cultural creativity of its inhabitants (in music, art, and science) during that period is the most visible manifestation. From most accounts, turn-of-the-century Vienna was a relatively safe city, a tolerant city – indeed a very pleasant city to live in – by the standards of the time. The Viennese coffee house, as a social institution, with its relaxed air and seeming openness to all, came to symbolize that era – an era that began to draw to a close at the start of the 1920s.

In our time, it has become fashionable to look back with nostalgia on this urban 'paradise lost,' giving rise to a Vienna-centred literature, of which Stefan Zweig's (1944) work was to be the first of many. In retrospect, Vienna's unique, seemingly inclusive, urban culture showed itself to be very fragile in the face of crisis. This cosmopolitan and tolerant city (or so it appeared outwardly) succumbed with little resistance to the Nazi regime. There is little evidence to show that opposition to racist policies and laws was any greater in Vienna than anywhere else within the German Reich.

Today, half a century later, Vienna faces new challenges, with the disappearance of the Iron Curtain, as it finds itself again a magnet for the populations of Central Europe and Metternich's 'Orient.' If the story of Vienna tells us anything, it is that we are still very far from understanding the underlying mechanisms, both past and present, that make diverse urban societies truly sustainable and inclusive. Outward appearances can be deceiving. It is a field of study that the researcher must approach with humility.

A Bridge (That Was) in Herzegovina

It is also entirely appropriate that this project should fall under the MOST Programme within UNESCO. Although MOST is the acronym for an English designation ('Management of Social Transformations'), 'most' equally means 'bridge' in many Slavic languages. By an unintentional twist of events, by evoking the current fate of the city of Mostar in Bosnia–Herzegovina, MOST again compels us to reflect on the fragility of cities as sustainable social structures. The town of Mostar, for example, takes its name from an old Turkish bridge (*stary* [old] *most*) that for three centuries bound the ethnically diverse parts of the city together. For centuries, Muslims, Catholics (Croats), and Orthodox (Serbs) lived together. The bridge survived both the First and the Second World War. It became a symbol.

Today the old bridge is gone, blown up by one of the belligerent parties in the recent war. The city is now totally segregated: Croats on one side of the river and Muslims on the other, most Serbs having since fled to other parts. If the reader will grant us poetic licence, the ultimate objective of this project may be described as the construction of (durable) urban bridges. Too many bridges have been destroyed in this century. Mostar is not unique. There are many cities in the Eastern Mediterranean that were once multicultural but are now either monocultural (or at least much less heterogeneous) or sharply divided. Alexandria, Istanbul, and Beirut immediately spring to mind. Perhaps there was something in the political philosophy of the old Ottoman Empire (as in the Habsburg Empire) that bred a respect for diversity. But these were national or, rather, imperial policies. The uniqueness of the approach taken in this book – as we are about to explain – lies in the emphasis we place on the role of *local* policies, as distinct from national policies, in creating socially sustainable cities for the future.

A Diverse Tale of Many Cities

This book, and the project that gave rise to it, build on an internationally comparative approach, comprising a diversity of situations. We have chosen ten cities for our study, two each in Canada, the United States, Western Europe, Africa, and Latin America. Let us begin with a few words on the cultural and social attributes of the ten cities that represent our universe for comparison.[1]

Starting with North America, Montreal and Toronto, in Canada, are at the same time very much alike and very different. Both harbour large immigrant populations, but Toronto stands out in having probably the highest proportion of foreign-born residents (approximately 42 per cent) of any major city in the Western world.[2] Few cities in modern times have faced greater challenges with respect to the integration of immigrants into urban life. Montreal, on the other hand, is a unique example of the (largely peaceful) cohabitation of two peoples over two centuries (French and English) within an increasingly diverse population consisting of groups from many other cultural and linguistic origins. Montreal is perhaps the only truly functionally bilingual city among major Western cities.

Turning to the United States, we examine Miami and Baltimore. Miami is today the most concentrated point of urban contact between the Anglo-Saxon and Hispanic worlds, acting also as a major point of entry for other groups (West Indians and Haitians, for example). In terms of its economic functions, specifically as a financial centre, Miami is as much a Latin American and Caribbean city as an American one. Miami comes the closest in the United States to being a functionally bilingual city. Baltimore, on the line between the American 'North' and 'South,' was one of the country's leading port and industrial cities until the 1950s. After that, it lost population to the suburbs (like many other American cities), and began to experience the effects of severe social and political polarization. The most important dimension of this polarization is reflected in a central city that in the late 1990s has a population that is almost two-thirds black, and a suburban region in which 87 per cent of the white population lives. Sustainability in Baltimore is largely a problem of responding simultaneously to central city poverty and decline, and to the overarching problem of race relations.

In Europe, we focus on Geneva, Switzerland, and Rotterdam, Holland. Because of the great diversity of political and administrative traditions, we will discover that European local authorities have approached the challenge of social sustainability in very different ways. Switzerland, most notably Geneva, has continued for decades to act as a magnet for foreigners. The very local and decentralized nature of entry and residence controls makes the Genevan case different from that of other European jurisdictions. Rotterdam has become increasingly cosmopolitan and multiracial in recent years, in part because of the traditional openness of Dutch society, with its long maritime history, but also because of the influx of migrants from former colonial territories, such as Surinam and Indonesia, and from European Union countries as well as from North Africa and the Eastern Mediterranean.

The situation experienced by cities in developing countries is different again, chiefly because of the lack of local resources and rapid rates of urban growth, but also because of the traditional weakness of local government and civil society. In Latin America, where we examine São Paulo and San Salvador, the challenge is not so much one of conflicts arising from cultural and racial diversity (although these are factors, specifically in São Paulo, in our case), but of harsh social inequalities. On average, the poorest 20 per cent of the Brazilian and Central American populations (excluding Costa Rica) receive between 2.1 and 2.7 per cent of national income, compared with 5.7 per cent in Canada and 8.2 per cent in the Netherlands (World Bank 1994, table 30). In sum, income disparities are between two and four times greater in the former than in the latter group of countries. São Paulo, today the largest city in the developing world (with a population estimated at 17.8 million by the end of the century), has for decades been the chief magnet for internal migration in Brazil, throwing together the populations of the more prosperous south and the desperately poor (and more African) northeast. In recent years, following the return to democracy in the country and the new constitution of 1988, São Paulo has been witness to a unique experience in local political reform and urban planning. San Salvador, El Salvador's metropolis, has been overwhelmed by rural migrants in recent years; its population has more than tripled since 1960 and is now well over 1.5 million; that is, larger than that of Vienna, Rotterdam, or Geneva. San Salvador is now at the centre of a difficult healing process, as the country emerges from a long and ugly (and largely class-based) civil war.

In Africa, we have chosen Nairobi and Cape Town. Both are cities with significant divisions of race and class; they also face rapid rates of population growth. Nairobi, not unlike San Salvador, continues to attract rural migrants at an impressive rate, but from a much more culturally and linguistically diverse hinterland, as well as drawing refugees from the strife-torn regions to its north (Ethiopia, Somalia). Nairobi has a largely African population, but with a continuing European community (due to its colonial history and current international status) and an important South Asian (largely citizen) community. Nairobi's rate of growth is even more rapid than that of San Salvador, approximately doubling every ten years. Cape Town, our last city, is a unique story of cultural and racial diversity. First settled by Europeans in the seventeenth century, it has always had a hybrid population: Hollanders, Huguenots, Hottentots, Javanese, Malays, English, Jews, and Africans. One of the consequences of this mix has been the evolution of a new people, the (Cape) Coloured, who, at least until recently, have formed the most numerous group. Like Montreal, it is a bilingual city

(English and Afrikaans), but it will perhaps soon become trilingual (with Xhosa) as the African population grows.

But Cape Town also, in some ways, recalls the story of Vienna. Before the 1950s it, like *fin de siècle* Vienna, had acquired a certain reputation for tolerance and civility, at least within South Africa, despite continuing racial inequality. Yet rather than moving forward to greater equality, Cape Town fell prey, like the rest of South Africa, to apartheid, destroying bridges built over many generations of cohabitation. Civil rights were abolished, neighbourhoods demolished, and substantial populations resettled. Today, after the dimantling of apartheid, the time has come for rebuilding bridges and adding new ones. Perhaps nowhere is it clearer than in post-apartheid Cape Town that those bridges must be local ones, addressing issues of everyday urban life: new zoning, housing, and land-tenure ordinances must be implemented; urban transport systems must be redesigned and job locations reconsidered; new structures of urban governance and metropolitan integration need to be put into place.

Each of these cities represents a challenge (in some cases, many challenges) to social sustainability, but at the same time a particular historical, institutional, and social context within which policies must be developed and carried out. Some of these challenges are global, although interesting patterns of response at the local level are emerging, as we suggest below. By analysing these local responses, we can begin to build the elements of a comparative approach to social sustainability in urban management – an approach that, to date, has not been adequately considered.

Building Inclusive Cities: The Challenge of the Next Century

Cities, by definition, are places where large numbers of people live in close proximity to, and association with, one another. Throughout history, urban populations of vastly differing social, cultural, and ethnic backgrounds have learned to live together, or at least to coexist within a common local economic and institutional system, but with varying degrees of success, as we have noted above. Geographical proximity has been a source both of social stress and of social innovation – the latter is the chief strength of the city, the former its greatest challenge. In his major recent book, *Cities and Civilizations*, Sir Peter Hall argues that, contrary to gloomy predictions of decline, many of the largest cities of the Western world have also served as platforms for the highest levels of innovation and creativity. While 'no one kind of city, nor any one size of city, has a monopoly on creativity or the good life ... the biggest and most cosmopolitan cities, for all their evident disadvantages and obvious problems, have throughout history been the places that ignited the sacred flame of the human intelligence and the human imagination' (Hall 1998, 7).

In the 1990s, in the context of massive global forces that move technology, culture, capital, and labour across national boundaries on an ever-broadening scale, cities are becoming focal arenas of social transformation. Indeed, it is in the world's cities – increasingly home to the majority of the population (the demographers tell us that around the year 2007 half the world's population will be urban) – that many of the major questions and challenges of our civilization are being raised. Perhaps paradoxically, some of the largest and most developed cities are in the throes of the most rapid change. A recent description of Los Angeles stresses the transformative influences of social diversity:

> Most studies of world city formation have emphasized the concentration of global financial control functions. For the exceedingly heterogeneous world city of Los Angeles, this focus must be expanded to include not only the huge industrial base ... but even more emphatically the extraordinarily global labor force, especially in the corona of diverse ethnic communities that surrounds and sustains the downtown financial, commercial, and government complex. This inner ring is the heartland of the Los Angeles Cosmopolis, a special type of world city where the very nature of urban cosmopolitanism, glocalization, and modern world cityness is currently being redefined. (Soja 1996, 443)

Many social scientists have observed that, even as cities develop, and as differences widen among regional urban systems, the degree of social inequality, cultural conflict, and political fragmentation experienced within urban boundaries has increased, and even sharpened, over the last decade or more. These discontinuities are related to many factors, but among the most powerful of these must be the combination of increasing international migration, public-sector cutbacks, and labour-market restructuring arising from technological change and international economic integration. In the developed world, cities face massive social, demographic, and lifestyle changes as well as ethnic transformation through immigration. While some cities in developing regions become poorer – and more insecure – many of their most able and best-trained citizens leave for distant shores. Once they arrive in the north, however, new immigrants often must cope with adaptation to new cultural realities; to local populations with varying levels of tolerance for newcomers under uncertain economic conditions; and to increasing feelings of anxiety over crime, unemployment, and disease.

Even in cities in the developing world that are not receiving international migrants, pressures of population growth, internal migration, and sometimes economic development, exceed the ability of urban managers to supply adequate infrastructure and public services in order to keep the urban economy functioning efficiently. The failure of public management at the city level not only leads to the privatization of many public services (such as water supply, waste management, education, and health), but also contributes to the consolidation of spatial and ethnic communities to resist deterioration, to respond to discrimination while preserving cultures and languages, and to cope with a more fragmented local environment. The struggle to survive – felt most intensely by the poorest and most disadvantaged of the urban populations in both the north and the south – is a result of both heightened environmental hazards and more desperate living conditions; but this struggle also contributes to further environmental degradation.

At the same time as these challenges are being faced, many new, and even hopeful, patterns are emerging. For example, international migration has made some cities in the northern hemisphere measurably more vibrant culturally, while at the same time infusing their stagnant economies with new sources of both investment capital and entrepreneurial talent. The cases of Montreal, Miami, and Toronto, cited above, are certainly examples of this. And for many cities in the south, the burgeoning of the informal sector has led to a revitalization of the popular economy; the reinforcement of social networks that provide a haven for those who are otherwise left behind by formal, bureaucratic structures of government and employment; and a source of new initiatives in housing, urban planning, food distribution, transport, and the production and sale of consumer goods. São Paulo and San Salvador would certainly fall into this category.

The emergence of this social economy coincides with a powerful drive in many countries of Africa, Asia, and Latin America, and even in industrialized nations, to restructure and democratize local government, and to wrest control of local urban communities away from national political forces that limit urban political activity.[3] Along with these trends – expressed in popular social movements, new cultural forms, and an enhanced awareness of the importance of gender in everyday life – innovative approaches to urban management are developing. These approaches are at once more broadly consultative and inclusive than was the case in the past, in both the north and many southern regions, and beginning to pay more attention to the social, cultural, and institutional realities that give deeper meaning to urban life. Important examples of these approaches featured in the chapters that follow include the setting up of a National Low-Cost Housing Fund in Brazil as a result of pressures from non-governmental organizations (NGOs), human rights groups, and a wide variety of citizen housing movements; the emergence in Nairobi, Kenya, of the Nairobi Action Plan, promulgated by the popularly organized Nairobi City Convention in 1993; and the reorganizing of the local government system in South Africa to incorporate formerly white municipalities and non-white townships within the same democratically elected councils. In northern cities such as Toronto, Rotterdam, and Montreal, there are continuous attempts to reorganize metropolitan government in order to reduce the differences between more advantaged and less advantaged areas, and in order to incorporate, within a common institutional and local policy framework, newly developing and fringe areas of the larger urban region.

A New Approach to Local Policy Analysis

The manner in which the modern city is organized and managed as a social entity is both a response to local circumstances and a statement – often to be understood in a national context – of important objectives on behalf of the society as a whole. Understanding these patterns and their variations across cultures and regions can reveal a great deal about the strengths and weaknesses of particular cities, but also about the larger society in which cities are placed. In an increasingly internationalizing (some would say 'globalizing') world, large cities play a crucial role, whether they are 'global cities' (such as Tokyo, London, and New York),[4] 'megacities' (Gilbert 1996),[5] or 'world cities' – a term made popular by John Friedmann.[6] The World Bank (1991, 14) holds that, in general, cities 'are the locus of productive economic activities and hope for the future.' For Jordi Borja and Manuel Castells (1997, 90), cities are the 'protagonists of our epoch,' taking an increasingly prominent and active role in politics, economics, the media, and cultural life. They then go farther, arguing that the management of ethnic and cultural diversity is one of the central functions of large cities today: 'our societies, in all latitudes, are and will be multicultural, and the cities (especially the large cities) are the places in which the greatest diversity is concentrated. Learning to live with this situation, succeeding in managing cultural exchange on the basis of ethnic difference and remedying the inequalities arising from discrimination are essential aspects of the new local policy in the conditions arising out of the new global interdependence' (1997, 89).

Few studies have looked comparatively at the range of local policies and political choices available to large cities in our globalizing world. Fewer still have attempted – again, comparatively – to sketch out the structural basis of local policies in relation to the challenge of cultural and ethnic diversity. But some recent comparative analysis has begun to lay the groundwork for a more systematic approach to local policy. Thus, an important recent book edited by Nigel Harris and Ida Fabricius (1996) looks at the effects of structural adjustment on eleven cities in the north and the south. On the one hand, as Harris argues, cities in both the north and the south have reacted to structural adjustment and the ensuing 'package' of macro-economic reforms (privatization, downsizing of the public sector, loosening of regulations, freeing of exchange rates) by taking a more active role in thinking about their future; creating new public/private coalitions; developing plans for the improvement of modern urban infrastructure; and promoting themselves internationally through conventions, sports, and cultural events (Harris 1996). On the other hand, one of the synthesis chapters in the same book points out that the comparison does not yield easy conclusions:

Although there have been many attempts to identify good practice by city governments, and by public–private partnerships, in confronting the problems that result from economic structural adjustment, the transfer of policies from one context to another is a process with some dangers. Differing resource levels, political and administrative structures, and even geographical locations may mean that an approach or a policy successful in one city may be less successful, or just infeasible, elsewhere. Although the problems of cities undergoing structural adjustment may be easy to identify and fairly ubiquitous – a decline in manufacturing, rising unemployment, inner-city decay and dereliction in industrial and port areas, and strong negative social effects – a single policy prescription is unlikely to meet the needs of all, or even most cities. (Lever 1996, 93)

The response of cities to structural adjustment reflects, at a broader level, the response of cities to global economic forces. Here, there is a burgeoning literature. One important stream of work looks at the way cities have organized themselves and designed local policies in the context of globalization and economic restructuring processes. For some writers, this is a 'new localism,' in the context of which cities all over the world organize themselves politically to opt for certain solutions to the challenges of attracting new investment and employment creation. One important premise of this approach is that – far from losing their importance to national or supranational entities – cities have become crucial decision-making agents in a more complex, interdependent system.

Advising cities on how they can 'cope' with global challenges has become a growth industry. In her widely read book *World Class*, Rosabeth Moss Kanter (a former editor of the *Harvard Business Review*) explores the responses of local governments in partnership with business since the 1980s (Kanter 1995). Based on impressive research in five major urban areas of the United States (Seattle, Miami, Cleveland, Boston, and Greenville/Spartanburg in South Carolina), she argues that cities that are successful in meeting global challenges (i.e., those that are 'world class') must excel in at least one of three main roles: as 'thinkers' (developers of concepts and ideas), as 'makers' (manufacturers or producers), or as 'traders' (making connections between cultures and countries). Institutions, political coalitions, and local infrastructure must be organized to reflect the best way of achieving the optimal approach.

In a recent comparative study – in this case, of fifteen medium-sized American cities – Susan Clarke and Gary Gaile (1998) take a closer and 'more nuanced' look at the urban response to global economic restructuring. Their findings stress the new reality of the local-policy context as it has been differentially shaped by a variety of external and internal forces. Taking their cue from Robert Reich (1991), whose book *The Work of Nations* shows how nations must change their policy agenda in the face of a new global capitalism, Clarke and Gaile argue that the 'work of cities' must also change. Not only will decision-making power shift from national arenas to both supranational and local/regional arenas, but the successful communities will be those that are able to 'reinvent local citizenship' through policies which value and reward education and training, at the same time mitigating social polarization and segregation. But in this enabling – and also risky – environment, cities will choose contextually specific paths, 'in part because their constitutional, economic, and social features vary, but also in response to political configurations at the local level. [Thus] there is no "silver bullet" promising successful local adaptation to a global era' (Clarke and Gaile 1998, 8). But if no single solution can apply to all cities, then more comparative knowledge about the key factors that make urban policies successful or unsuccessful – within both specific and generalizable contexts – is urgently required by the international social-science community.

Until now, much social theory dealing with major issues of social and economic change has tended to remain at a macro-level, often ageographic and aspatial. But as Clarke and Gaile and other writers have begun to realize in recent years, people live in real places. And as Henri Lefebvre has maintained, local places connect with society: 'Space is permeated with social relations; it is not only supported by social relations, but it is also producing and produced by social relations.'[7] Policy analysis has equally all too often ignored the day-to-day realities of territorially based management issues. Yet, the capacity of urban environments to be 'inclusive,' and to promote social sustainability, will to a significant degree depend on such seemingly prosaic matters as the design of streets, the removal of garbage, the pricing of public transport, the adequate registration of property rights, the location of employment nodes, the management of school districts, as is pointed out in the case of post-apartheid Cape Town. These policies work with, and through, social structures and institutions. Our emphasis must be on *local* policies and on *local* institutions, even though the broader forces conditioning the dynamic of urban change incorporate complex elements from larger and more inclusive systems. In the case-study chapters that follow, we have concentrated on a number of specific policy areas, each of which has a particular institutional expression in the cities chosen. As these institutions – and the local policies that function through and around them – interact with territorial factors, we can begin to understand some of the major elements of urban social sustainability. But what, precisely, do we mean by social sustainability?

Analysing the Social Sustainability of Cities

Since the publication of *Our Common Future*, the Brundtland Report on Environment and Development in 1987, the idea of 'sustainable development' has become a widely accepted objective of countries in both the north and the south. In *Our Common Future*, sustainable development was defined as 'development that meets the needs of the present without compromising the ability of future generations to meet their own needs' (World Commission on Environment and Development 1987, 43). Behind this apparently ambivalent terminology was a major conflict: between environmentalists concerned to safeguard the biosphere, and proponents of economic growth concerned to increase and expand production. A considerable literature has accumulated since the late 1980s, dealing with approaches to the sustainable development of countries and sectors – including cities.[8] But with a sharper focus on the global context of cities that is characteristic of the late 1990s, an additional factor has entered the discussion: the social geography of cities, and the relation of this social geography to the matrix of factors that serve as prerequisites to, and policy reflections of, sustainable development in relation to the natural environment.

The connection between social factors and the environment is particularly clear in the development discourse. Thus, the approach of many southern countries to the urban environmental challenge forms part of what is often called the 'brown agenda' – meaning that, in poor countries, environmental considerations cannot be approached solely through such 'green' concerns as biodiversity, the protection of the ozone layer, and the creation of wildlife and forest preserves, but must first be channelled through far-reaching programs to reduce poverty – in particular, urban poverty. This means urban infrastructure, education, and improved health programs for the urban poor as a bare minimum. But programs to improve the life chances of the urban poor and other disadvantaged groups must be premised on their effective incorporation into the body politic, and on the validation of their social and cultural institutions as well. Without social policy, there can be no effective environmental policy.

The same argument can be made for cities in the north, where it has been shown[9] that the poor, and the socially and culturally marginal, live under conditions most at risk for environmental hazards. To be environmentally sustainable, cities must also be socially sustainable. We can therefore state our central premise in the following way: For the management of a city to be successful (all other factors being equal), its policies need to be conducive to 'social sustainability.' Social sustainability for a city is defined as *development (and/or growth) that is compatible with the harmonious evolution of civil society, fostering an environment conducive to the compatible cohabitation of culturally and socially diverse groups while at the same time encouraging social integration, with improvements in the quality of life for* all *segments of the population.*

Social sustainability is strongly reflected in the degree to which ine-qualities and social discontinuity are reduced. And, as international research has revealed, not only do socially sustainable policies reduce urban decay and violence, but they may also serve to distinguish between cities that can effectively respond to globalizing trends and those that cannot.

To achieve social sustainability, cities must reduce both the level of exclusion of marginal and/or disadvantaged groups, and the degree of social and spatial fragmentation that both encourages and reflects this exclusionary pattern. Social sustainability, in this respect, may be seen as the polar opposite of exclusion, both in territorial and social terms. *Urban policies conducive to social sustainability must, among other things, seek to bring people together, to weave the various parts of the city into a cohesive whole, and to increase accessibility (spatial and otherwise) to public services and employment, within the framework, ideally, of a local governance structure which is democratic, efficient, and equitable.* This is all about building durable urban 'bridges,' as we have said, capable of standing the test of time. In the following section, we discuss six policy areas that are central to the ability of cities to deal effectively and equitably with social and cultural diversity.

Six Policy Areas: The Institutional–Territorial Nexus

To understand social sustainability in a comparative framework, we have chosen to examine six major policy areas that are normally (at least in part) the responsibility of local levels of government dealing with large or medium-size cities. These policy areas (governance, social and cultural policy, infrastructure and public services, urban land and housing, urban transport, and employment and economic revitalization) cover the major functions of most local goverments: representation and the maintenance of order, social support, the operation of infrastructure and public services, land regulation and development, and the encouragement of local economic development. The specificity of our approach lies not so much with the choice of particular policy areas – which are fairly classic in urban studies because they incorporate most of what local governments generally do – but with our attempt to link them to social sustainability. Our basic working hypothesis is that *the social sustainability of cities is affected not only by nationwide aspatial policies (social legislation, fiscal policy, immigration laws, and the like) but also, if not chiefly, by policy decisions and implementation at the local level, often in sectors which a priori appear to be relatively banal and prosaic.* Local affairs *do* matter.

1. Governance

The governance of cities and local communities has become a major issue over the last decade. By 'governance' we mean the relationship between governments and state agencies, on the one hand; and communities and social groups, on the other. 'Governance' is thus a broader and more inclusive term than 'government,' just as 'local governance' is a more inclusive term than 'local government,' in that it encompasses the activities of a range of groups – political, social, and governmental – as well as their interrelationships. 'Local governance' thus subsumes the operations of local governments, their relationships with the societies within which they operate, and even the technical area of 'urban management,' the term that has come to connote the actual management of local government services and infrastructure.

The emergence of 'local governance' as a key issue in the discussion of policies for human settlements over the last decade may be ascribed to four major factors:

- the elaboration and implementation of a policy of decentralization by many formerly centralized countries;
- the breaking down of one-party states, and governmental systems, that were in the hands of military groups, toward a system of democratic elections at both the national and the local levels;
- the increased importance of urban social movements, combined with the growth of a worldwide environmental movement that has produced a tendency to place greater emphasis on local control and involvement in decisions having to do with land use and industrial emissions;
- the emergence of local 'policy communities,' or networks of governmental officials, representatives of groups in civil society, researchers, and other experts in local questions, which tend to coalesce in response to problems in local communities.

It should be understood that these trends have had an impact on cities in both the north and the south. The trends have interacted with each other as well. In the case of decentralization, for example, probably the most important single factor influencing the devolution of power and administrative authority to cities in francophone African countries was the French initiative to decentralize from the national to the departmental level, beginning with the law of 2 March 1982. According to observers, this legal decentralization has now become part of the French political 'game,' and thus has been incorporated into its political culture.[10] Local elections in French departments and communes are much more important now than they were two decades ago. This sea change has had a profound effect on municipal policy in francophone countries outside France, although other factors – such as the movement towards democratic, multiparty government, and the influence of donor agencies – have played a role as well. In any case, decentralization is 'currently a worldwide phenomenon' (Prud'homme 1989, 71) to be found in northern countries (such as France, Italy, and Denmark) as well as in many southern countries (such as Brazil and the Philippines).

There is a lively, ongoing discussion about the proper meaning of the term 'governance.' As we have stated above, we would prefer to understand the concept as a relationship, rather than as a variable. Many commentators have escaped from the neutrality of such a definition to focus on what they call 'good governance.' While we must be careful not to reproduce in such a value-laden concept all the sociocultural and institutional prerequisites of government in northern countries, the notion of 'good governance' carries with it a premise of institutional design that is at once open and accountable to civil society in general, and effective in terms of financial management and policy implementation. Good governance involves an effective balance between the raising of revenue and the proper expenditure of this revenue on services and investments that are based on accountable decisions. This model, in turn, implies that many levels of government, and many local stakeholders and social groups, will be involved. Thus, questions of governance raise numerous issues on the impact of different local government structures, on urban finance, on local–central relations, on the relative access of different groups to the decision-making process, and on generalized attitudes to government performance. To the extent that groups are openly brought into this process, experience suggests that local environmental issues can more effectively be addressed, and the urban political system can more effectively deal with sensitive issues such as race relations, and the role of the state in relation to the poor. 'Good governance' may also lay the groundwork for creative intellectual activity, a prerequisite for managing large cities in the late twentieth century.

Three of the case studies in the book specifically address questions of governance, although most of the cases at least implicitly deal with some aspects of the relationship between local government and civil society. In the Miami case study, for example, we are presented with an intriguing argument: in a city where the control over local criminal activities has become a key issue in electoral politics (because of the implications of violent crime for the city's position as a trading, investment, and tourist centre), Jonathan Simon suggests, local officials have labelled certain groups (especially the low-income black population) as being prone to violence and crime, and effectively governed in punitive terms rather than through measures of constructive social policy. This approach to governance responds to real problems of bringing about the effective integration of vastly disparate socio-economic groups within a neo-conservative ideological framework, but, as the author argues, the dangers include disenfranchising and alienating large numbers of minority citizens, the creation of 'gated communities' that ignore the laws of the larger municipal authorities, and the generation of 'a large and more powerful managerial apparatus which threatens to limit individual rights and the free and open access to public spaces long deemed essential to the reproduction of democratic will.'

The case of Toronto, Canada's largest and commercially most important city, is in some important respects a mirror image of the Miami situation as described here. While it has a large immigrant population, Toronto has a very low crime rate (at least as compared with American cities of similar size) and has achieved a good residential and occupational level of integration for its major groups. While some difficulties have occurred (for example, in the ineffective integration of some recent refugee groups), overall the governance system has worked to disperse major ethnic and cultural groups around the city, and to provide opportunities for them to take part in the economic prosperity of the larger metropolitan area. As Frances Frisken, L.S. Bourne, Gunter Gad, and Robert Murdie argue, some of this is a result of public policies: for example, the promotion of mixed-income public housing in dispersed areas around the city; and the support for an extensive, one-fare public transit system that links the suburbs with the downtown core. But another major structural condition for success has been the continued economic and social vitality of the downtown core, a factor attributable at least as much to historical patterns of immigration (largely in the hands of the national government) as to the prescient policies of the local government.

The success of Toronto, a relatively wealthy northern city, in dealing with social diversity underlines the importance of two major factors: a relatively buoyant economy, and an open, transparent system of governance that has been able to respond to the needs of a constantly changing society. Nairobi, Kenya's capital city, illustrates a very different and less successful adaptation to social change. In the first place, Nairobi is located in one of Africa's (and the world's) poorest countries. In spite of its having the highest level of industrial and commercial development in Kenya, the overall resources which the Nairobi City Council can mobilize on a per-capita basis for services and infrastructure are very limited, by international standards. But a socially diverse, and increasingly politically conscious population has begun both to resist government restrictions against informal housing, commerce, and agriculture, and to demand higher levels of service and accountability at the local and national levels. As Diana Lee-Smith and Davinder Lamba show, the city will remain deadlocked politically so long as the locally elected city councillors are severely limited by the controls exercised by the central government. Political controls are also in place to limit the activities of residents in informal slum areas, citizens' groups, and NGOs. But as Nairobi lives through what the authors see as a 'social transformation,' the pressures on the governing regime, and on the institutional structure, to respond to new realities are intense.

2. Social and Cultural Policies

If 'governance' refers to the relationship between civil society and formal institutions of government, we must equally pay attention to the nature of social organization that makes this relationship possible. In his now-classic study of territorial decentralization in Italy, the political scientist Robert Putnam (1993) places considerable emphasis on the prerequisite of what he calls 'social capital.' In Putnam's usage, social capital refers to 'features of social organization, such as trust, norms, and networks, that can improve the efficiency of society by facilitating coordinated actions' (p. 167). As have others, Putnam is able to show that territorial decentralization operates best in regions of Italy where there is a long tradition of social trust and organization; by contrast, regions that have a weak tradition of social cooperation cannot easily manage their own affairs. Subsequently, and using the same logic, Putnam (1995) has argued that a decline in civic engagement in the United States may very well be associated with a parallel decline in participation in a wide range of associational activities, due at least in part to the advent of television. The same line of argument is subtly deployed by the late Christopher Lasch (1996), who suggests that American democracy is being undermined by the behaviour and value of its elites. While Lasch's larger argument is complex, one important element in his analysis is the decline of 'institutions that promote general conversation across class lines.' But, he continues,

> civic life requires settings in which people meet as equals, without regard to race, class, or national origins. Thanks to the decay of civic institutions ranging from political parties to public parks and informal meeting places, conversation has become almost as specialized as the production of knowledge. Social classes speak to themselves in a dialect of their own, inaccessible to outsiders; they mingle with each other only on ceremonial occasions and official holidays. Parades and other such spectacles do not make up for the absence of informal gatherings. Even the pub and the coffee shop, which at first appear to have nothing to do with politics or the civic arts, make their contribution to the kind of wide-ranging, freewheeling conversation on which democracy thrives, and now even they are threatened with extinction as neighborhood hangouts give way to shopping malls, fast-food chains, and takeouts. Our approach to eating and drinking is less and less mixed with ritual and ceremony. It has become strictly functional: We eat and drink on the run. Our fast-paced habits leave neither time nor – more important – places for good talk, even in cities the whole point of which, it might be argued, is to promote it. (Lasch 1996, 117–18)

In a wide-ranging study, Francis Fukuyama (1995) argues that the decline of social capital in the contemporary United States is a serious disadvantage to that country in an age of competitive international capitalism. In general, social capital and whether or not it is actually a diminishing asset in the United States is a subject of lively scholarly contestation.[11]

Whatever one concludes about the viability and political importance of close social ties, it is at least an arguable proposition that government policy can either strengthen or undermine the ability of cities and local communities to accumulate social capital. The sustainability of cities and the quality of life they provide for all their citizens are shaped not only by the quality and distribution of 'hard' public services (such as water, sanitation, roads, and transport), but by policies that address social activities. These social activities, by the very nature of modern life, are often undergirded by cultural institutions that give support both at the level of individual ethnic and regional groups (for example, language training for immigrants, support for ethnic language training after hours in public schools, employment counselling to those seeking work in a new country for the first time), and at the level of the whole urban community. Support (or lack of support) for theatres, symphony orchestras, museums and art galleries, ballet companies, exhibitions of local artists, and community cultural centres may play an important role both in creating a sense of urban pride and common purpose, and in attracting, and keeping, the kinds of highly paid international professionals that accompany the development of large-scale financial institutions which are emerging in the global economy.[12]

Support for cultural institutions, and the diverse impact these institutions may have on various ethnic and immigrant groups in the community, may also translate into commercial advantage. Every summer for twenty-eight years, for example, the city of Toronto has played host to a major festival known as Caribana – involving an organized parade of elaborate Caribbean floats and costumes, accompanied by other festivities such as displays of dances, a picnic, and musical shows – that attracts hundreds of thousands of tourists to the city from all around eastern North America. A survey in 1990 showed that 55 per cent of those attending the festival came from outside the city of Toronto (Decima Research 1991, 10). Over the last several years, the average number of people watching the parade has been estimated at 1.2 million. Another cultural festival that attracts tourists and many local people is a 'caravan' held over a nine-day period in June, at which more than thirty different ethnic groups prominently represented in the city offer food, crafts and visual displays, and entertainment to guests in some forty 'pavilions' scattered throughout the city. Overall, the Toronto Convention and Visitors' Association estimates that there are at least 153 yearly 'multicultural events' taking place throughout the city.[13] These kinds of events not only tend to validate the cultural legitimacy of a wide variety of different groups in a polyglot city, but add density to the texture of local economic activity as well.

3. Social Infrastructure and Public Services

Social infrastructure (such as crèches, schools, hospitals and clinics, and community centres) and public services (such as water, telecommunications, public transport, and electricity) are extremely important in the day-to-day operation of urban communities. First, the proper functioning of these services has an economic impact – good services and infrastructure attract investment, and poor or decaying infrastructure and badly functioning services result in costs to existing businesses. A classic study of Nigerian infrastructure by Kyu Sik Lee and Alex Anas (1989) shows how unreliable services and infrastructure impose high costs on manufacturers. For example, the authors point out, 'virtually every manufacturing firm in Lagos has its own electric power generator to cope with the unreliable public power supply. These firms invest 10 to 35 percent of their capital in power generation alone and incur additional capital and operating expenses to substitute for other unreliable public services' (Lee and Anas 1989, quoted in World Bank 1991, 38). In Nigeria and many other low-income countries, manufacturers' high costs of operation prevent innovation and adoption of new technology and make it difficult for them to compete in international markets (World Bank 1991, 38).

But, second, aside from the obvious economic costs of poor services and infrastructure, there is also the problem of relative access by different economic and social groups. In many developing countries, the poorest and most recently arrived migrants live on the outskirts of the large cities, where infrastructure (such as water, paved streets, electrical supply) is minimal or absent, and where access to public transport and such social infrastructure as hospitals and schools is extremely limited. Municipalities facing this gap in the provision of services and infrastructure must now face the severe problem of finance, in that the poor, peripheral areas rarely generate the local tax resources, or the fees for service, that would sustain a major program of infrastructural investment. The problem often becomes more severe with the tendency throughout the world towards privatization of public services. In the end, those who most need the services are least able to pay for them.

The case of Montreal offers an interesting illustration of possible ways by which government – in this case national, provincial, as well as local government – policies have (albeit not always intentionally) diffused the connection between poverty and ethnic concentration. As Anne-Marie Séguin and Annick Germain explain in chapter 2, new forms of poverty are very much present in the city, particularly in the central areas of the urban agglomeration. But, that the characteristics of poverty have not attached themselves primarily, or even noticeably, to one group rather than another in a city in which immigration from outside the country has created an overlay to the continuing contestation between French and Anglo-Saxon cultural choice, is – as economists would say – a non-trivial accomplishment. As the authors suggest, two aspects of neighbourhood life seem to explain the extensive interethnic mixing that is a hallmark of the lively quality of urban existence in Montreal: a strong associational life by ethnic communities, and a well-placed (and well-used) network of public spaces (including metro stations, parks, and commercial centres). While national and provincial governments have contributed – through support for health and educational facilities – to the evening-out of opportunities for the rich and poor, local policies have supported the construction of an excellent public transit system (by North American standards), the dispersion of low-cost public housing, and the reinvestment in central-city housing – often in poor areas – by contractors who have built for the middle-income market. A particular form of housing common in the central area of Montreal, known as the 'plex,' keeps resident landlords in place while providing one or two floors of rental accommodation for tenants who are often newcomers or immigrants. But whether Montreal can continue to be a socially sustainable city is a question that the authors leave open.

In South Africa, the particular problem of the 'dual city' – by which wealthy, well-endowed formerly 'white' municipalities must somehow work together with poor, formerly non-white townships almost totally bereft of services and infrastructure – will demand both sacrifice and forbearance if post-apartheid municipalities are to function effectively. In his discussion of Cape Town, John Abbott addresses this problem squarely. While the city has gone through the necessary political reforms by bringing formerly rich and poor municipalities into the same political system, and achieving a sensible balance between metropolitan and local-government functions, Abbott questions whether the current development focus of the metropolitan government will be sufficient to overcome past inequities. Examining the cases of master planning, transport planning, and housing, Abbott argues that the city has a long way to go. Like many other cities in Southern Africa, Cape Town has a strong tradition of physical planning; but in order to advance goals of social integration, a more sensitive approach to such issues as informal employment, and a more direct and thorough understanding of social problems must be achieved.

An additional complicating factor relates to gender. Studies are beginning to show that, during the period of structural adjustment and the current period of economic stagnation in many countries, those most affected have been poor women. While more women are working in the informal sector, their real wages have declined, and they are much more vulnerable than before.[14] Policies undertaken by municipalities need to add gender sensitivity to a sensitivity to the social and cultural needs of poor migrant groups, all within an economic framework in which resources at the centre are shrinking, and resources at the local level are very restricted.

4. Urban Land and Housing

Control over patterns of land and housing is a central function of urban-based management systems almost everywhere in the world. The manner in which housing and land markets function is a very important determinant of the capacity of households to choose where to live, and therefore of their ability to build up tangible future assets and make a commitment to the urban area in question. Successful policies in this field will have a strong relationship with the integration of immigrant groups into city life, with the development of a viable approach for environmental sustainability, and with the maintenance of viable neighbourhood life. Decreasing public funds in many nations have made it more difficult to implement public strategies for dealing with social exclusion in housing. Comparative research will, in part, aim at investigating the success (or lack of it) of local authorities in devising strategies for combating (or, on the contrary, contributing to) housing segregation and poverty.

One rather positive experience with housing policy is related in the chapter on São Paulo, Brazil. Tracing Brazil's experience with economic development during the aborted 'miracle' years under the military, Ana Amélia da Silva chronicles the extremes of wealth and poverty that characterize the country's largest city. Reflecting the high levels of precariousness within which many must exist, the city includes a huge homeless population, experiences (at least in the poorest areas) very high levels of violence and criminality, and cannot guarantee to large numbers of its citizens the most minimal access to education and health facilities. But emerging from the late 1980s, and from the movement towards democracy ushered in by the 1988 constitution, a new party – the Workers' Party – was elected to govern in the period from 1989 to 1992. The new mayor, Luiza Erundina, faced many challenges and conflicts, none more serious than conflicts over land and the housing. By promoting a housing policy that focused on developing collective responsibility on the part of the low-income communities for the land and the housing being built for them, the government succeeded in creating 40,000 low-income units by the end of its short term in office. The policy remained contentious during the life of the Erundina administration, so that, when a new political regime came to power in 1992, the earlier policy was discontinued in favour of investment in infrastructure projects such as new highways, tunnels, and high-rise apartments. Although the author is critical of the post-Erundina administration, she argues that the democratic reforms that swept Brazil by the early 1990s at least offered the possibility of creating 'a public space where the rights to citizenship can be extended to those situated on the "borders" of Brazilian society.'

Land-tenure and zoning ordinances are of crucial importance in understanding the underlying territorial mechanisms that create exclusion. Apartheid Cape Town is an extreme example of enforced (policy-driven) exclusion. Exclusion (i.e., of non-whites from the central areas) was largely achieved via strictly enforced zoning by-laws that determined who could live where and land-tenure regulations that defined who could own land in which areas. This is indeed an extreme case, although the cities of the U.S. South, including Baltimore and Miami, have similar histories, the exclusionary effects of which are still visible today, as in Cape Town. In more (apparently) liberal and modern societies, the exclusion (of supposedly undesirable groups) is often achieved through the subtle use of zoning by-laws and building regulations. If regulations are such, for example, for land-frontage (greenspace) requirements and use of building materials, that only the well-off are able to build on the land, then the de facto impact is to exclude lower-income families. These kinds of practices are all too prevalent in U.S. cities and are in turn linked to the issue of municipal autonomy.

The issue of *land* tenure (as opposed to housing per se) is especially crucial in developing cities. The vicious cycle of poverty and exclusion may in large part be understood in terms of the relative security (or rather, insecurity) of access to urban land. Simplified somewhat, the process may be summarized as follows. First, ownership of land on the urban fringe is ill defined with no clear property rights or with overlapping property rights. This is often a reflection of the incapacity of local government, in the face of rapid rural in-migration, to provide available land for urbanization at a sufficiently rapid pace. The results are all too evident in the outskirts of cities such as Nairobi and San Salvador, but also Cape Town and São Paulo. Because, in turn, tenure is insecure, the tenants, often living in makeshift housing, are open to political blackmail. Indeed, keeping tenure insecure is often an indirect means of exercising control over politically weak (and thus excluded) populations. Tenure becomes an object of political trading and influence.

The insecurity of tenure also makes it difficult for the municipality to harness local resources in the form of property taxes. Real-estate taxes cannot be levied unless property rights are clearly established. This failure to raise local revenues in turn means that the municipality is unable to provide the necessary services to newly urbanized areas: roads, sanitation, water, and so on (see also the other policy areas). These services are thus often procured, if at all, via informal means, which will generally be substandard and again be open to political-influence trading. The poor level of services will mean that the marginalized populations who live in these zones are actually paying more, in relative terms, for housing than are more well-established segments of the population. The insecurity of tenure also means that fewer opportunities to amass savings via investments in land and housing (in essence, creating assets for future generations) will be available to these marginalized populations. The 'formal' land market may equally be kept out of their reach by the type of zoning and building regulations discussed earlier. The result is a cycle of poverty and territorial exclusion that can be broken only via the introduction of new ways of managing urban land.

In developed cities, housing policies (frequently with the best of intentions) may in fact indirectly foster exclusion. Rent control, often aimed at helping the poor, may create a new privileged class (those who got there first), while at the same time impeding improvements in the 'controlled' housing stock and also fostering a parallel black market; that is, to the extent that the controlled price no longer reflects market prices. In the same vein, social or public housing, often equally aimed at helping the poor, may in fact indirectly foster segregation and exclusion. In so far as public-housing developments end up concentrating large populations of the same class (or ethnic group), they may in fact create ghettos. The 'exclusionary' effect will in part depend on the level of territorial concentration of such developments and the bureaucratic (or political) process by which access to public housing is determined.

At the same time, housing policy may operate to mitigate tendencies towards economic decline and social polarization, tendencies that are often a consequence – even in developed countries – of increasing globalization. Thus, Frans Dieleman and Robert Kloosterman, describing Rotterdam as a 'post-industrial city' and a 'gateway to the global economy,' show in detail how jobs declined in the aggregate from the 1970s through the early 1980s, while at the same time economic restructuring caused a shift from manufacturing to service employment. But as the economy of the city stagnated during the 1980s, the financial support system – heavily subsidized by the national government – was able to bolster social-policy initiatives to cushion the shock. In the current situation, immigrant groups are very strongly overrepresented among the unemployed in both Rotterdam and Amsterdam. But what the authors call 'the corporatist Dutch welfare state' has avoided the worst social consequences of such a situation by supplying housing, education, police services, and public transport at a relatively 'decent' level to the neighbourhoods where immigrants live. In addition, the Rotterdam municipal government has undertaken a number of initiatives to improve employment opportunities for the socially excluded. Low-income groups are also significant beneficiaries of a large stock of publicly owned rental housing, and, although direct subsidies to social housing have been cut, the central government has found other funding mechanisms to keep rent levels low for poor households. How long this welfare-state approach to maintaining social cohesion can be sustained will depend a lot on the local sense of togetherness in the city, and on new political arrangements at the regional level.

5. Urban Transport and Accessibility

Transport in most cities is both a public service (through municipal or state-controlled transport companies) and a mixture of private activity and public facilities (through pedestrian walkways, bicycle paths and rights of way, public roads for private cars and other vehicles). The organization and management of urban transport will have a major impact on the relative access of various sectors of the population to employment; and it will affect access to land and housing as well. The design of urban transport systems, for example, is a key factor in defining the access of women to labour markets and to urban services. In an

urban setting, the spatial organization of various infrastructure investments and amenities, some of which may impose obstacles to the
movement of persons (such as railway or highway overpasses or
industrial parks), may have a profound impact on the level of social
segregation.

Taking again the recent history of Cape Town as our extreme case (of
exclusion), apartheid was founded not only on zoning laws and land
tenure restrictions, but also on the functioning of an 'efficient' urban
transport system allowing whites and non-whites to live in distinct
areas, often separated by great distances. It is one of the ironies of
transport systems that they serve both to bring people together and to
divide them. This is nowhere more true than in urban areas. Modern
advances in transport technology, especially the introduction of the
automobile (more on this below), have increased the opportunities for
social and ethnic segregation by allowing households to 'choose' their
place of residence from a much wider geographical range, and to live
farther away from groups with which they do not wish to interact. Perhaps in no other policy area are the indirect (and often unforeseen)
consequences of policy choices on exclusion as important as in urban
transportation.

Of major importance is the impact of policy on intermodal competition, that is, on the relative position of alternative modes of transport.
Policies that give priority to the use of the automobile (as opposed to
public transport) can have very negative effects on the fight against
exclusion. The process, all too prevalent in American cities, may be
described thus. As local (or national) governments put more money
into urban road and highway infrastructures, relatively fewer funds
are available for public transport systems. The relative use of automobiles increases, in turn decreasing the demand for other modes of
transport, further decreasing the quality of public transport (also
increasing its unit costs). Decreased demand makes public transport
less profitable (i.e., more expensive to run) for public or private operators. Generally, for public transport to be 'affordable,' minimum levels
of demand must be maintained, given the high fixed costs of most systems. A bus or tram line can be maintained only if a sufficient number
of people use it. By implicitly subsidizing the use of the private automobile, policy-makers will often end up gravely weakening (if not
totally destroying) collective means of transportation. Automobile
users in cities are seldom made to pay the full social cost of their
behaviour: road pricing is still in its infancy as a policy option and

often difficult to apply (especially in cities in developing countries). The true costs of congestion and pollution are almost never charged.

The effects of the implicit subsidization of the automobile, however, go much further. Unless counterbalanced by other urban planning measures (such as zoning and density requirements), residential expansion based on the (almost) exclusive use of the automobile will lead to the development of dispersed, low-density, settlement patterns. This in turn can have two deleterious effects: first, the dispersed (low-density) nature of settlement will make it even more costly to reintroduce public transport systems should the population desire them. Indeed, it may make the use of public transport almost impossible. Second, it may create settlement patterns where people of different classes and different hues live very far apart. The result is an urban agglomeration where geographic mobility (except for short distances) requires the use of an automobile and where the poor and rich (or black and white) never meet, at least not in transport vehicles, and hardly ever see each other.

The exclusionary effects of patterns of urbanization of this nature are not difficult to imagine. They are observable in many American cities such as Miami, but are also beginning to appear in many Latin American cities; San Salvador is by no means an atypical case. The poorest elements of the population, most not able to own and maintain an automobile, will cling to neighbourhoods close to the centre of the city or other employment nodes, while the better-off will create their own residential zones. What there is of a public transport system will often be of low quality and will, with some exceptions, be generally reserved for the poorer sections of the population (creating another reason why the middle class will try to avoid public transport). In cities in developing countries, the use of mini-buses (*colectivos* in Spanish) will often play a useful role in filling the void, but this solution remains feasible only so long as demand remains sufficiently high, that is, only so long as the use of the automobile is limited to a small percentage of the population. As the use of the automobile rises, the mini-bus may also perish unless adequate urban transport policies are introduced.

The most excluded elements of society become veritable captives of their neighbourhoods. If the automobile is indeed a prerequisite for mobility, then women (and the elderly) are hit especially hard: the first group because mobility now means the need to own two autos (the male generally monopolizing the first), clearly beyond the means of most households; the second group simply because driving becomes impractical after a certain age. Yet, these (negative) outcomes are by no means inevitable. Many cities in our sample have gone a long way in implementing 'inclusive' transport policies that seek to lift as many restrictions as possible on the geographic mobility of the less well-off and the disabled (Montreal, Toronto, Geneva). Here again, much can be learned by comparing experiences.

6. Employment, Economic Revitalization, and the Building of Inclusive Public Spaces

The supply of remunerative employment in a city, while largely an effect of national and international economic forces, can also be affected by local policies. Given a city's particular demographic structure, how urban space is organized, zoned, or otherwise planned will have an important impact on the overall access of urban residents to employment. Urban governments provide employment in themselves, but their policies to attract industry and encourage medium and small enterprises (whether these policies are direct or indirect), and to regularize labour markets through local schemes or through cooperation with the national government, will also have a considerable effect on employment, and therefore on the overall economic performance of cities. To the extent that the local demand for employment lags behind the supply, cities will find themselves with more severe problems of crime, and with higher taxes and welfare expenditures. Comparative analysis must examine the impact of technological change on the spatial structure of employment within the city. Why have some urban regions been more successful than others in maintaining employment in the central parts of the city, avoiding inner-city decay?

Local decisions can have an important impact on the location of employment. Here again, poorly informed policies can have a major (but often unintentional) effect on the process of exclusion. Where commercial spaces are located and the manner in which they are planned will very much determine who works with whom and who shops where – in sum, who interacts with whom. It is one of the functions of a city-centre (or downtown) to be a meeting place, a bridge, a place where groups from various backgrounds and classes come together. In modern society, shopping and working are among the most important functions. The places where people shop and/or work will also often be near the places where they gather for other purposes (see 'cultural infrastructure,' above). The banks of the Seine would be bleak if there were no commercial activity, if the centre of Paris were not also an important place of employment. By the same token, the social dynamics of public spaces (such as parks and squares) cannot be separated from the workplaces nearby.

Decisions surrounding the location and development of commercial space can set in motion a process of either inclusion or exclusion. San Salvador currently appears to offer an unfortunate example of a process of spatial polarization of employment and commercial activity. By leaving the old commercial centre largely unattended (already damaged by an earthquake), but, more important, by promoting the development of new commercial zones and office parks in other areas (farther west), local authorities have in fact created two San Salvadors: the old centre, largely left to the poor, filled with street vendors and informal markets (and some informal industry); a new centre to the west, with modern shopping malls, offices, parking spaces, and a high proportion of white-collar employment. Basically, two economic worlds coexist within the same urban agglomeration, separated by both social and geographic space. It is difficult to argue that this is conducive to social sustainability. As Mario Lungo argues in chapter 9, however, it is not only economic revitalization that is needed. Rather, he calls for an integrated recovery plan, which combines physical reconstruction with the restoration of public space and residential functions. The effectiveness of such a plan can be assured only by an urban-management system that is more democratic and participatory.

A good northern example of the promotion of policies for the economic revitalization of the central city is contained in the chapter on Baltimore. An apparent textbook case of the successful redevelopment of the downtown harbour area, Baltimore attracted praise for its tourism strategy, and was ceaselessly promoted as a 'Renaissance City' by its mayor during the 1970s and 1980s. But by the mid-1990s, the glitter had worn off, and the city was revealed for what some felt it had always been – three cities. One was a city of luxury hotels, sports stadiums, and waterfront tourist facilities such as the Hard Rock Café and Planet Hollywood restaurant. Another was the growing and prosperous suburbs where both the white and the black middle class had been settling since the 1950s. But the third was what Marc Levine calls the 'Underclass City,' composed of 'desolate neighbourhoods marked by social exclusion, high rates of crime and drug abuse, deepening ghetto poverty, and dilapidated or abandoned housing.' As is the case in many other North American cities that have used prestige projects as a lure for outside investment, the Baltimore development strategy produced a 'casino economy' that utterly failed to connect with the needs of the increasingly marginal residents of the inner city. In reflecting on this experience, the author raises questions about aesthetics, about social justice, and about fiscal sustainability. The chapter concludes that the city needs a culture of 'socially just regionalism' to overcome 'the polarizing effects of U.S.–style metropolitan fragmentation.'

San Salvador and Baltimore are very different from other cities studied in this volume, which have, it would appear, been much more successful in promoting an integrated economic space and labour market, essentially through the explicit promotion of a strong and economically diversified city-centre. In the cases of cities such as Geneva and Montreal, there is little doubt that the centre remains the centre, the meeting place of workers, shoppers, and strollers from all parts of the larger agglomeration. While, as Antoine Bailly reminds us in the case of Geneva, wealth does not ensure social sustainability, the successful organization of city-centre economies should be a major objective of planning, and are often the direct result of policy decisions concerning employment location and promotion. A strong central city does not preclude the existence of industrial districts in more outlying areas, provided access is assured. The successful creation of a truly integrated urban labour market, conducive to social integration, requires coordination between the various policy areas discussed here: in particular urban land planning, infrastructure, and governance. As was stated earlier, social sustainability, to be successful, requires that we go beyond a purely sectoral approach.

Finally, what may often appear as very banal matters in terms of employment codes and commercial regulations and by-laws can again have important impacts on the process of exclusion: the pricing and licensing of street vendors; the licensing of open-air activities; the leasing of public market space; the pricing and servicing of industrial parks; regulations surrounding trucking and storage; and so on. To this we may add the physical impact of industrial developments on the division of social space. Industrial zones also act as physical barriers. Environmental regulations with respect to pollution and industrial waste (collection and disposal) will equally have an impact, both on the location of economic activity and on the relative quality of life in different parts of the agglomeration.

In sum, then, what we are proposing in this volume is a closer look at the many and intricate ways in which local policies affect – or might affect – social sustainability. At the threshold of the twenty-first century, massive urbanization and increasing social diversity are two central, and ineluctable, trends. How cities manage diversity, so that cultural and social variety becomes a driving force behind, rather than an impediment to, development, is one of the most important questions we can pose. As the essays in this book illustrate, each city has its own history of dealing with these social trajectories; what is appropriate, or even what has failed in one, may be instructive to others, but it can never be fully determinant. Not only are cities growing and changing, but policies are responsive over time, and contexts are fluid. We need case studies of how cities deal with their diversities, but we also need a more nuanced and complex perspective on this important phenomenon. As all the chapters in this volume are written by researchers who live and work in the countries or cities they describe, we hope that at least part of this perplexing, worldwide reality will begin to emerge.

Notes

Others who have contributed to earlier versions of this text are: Annick Germain, Anne-Marie Séguin (both of INRS-Urbanisation) and Jeanne Wolfe (of McGill University).

1 The choice of the ten cities in our sample was based on three major criteria: (a) our sense of which cities were representative of a range of social and planning problems in the five major countries and regions we were able to discuss; (b) our access to scholars and/or local institutions that had a 'track record' in the study of this general area, and their agreement to attend meetings and to write a paper in English on the subject; and (c) our subjective judgment that their work would be of high quality and of interest to an international audience. Clearly, a large list of other cities might also have satisfied criteria (a) and (c), but logistical and funding factors influenced the choice of cities according to criterion (b).
2 The term 'city,' as it is used here, refers to the entire metropolitan area, or census metropolitan area, as the term is employed by Statistics Canada.
3 As *The Economist* put it in a special survey, 'city halls around the world are beginning to feel the effect of an unheralded revolution. New mayors with new policies are coming in. National governments are starting to loosen their grip. The result is a yeasty period of experimentation which may yet prove that the problems of cities can be overcome' (*The Economist* 1995, 17).

4 On the notion of 'global' cities, see the path-breaking study by Saskia
   Sassen (1991). More recently, the same author has argued that, in spite of
   the powerful economic and social forces of globalization, questions of
   governance (including regulation) and accountability in cities that are the
   sites of the localization of these forces are very much open to the influence
   of democratic policies (Sassen 1998).

5 While noting that there are many definitions of the 'megacity,' Gilbert says
   that most are based on large size. His own criterion draws from the United
   Nations Department of International Economic and Social Affairs
   (UNDIESA) definition, first enunciated in 1986: cities that are expected to
   have populations of at least 8 million inhabitants by the year 2000.

6 On 'world cities' see John Friedmann and Goetz Wolff 1982; Friedmann
   1986; and Paul Knox and Peter Taylor 1995. Knox defines world cities as
   'centres of transnational corporate headquarters, of their business services,
   of international finance, of transnational institutions, and of telecommunications and information processing. They are basing points and control
   centres for the independent skein of financial and cultural flows which,
   together, support and sustain the globalization of industry' (1995, 6).

7 Henri Lefebvre, *The Production of Space*, tr. Donald Nicholson-Smith
   (Oxford: Basil Blackwell, 1991), p. 286; cited in Dolores Hayden 1995, p. 41.

8 See, for example, two books co-edited and co-written by one of the present
   authors: Richard Stren, Rodney White, and Joseph Whitney 1992; and
   Richard Gilbert, Don Stevenson, Herbert Girardet, and Richard Stren 1996.
   Many other books and articles have dealt with similar and complementary
   themes.

9 See, for example, Willem van Vliet– 1992, pp. 169–204.

10 An authoritative survey of local administration in France concludes that
   'the decentralization of laws of 1982 and 1983 brought with them a major
   change in both the legal framework and the relations between the state and
   local authorities ... Recalling the sharp criticisms of the reform, which certain experts thought were well taken at the time, we must admit, ten years
   later, that those who were most sharply critical of the measures taken have
   become veritable apologists of the same measures. Decentralization seems
   thus to have been unanimously accepted' (Terrazzoni 1993, 166).

11 For arguments that challenge Putnam's premise that social capital in the
   United States is in decline, see Schudson 1998 and Wuthnow 1998.

12 On the emergence of this new class of transnational professionals and their
   impact on cultural institutions, see Sassen 1991.

13 Metropolitan Toronto Convention and Visitors Association (1995). Many of
   these events are religious in nature, but most are open to the general public.

14 See, for example, Giovanni Andrea Cornia, Richard Jolly, and Frances
    Stewart 1987, especially chapter 1; and articles in the special issue of
    Environment and Urbanization (1995).

References

Borja, Jordi, and Manuel Castells. 1997. *Local and Global: Management of Cities in
    the Information Age*. London: Earthscan.
Clarke, Susan E., and Gary L. Gaile. 1998. *The Work of Cities*. Minneapolis:
    University of Minnesota Press.
Cornia, Giovanni Andrea, Richard Jolly, and Frances Stewart. 1987. *Adjustment
    with a Human Face: Protecting the Vulnerable and Promoting Growth*, vol. 1.
    Oxford: Clarendon Press.
Decima Research. 1991. *A Report to the Caribbean Cultural Committee on Caribana
    1990 Survey*. Toronto: Decima Research.
Economist, The. 1995. 'Special Survey on Cities.' 29 July.
Environment and Urbanization. 1995. 'Urban Poverty: Characteristics, Causes
    and Consequences.' Special issue 7/1.
Friedmann, John. 1986. 'The World City Hypothesis.' *Development and Change*
    17/1: 69–84.
Friedmann, John, and Goetz Wolff. 1982. 'World City Formation: An Agenda
    for Research and Action.' *International Journal of Urban and Regional Research*
    6/3: 309–44.
Fukuyama, Francis. 1995. *Trust*. New York: Basic.
Gilbert, Alan. 1996. *The Mega-City in Latin America*. Tokyo: United Nations
    University Press.
Gilbert, Richard, Don Stevenson, Herbert Girardet, and Richard Stren. 1996.
    Making Cities Work: Local Government and Sustainable Development. London:
    Earthscan.
Goetz, Edward G., and Susan E. Clarke, eds. 1993. *The New Localism: Compara-
    tive Urban Politics in a Global Era*. Newbury Park, CA: Sage.
Hall, Peter. 1998. *Cities in Civilization*. New York: Pantheon.
Hayden, Dolores. 1995. *The Power of Place: Urban Landscapes as Public History*
    Cambridge, MA: MIT Press.
Harris, Nigel. 1996. 'Introduction.' In *Cities and Structural Adjustment*, ed.
    Nigel Harris and Ida Fabricius, 1–12. London and Bristol, PA: UCL
    Press.
Harris, Nigel, and Ida Fabricius, eds. 1996. *Cities and Structural Adjustment*.
    London and Bristol, PA: UCL Press.

Kanter, Rosabeth Moss. 1995. *World Class: Thriving Locally in the Global Economy.* New York: Simon and Schuster.

Knox, Paul. 1995. 'World Cities in a World System.' In *World Cities in a World-System*, ed. Paul Knox and Peter Taylor, 3–20. Cambridge: Cambridge University Press.

Knox, Paul, and Peter Taylor, eds. 1995. *World Cities in a World-System.* Cambridge: Cambridge University Press.

Lasch, Christopher. 1996. *The Revolt of the Elites and the Betrayal of Democracy.* New York: W.W. Norton.

Lee, Kyu Sik, and Alex Anas. 1989. *Manufacturers' Responses to Infrastructure Deficiencies in Nigeria.* INU Discussion Paper no. 50. Washington, DC: World Bank.

Lever, William F. 1996. 'Summing Up.' In *Cities and Structural Adjustment*, ed. Nigel Harris and Ida Fabricius, 93–101. London, Bristol, PA: UCL Press.

Metropolitan Toronto Convention and Visitors Association. 1995. *Around the World: A List of Multicultural Events in Toronto.* Toronto: Metropolitan Toronto Convention and Visitors Association.

Prud'homme, Remy. 1989. 'Main Issues in Decentralization,' in The World Bank, *Strengthening Local Governments in Sub-Saharan Africa*, 71–5. Washington, DC: The World Bank.

Putnam, Robert. 1993. *Making Democracy Work: Civic Traditions in Modern Italy.* Princeton, NJ: Princeton University Press.

– 1995. 'Tuning In, Tuning Out: The Strange Disappearance of Social Capital in America.' *PS: Political Science and Politics* 28/4: 664–83.

Reich, Robert. 1991. *The Work of Nations: Preparing Ourselves for the 21st Century.* New York: Knopf.

Sassen, Saskia. 1991. *The Global City: New York, London, Tokyo.* Princeton, NJ: Princeton University Press.

– 1998. 'The State and the Global City: Notes Toward a Conception of Place-Centered Governance.' In *Globalization and Its Discontents*, 195–218. New York: New Press.

Schudson, Michael. 1998. *The Good Citizen. A History of American Civic Life.* New York: Free Press.

Soja, Edward W. 1996. 'Los Angeles, 1965–1992: From Crisis-Generated Restructuring to Restructuring-Generated Crisis.' In *The City: Los Angeles and Urban Theory at the End of the Twentieth Century*, ed. Allen J. Scott and Edward W. Soja, 426–62. Berkeley and Los Angeles: University of California Press.

Stren, Richard, Rodney White, and Joseph Whitney, eds. 1992. *Sustainable Cities: Urbanization and the Environment in International Perspective.* Boulder, CO: Westview.

Terrazoni, André. 1993. *L'administration territoriale en France*. Paris: Librairie générale de droit et de jurisprudence.

van Vliet–, Willem. 1992. 'The United States.' In *Sustainable Cities: Urbanization and the Environment in International Perspective*, ed. Richard Stren, Rodney White, and Joseph Whitney, 169–204. Boulder, CO: Westview.

World Bank. 1991. *Urban Policy and Economic Development: An Agenda for the 1990s*. Washington, DC: World Bank.

– 1994. *World Development Indicators*. Washington, DC: World Bank.

World Commission on Environment and Development. 1987. *Our Common Future*. Oxford and New York: Oxford University Press.

Wuthnow, Robert. 1998. *Loose Connections: Joining Together in America's Fragmented Communities*. Cambridge, MA: Harvard University Press.

Zweig, Stefan. 1944. *Die Welt von Gestern* (The World of Yesterday). Stockholm: Bermann-Fisher Verlag.

2 The Social Sustainability of Montreal: A Local or a State Matter?

ANNE-MARIE SÉGUIN and ANNICK GERMAIN

This book is about building inclusive cities through local policy. Local affairs *do* matter, or so Mario Polèse and Richard Stren write in chapter 1. For the past two decades, decentralization has been regarded highly in many advanced industrial countries. Notable among its many perceived advantages is the potential to increase efficiency in the delivery of public services, making them more accessible to the population while enhancing local democracy. According to this vision of decentralization, local power appears headed for a bright future.

To what point, however, should we encourage decentralization? And, even more important, what should we decentralize? For some, control and management of social services, including health and education, and certain aspects of economic development should be transferred to the local level. Local leaders frequently support this position, looking to decentralization as a means to achieve greater managerial autonomy. The approach also suggests that cities should be given a larger role in the establishment of policies to protect the social fabric from the negative effects of development. In other words, the local level is assumed to be the most efficient for maintaining a socially sustainable milieu.

Opinions on decentralization, however, are still far from consensus. Some researchers point out that decentralized systems have not yet provided evidence of their ability to guarantee equity and social justice, and many believe that decentralization is just a subtle way for higher levels of government to reduce spending on the welfare state (Derycke and Gilbert 1988; Lemieux 1996). In a sense, equity must become a precondition for local autonomy.

In this chapter we review arguments praising the merits of decentralization and of local power by exploring the importance of different levels of government in the production of a socially sustainable metropolis. We will do this by examining the role of policies applicable at the local scale but emanating from government at separate levels.

Let us first examine what we mean by a socially sustainable city. With the exception of that proposed by Polèse and Stren, most definitions of similar concepts tend to stress what social cohesion *is not* rather than what it is. This is especially obvious in American literature on urban underclass neighbourhoods, which are perceived as synonymous with areas of social marginalization (Wackant and Wilson 1989; Hughes 1990; Greene 1991; Herpin 1993; Massey 1994). Social marginalization or social exclusion comprises several dimensions: economic, political, and social. Social exclusion implies deprivation of financial resources, and limited access to basic collective social goods and services. Social exclusion also harbours the notion of social 'disaffiliation' (Castel 1991); in other words, a socially excluded individual is someone removed, or symbolically exiled, from kinship and social networks that would provide a sense of security and belonging within a family, a neighbourhood, a city, or a workplace. Finally, social exclusion can mean the loss of one's sense of belonging through the loss of citizenship (Taboada Leonetti 1995; Strobel 1996).

Starting with these defining elements of social exclusion, we can deduce the characteristics of a socially sustainable city. Such a city's inhabitants should be assured a basic level of financial resources, as well as access to public goods and services in areas such as education, health, and culture; the socially sustainable city would also stimulate social integration by providing dynamic arenas for social and community interaction. In larger cities, the possibility for individuals and groups of different ethnocultural backgrounds or socio-economic status to share urban space without experiencing marked sociospatial segregation could also serve as an accurate index of social sustainability. At one time, family, religion, and employment provided individuals with a sense of social integration and belonging. Postmodern societies, however, splintered by the gradual erosion of these social institutions, have come to be defined by a social-cohesion crisis (Ghorra-Gobin 1996). In this way, the integration of differences has become a sensitive issue. As pointed out by Jean Remy and Liliane Voyé (1992), the social model of harmony born from hierarchy has given way to a social model of competition for equality. This reversal of fortune has exacerbated tensions on the issue of the treatment of differences. The 'social question' no longer boils down to issues of distributive justice, as was the case in the 1960s; rather, it is henceforth inextricably bound to how well economic and sociocultural differences can coexist.

The case of Montreal illustrates many of the issues presented above. First, Montreal exhibits many of the paradigmatic attributes of a socially sustainable city while simultaneously facing difficult challenges: poverty and unemployment, as well as an ever-increasing share of immigrants admitted to the province of Quebec, to say nothing of what is referred to as the 'national question' of provincial–federal relations between Quebec and Canada. Furthermore, the complexity of Montreal's urban society draws upon its historical duality between French-speaking Catholics and Anglo-Protestants.

In this chapter, we will argue that Montreal's social sustainability derives from a combination of factors, the most important being governmental (primarily provincial) intervention in key areas, notably in financial support to health services, to education, and to the very poor. While municipal and regional policies have played, and continue to play, a role in these areas, they are of less significance. In addition to these political and administrative factors, the role of history has been very important in the development of Montreal's social sustainability, although historical factors are only briefly discussed here.

After introducing the Montreal metropolitan area, we focus on examining the city's social fabric in order to argue that, despite relatively high poverty levels, Montreal has not developed any ghettos or socially marginalized neighbourhoods such as those found in a number of American cities.

We then highlight some of the factors that have contributed to the relative success of Montreal in terms of social sustainability by looking into the respective roles of different levels of government, while giving special attention to national policies addressing social equity. Finally, we recall some historical factors that may also have played a part in making Montreal what it is today.

A City, an Island, and a Region

Founded in 1642 by Messieurs et Dames de la Société Notre-Dame de Montréal, the city was born of a missionary project, the conversion of the Amerindians of New France. Following the conquest of the colony by the armies of the British Empire in 1760, Montreal became a bilingual city (with anglophones in the majority between 1831 and 1866) and a city of many cultures. From the middle of the nineteenth century, Montreal developed into the industrial cradle of what would become, in 1867, the Canadian confederation. It remained Canada's unrivalled metropolis until the middle of the twentieth century, being surpassed by Toronto in the 1960s. Montreal, in geo-economic terms, went from being the metropolis of Canada to the metropolis of the predominantly French-speaking province of Quebec.

Since the 1960s, Montreal's population growth has been much slower than in the first half of the twentieth century. This moderate growth rate distinguishes it from Toronto and Vancouver (although Vancouver is still smaller than Montreal in population size), but the demographic slowdown has, in many ways, allowed the preservation of its urban and social fabric. Montreal is, in fact, a metropolis of average size, mostly devoid of the inconveniences often associated with large cities. The sense of community in many of its neighbourhoods and in the city-centre has undoubtedly benefited from its relative demographic stability.

The suburbanization processes throughout this century have resulted in Montreal spreading out beyond the original Island of Montreal to create a polynucleated urban agglomeration. Greater Montreal is a city-region of, in 1996, 3,326,510 inhabitants.[1] It is highly fragmented, with 113 municipalities of different sizes each defending its own autonomy, especially since the dominant municipality, the City of Montreal, has 1,017,669 inhabitants, or almost a third of Greater Montreal's total. The population heart of the metropolitan area is the Island of Montreal, on which are twenty-nine municipalities, including the central city. These were joined in 1969 in a federation called the Montreal Urban Community (MUC), which had 1,775,846 inhabitants in 1996. The second-largest island, Jesus Island, is located just to the north, and forms the territory of the municipality of Laval, the second-largest municipality in the province of Quebec, after Montreal.

The scope of the MUC's responsibility is relatively limited: property-tax evaluation, public security, food inspections, and the establishment of regional-development plans. Over the course of time, the MUC has intervened in other areas: the battle against pollution, water purification, public transportation, and the establishment and improvement of regional parks. Collectively, the other municipalities of the metropolitan area form another supra-municipal structure, the regional county municipalities (MRCs); these are quite limited in their powers and

Table 2.1: Incidence of Low Income by Area, Montreal, 1990

	Low-income pop'n./Total pop'n. (%)	Low-income families/Total families (%)	Low-income unatt.persons/ Total unatt. persons (%)
Montreal Metropolitan Area	22.0	18.5	44.9
City of Montreal	33.3	27.9	49.8
MUC–East	25.7	22.5	47.8
MUC–West (West Island)	18.3	15.3	37.3
Laval	16.1	13.8	39.2
North Shore	14.1	13.1	42.0
Longueuil	24.3	21.5	41.1
Rest of the South Shore	11.7	10.4	35.8

Source: Data from Census of Canada, 1991, electronic product, compiled by the authors

spheres of action, their primary role being the establishment of regional development plans. The Montreal metropolitan region is of enormous importance in Quebec as it represents 45.3 per cent of the entire provincial population.

Poverty and the Social Division of Urban Space

Over the past several years, the Montreal metropolitan area has been severely stricken by poverty. In 1990, according to Statistics Canada,[2] low-income people represented a staggering 22 per cent of the total population.[3] Nineteen per cent of all families and 45 per cent of unattached individuals in Montreal's metropolitan area were categorized as low income. In other words, more than one in five people, just under one in five families, and slightly fewer than one in two unattached individuals lived in relative poverty.

Geographically speaking, this low-income population was not evenly spread across the metropolitan region. Data from 1990 indicate a very neat social division in Montreal's metropolitan spatial layout. The central city (we refer here to the city of Montreal) is clearly distinguished from the rest of the metropolitan area; more than one-quarter of its families and half of its population of unattached individuals are poor (see table 2.1 for detailed data, and figure 2.1 for location of the urban areas). Poverty is also slightly overrepresented in the city of Longueuil and in the eastern part of the island of Montreal (MUC–

Figure 2.1 Montreal Metropolitan Area, 1991
Source: INRS–Urbanisation

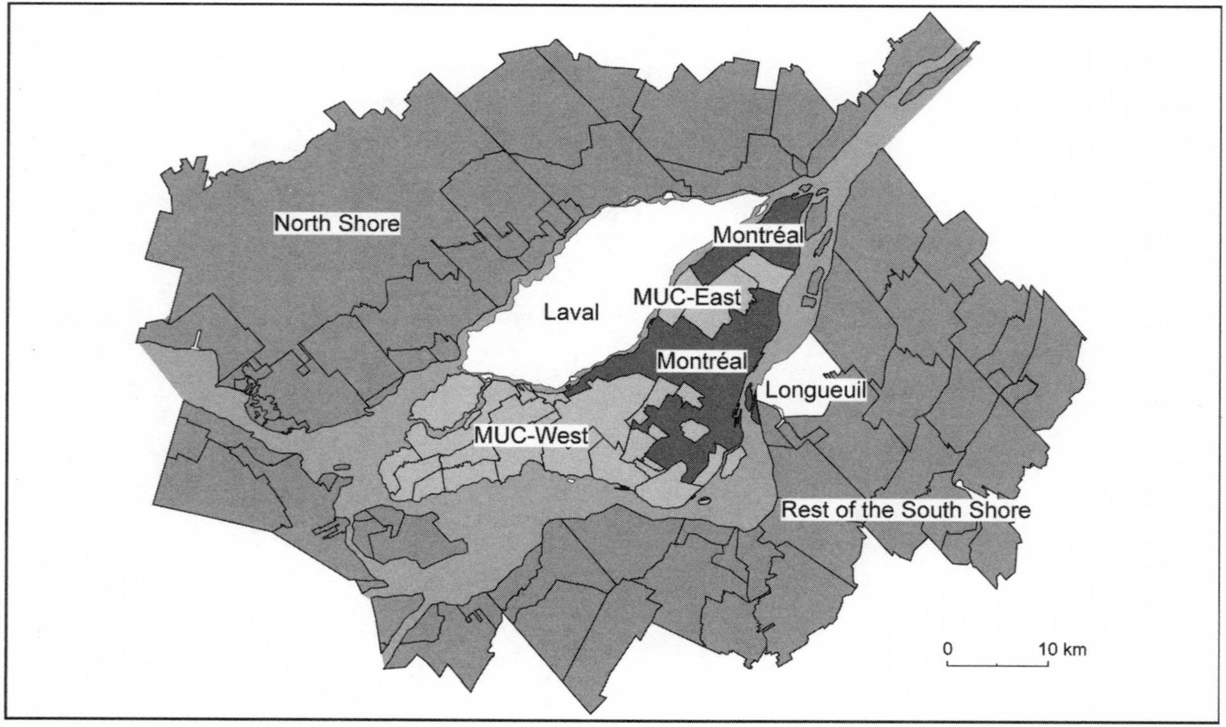

East). Laval, the western part of the island of Montreal (MUC–West), the North Shore, and the rest of the South Shore, the other largest components of the agglomeration, show poverty levels lower than those for the overall region. This means that the burden of supporting poor populations is not evenly distributed across the metropolitan area.

The social division of the metropolitan area appears even more clearly at a more disaggregated level, that of census tracts (figure 2.2).[4] The central city stands out with a concentration of census tracts showing a significant proportion of low-income groups. In 1990, for the metropolitan area, 115 of the 130 census tracts with 40 per cent or more of low-income persons in their population were located in the central city, which also exhibited a high proportion of the sectors with a low-income population of 30 per cent to 39 per cent. These census-tract categories are almost absent in the outlying suburbs (Séguin and Termote 1997).

It could readily be expected that the high level of economically disadvantaged people in Montreal's population and the concentration of low-income households in certain areas would have a negative impact on the social sustainability of the metropolis. How, therefore, can Montreal be considered a socially sustainable city? One factor among others is the fact that this social division based on income masks a complex reality that merits closer scrutiny.

Poor Neighbourhoods Are Still Socially Mixed

On an aggregate basis, areas of poverty have a relatively heterogeneous population profile, reflecting the social diversity of these localities. If we combine the Census Metropolitan Area's (CMA's) census tracts that show a low-income rate of 40 per cent or higher, we see that the population profile within these areas does not differ strongly from the overall metropolitan profile. Montreal's poor neighbourhoods are not characterized by a homogeneous population of unemployed, inactive, or uneducated people, or of single-parent families (single mothers), or of recent immigrants. In fact, for the following variables – male and female activity rates, male and female unemployment rates, the percentage of persons aged fifteen and over with less than a Grade 10 or less than a Grade 14 level of education, the percentage of single-parent families in total households, and the percentage in the population of recent immigrants (living in the country for less than ten years) – if we aggregate all the poorest census tracts (those with a low-income rate of 40 per cent or

Figure 2.2 Percentage of Low-Income Population in Total Population in 1990 by Census Tract, Montreal Metropolitan Area

Source: INRS–Urbanisation

% of low   number of
income   census tracts

1.9 - 9.9   (104)

10   - 19.9   (205)

20   - 29.9   (179)

30   - 39.9   (116)

40   - 87.2   (130)

no data   (15)

0   10 Km

more) and compare the value obtained for each variable with the value for the overall metropolitan area, the gap between the two values is always of ten points or less (Séguin 1998). These findings, which initially seem surprising, are an index to the social diversity prevalent in the poorest areas of Montreal. They are also consistent with studies that have uncovered the existence of new forms of poverty in Quebec (Tremblay 1990; Conseil des Affaires Sociales 1991).

These new forms of poverty are the result of many factors. One major factor is the increasing instability of employment, manifested in involuntary part-time employment, short-term contractual employment, and de-skilling. Second, as the average age of the population rises, so do poverty levels; as people live longer, many exhaust their savings during retirement. The trend towards the prolongation of education is another source of poverty; as students extend their academic careers, more and more poor households are student households. Finally, the inadequacy of the minimum wage is a new trigger of poverty; many low-income households are those of minimum-wage workers. We can see from these factors that the population of Montreal's poor neighbourhoods is not composed entirely of socially marginalized or excluded individuals, but is quite heterogeneous.

We will now examine the question of immigration in Montreal, where, as in many European and North American metropolitan areas, international immigration poses new challenges to social cohesion.

Living with Ethnic and Cultural Diversity

Metropolitan areas of industrialized countries have pride in their cosmopolitan character, but the size and composition of migratory flows, as well as national policies and attitudes, have made immigration into a highly contentious issue over the past two decades. The growing concentration of immigrants in large cities increases the frequency of contact between individuals of different cultural backgrounds, and the question of shared space arises as a central issue. This pattern is underscored by the increasing diversity of immigrants' national and ethnocultural origins. Montreal makes a particularly interesting subject for the study of cosmopolitanism because of its higher level of multi-ethnicity coupled with its status as the metropolis of a divided society. Montreal's history is framed by a narrative of contention and opposition between French and Anglo-Saxon cultures. The debates surrounding the issue of national unity, as well as the cultural and linguistic divisiveness that thread throughout Montreal's history, have come to bear heavily on immigration issues and, notably, around the French or English language choice of the immigrants.

Until the 1970s, Montreal's cosmopolitanism developed peacefully, far from the usual cultural, linguistic, and political controversy. The situation is very different today. The last referendum on Quebec independence, in 1995, revealed the lack of consensus among francophones, anglophones, and New Québécois, a situation exposing the Island of Montreal as an electoral entity separate from the rest of the province.

It was only at the end of the 1960s that Quebec began to realize the impact of immigration on the evolution of the linguistic profile. In the second half of the 1970s, the Quebec government adopted legislative measures specifically intended to stop the anglicization of immigrants; Bill 101 made attendance at French elementary and secondary schools compulsory for all children settled in the province, with the exception of children whose parents were educated in English in Quebec or in another Canadian province. Bill 101 is now well accepted. It reversed the trend of minority attendance at English-language schools. The legislative changes did not, however, eliminate the ambivalence permeating the context in which immigrants develop their strategies for integration into a host society that remains dominated, particularly in Montreal, by tension between two cultural and liguistic worlds. The central role of immigrants in maintaining the French character of Quebec is also amplified by demographic changes leading to a serious decline in the French-speaking population that can be countered only by vigorous policies to encourage an increase in fertility rates along with very high levels of international immigration.

Quebec has a high rate of international immigration, and 88 per cent of the province's immigrants reside in the Montreal metropolitan area. The City of Montreal represents the reception area for 40 per cent of the immigrants admitted to Quebec, and almost a quarter of the city's inhabitants are of foreign origin – in other words, born outside Canada (Ministère des Affaires Internationales, de l'Immigration et des Communautés Culturelles [MAIICC 1994]). There are many indications that Montreal's ethnic mix colours daily life in a positive way, suggesting that immigration is, so far, a success story.

Let us first briefly explore the evolution and governing framework of Montreal's multi-ethnicity. Until the end of the nineteenth century, 98 per cent of Montreal's population was of either French or British origin. Unlike many cities in North America, Montreal was not recognized as cosmopolitan, but rather as a city populated by British, Scottish, Irish, and French inhabitants. At that time, each cultural group was organized in distinct social and institutional networks, each living in segregated areas of the city, a clearly fragmented ethnocultural landscape. Montreal's cosmopolitanism built upon this splintered urban and social bedrock, first triggered at the turn of the twentieth century by the arrival of European immigrants, and later nourished by primarily non-European waves of immigration which started during the mid-1970s. This 'new' immigration left a marked imprint on Montreal's ethnic landscape. While European immigrants (notably Jews from Eastern Europe, Italians, Greeks, and Portuguese) have jointly contributed to the creation of 'ethnic neighbourhoods' that sometimes function as economic enclaves (Olson 1991) within the heart of Montreal, migratory waves over the past two decades have promoted the multi-ethnic character of urban neighbourhoods which have spread more widely across the metropolitan area.[5]

Today, immigrants (and more generally individuals of ethnic origin other than French or British) live in a wide range of housing types (Germain and Blanc 1998). Multi-ethnic areas can be poor neighbourhoods in the centre of the agglomeration, or affluent suburbs, or a whole gamut of situations in between. However, these areas are far less common in suburbs at the periphery of the metropolitan area, where French-Canadian middle-class families still form the majority (Mongeau and Séguin 1993). Therefore, while there is a division of metropolitan space along ethnic lines, there is also a progressive spreading out of immigration, especially 'new wave' immigrants, which is causing shifts in the established residential patterns associated with immigration.

Several studies have attempted to identify patterns of interethnic mixing in a variety of contexts. One of these studies explores the modes of interethnic coexistence in seven neighbourhoods, among the most multi-ethnic of the metropolitan region (Germain et al. 1995); it analyses two aspects of neighbourhood life – participation in community life and forms of social interaction in public spaces. Without repeating our results, let us simply say that detailed analysis of voluntary associations involved in each of the neighbourhoods – and more specifically of the community networks that have developed in most of them – reveal the importance of ethnic groups in community action. Ethnic groups are often the first to set up community structures to help out economically disadvantaged, marginalized, or recent immigrant residents of their neighbourhood. Today, neighbourhoods in Montreal boast a number of associations run by ethnic groups, which cater either exclusively to their own community or to the larger population as well. In the past few years, these as well as non-immigrant associations have worked at coordinating their actions. This dynamism is not surprising as Montreal possesses a well-established and vigorous associative tradition.

Regarding forms of sociability in public spaces (such as parks, public squares, subway stations, commercial thoroughfares, commercial centres, and the like – in short, meeting places), systematic observation of the social life in some thirty public spaces reveals a common pattern that could be described as a peaceful but distant cohabitation of users of diverse ethnic origins. In these spaces, residents seem to respect a code of civility, which enables them to enjoy the diversity of social contact offered within these spaces, while maintaining distance from other users. Social interactions are found to be segmented along ethnic lines, with the exception of pre-school children.

This points to the existence of a *modus vivendi* that is not exempt from sporadic tensions, but that nevertheless allows for generally peaceable and non-conflictual sharing of public space. Community groups also play an active role in the resolution of those difficulties that do arise, especially in densely populated urban areas, when people of diverse origins are brought together.

On a different note, to the extent that one finds immigrants in the poorest districts of the city, and given that Montreal exhibits at least some residential concentration of several different ethnic groups (McNicoll 1993) – a process that promotes the emergence of an increasing number of multi-ethnic neighbourhoods – we cannot speak of ethnic ghettos, in the literal sense of the term. Furthermore, over the years immigrants have had a higher economic success rate than that of Canadian-born Quebecers (Gagné 1989). Consequently, no direct correlation can be established between immigration and social exclusion. Immigrants seem to find their place in the labour market; they are not confined to specific areas; and neighbourhoods where they live are often charged with a dynamic and flourishing social life (Germain et al. 1995). A recent study reveals, however, that newly landed immigrants have experienced a lower level of economic integration (Gagné 1995). This fact is not unrelated to the narrowing of the labour market that affects all workers, regardless of their origin, or to the relative inaccessibility of the public sector to those who are not long-established francophones.

Factors Contributing to Montreal's Social Sustainability

Despite the presence of a significant low-income population and the social divisions fragmenting the metropolitan area, and despite the fact that new waves of immigrants are faced with increasing difficulties in their attempts to achieve economic integration, Montreal can still be described as a socially sustainable city. How can we explain this paradox?

A combination of political and historical factors seem to be working together to prevent inner-city neighbourhoods and other poor districts from becoming areas of exclusion. First, Montreal's social sustainability owes a great deal to both federal and provincial aspatial policies, that have provided for a decent level of redistribution of social wealth within both the province and the country. This redistribution process has taken different forms: financial assistance to the poor; the financing of health and education services, and various infrastructure investments necessary for the maintenance and improvement of older urban residential areas. The local government has also played a smaller, but nonetheless important, role in the redistribution process through the establishment of policies related to housing and the general quality of life, and through the planning and development of a public transport system that is significantly more efficient than those of many other metropolitan areas in North America. The social sustainability of the Montreal urban area results, therefore, at least in part, from the effects of aspatial policies; and Montreal thus illustrates the proposition that local problems are not always remedied by exclusively local means.

The Localized Effects of National Policies

Pierre Strobel (1996, 202) insists on the importance of social protection in the battle against social exclusion. This opinion is relevant in the case of Montreal. Let us first recall that, at the beginning of this century, state intervention was very limited and that social institutions were controlled by both public and private local agencies. The situation began to change in the 1930s, as municipalities were assailed by the economic ravages of the 1929 stock market crash, and suffered from the results of speculative policies born of the boosterism that had permeated local politics since the end of the nineteenth century.

In Quebec, it was not until the 1960s and 1970s, with the entrenchment of important measures of financial support for low-income households, that an actual system of social protection was developed. This social safety net was set in place at both the provincial and the federal level of government through different programs, regardless of matrimonial status, type of household, race, ethnic or national origin. It continues to be a fundamental agent in the battle against exclusion. The centralization of its management[6] and of its finances allows the poor access to the same level of support wherever they live. A further result is that the concentration of low-income populations in certain municipalities has not significantly burdened municipal budgets.

Health and Education

The role of national policies is not confined to financial support for the very poor. Areas as important as health care and education are also completely (as with health care) or in large part (as with education) financed by superior levels of government.[7] Also, like the rest of the population, disadvantaged households have free access to a universal health-care system. And, even though some services that used to be covered by health insurance now have to paid for by the users, and despite the increasing frequency with which private health services are used, no major social disparity can be said to plague the health-care system.[8]

In the education system, all children have equal access to public schools that provide a virtually cost-free education up to the university level.[9] And while both public and private universities charge tuition fees, they, too, are in large part financially supported by the state. While Quebec's tuition fees are still among the lowest in the country, the cost of tuition has increased substantially over the last few years. In addition to the public school system, a network of private primary, secondary, and college-level schools are also funded, in major part, by the state, even though they are less accessible to families from more modest financial backgrounds. Public and private education programs should not differ much from one another, since, theoretically speaking, the standards and the content of course material must conform to the regulations imposed by the Quebec Ministry of Education. Moreover, the provincial government has launched different programs on the Island of Montreal, designed to provide stronger support to schools in low-income areas[10] or to schools catering to a large proportion of immigrant students. These programs aim to ensure that differences in children's social environments will not threaten the quality of education or the students' achievement levels.

The efforts aimed at reducing provincial- and federal-government expenditures since the mid-1990s have, however, put a number of services in jeopardy. Consequently, the quality of health-care programs has deteriorated over the years, and critics fear that this type of degeneration might affect other areas of government programs. Is it possible that the underlying qualities of Montreal's social sustainability will be threatened by government cutbacks?

The redistribution of social wealth supported by higher levels of government has until recently enabled the poor to satisfy their basic needs, to gain access to education and to benefit from a public system of health care. This redistribution has had a significant impact on the residential geography of the middle class. In countries, provinces, or those U.S. states where support to the poor and to health and education is subsidized by local or regional governments (municipalities or counties, for example), middle- and upper-class households tend to move away from areas or municipalities where the poor are concentrated in order to reduce their own fiscal burden, whether based on property tax or on income tax. They consider the poor as creating social expenditures, while contributing little to government revenue through either property or income taxes (Ashton 1978). However, in the province of Quebec, and therefore in Montreal, since social security, health care and education, which represent such substantial elements in the budget of modern states, are financed by higher levels of government, moving is not an answer for families seeking to reduce their fiscal contribution by a significant margin. This situation has no doubt worked towards maintaining a social mix in the central city. Conversely, it has also undoubtedly helped to make suburban municipalities more likely to allow or tolerate a certain level of social diversity by accepting, for instance, the construction of private rental housing for modest-income families. Policies of higher levels of government, therefore, while they are essentially aspatial, have yielded spatial consequences by preventing stronger social divisions within the metropolitan region and, most of all, a drastic social fragmentation of space.

It is likely that a 'municipal welfare state'[11] would have created a very different situation.

Infrastructure and Housing

Higher levels of government have also contributed to the battle against social exclusion by establishing financial support programs for collective services and facilities such as public libraries, sports facilities, and local cultural and community centres.[12] These programs have provided the central city and other low-income areas with high-quality public facilities that, without the programs, would have been exclusively destined for wealthier municipalities.

In addition, higher levels of government have indirectly contributed to upholding a vibrant associational life in many neighbourhoods, including poorer areas in Montreal and other municipalities, through financial-support programs for community groups, which have frequently taken over the former role of religious organizations in activities designed to help the poor. Community organizations, since the end of the 1960s, have also been very active in urban social movements. Acting on behalf of the poor, they have been vocal advocates to local governments, especially for the renovation of older, rundown neighbourhoods.

The impact of higher levels of government on the central city and other older municipalities has also been felt through housing policies, which can be divided into two categories: those that focus on helping families with relatively modest incomes gain access to home ownership, and those that concentrate on the renovation and restoration of the environment and housing in older, declining neighbourhoods. The first set of these policies has generally had a negative impact on old neighbourhoods by indirectly encouraging urban expansion and prompting many families to move to the outer suburbs where housing is cheaper, thereby draining part of the rental housing stock's clientele from the central city and from other contiguous, and equally vulnerable, municipalities.

The second set of policies, geared towards the restoration of older buildings and the renovation of neighbourhoods, has conversely had a beneficial impact. Not only have these policies succeeded in improving the quality of housing in old, and therefore often low-income, neighbourhoods, but they have also contributed to the social diversity of these areas. The projects have provided neighbourhoods with qualities desirable to middle-class families, thereby dissuading them from moving away (Séguin 1992). In terms of housing policies, therefore, senior-government intervention has been both beneficial and detrimental to the battle against exclusion. We should add, however, that while the provincial housing authority (Régie du Logement du Québec) is mainly responsible for the arbitration of rent increases, it has probably also helped to maintain housing prices at a reasonable and affordable rate. Without the housing authority's intervention, poor families are likely to have been relegated to a limited segment of the rental-housing market.

Public policy concerned with immigration, at both the federal and the provincial level since 1978, has also helped to maintain Montreal's social sustainability. Immigrants (more specifically permanent residents)[13] have access to income support as well as to the public school system and the public health-care network. Given the high rate of unemployment affecting the whole of the population (immigrants as much as non-immigrants), and given the consequent strain on social programs, the large numbers of newly arrived immigrants[14] could have exacerbated tensions with local citizens; this potential situation, however, is not reflected in recent opinion polls (Joly 1996).

Federal and provincial authorities have only rarely intervened directly in immigrants' urban settlement patterns, as they have in the case of specific refugee groups. Finally, given the stagnation of Montreal's employment situation, and the fact that immigrant mobility is not restricted within Canada, many have opted to move to other provinces.

The Role of Local Urban Management

This section will focus on the central city of Montreal. Montreal adopted an urban plan only in 1992; it is therefore not a 'planned' city, in the strict sense of the term. Nevertheless, Montreal's development has largely been directed by policies that have sometimes strengthened and at other times undercut the city's social sustainability. Several types of policy intervention are examined here, in the areas of public transportation, urban renewal, and housing, for the most part social housing.

In the early 1960s, the City of Montreal embarked, unaided, on the construction of a subway system, which, with subsequent financial support from the provincial government, has undergone several phases of expansion. Since 1970, public transportation has been under the jurisdiction of the MUC. Parallel to the development of the subway, authorities opted for maintaining bus networks and, more recently, for creating a suburban train network. By North American standards, the metropolitan area is well served by public transportation (Bussière and Dallaire 1994), but the Quebec government's massive withdrawal of financial support over the last few years has put a great deal of pressure on the regional authority of the MUC, which is responsible for operating costs, for a significant portion of maintenance costs, as well as for equipment-replacement costs (Frisken 1994). As the hub of the subway system is located in the downtown core, and given that buses and suburban trains feed into subway stations, the construction of the subway system has allowed the downtown core to retain a high proportion of the region's employment, especially in higher-level services (Coffey, Polèse, and Drolet 1996). In contrast to the general North American trend of economic activities moving away from the city-centre to the suburbs, Montreal's downtown area has preserved its status as the city's commercial and entertainment nucleus. Moreover, the quality of the public transportation system gives lower-income populations better access to the range of employment available throughout the Island of Montreal and surrounding municipalities.

Municipal interventions in the City of Montreal's most vulnerable areas have taken a variety of forms, beginning with urban-renewal projects in the 1960s and in the early 1970s. The impact of these interventionist projects have, fortunately, been fairly limited. This is undoubtedly due, at least in part, to the lack of financial involvement by large foreign real-estate investors, but also because Montreal had at the time a relatively slow rate of both demographic and economic growth. The urban-renewal movement gave way to a different approach towards the mid-1970s: the restoration and improvement of rundown housing stock and old neighbourhoods that a decade earlier would have been destined for total demolition.

From the middle of the 1970s, the City of Montreal, along with other older municipalities containing old and deteriorated neighbourhoods, has benefited from several federal and/or provincial programs geared to improve older residential areas; programs, that is, for the restoration of rented or owner-occupied buildings. Montreal and other cities were also able to take advantage of district renovation programs (Société d'Habitation du Québec [SHQ] 1988). While these were frequently locally managed, municipalities invested very little in their operation. Community groups played an important role here, demanding that program funds be invested in the improvement and rehabilitation of residential areas for the benefit of the poor.

Starting in the 1980s, the City of Montreal has also developed its own housing policies, with the main objective being to retain or bring back the middle-class population to the central city (Ville de Montréal 1990). One city-funded program, Opération 20,000 Logements, made available to building contractors vacant lots scattered throughout the city, as a means of aggressively encouraging housing construction. More recently, a paramunicipal agency responsible for housing and development in Montreal has been mandated to acquire residential buildings heading for rapid social and/or physical deterioration, in order to restore them and assure their proper management and care. Frequently undertaken in poorer areas, this type of interventionist program has prevented the decay of large apartment blocks and rental buildings whose deterioration would have had a very negative impact on their surroundings through declines in property value and harm to the social fabric.

Similarly, since the beginning of the 1980s the City of Montreal has introduced a series of measures designed to encourage contractors to invest in the central city, and to lure middle-class families back into the central area. As an incentive, the city has set up property-tax refund programs for buyers of new residential units. More recently, in selected districts, Montreal has offered a $10,000 grant for each newly built residential unit, in the hope of reducing the sale price to levels competitive with those in suburban areas. These incentives were heavily criticized, mostly by pressure groups who believed them to benefit the middle classes disproportionately, and to the detriment of rehabilitation programs for rundown neighbourhoods. In time, and in a context where decentralization is becoming an increasingly important issue, and given the minimal growth rate of new families in the urban region, the presence of a more credit-worthy clientele will prove to be a positive factor for inner-city neighbourhoods. This clientele will help to replenish municipal coffers while simultaneously contributing to the prosperity of neighbourhood businesses. It is also important to note that the moratorium on the conversion of rental properties to co-ownership (condominiums), only very recently lifted, has operated as a safeguard, helping to maintain a stock of good-quality rental housing and to protect renters who cannot afford to purchase their units.

In terms of social housing, the City of Montreal's decision[15] to disperse the low-cost public housing projects known as HLMs (*habitations à loyer modique)* throughout the municipality, has clearly contributed in a positive way to the evolution of old neighbourhoods. In Quebec, HLMs accommodate very poor families who rely almost exclusively on social-welfare programs or on old-age pensions[16] as their sole source of income. Concentrating these households in certain areas of the city would have greatly impoverished those districts. Following construction in the 1960s of two large-scale projects (800 and 500 housing units each), the city opted for more modest projects, which it attempted to disperse throughout the municipality. From the beginning of the 1980s, the city has encouraged two kinds of housing projects: very small ones (of 10, 20, or 30 units) that fit into the existing urban fabric, and larger projects consisting of 100–150 units each. The latter are receiving more and more criticism as they lead to the concentration of approximately 400–500 very poor people, leading to problems of integration in these socially mixed environments (Dansereau and Séguin 1995).

As far as the management of ethnic diversity is concerned, municipalities are somewhat new to the field. Over the last few years, some municipalities, like the City of Montreal and the City of Brossard on the South Shore, have been attempting to introduce measures to facilitate the integration of immigrants. Among these measures, employment-equity programs[17] have had very limited results, notably because they were set in motion at a time when the municipal government had suspended the hiring of new personnel.

The Weight of Historical Factors

In parallel with the social policies imposed by the higher levels of government and local policies in the area of housing and development, Montreal's social sustainability seems to owe much to factors that, for want of a more precise term, we can call 'historical.' These factors are multifaceted. We have already discussed the city's relatively slow rate of demographic growth since the beginning of the 1960s, a rate that has ensured the relative constancy of the social and urban fabric, while unrestrained growth in other large metropolitan areas has scarcely been able to avoid eroding the social fabric.

Residential characteristics and urban morphology are also both worthy of mention. Contrary to the experience of American cities, major Canadian urban areas have succeeded in protecting the density and vibrancy of their central cities. In Montreal, central districts that saw their population decline until the 1980s, surround a vast downtown core that operates as the central destination for the majority of Montreal residents for employment, leisure, and university education. Moreover, before 1950, residential areas were dominated by a very characteristic form of housing – the 'plex,' which consists of row housing, with dwellings stacked on two or three levels. This structure has become exemplary of vernacular Montreal architecture. At the end of the nineteenth century, the plex type of housing was prevalent mostly in the affluent neighbourhoods of the Anglo-Protestant bourgeoisie, but in the first half of the twentieth century it became the dominant architectural form (with certain variations) in all central districts. The landlord often lives on the ground floor, while the first and second floors each consist of either one or two units that are rented out. This residential model has encouraged social diversity in the central city, while providing a relatively cost-efficient housing formula. The model demands that the landlord be credit-worthy and financially secure; the tenants, by contrast, could be on the lower rungs of the economic hierarchy. A further benefit of this formula is that, because it involves the presence of resident landlords, it has also contributed to the protection of the social and residential environment of older city districts.

Overall, the housing stock of the central city is characterized by a large supply of housing at relatively moderate or low cost. The great fluidity of the Montreal real-estate market has been ensured by the high level of residential mobility of Montrealers and by high vacancy rates in rental properties over the last few years. This fluidity is not unrelated to the virtual absence of ghettos, and probably also facilitates the moving process for newly landed immigrants. However, the availability of relatively low-cost rental housing has also undoubtedly slowed the entry of middle-class households, and especially single-person households, to property ownership, for which they often have to leave the central city.

Finally, a well-established neighbourhood life, combined with an ethnically segmented urban fabric, has contributed to the formation of a multi-ethnic mosaic expressing a rich mixture of cultures. This relatively comfortable coexistence is perhaps due to the fact that in Montreal, unlike in the French system, immigration has no colonial connotation; rather, immigrants come from a broad spectrum of cultural backgrounds. Moreover, there is no racial tension comparable to that found in the United States. On a more negative note, the linguistic controversies associated with the national-unity debate tend to surface when immigration issues are at stake, especially around election time, and frequently involve the overpoliticization of immigrant integration issues. However, these controversies have only rarely degenerated into violent confrontation during the last twenty or so years.

We could also add that, generally speaking, Canada's crime rate is consistently much lower than that of the United States. Statistical disparity testifies to fundamental differences between the Canadian and American national characters. While American mythology exalts the primacy of the individual, Canada's national identity is built upon conservative principles of peace, order, and good government. Of course, there is much more historical evidence to explain the two countries' divergent experience of violence. The discussion lies outside the scope of this chapter, but we mention these factors to support our central thesis that the role of central governments is instrumental in the maintenance of urban social sustainability.

Conclusion

The social sustainability of cities is the product of many contributing factors. We have focused in recent years on the role and effectiveness of local policies, but in doing so we may have lost sight of the decisive role of central governments in protecting our cities' social fabric. The case of Montreal provides an interesting illustration of the debate surrounding decentralization. In a metropolitan context marked by a high degree of municipal fragmentation, the Montreal example highlights the benefits of a centralized system in its provision of social equity and protection, factors crucial to the development of social sustainability. The aspatial policies of higher levels of government in Canada, designed to provide an adequate social safety net, a universal system of health care and education, housing programs, and the like, seem to have had beneficial effects on the social division of urban space to the extent that Montreal is not marked by zones of social exclusion. If some segmentation of social groups is evident in the Montreal urban area, with poverty concentrated in the central city, it is also evident that these same districts boast a significant level of social diversity.

These conditions have also undoubtedly allowed immigrants to take their place in Montreal's urban landscape without too many difficulties. Since legislation was adopted to impose French as the only official language in Quebec, and language laws have forced immigrants to send their children to French-speaking schools, Montrealers seem to have adopted an attitude of accommodation in their day-to-day lives. The city's French character coexists with de facto bilingualism, and younger generations (especially first-generation immigrants) are eagerly experimenting with trilingualism. But Montreal remains a sensitive area of national debate. In fact, the image of division projected by political discourse on the principles upon which the cohesion of Quebec society is built conflicts with the *modus vivendi* prevailing in the daily neighbourhood life of Montrealers. In other words, Montreal has sown the seeds of cosmopolitanism, and interethnic cohabitation is relatively peaceful. Of course, the city is not entirely without discriminatory or intolerant attitudes, but analysis so far does not suggest a socially fragmented milieu.

While various historical factors have contributed to the relatively harmonious pattern of ethnic integration, it has been possible in this chapter only to touch upon these as support for our argument. Our core contention, however, challenges the overly optimistic assessment of the potential benefits of decentralization for urban social sustainability.

Today, decentralization appears in a mostly detrimental context, as central governments pull out of many social programs in response to the budgetary pressures of deficit reduction. Decentralization is therefore only rarely associated with issues of local democracy; it is more commonly tied to the exploitation of local civil society's available resources (Germain 1996a). As a consequence, the conditions that promote social equity, specifically the redistribution of resources, are often neglected.

As Quebec's population ages and the effects of the baby boom diminish, the working-age population will decline. We can no longer count on a demographic balance. Negotiations over resource allocation cannot be left to local governments as these are generally more conservative than policy-makers at either the provincial or the federal level of government.

Nor can we ignore the historic features of the *Trente Glorieuses*, the period that witnessed the development of the welfare state in Quebec, a system that contrasted sharply with previous approaches to the management of the social fabric. The public policies in effect since the beginning of the 1960s are inextricably linked to the sustained levels of economic growth and the remarkable expansion of the state apparatus characteristic of this period. To a large extent, the discourse surrounding decentralization is born from this period of abundance. Today, however, the content of this discourse is much altered. Perhaps we are entering a new era, one still cloaked in the shadows of the unknown, yet charged with the promise of unprecedented change. In this context, can Montreal continue to be a socially sustainable metropolis?

Notes

1 Population figure for the Census Metropolitan Area (CMA) as defined by Statistics Canada.

2 This and the following section draw many ideas from Anne-Marie Séguin 1998.

3 Every four years Statistics Canada conducts a survey of expenditure patterns of Canadian families called the Family Expenditure Survey (FAMEX). Low-income cut-offs are based on FAMEX data, from which the Canadian average family expenditure on food, shelter, and clothing is calculated. This is expressed as a percentage of pre-tax income. Base-year low-income cut-offs are set where families spend 20 percentage points more of their income than the Canadian average on food, shelter, and clothing. The FAMEX data are then analysed to determine the income levels where families spend this percentage on the basics (i.e., the overall Canada percentage plus 20 percentage points). These income levels, differentiated by size of area of residence and by family size, become the base-year low-income cut-offs. Low-income cut-offs are updated annually by the Consumer Price Index (annual average, all-items) (Statistics Canada 1997).

4 According to the 1991 census, the metropolitan region contained 738 census tracts. Each of these corresponds to a small fraction of the metropolitan region, and contains approximately 500 to 2,000 households.

5 The 1996 census showed the proportion of immigrants in the Montreal area to be 17.8 per cent, while the proportions in the Toronto and Vancouver metropolitan regions were 42 per cent and 35 per cent, respectively.

6 We must, however, note a small exception. The City of Montreal exercises local management responsibility for the distribution of allowances from the office of income security to eligible households within its area of jurisdiction. The standards, level of allowance, and eligibility criteria are, however, established by the provincial government.

7 In education, for example, of the budgets allowed to local-authority school boards responsible for the management of education in 1996–7, 80 per cent came from the Quebec Ministry of Education (Maheu 1998), 13 per cent from property taxes, and 7 per cent from other sources. Here, it is important

to specify that the standard and content of teaching material is defined by the ministry. We can therefore speak of a centralized intervention process, where only the management function is delegated to local authorities. In health, all of Quebec's inhabitants can consult a doctor of their choice, at no charge. The regional health offices are responsible for dividing funds among hospitals and among the local community health clinics (LCHCs). However, the criteria, standards, and financing are decided by the Ministry of Health and Social Services. The health system is, therefore, centralized; only its management is decentralized (Lemieux 1996). It is important to add that the ministry has a weighting system, allocating a higher per-capita rate to the LCHCs located in Montreal's inner-city neighbourhoods. This differentiation has sparked a number of demands from other communities, notably from the LCHC on Montreal's South Shore, where the population is more affluent.

8 The establishment of private health clinics that impose service charges is still rare. It does not allow us to conclude that one health-care system is restricted to the rich, and one to the poor. In general, the health-care system remains accessible to everyone, at no direct cost.

9 In 1996–7, 96 per cent of pre-school children, as well as 92 per cent of primary and secondary school students, attended a public institution (Ministère de l'Education du Québec [MEQ] 1998).

10 Inclusion in the list of schools in distressed areas is an important political issue that divides local authorities. It is therefore the school board of the Island of Montreal that draws up the map of distressed areas, but, to prevent any stigmatization, special budgets for students living in distressed areas are allocated directly to the schools that they attend (Germain 1996b).

11 The term is borrowed from Dominique Mathieu (1993).

12 These programs cover the costs of construction and the acquisition of basic facilities and equipment. Operating and maintenance costs are generally covered by the municipalities, which also decide on location.

13 Those who request refugee status are also covered by a federal health insurance plan, and their children have free access to public schools. They are not, however, eligible for income-security payments. Under exceptional circumstances, the minister may ensure that they receive money from the income-security plan when necessary. In reality, in Quebec, 85 per cent of those who claim refugee status receive this income, although the assistance is not theirs as a matter of law. Immigrants who have been sponsored by a member of their family in Canada have access to the income-security plan, but only if they prove that they have taken steps to obtain help from their

relatives. If the relative defaults, the income-security office will make payments at a basic level and will try to obtain an undertaking for repayment in the future.

14 Since the end of the 1980s, the immigration rate has been relatively high in order to compensate for Quebec's low birth rate, one of the lowest in the world. However, the immigration rate does not ensure the renewal of the Quebec population.

15 Here, it is important to note that, while the construction of low-cost public housing was, until recent years, financially backed by senior levels of government, it was, and continues to be, managed by the local level. While cities are requested to contribute something, the operating costs of these programs are also primarily covered by senior levels of government.

16 Lack of economic resources is the first criterion for determining which households can access an HLM. Furthermore, rent levels are set at 25 per cent of the total income of all members of the household, with no upper limit. This has the effect of driving away those households that have improved their economic situation, as they can find housing at lower cost in the private rental market.

17 Civil-service positions at the provincial and municipal levels are, for all practical purposes, reserved to long-established French-speaking people; and these positions represent a very high proportion of the employment created since 1970.

References

Ashton, P.J. 1978. 'Urbanization and the Dynamics of Suburban Development under Capitalism.' In *Marxism and the Metropolis*, ed. William K. Tabb and Larry Sawers, 54–81. New York: Oxford University Press.

Bussière, Yves, and Yves Dallaire. 1994. 'Étalement urbain et motorisation: où se situe Montréal par rapport à d'autres organisations?' *Cahiers de géographie du Québec* 38/105: 327–44.

Castel, Robert. 1991. 'De l'indigence à l'exclusion, la désaffiliation. Précarité du travail et vulnérabilité relationnelle.' In *Face à l'exclusion. Le modèle français*, ed. J. Donzelot, 137–68. Paris: PUF.

Coffey, William, Mario Polèse, and Réjean Drolet. 1996. 'Examining the Thesis of Central Business District Decline: Evidence from the Montreal Metropolitan Area.' *Environment and Planning A* 28/10: 1795–814.

Conseil des Affaires Sociales. 1991. *Pour combattre la pauvreté: Culture et développement social*. Sillery, Quebec: Avis du Conseil des Affaires Sociales.

Dansereau, Francine, and Anne-Marie Séguin. 1995. *La cohabitation intereth-nique dans le logement social au Québec*. Research report submitted to Société d'Habitation du Québec. Montreal: INRS-Urbanisation.

Derycke, Pierre-Henri, and Guy Gilbert. 1988. *Economie publique locale*. Paris: Economica.

Frisken, Frances. 1994. 'Provincial Transit Policymaking for the Toronto, Montreal and Vancouver Regions.' In *The Changing Canadian Metropolis: A Public Policy Perspective*, vol. 2, ed. Frances Frisken, 497–539. Berkeley, CA: Institute of Governmental Studies Press.

Gagné, Madeleine. 1989. 'L'insertion de la population immigrée sur le marché du travail au Québec. Eléments d'analyse des données de recensement.' *Revue internationale d'action communautaire* 21/61: 153–63.

– 1995. *L'intégration des immigrants au Québec: Choix et illustration de quelques indicateurs*. Communication presented to 8ᵉ Entretien du Centre Jacques Cartier, Rhône-Alpes, 'Anciennes et nouvelles minorités: Démographie, culture et politique,' Colloquium, 5–8 December.

Germain, Annick. 1996a. 'Le local: Concept d'analyse ou concept de combat?' In *Acteurs, institutions, enjeux, politiques*, vol. 1, ed. N. Boucher, 19–23. Ste. Foy: Presses de l'Université Laval.

– 1996b. 'Le milieu et la concentration de la défavorisation. Des concepts qui parlent.' In *La défavorisation dans les écoles primaires*, ed. A. Côté, A. Germain, J. Matte, and M. Saint-Jacques, 15–24. Montreal: Conseil Scolaire de l'Île de Montréal.

Germain, Annick, and Bernadette Blanc. 1998. 'Les quartiers multiethniques et leur vie de quartier.' *Revue européenne des migrations internationales* 14/1: 141–58.

Germain, Annick, with Julie Archambault, Bernadette Blanc, Johanne Charbonneau, Francine Dansereau, and Damaris Rose. 1995. *Cohabitation interethnique et vie de quartier*. Études et recherches no. 12. Quebec: Ministère des Affaires Internationales, de l'immigration et des Communautés Culturelles.

Ghorra-Gobin, C. 1996. 'La crise de la cohésion sociale.' *Le livre de l'année*. Paris: Larousse.

Greene, Richard. 1991. 'Poverty Concentration Measures and the Urban Underclass.' *Economic Geography* 67/3: 240–52.

Herpin, Nicholas. 1993. 'L'urban underclass chez les sociologues américains: Exclusion sociale et pauvreté.' *Revue française de sociologie* 34: 421–39.

Hughes, Mark Alan. 1990. 'Formation of the Impacted Ghetto: Evidence from Large Metropolitan Areas, 1970–1989.' *Urban Geography* 11/3: 265–84.

Joly, Jacques. 1996. *Sondage d'opinion québécoise sur l'immigration et les relations interculturelles*. Etudes et recherches no. 15. Quebec: Ministère des Relations avec les Citoyens et de l'Immigration.

Lemieux, Vincent. 1996. 'L'analyse politique de la décentralisation.' *Canadian Journal of Political Science/Revue canadienne de science politique* 29/4: 661–80.

Maheu, Robert. 1998. *Indicateurs de l'éducation, édition 1998*. Quebec: Ministère de l'éducation du Québec, Direction générale des services à la gestion.

Massey, Douglas S. 1994. 'America's Apartheid and the Urban Underclass.' *Social Service Review*, December: 471–87.

Mathieu, Dominique. 1993. 'La spécialisation spatiale à Los Angeles.' *Annales de géographie* 569: 32–52.

McNicoll, Claire. 1993. *Montréal, ville multiculturelle*. Paris: Bélin.

Ministère des Affaires Internationales, de l'Immigration et des Communautés Culturelles (MAIICC). 1994. *Population immigrée dans la région métropolitaine de recensement de Montréal, 1991*. Collection Statistiques et indicateurs no. 6. Quebec: Les publications du Québec.

Ministère de l'Education du Québec (MEQ). 1994. *Rapport annuel, 1993–1994*. Quebec: Publications du Québec.

Mongeau, Jaël, and Anne-Marie Séguin. 1993. *Les profils résidentiels des ménages immigrés et non immigrés dans la région Montréalaise selon le recensement de 1986*. Notes et documents no 3. Report submitted to the Ministère des communautés culturelles et de l'immigration du Québec. Montreal: INRS-Urbanisation.

Olson, Sherry. 1991. 'Ethnic Strategies in the Urban Economy.' *Canadian Ethnic Studies* 33/2: 39–60.

Remy, Jean, and Liliane Voyé. 1992. *La ville, vers une nouvelle définition?* Paris: L'Harmattan.

Séguin, Anne-Marie. 1992. 'Les politiques de logement récentes: leur impact sur le devenir de la ville-centre.' Research report submitted to the City of Montreal, December.

– 1998. 'Les espaces de pauvreté.' In *Montréal 2001: Visages et défis d'une métropole*, ed. C. Manzagol and C. Bryant, 221–36. Montreal: Presses de l'Université de Montréal.

Séguin, Anne-Marie, and Marc Termote. 1997. *L'appauvrissement des populations québécoise et montréalaise*. Research report submitted to the Fédération des Caisses populaires de Montréal et de l'Ouest du Québec. Montreal: INRS-Urbanisation.

Société d'Habitation du Québec (SHQ). 1988. *Les programmes d'aide à l'habitation au Québec*. Direction de la planification et de l'évaluation, SHQ. Quebec: Publications du Québec.

Statistics Canada. 1997. *Low Income Cut-offs*. Catalogue 13–551-XPB. Ottawa: Ministry of Supply and Services.

Strobel, Pierre. 1996. 'De la pauvreté à l'exclusion: société salariale ou société des droits de l'homme?' *Revue internationale des sciences sociales* 148: 201–18.

Taboada Leonetti, Isabelle. 1995. 'Intégration et exclusion dans la société duale. Le chômeur et l'immigré.' *Lien social et politiques: RIAC* 34: 93–103.

Tremblay, Diane-Gabrielle. 1990. *Economie du travail: Les réalités et les approches théoriques*. Sainte-Foy, PQ: Télé-Université et Editions Saint-Martin.

Ville de Montréal. 1990. *Habiter Montréal. Politique d'habitation*. Montreal: Service de l'habitation et du développement urbain.

Wackant, Loïc J.D., and William Julius Wilson. 1989. 'The Cost of Racial and Class Exclusion in the Inner City.' *Annals of the American Academy of Political and Social Science* 501: 8–25.

3 Governance and Social Sustainability: The Toronto Experience

FRANCES FRISKEN, L.S. BOURNE, GUNTER GAD, and ROBERT A. MURDIE

Within North America, Toronto often serves as a model of effective urban governance primarily because of three characteristics that imply a high level of social sustainability: the economic vitality and social well-being of its downtown business and residential districts; a public transit system that has performed more effectively and efficiently than all others in North America; and the relatively uniform quality of local public goods and services provided in all parts of the metropolitan region. These three characteristics make Toronto an ideal setting in which to investigate the contributions that governance, broadly defined, can make to urban social sustainability.

Any such investigation must take account of the different scales at which Toronto can be defined. Until recently, the name 'Toronto' could signify one of three quite different geographical entities (see figure 3.1). The first was the old City of Toronto, the historic core city of a rapidly expanding urban region. Incorporated as a city in 1834, this municipality grew by annexing adjacent suburban districts until 1914 (Lemon 1985). After that date its boundaries remained unchanged until the end of 1997. It is this Toronto that stirs admiration in visitors for its vibrant downtown business district (still the primary employment centre for the Toronto area) and its well-kept middle-class neighbourhoods. Unlike the deteriorated 'inner cities' found in many urban regions in the United States, it does not have extensive slums characterized by physical deterioration, disinvestment, and social malfunction (Board of Trade of Metropolitan Toronto 1996, 195–6; Lemon 1996, 142–294; Precourt and Faircloth 1996).

The second Toronto was the Municipality of Metropolitan Toronto (commonly referred to as 'Metro'), a two-tier federation of thirteen

Figure 3.1 The Greater Toronto Area
Source: City of Toronto UPDS Graphics and Presentations

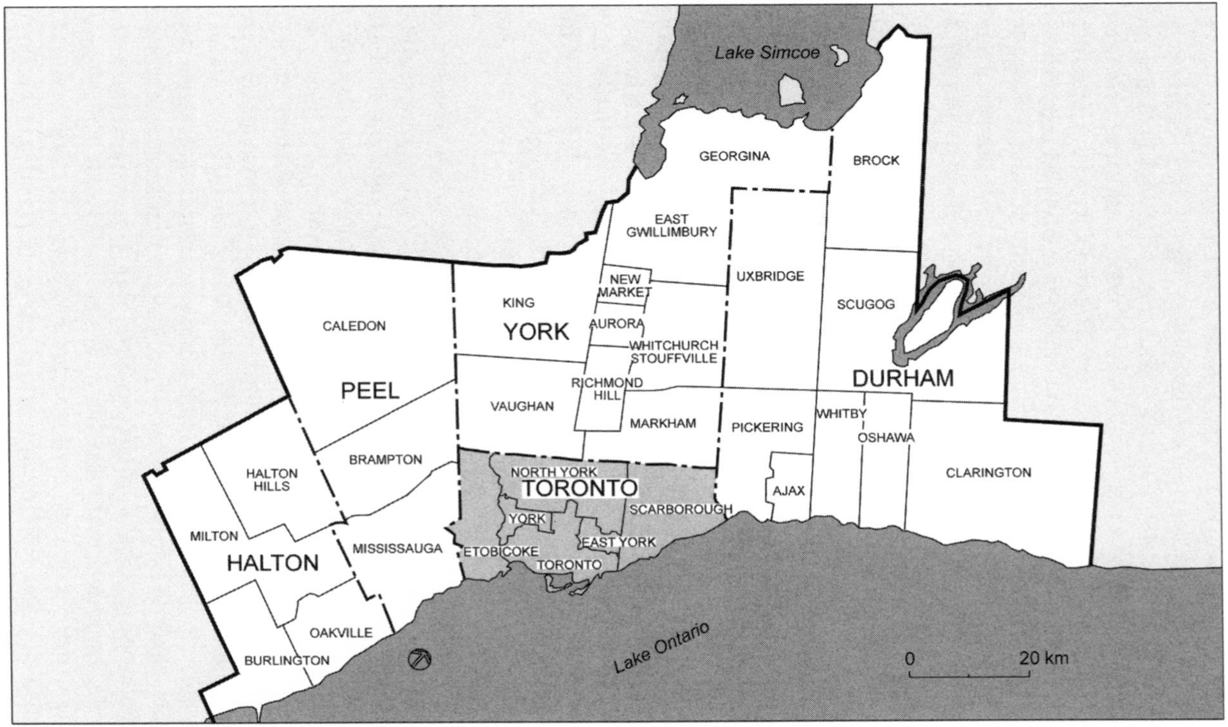

municipalities created in 1953 to provide physical infrastructure to rapidly growing suburban districts out of pooled local tax revenues. In 1966 the government of the Province of Ontario consolidated the thirteen municipalities into six (Etobicoke, North York, Scarborough, York, East York, and the City of Toronto; see figure 3.1). Then, in 1998, it merged Metro with its six constituent municipalities into a new, greatly enlarged City of Toronto. The old City of Toronto disappeared as a legal entity.[1] Because this chapter is concerned primarily with how Toronto acquired its reputation as a socially sustainable city, it refers to the political structure of Metro before the 1998 merger. Thus it treats Metro as an entity distinct both from the old City of Toronto and from the inner ring of five older suburban municipalities (the within-Metro suburbs) that surrounded the core city before the merger took place.

The third Toronto is the much larger Toronto urban region. This entity has no legal existence at present; it serves only as a basis for collecting data and analysing trends and issues associated with Toronto-related expansion. It is defined in two major ways. The definition most commonly used by Toronto area governments since the mid-1980s depicts a Greater Toronto Area (GTA) composed of five upper-tier regional municipalities (identified as Halton, Peel, York, Durham, and Toronto – the former Metro – in figure 3.1). Another definition, based on journey-to-work criteria, is that used by Statistics Canada to describe the Toronto Census Metropolitan Area (CMA). While CMA boundaries have moved outward since the concept was first used in 1951, the statistical region as defined in 1996 was still somewhat smaller in area and population than the five-region GTA.

In this chapter we treat 'Toronto' as an urban region comprising three zones of analysis, the inner core (referred to here as the old City of Toronto), the five municipalities that made up the rest of Metropolitan Toronto before 1998 (the older, within-Metro suburbs), and the four outer suburban regions or outer suburbs, containing twenty-four local municipalities. Our analysis suggests that a system of governance comprising local, metropolitan/regional, and provincial government institutions has contributed to conditions conducive to social sustainability in the Toronto area in a number of important ways. As the area has expanded outward, however, that system has undergone changes that appear to be eroding Toronto's ability to remain socially sustainable. To understand why this might be the case, it is necessary to consider the various ways in which a government system might address problems that work against social integration and social harmony.

Requirements for Socially Responsive Local Governance: Alternative Perspectives

The identification of cities and city-regions as significant actors in the global economy has led some writers to suggest that it is now local governments, or systems of local government, that are most responsible for deciding the social character and quality of life in their jurisdictions. Such writers can justify their case for local action by drawing on a tradition of urban political analysis that maintains that municipal governments, being chosen by and accountable to citizens in their local communities, are the governments that are best able and most likely to do what is needed to integrate socially and culturally diverse groups into harmonious communities. This socially benign view of local government also supports the idea that representatives of the many and varied municipalities that make up metropolitan areas can agree among themselves about ways to reduce threats to social sustainability.

The evidence suggests, however, that few local governments are inclined to initiate or agree to policies intended to make life easier for the less advantaged members of the metropolitan community. Instead, research has discovered a generalized tendency for local governments to use their powers (particularly their powers to control land use and to regulate buildings) to discourage or exclude activities or types of residents considered 'undesirable' for financial or social reasons, and to attract only those people and activities likely to benefit the municipality (Danielson 1976). Three motives seem to underlie this type of behaviour. One is the desire of municipal governments to enhance their tax bases, or at least to protect them from demands for new services or from changes that might pose a threat to property values. A second is a desire not to drive residents away to other municipalities where taxes are lower, and to avoid attracting new residents by offering services they cannot get elsewhere. The third is a politically motivated concern to protect local residents (and voters) from perceived threats to the preferred (usually middle-class) lifestyle of homeowning majorities (Filion 1992; Hawley 1976).

Suburban governments and many city neighbourhoods are particularly resistant to senior government policies intended to promote a city-wide or region-wide distribution of low-rent housing, or to undertake such policies on their own, as a way to end the isolation of the urban poor in ghetto conditions and to promote their integration with the rest of the urban community. This resistance has been well documented in the United States, where a 'fair share' distribution of low-rent and socially assisted housing within metropolitan areas has been identified as important to improving the life chances of the urban poor, and reducing problems of physical decay and social disharmony in older cities. Policies having a similar purpose are those aimed at offset-ting disparities in municipal tax bases (through local revenue sharing or a sharing of some portion of the local tax base) and transportation policies that allow people without automobiles to move easily between residential and employment sites in all parts of an urban region (Peirce, Johnson, and Hall 1993; Downs 1994; Rusk 1995; Dodge 1996).

If a national or state/provincial government decides that it wants any or all of these matters dealt with in the interest of distributing the costs and benefits of urban growth and change more equitably throughout a metropolitan region, and if it becomes clear that few of an area's municipalities are prepared to act on them, it may either exer-cise its legal right to make policies on its own, or create some form of metropolitan or regional government and give it the authority to do what it wants done. The latter approach is the one most favoured by urban political analysts because it keeps decisions affecting the physi-cal and social development of an expanding city-region in the hands of people who represent local constituencies and who deal specifically with issues that affect people in their daily lives.

In principle, metropolitan governments can take a wide variety of forms, ranging from a unified, monolithic structure with full authority to manage the affairs of an entire region, to loosely structured gather-ings of public officials who can decide what needs to be done and make recommendations to municipal or senior governments. Ulti-mately, however, it is the government responsible for municipal insti-tutions (which in the case of Toronto is the provincial government of Ontario) that determines how much will be done in an urban region to promote social sustainability. If it decides to do nothing – that is, if it lets municipal governments deal as best they can with the social prob-lems they cannot avoid, and avoid as many problems as possible by shifting them to other municipalities – it is making a choice that will be just as important for that region's social character as if it had acted more purposefully.

The Toronto area is a good setting in which to examine what differ-ent approaches to metropolitan governance are likely to mean for urban social sustainability. It has undergone a succession of changes in its system of governance that have meant different levels of involvement by central (provincial), regional, and municipal institutions at different times. In this chapter, we assess the ways in which the three levels of government have dealt with the three activities earlier described as important to achieving social sustainability in metropolitan areas: promoting a relatively uniform quality of public goods through local revenue-sharing; the distribution of social housing on a 'fair share' basis; and providing a transit choice for those area residents without access to an automobile or who cannot drive. Before looking at how these policies have evolved in the Toronto area, however, we consider the extent to which that area has experienced the social and spatial fragmentation that such policies are expected to alleviate.

How the Greater Toronto Area Has Evolved

Population Growth

Toronto is Canada's largest urban region, having pulled ahead of the Montreal area in 1976. It has been growing steadily in both areal extent and population since 1951. By 1996, the five-region GTA encompassed over 7,200 square kilometres and the GTA's population was more than 4.6 million (see figure 3.1 and table 3.1). Between 1986 and 1996, the GTA's population increased by 24 per cent. As noted in table 3.1, this growth was not uniform across the region. Population in the outer (regional) suburbs increased by almost 50 per cent during this period, while growth in the inner core (City of Toronto) and the older within-Metro suburbs (Scarborough, East York, North York, York, and Etobicoke) was much more modest. Two trends are particularly noteworthy in the context of this chapter. First, Metro's share of the GTA population has continued to drop over time, from 71.6 per cent in 1971 to 58.7 per cent in 1986 and 51.5 per cent in 1996. Second, in contrast to many American metropolitan areas that have suffered serious declines in the populations of their core areas, the population of Toronto's inner core increased slightly (by 6.8 per cent) during the 1986–96 decade. This increase is largely attributable to the construction of new housing, especially high-rise condominiums and socially assisted non-profit and co-operative units.

A Changing Socio-economic Structure

Within this rapidly expanding urban envelope, a major restructuring

Table 3.1 Population Growth in the GTA and Its Components, 1986–1996

	Population (in 000s)			
	1986	1991	1996	% change 1986–96
GTA	3,733	4,236	4,628	24.0
Regional suburbs	1,540	1,960	2,243	45.7
Metro Toronto	2,192	2,276	2,385	8.8
City of Toronto	612	635	654	6.8
Scarborough	485	525	559	15.3
East York	101	103	108	6.6
North York	556	563	590	6.0
York	135	140	147	8.2
Etobicoke	303	310	329	8.5

Source: Census of Canada

of the social and economic landscape has occurred, both within the geographical area of the former Metro Toronto and within the outer suburban regions. In 1961 'blue collar' workers accounted for 40 per cent of the old City of Toronto's resident labour force, and 36 per cent of the resident labour force of the within-Metro suburbs and outer suburbs combined. By 1991 the percentage of 'blue collar' workers had fallen to 15 per cent in the old City of Toronto, compared with 21 per cent in the suburbs. The situation for persons in managerial/professional occupations changed in the opposite direction. Persons in these occupations living in the old city rose from 16 per cent in 1961 to 42 per cent in 1991, but only from 25 per cent to 33 per cent in the old and new suburbs combined. While changes in the service, clerical, and sales occupations were less dramatic, these occupations also accounted for a lower share of the resident labour force in the old City of Toronto than in the suburbs.

   Shifts in the distribution of the resident labour force, combined with changes in household composition, help explain the persistent economic and social well-being of the Toronto core. The old City of Toronto's average census family income in 1991, while below the average for sixteen of the twenty-four municipalities in the GTA's four outer regions, was the highest in Metro.[2] Its average family income had increased relative to the Metro average (from 91 to 108 per cent) since 1971 while that of all other Metro municipalities had declined.[3] Its average per-capita income not only was higher than that in any other Metro municipality, but also exceeded the average for all but five municipalities in the GTA. Only average household income was slightly lower than Metro's and considerably below that of the GTA as a whole, undoubtedly because the City of Toronto had a much higher percentage of one-person households (37.8 per cent) than did Metro (27.4 per cent) or the entire GTA (21.4 per cent). Even so, Toronto was the only central city in Canada not to experience a decline in household income relative to the rest of its Census Metropolitan Area (CMA) between 1970 and 1990 (Bourne 1997, 139).

There was and still is substantial poverty in the core city nonetheless (Bourne 1997; Murdie 1996, 1998). The 22.4 per cent of the old City of Toronto population classified as 'low income' by Statistics Canada in 1991 exceeded that of Metro as a whole (18.9 per cent) and was considerably higher than the proportion (8.3 per cent) living in the four suburban regions (Metropolitan Toronto Planning Department, Research and Special Studies Division [n.d.], 77). Only the City of York, an older inner suburb, had a similar proportion of persons in this category. In contrast to the old City of Toronto, however, York also had the lowest average income in Metro. The old City of Toronto, moreover, had the highest index of income disparity, measured as the ratio of low-income to high-income households, and thus the highest level of social polarization.

Changes in the social geography of Metropolitan Toronto have thus resulted in a complex pattern. While many of Toronto's most disadvantaged residents still lived in the old City of Toronto, this core city differed in important respects from the image of the impoverished and socially troubled 'inner city' so prominent in writings about North American cities. Further analysis shows, however, that within-Metro suburbs had suffered a relative decline in socio-economic status in terms of average household income and of characteristics of the resident labour force while the rest of the Census Metropolitan Area (CMA) experienced a relative increase. In combination those changes suggested a troubling increase in social polarization both within the core city and between the old and new suburbs within the CMA. This polarization, in turn, raises concerns about increased social friction in the future.

Social and Ethnic Transformation

The decline in the relative socio-economic status of within-Metro suburbs resulted in part from a steady increase in the number of low-income immigrants and refugees living there. The Toronto CMA, Canada's most important immigrant reception area, has been the intended destination for approximately 30 per cent of all immigrants to Canada in each year since 1971.[4] By 1996, 42 per cent of the area's population was born outside the country, an increase from 38 per cent in 1991. The origins of Canada's and Toronto's immigrant population had also changed dramatically. Until the late 1960s most (roughly 80 per cent) of Toronto's immigrants were from Britain and other European countries. Since then there has been a substantial increase in immigrants and refugees from South, East, and Southeast Asia; the Caribbean; Africa; and Central and South America (see figure 3.2). By the 1990s, over 80 per cent of immigrants were from these non-traditional sources.

Recent immigrants have settled in all parts of the former Metro and, lately, in many of the newer suburbs outside Metro. This settlement pattern contrasts with that of older groups, such as Italians and Portuguese, that first settled near the downtown core before moving to the suburbs. The shift in the spatial distribution of new immigrants has resulted from several factors, including the changing characteristics of immigrants and the development of a wider variety of housing tenure in the suburbs. Business immigrants from Hong Kong, for example, have the resources to move directly into relatively high-priced housing in the newer suburbs. In contrast, low-income immigrants and refugees have little choice in housing and are often forced to live in public housing or lower-rent private dwellings that were built on relatively inexpensive suburban land inside Metro during the 1960s and 1970s.

Changing Structure and Distribution of Employment

According to census figures, employment expanded considerably in the Toronto CMA between 1971 and 1991, from about 1.16 million to 2.02 million jobs. While job growth occurred in all parts of the metropolitan area, it was more vigorous outside than inside the former Metro. Consequently, the old City of Toronto's share of total CMA jobs declined sharply, from 48 per cent to 31 per cent, between 1971 and 1991. The share of total CMA jobs in the within-Metro suburbs fell slightly, from 35 per cent to 33.7 per cent, and the share in the outer suburbs more than doubled, from 17 per cent to 35.5 per cent. This pat-

Figure 3.2 Place of Birth by Period of Immigration, Toronto CMA, 1996

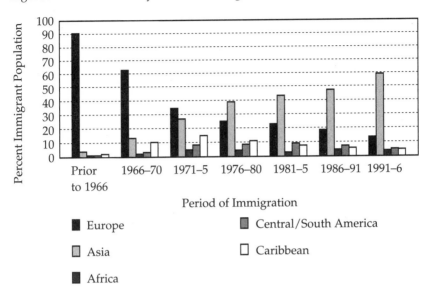

Source: Census of Canada, 1996

tern of relative employment decentralization persisted during the recession that began in 1989. While the old City of Toronto and within-Metro suburbs lost a large number of jobs and had not yet recovered to the 1989 level by late 1997, the outer suburbs lost fewer jobs and regained them more quickly.

Not only did different 'industries' or sectors of the economy grow at widely varying rates between 1971 and 1991, but their growth and decline were distributed unevenly within the Toronto region. The City of Toronto, the City of York, and the Borough of East York suffered heavy losses in manufacturing, resulting in an absolute decline of manufacturing jobs for Metro Toronto as a whole. At the same time, strong growth in the transportation/utilities and the trade sectors in within-Metro suburbs more than compensated for losses in these sectors in the City of Toronto. While Metro as a whole showed a considerable increase in jobs in sectors with a strong blue-collar component, that increase occurred outside the old City and the two innermost suburbs.

The sectors composed mainly of white-collar work showed absolute increases in both the City of Toronto and the rest of Metro.

In the outer suburban ring, jobs in manufacturing showed strong growth over the same period, continuing the outward movement of manufacturing that began in the 1960s. All other economic sectors also grew strongly in this outer ring, especially other sectors with a high content of blue-collar work (construction, transportation, and utilities) or those oriented towards the expanding residential population (trade and community services). The only sectors where absolute growth was relatively small were the finance, insurance, and real estate (FIRE) sector and the business-services sector. These remain the most spatially concentrated sectors (in the downtown core and a few suburban nodes) of the regional economy.

Changes in both the sectoral and occupational structures of the economy have produced clearly recognizable trends in the geography of job quality. 'High-level' (i.e., professional/managerial) jobs are concentrated in the core of the region, with the old City of Toronto having nearly 39 per cent of these jobs but only 31 per cent of all jobs, while the continuous deconcentration and decentralization of the manufacturing sector has led to a dispersal of blue collar employment. Fully 45 per cent of these blue collar jobs are now found in the outer suburbs and 36 per cent in the within-Metro suburbs.

Overview

Within the rapidly expanding Toronto urban region, the diverse social landscape of the urbanized core has been refined, replicated, and extended into suburban areas, including newer suburbs outside Metropolitan Toronto. The region has also undergone a dramatic shift in ethnocultural composition, especially in terms of rapidly increasing numbers of new visible minorities, largely because of steady immigration. These changes are evident in the patterns of two social indices: the distribution of average household income and poverty levels (see figure 3.3), and the concentration of immigrant and low-income populations (see figure 3.4). Here we can clearly observe the social transformation of the suburbs, particularly that brought about by the emergence of new concentrations of low-income households, recent immigrants, and non-traditional families. While this social transformation has been particularly apparent in the 'old,' or within-Metro, suburbs, it has also been occurring rapidly in many parts of the outer

Figure 3.3 Low-Income Households in the Toronto CMA, 1991,
by Enumeration Area
Source: Ranu Basu, from Census of Canada, 1991

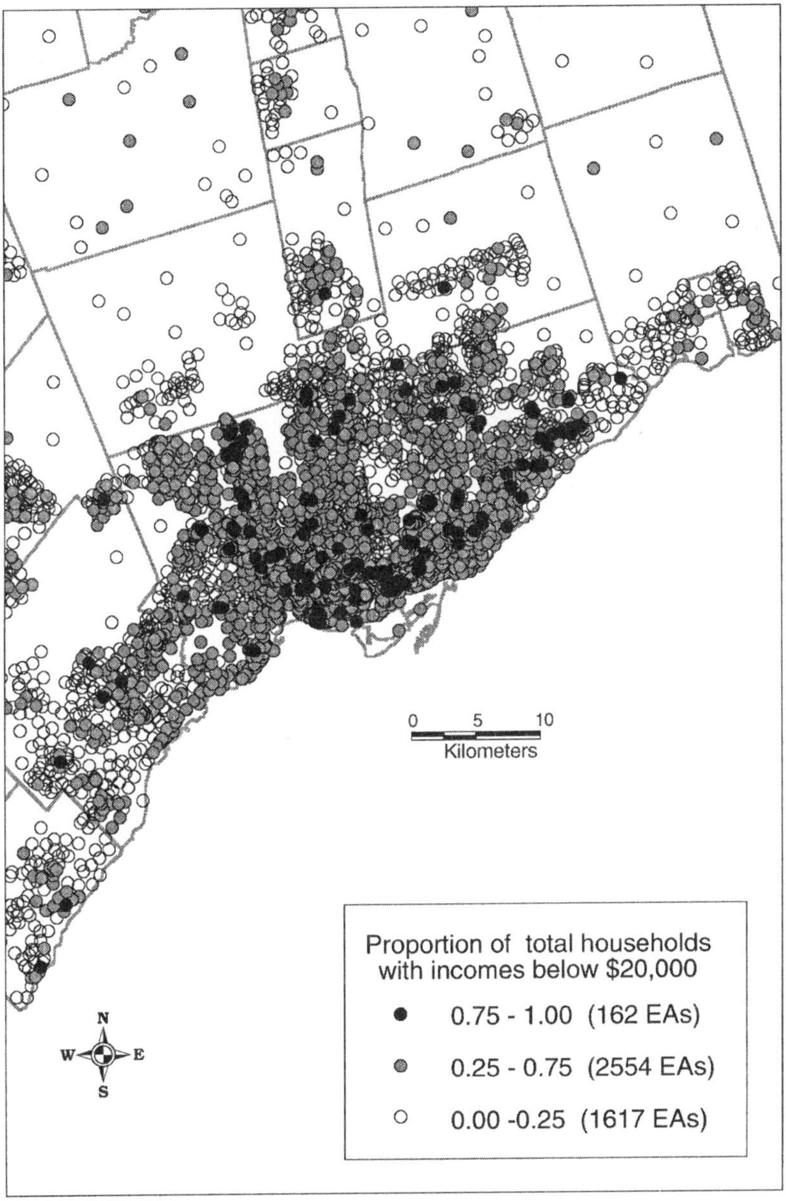

0   5   10
Kilometers

N
W ◆ E
S

Proportion of total households
with incomes below $20,000

●   0.75 - 1.00   (162 EAs)

◉   0.25 - 0.75   (2554 EAs)

○   0.00 -0.25   (1617 EAs)

Figure 3.4 Enumeration Areas with Both a High Proportion of Low-Income Households and a High Proportion of Recent Immigrants, Toronto CMA, 1991
Source: Ranu Basu, from Census of Canada, 1991

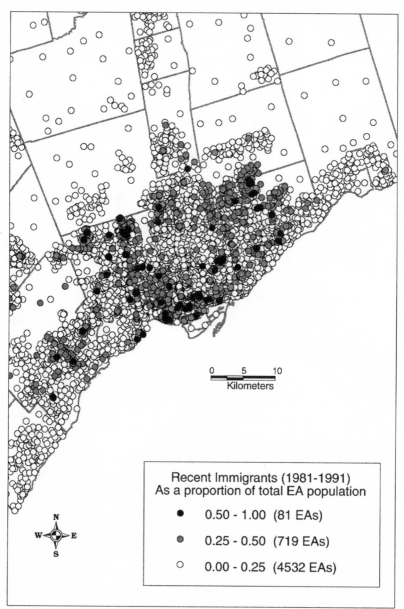

suburban ring. The areas of most concern are those where high levels of immigration coincide with concentrations of low-income populations.

As for employment restructuring, the old City of Toronto still had the most favourable job-to-resident ratio of any municipality in the Toronto CMA in 1991. Its jobs were increasingly in offices, however, and tended to be higher-paying. Also, they were concentrated in the central area and other nodes along the north–south subway line. At the same time, lower-paying jobs as a proportion of all jobs tended to be increasing slowly in both the within-Metro suburbs and the outer suburbs, where employment also tended to be much more dispersed.

Despite increasing socio-economic diversity and the decentralization and dispersion of blue-collar employment, differences in income levels between central and outer municipalities have so far remained relatively low by North American standards. It is now time to ask how governmental arrangements and policies influenced the development of this socio-economic structure, and how governments have responded to the challenges to social sustainability posed by changes occurring within the social and economic spheres.

The Contributions of Governance to Toronto's Spatial Structure

Background

The government of the Province of Ontario exercises its constitutional authority for municipal governance through legislation, through the guidelines and regulations administered by its various departments, and through an appointed, quasi-judicial agency, the Ontario Municipal Board (OMB). This body has authority to approve municipal capital expenditures and to settle disputes related to aspects of municipal administration, including land-use planning. It was the OMB that recommended the creation of Metropolitan Toronto in 1953 as a way to deal with the area's rapid growth (Ontario Municipal Board 1953). Issues of municipal finance were prominent, then as later, in discussions leading to the area's political reorganization. Many of these issues related to the tax on municipal property (land and buildings), the principal type of own-source revenue available to Canadian municipalities. Prominent among them were large intermunicipal variations in taxable wealth, as indicated by variations in the assessed value of residential and commercial properties, and thus in the ability of municipalities to finance local services and public education.

Despite its innovative features, the two-tier system of local administration recommended for Metro Toronto by the OMB, and largely
implemented by the province, fell far short of being the unified
arrangement favoured by proponents of metropolitan government.
Metro Council became responsible for property assessment, major
physical infrastructure, metropolitan parks, and the administration of
justice. Thirteen municipal councils continued to provide physical services within their own boundaries, and looked after local parks, social
welfare, public health, fire protection, libraries, and property-tax collection. The Metropolitan Toronto School Board took over some aspects of
education finance, but eleven local boards operated the schools, deriv-
ing most of their revenues from local property taxes. Other services
were provided by appointed boards and commissions: the Toronto
Transit Commission; a Metropolitan Toronto Planning Board and local
planning boards; a Metropolitan Toronto Housing Authority and a City
of Toronto Housing Authority; and, after 1957, a Board of Police Commissioners with a majority of provincial members.

Because it remained institutionally fragmented, Metro Toronto's ability to function depended on the willingness of the locally elected and
appointed officials who served on its various units to cooperate in
devising common policies. Cooperation did occur during Metro's early
years, when metropolitan institutions moved rapidly to provide much-
needed physical infrastructure to the rapidly growing suburbs. It broke
down, however, when local representatives on the Metropolitan Toronto Council and Metropolitan Toronto School Board began to debate
ways to deal with growing gaps in spending on local services (particularly social assistance and public education) resulting from persistent
intermunicipal disparities in property assessment. Metro institutions
also showed little interest in enlarging Metro's area of jurisdiction to
take in developing suburban districts outside its boundaries.

It was the provincial government that began to respond to intermunicipal disparities and Toronto-area expansion in the 1960s with
regional planning initiatives, local-government restructuring, increased
grants to local governments, and the takeover of some local functions.
Its interventions resulted in a governmental system for the Toronto area
that was even more fragmented than the system that presided over
Metro's development in the 1950s. As will be shown below, it also managed several important issues of regional administration very differently outside Metro Toronto than these had been managed for Metro
alone.

Tax Sharing

From the beginning, the Metropolitan Toronto Council covered the costs of functions assigned to it by levying charges on member municipalities based on the size of their property assessments. In other words, assessment-rich municipalities paid more per capita into Metro than did poorer ones. This arrangement allowed Metro to proceed quickly with the construction of new physical infrastructure. It did not make the thirteen municipalities more equal in their own tax resources, however, or in their ability to provide those services for which they remained responsible. In the decade after Metro's 1953 creation, the thirteen municipalities became more unequal in their per-capita assessments and in their spending on local services (Royal Commission on Metropolitan Toronto 1965, 172). Both Metro Council and the Metro Toronto School Board debated this issue at length without agreeing to act on it. The provincial government then took the initiative when it reorganized Metro Toronto in 1966. It reduced the number of lower-tier units from thirteen to six by consolidating some of the smaller municipalities into larger ones (see figure 3.1). It also transferred responsibility for social services from local councils to the metropolitan council and empowered the restructured Metropolitan Toronto School Board to finance public education out of pooled local taxes.

The redistribution of property-tax revenues for social services and public education not only helped to reduce disparities in these services, but also allowed the governments of Metro's poorer municipalities to provide a higher standard of local services than they would have been able to provide otherwise. And it did so without obvious harm to the City of Toronto, which not only had the highest total assessment per capita after Metro's restructuring in 1966, but also experienced an increase in that assessment base relative to other Metro municipalities after that date.

Between 1969 and 1974, the provincial government consolidated local school districts and municipalities into larger units, and created two-tier regional municipalities in many parts of the province. These changes applied the principle of tax sharing to regional municipalities separately, but not to the five-region GTA as a whole (see figure 3.1). In 1997 the provincial government announced a new round of changes to local governments that involved taking education off the residential tax base altogether. In exchange, municipalities took over all, or large shares of, the costs of local services, including social services, for which the province had been paying between 50 and 100 per cent of total costs. Coming as it did immediately after the provincial government's decision to amalgamate Metro into a single city, this announcement both strengthened opposition to amalgamation and created intense anxiety about Metro's long-term well-being. In response to objections (some coming from its own supporters), the province restored nearly 20 per cent of the cost of education to the residential property tax, reduced some of the social-service costs to be 'downloaded' onto local governments, and set aside money to repair social housing.

Despite these changes to the downloading legislation, city officials continued to insist that the shift of social-service costs to municipalities implied higher relative costs for the new City of Toronto than for most other Ontario municipalities. After strong lobbying from prominent Metro interests, the Commissioner of Community and Social Services, the Board of Trade, and some of the government's more prominent supporters, the Minister of Municipal Affairs said the government would find a way to pool local property taxes across the GTA to pay for the local share of social services and public health. This announcement brought immediate objections from suburban officials, who maintained that they should not have to pay for services that would benefit a disproportionately large share of Metro residents. The government changed course once again, saying that only the costs of welfare and social housing would be pooled; municipal governments would be separately responsible for providing all other social services (including public health, ambulance services, and child welfare). The government has also said that the Greater Toronto (GT) Transit commuter system will be financed out of a pool of local tax revenues from across the entire region (including Hamilton–Wentworth, the regional municipality to the west of Halton).

Concerns about the implications of provincial downloading for Toronto's financial well-being and social sustainability rests on an awareness of the increasing differences between the new city's socio-economic structure and that of the suburban regions, in particular the relative decline in the socio-economic status of the within-Metro suburbs compared to the outer suburbs. Past government policies contributed to those differences by helping to make Metro the principal provider of lower-priced rental housing in the GTA. Recent provincial government policies have ensured that the new City of Toronto will retain that role.

The Provision and Spatial Distribution of Low-Cost Housing

The City of Toronto helped initiate deliberations leading to the creation of Metropolitan Toronto in 1953 in part because of its concern that residential overcrowding in central neighbourhoods was impeding the redevelopment and renewal of the downtown core (Rose 1972, 10–19). The city had initiated Canada's first family public housing development (Regent Park North) immediately after the Second World War, and faced the prospect of having to accommodate most of the area's poorest households unless low-cost housing were built in the suburbs. Suburban governments had little or no interest in sponsoring public housing, however, nor in providing the social and community services that low-income residents were likely to need.

In creating Metropolitan Toronto, the provincial government gave both Metro Council and local councils the right to negotiate with federal and provincial authorities for public-housing assistance. Little public housing was built during Metro's first ten years, but Metro planners did persuade reluctant suburban governments to identify or agree to potential sites. Thus, when the provincial government created the Ontario Housing Corporation (OHC) in 1964 to use recently announced federal funds to invigorate the public-housing program, the groundwork had been laid. By 1973, with 24 per cent of the province's population, Metro had about 60 per cent of its total supply of family public housing (Rose 1980, 175). Two-thirds of that housing was in the within-Metro suburbs, which by then also contained two-thirds of Metro's population.

Because suburban governments would approve higher-density forms of housing in only a few districts, and because federal and Ontario governments placed severe constraints on unit costs, most public housing took the form of concentrated clusters of apartment buildings, usually high-rise and often on isolated sites. These same districts also absorbed much of the private low-rental housing and lower-priced condominiums built in the suburbs. These are the districts that now house some of Metro's lowest-income residents, including recent immigrants and refugees.

The location of a significant proportion of the public-housing stock outside the City of Toronto indirectly helped maintain the attractiveness of the inner city for commercial redevelopment and residential rehabilitation. It also prevented the entrapment of the area's poorer residents in inner-city ghettoes, as was happening in many American cities during this period. At the same time, however, formulae used for its allocation resulted in high concentrations of low-income, often single-parent and/or new immigrant families in high-rise towers and other forms of high-density housing in the suburbs. This trend produced a political backlash among suburban residents, making municipal councils both inside and outside Metro increasingly reluctant to approve any type of higher-density housing for rental use.

Much less rental housing was built in the outer suburban regions than in Metro, and little of it was public housing. Although the OHC was a provincial, not a Metro agency, it did not have a mandate to decide where public housing should go. It acted only on requests from municipal governments, and few such requests came from municipalities outside Metro. A mid-1970s shift in social-housing assistance to non-profit and cooperative housing for families with a range of incomes did little to change the situation. The only municipalities to take advantage of the new programs were the City of Toronto, Metro Toronto, and the Regional Municipality of Peel. Not until the late 1980s did the other three regional municipalities initiate social-housing programs, and then only in response to evidence of local need. Thus, by 1992 Metropolitan Toronto, with 58 per cent of the GTA's total housing stock, had 97 per cent of all public-housing units in the GTA and nearly 80 per cent of the GTA's stock of rent-geared-to-income housing (Metropolitan Toronto Planning Department 1993, table 2.3).

Since then, an end to federal and provincial financial assistance has brought new social-housing construction to a halt. The Ontario government has said it will make municipal governments fully responsible for administering social housing and paying that share of operating costs (mainly rent subsidies) not covered by the federal government. It has done away with unpopular legislation, enacted and then strengthened by previous governments, requiring new residential developments anywhere in the province to include a specified component of 'affordable' housing. It has also revoked legislation giving homeowners the right to convert parts of their homes to accessory rental apartments without first seeking municipal approval. Suburban municipal governments are again free to restrict residential development in their communities to single-family homes on separate lots, or higher-priced townhouses and condominium apartments.

While the core city/outer suburb differences in housing quality and tenure mix are still small in comparison with those found in many metropolitan areas in the United States, they nonetheless suggest that the new City of Toronto will be home to a growing share of GTA house-holds who either cannot afford to purchase housing or cannot afford to pay high-end-of-market rents. How well members of such households are able to participate in the expanding regional economy will depend to a significant degree on the quality of local public services, and on how well the transportation system serves their travel needs.

Core-Oriented Rapid Transit

Like the public-housing program, Metro Toronto's public transit system began with a City of Toronto initiative – a 1946 decision to replace a heavily used streetcar line on Yonge Street, Toronto's main north–south artery, with a full-capacity subway. After the city-owned Toronto Transportation Commission was reconstituted in 1953 as a metropolitan agency, the Toronto Transit Commission (TTC), the metropolitan council took over and increased that agency's capital debt so that the TTC could acquire several suburban bus lines and integrate them with the city system.

Because of the immediate success of the Yonge Street subway, transit occupied a more important place in planning proposals for Metro Toronto than it did in plans prepared for most other North American urban regions in the 1950s and 1960s. Nonetheless, Metro planners assigned subways a limited and well-defined role in the long-range transportation system: to carry passengers between densely populated central neighbourhoods and the downtown core (Metropolitan Toronto Planning Board 1959, S4). The private automobile would serve the more dispersed trips made outside that district. This philosophy underwent gradual change in succeeding years, however, as a result of political struggles within Metro Council that culminated in Metro and provincial government decisions to pay the full capital costs (on a 25–75 per cent basis) and to cover the operating deficits (on a 50–50 per cent basis) of the transit system. These decisions allowed the TTC to extend subway lines into the suburbs and to introduce new suburban bus lines to bring passengers to subway stations. They also prompted Metro Council (which had a majority of suburban members after 1966) to replace a zone fare system with a single, uniform, Metro-wide fare, and with unlimited transfer rights among vehicles travelling within Metro. As a result of these changes, it became both easier and cheaper for suburban residents to travel to jobs in downtown Toronto. It also became easier for City of Toronto residents to travel by transit to jobs and other sites, such as university campuses, in the within-Metro suburbs. While new subway and bus lines were seldom designed to improve transit services within and between suburbs, they did provide most Metro residents with the option of using transit to get to other parts of Metro if they had no travel alternatives.

Despite its large financial contributions to transit, the provincial government left it up to municipal governments to decide how to operate their transit systems and invest capital subsidies. In Metro, where suburban representatives formed a majority on Council after 1966, the role of rapid transit underwent gradual redefinition. No longer was it to be just a way to get people to downtown Toronto; it was also to aid the development of, and then provide access to, suburban office/commercial nodes or 'town centres.' Metro planners incorporated this 'nodal' concept into proposed revisions to the 'unofficial' Metropolitan Toronto plan during the 1970s.[5] They also proposed additions to the rapid-transit network that would serve these nodes, enhance service in and between the within-Metro suburbs, and bring subway lines to Metro's boundaries.

Members of Metro Council could not agree where new transit lines should go and which should have priority. They could agree, however, that Metro should not have to pay for subway extensions that benefited people living in outer suburban municipalities. Thus the transit plan ('Network 2011') that Metro Council approved in 1986, six years after it had endorsed the nodal concept, depicted separate subway spurs heading east and west from points on the north–south subway to developing or proposed suburban nodes within Metro. All these lines stopped well short of the Metro boundaries. Four years later, in 1990, the provincial government countered with its own proposal for a transportation network ('Let's Move') for the whole Toronto area that included Network 2011, but with three of its lines extended to the Metro boundary (Ontario Ministry of Transportation 1990). It allowed Metro to proceed with construction of two of its preferred lines, however, in the interest of job creation.

The provincial government was more actively involved in the development of the regional GO Transit commuter system (now GT Transit), to which it contributed 100 per cent of capital and operating costs not covered by fare-box revenues. GO rail and bus routes, which increased steadily throughout the 1970s, originated in downtown Toronto or at terminals on the Metro subway system, and were designed primarily to bring outer suburban commuters into the city.[6] Thus, they both reinforced the core orientation of the TTC system and supported residential development in the outer suburbs.

Because of its own and local concerns about potential costs, the provincial government did not create regional transit authorities when it set up regional governments in the early 1970s. By the 1980s, therefore, there were fourteen separate local bus systems operating in the four suburban regions. Only a few of them had direct connections to the GO system or carried passengers across the Metro boundary to TTC subway terminals. Those that provided such services did so to help commuters make the trip to and from downtown Toronto, not to help Metro residents travel to dispersed suburban job sites. Moreover, GO services operated on a fare-by-distance basis, in contrast to Metro's uniform-fare system. Efforts to integrate transit services and rationalize fare structures began in the early 1970s and have continued into the 1990s, with only limited success. Municipal officials and local transit operators, worried about potential cost increases and loss of control, were never cooperative, and the provincial government was unwilling to impose its own solution.

The recent situation for public transit in the Toronto area has changed dramatically, and its future has become even more uncertain, as a result of changes made by the provincial government to transit financing and administration. In 1996 the government withdrew its financial support from one of the two new Metro subway lines on which work had already begun. Then in 1997 it made municipalities fully responsible for all future capital and operating costs of public transit, including the full costs of GO Transit. These decisions left the GTA with a transit system strongly oriented to downtown Toronto but poorly equipped to transport either city or suburban residents to non-central locations. Because transit riders and potential riders are an unorganized minority with little or no representation on most municipal councils, their travel requirements will likely count for little when weighed against the advantages (to those councils) of spending local tax dollars on services with wider voter appeal. These same decisions also mean that transit systems will have fewer financial resources on which to draw to improve their systems and the level of accessibility provided to residents of the GTA.

Summary

Metro-wide distribution of low-cost housing, relatively uniform local services, and an integrated public transit system contributed to the social and economic health of the old City of Toronto and to its ability to sustain social cohesion and interaction. They did so by helping to keep the core city an attractive site for new commercial and residential investment.[7] These features also enabled some of Metro's lower-income residents, including recent immigrants, to live closer to decentralized job sites in within-Metro suburbs and to travel by transit to all parts of Metro for a single fare. They did not end poverty or inequalities, however, although they helped make these conditions less visible to visitors from outside the area and to many Metro residents. Nonetheless, policies that used pooled tax resources to provide a relatively uniform standard of municipal services and public schooling throughout Metro Toronto were critically important to the social well-being of those living in lower-priced suburban housing. Suburban public transit also benefited from the use of pooled taxes for area-wide purposes in so far as Metro's capital expenditures on subways resulted in improvements to suburban bus services. In both cases, those policies acted to reduce social inequalities when measured in 'real' income.

Metropolitan Toronto institutions were important in developing and implementing the policies that helped determine Metro's character and quality of life. They seldom did so on their own initiative, however, nor did their existence necessarily stimulate intermunicipal cooperation. Local politicians who served on Metro decision-making bodies were more likely to resist than support any policy change or innovation that implied the transfer of benefits and costs from some municipalities to others. It was typically central (provincial) government intervention, in the form of local government restructuring, legislated requirements, regulations, grants, or direct takeover of a service that brought such policies into effect. While that intervention only partially counteracted the unequal distribution of advantages and disadvantages among different parts of Metro Toronto, it went further than municipal governments, or their representatives on metropolitan institutions, were ever willing to go on their own.

As a result of tax-pooling, housing, and public-transit policies, the City of Toronto and within-Metro suburbs gradually became more alike in their population characteristics, though not in their taxable assessments. While this convergence was taking place, Metro Toronto began to diverge from the newer suburban regions in two important ways: average family income declined relative to that of the GTA as a whole while it increased in the suburban regions, and Metro's population became much more diverse in social and ethnocultural terms.

Metro's divergence from the suburban regions occurred as development in those regions followed patterns similar to those found in metropolitan areas throughout North America, although at somewhat higher densities and in relatively more compact form. These outer suburbs are now characterized by: (1) a predominance of privately owned single-family homes on individual lots and a limited supply of lower-priced housing either for rent or for sale; (2) large homogeneous employment districts (industrial or office parks, commercial zones) typically isolated from residential areas; and (3) relatively poor local transit connections to the regional commuter system, to rapid transit stations within Metro, or between suburban residential and employment districts. Yet it is the suburban employment districts that are absorbing most of the new job growth in the Toronto area, including a disproportionately large share of the blue-collar jobs. There is thus a growing spatial mismatch between housing and transportation options for less-well-off GTA residents, on the one hand, and the distribution of employment opportunities, on the other. If core residential districts remain attractive to higher-income households, the majority of the GTA's less-affluent residents will be accommodated in pockets of 'affordable' housing, including concentrations of social housing and private low-rental units, in the less attractive parts of the new City of Toronto (the old city and within-Metro suburbs) with little or no transit access to emerging job concentrations in the outer suburbs.

The Political Dynamic and Its Implications

Toronto's experience is consistent with the argument that local governments on their own are unlikely to pursue policies that maintain social sustainability in an urban region. In fact, most local governments in both Metropolitan Toronto and the outer suburbs have resisted or opposed such policies if they implied extra costs for their taxpayers or if they considered them to be inconsistent with the community character to which their residents aspired. The enactment and implementation of such policies required the intervention of a senior government with the authority to decide the structure and responsibilities of municipal institutions – in this case the government of the Province of Ontario. In recent years, however, the provincial government has weakened or withdrawn its legal and financial support for the types of policies that helped in the past to harmonize residential, travel and job opportunities within Metropolitan Toronto.[8] Moreover, it has acquiesced in, or even encouraged, suburban policies that foster dispersed development patterns (sprawl) and that largely exclude any type of housing that is affordable to the less affluent members of the urban community.

The most common explanation for the provincial government's behaviour is the neo-conservative ideology and the electoral commitments of the Progressive Conservatives, who came to office in 1995. This explanation implies that a future government coming to power with a different ideology and a different agenda might adopt policies that are more conducive to promoting social integration and maintaining social harmony within the GTA. Support for this assumption comes from the fact that two earlier governments, one headed by the provincial Liberal party, the other by the provincial New Democratic Party, had begun to adopt policies to encourage more compact, more socially mixed and more transit-supportive forms of suburban development.

A longer-term perspective suggests, however, that the underlying political dynamic shaping Toronto area governance cannot simply be attributed to the vagaries of party politics and political ideology, or even to the recent ascendancy of neo-conservative ideas in urban policy making. Provincial policies for the extended Toronto metropolitan area began to diverge from those implemented in Metropolitan Toronto in the 1960s, when the province became directly involved in administering or funding services (including social housing and public transit) that had previously been left to local governments, and when it began to create two-tier systems of regional government in the outer suburbs. That divergence contributed to the differences between the inner and outer parts of the GTA that are becoming increasingly apparent today. The motives underlying provincial policies for the outer suburbs were nonetheless similar to the motives that prompted the decision to create Metropolitan Toronto – an interest in ensuring that the metropolitan area had the services needed to support continued economic growth, a desire to minimize the costs of new local services to the provincial budget by enhancing the capacity of local governments to pay for them, and a perceived need to respond to political pressures to act on one or more immediate problems (such as transportation congestion and a housing shortage). To retain electoral support, the government also had to adopt policies that did not alienate too many voters.

It was not always easy or even possible to reconcile these motives, but the government's efforts to do so changed as the urban area expanded. An interest in preserving the economic and social health of the core city was most evident in policies adopted during Metro's first two decades, when the City of Toronto was still the area's primary employment centre and a strong magnet for new economic growth. With provincial urging or support, Metro pursued policies that helped to counteract the tendency of individual municipalities to act in ways that would confine and isolate the region's poorer residents in older central districts. These policies not only benefited the city, but also gave the area's poorer households access to a broader range of housing, schools, transportation, employment, and other opportunities located within Metro.

These policies undoubtedly did contribute to social well-being. They did not, however, take account of the way that policies for the rest of the metropolitan area were affecting, or were likely to affect, the opportunities available to those households as development shifted to the outer suburbs. Moreover, the concentration of social housing (and low-cost private housing) at high densities in relatively few districts hardened community attitudes against all forms of lower-priced housing. These attitudes have been especially influential in the outer suburbs, where there have been few attempts to provide an affordable housing mix. As outer suburban municipalities gain population relative to Metro, any political party that wants to win election in Ontario will have to take such attitudes into account.[9] Furthermore, continued job growth in the suburbs can be taken to mean that the region's economic future lies primarily in the suburbs, and that is where new public investments should be made. Some suburban governments already argue this point of view. As suburban populations and economies continue to grow, such arguments and the attitudes on which they are based are likely to become increasingly persuasive, both with senior governments and within regional forums.

The only regional forum the provincial government has been willing to create is a Greater Toronto Services Board (GTSB) with a mandate to decide what cross-boundary services are needed and how their costs should be allocated among local governments. That body, formally established in January 1999, is composed entirely of local officials, and its performance will depend on the willingness of those officials to tackle regional issues cooperatively. It has only one prescribed function: to oversee the operation of GT Transit, for which it must collect money from the area's local governments to pay operating deficits. Otherwise its job is to 'promote and facilitate coordinated decision making among the municipalities of the Greater Toronto Area' (Government of Ontario 1998).

The new City of Toronto government must therefore overcome formidable obstacles if it is to function successfully in this highly competitive and often unsympathetic environment in a manner that is conducive to social sustainability. In the absence of provincial support, it will have to find ways to house a growing proportion of the GTA's neediest residents and provide them with most of the services they need to become productive members of Canadian society and the regional economy. To do this successfully, it will have to avoid actions likely to increase social polarization both within the city and between the city and the suburban regions. It will have to find ways to keep the new city relatively safe, vibrant and appealing to business and middle-class homeowners. It will also have to find ways to ensure that public goods and services continue to be provided in a relatively equitable fashion.

To accomplish these tasks, the new city's officials will have to convince the federal government, the provincial government, and other municipal governments in the GTA that policies likely to result in the core city's impoverishment are in nobody's long-term interest. Given the pressures and constraints felt by all local governments in the region, and the short time horizons that guide municipal decisions, it is doubtful that the city government and city supporters can build their case entirely on abstract assertions of the importance of the core city to the regional economy. Metro's experience suggests that the economic and social well-being of a core city remains important in the eyes of local governments in an urban region only if those governments derive short-term and easily perceptible benefits from policies that also help the city.

Notes

This chapter is a condensed version of an earlier research paper (Frisken, Bourne, Gad, and Murdie 1997). Because of restrictions on space, most of the tables and figures in the earlier report could not be included here.

1 The Canadian constitution gives Canada's ten provincial governments exclusive jurisdiction over 'municipal institutions.'

2 At time of writing, only population and immigration counts were available from the 1996 census. For other types of data, 1991 figures have been used.

3 Based on census data included with Social Planning Council of Metropolitan Toronto 1975, Map 5, and by Board of Trade of Metropolitan Toronto 1996, 130.

4 Figures on immigration are collected by Citizenship and Immigration Canada for the Toronto area.

5 Metro Council had refused to ask the province to give its plan legal, or 'official,' status after debating it in 1966.

6 The GO system carried about 36 million passengers in 1997, compared with the 385 million carried by the TTC.

7 Because of space limitations we have not been able to include a discussion of the contribution made by Canada's health-care system, for which costs are shared by the federal and provincial governments, to lessening the social impacts of income disparities throughout the GTA.

8 The one exception is public education, over which the province wants to exercise full control. In the United States, the declining quality of city schools has been identified as an important reason for the suburban migration of the urban middle class. Thus, the way the provincial government administers the public schools, including the extent to which its policies take account of the special needs of Metro's low-income and immigrant populations, is likely to be important to the new City of Toronto's ability to retain a socially mixed population.

9 The New Democratic Party (NDP) government (1990–5) ignored community sentiments when it adopted planning legislation that both supported higher suburban densities and promoted the inclusion of an affordable-housing component in new developments. While it is impossible to attribute the results of an election to any one cause, it is worth noting that the NDP not only lost heavily to the Progressive Conservatives in the 1995 election, but lost every seat it had held in the four suburban regions.

References

Board of Trade of Metropolitan Toronto. 1996. *1996/97 Toronto Region Business and Market Guide.* Toronto: Board of Trade of Metropolitan Toronto.

Bourne, L.S. 1997. 'Social Polarization and Spatial Segregation: Changing Income Inequalities in Canadian Cities.' In *Contemporary City Structuring,* ed. R. Davies, 134–47. Cape Town: University of Cape Town.

Danielson, Michael N. 1976. *The Politics of Exclusion*. New York: Columbia University Press.

Dodge, William R. 1996. *Regional Excellence: Governing Together to Compete Globally and Flourish Locally.* Washington, DC: National League of Cities.

Downs, Anthony. 1994. *New Visions for Metropolitan America*. Washington, DC: The Brookings Institution.

Filion, Pierre. 1992. 'Government Levels, Neighbourhood Influence and Urban Policy.' In *Political Arrangements: Power and the City*, ed. Henry Lustiger-Thaler, 169–83. New York: Basic Books.

Frisken, Frances. 1993. 'Planning and Servicing the Greater Toronto Area: The Interplay of Provincial and Municipal Interests.' In *Metropolitan Governance: American/Canadian Intergovernmental Perspectives*, ed. Donald N. Rothblatt and Andrew Sancton, 153–204. Berkeley, CA: Institute of Governmental Studies Press.

Frisken, Frances, ed. 1994. *The Changing Canadian Metropolis: A Public Policy Perspective*. Berkeley, CA: Institute of Governmental Studies Press, University of California, and Toronto: Canadian Urban Institute.

Frisken, Frances, L.S. Bourne, Gunter Gad, and Robert Murdie. 1997. *Governance and Social Well-Being in the Toronto Area: Past Achievements and Future Challenges*. Research Paper 193. Toronto: Centre for Urban and Community Studies, University of Toronto.

Gad, Gunter. 1991. 'Office Location.' In *Canadian Cities in Transition*, ed. Trudi Bunting and Pierre Filion, 432–59. Toronto: Oxford University Press.

– 1991b. 'Toronto's Financial District.' *Canadian Geographer* 35: 203–7.

Hawley, Willis D. 1976. 'On Understanding Metropolitan Political Integration.' In *Theoretical Perspectives on Urban Politics*, ed. Willis D. Hawley and Michael Lipsky, 100–45. Englewood Cliffs, NJ: Prentice-Hall.

Lapointe Consulting and Robert Murdie. 1995. *Immigrants and the Canadian Housing Market: Background Report*. Ottawa: Canada Mortgage and Housing Corporation.

Lemon, James T. 1985. *Toronto Since 1918: An Illustrated History.* Toronto: Lorimer.

– 1996. *Liberal Dreams and Nature's Limits: Great Cities of North America Since 1600*. Toronto: Oxford University Press.

Metropolitan Toronto Planning Board. 1959. 'The Official Plan of the Metropolitan Toronto Planning Area' (Draft).

Metropolitan Toronto Planning Department. 1993. *Metro's Changing Housing Scene, 1986–91*. Toronto: Metropolitan Toronto Planning Department.

– Research and Special Studies Division. [n.d.]. *Metropolitan Toronto and the*

Greater Toronto Area. 1991 Census Atlas. Series B Data. Toronto: Metropolitan
Toronto Planning Department.

Murdie, Robert A. 1994. 'Social Polarisation and Public Housing in Canada: A
Case Study of the Metropolitan Toronto Housing Authority.' In *The Changing
Canadian Metropolis: A Public Policy Perspective*, vol. 1, ed. Frances Frisken,
293–339. Berkeley, CA: Institute of Governmental Studies Press, University
of California and Toronto: Canadian Urban Institute.

– 1996. 'Economic Restructuring and Social Polarization in Toronto.' In *Social
Polarization in Post-Industrial Metropolises*, ed. John O'Loughlin and Jürgen
Friedrichs, 207–33. Berlin and New York: Walter de Gruyter.

– 1998. 'The Welfare State, Economic Restructuring and Immigrant Flows:
Impacts on Socio-spatial Segregation in Greater Toronto.' In *Urban Segregation and the Welfare State: Inequality and Exclusion in Western Cities*, ed.S. Musterd and W. Ostendorf, 64–93. London: Routledge.

Ontario, Government of. 1998. Bill 56: *An Act to Establish the Greater Toronto Services Board and the Greater Toronto Transit Authority and to Amend the Toronto
Area Transit Operating Authority Act*. 2nd Session, 36th Legislature, Ontario.
47 Elizabeth II. 2nd Reading.

Ontario Ministry of Transportation. 1990. *Let's Move: Transportation Solutions for
the 90s*. Toronto: Ministry of Transportation.

Ontario Municipal Board. 1953. *In the Matter of Sections 20 and 22 of 'The Municipal Act'* ... *Decisions and Recommendations of the Board*. Toronto: Queen's
Printer.

Peirce, Neal, Curtis Johnson, and John Stuart Hall. 1993. *Citistates: How Urban
America Can Prosper in a Competitive World*. Washington, DC: Seven Locks.

Precourt, Geoffrey, and Anne Faircloth. 1996. 'Best Cities: Where the Living is
Easy.' *Fortune*, November, pp. 127–49.

Rose, Albert. 1972. *Governing Metropolitan Toronto: A Social and Political Analysis*.
Berkeley: University of California Press.

– 1980. *Canadian Housing Policies, 1935–1980*. Toronto: Butterworths.

Royal Commission on Metropolitan Toronto (Carl Goldenberg, Commissioner). 1965. *Report*. Toronto: Queen's Printer.

Rusk, David. 1995. *Cities without Suburbs*, 2nd ed. Washington, DC: Woodrow
Wilson Center Press.

Social Planning Council of Metropolitan Toronto. 1975. *Metropolitan Profile:
Metropolitan Toronto – Planning Facts*. Toronto: Social Planning Council of
Metropolitan Toronto.

4 Miami: Governing the City through Crime

JONATHAN SIMON

Crime and the Postmodern City

Crime is often recognized as one of our oldest 'urban problems' (Silver 1967, 1). Indeed, in many respects crime has been a constitutive feature of the modern city. Representing crime helped give rise to the mass urban newspaper of the nineteenth century (Leps 1992). Analysing crime was a primary focus of the new social science of sociology as it began to establish itself as a distinctively urban discourse at the beginning of the twentieth century (Durkheim 1933; Park, Burgess and McKenzie 1925). Fighting crime has frequently been the context for important efforts at urban reconstruction, including initiatives to clear 'slums,' construct great avenues (Chevalier 1973), and reorganize municipal boundaries and political structures (Monkonnen 1988).

In the postmodern city, crime looms larger than ever (Harvey 1989; Jameson 1992). For much of the twentieth century, fighting crime meant addressing deeper social problems such as industrialization, immigration, and segregation. Today, it is increasingly the case that crime itself, and the host of responses to it, have become a locus for regulating urban life, influencing the siting of housing, transportation, and commercial development. It is obvious that crime poses a threat to the social sustainability of cities. No urban leader in the world needs to be convinced of that. What is less well understood is how crime, and our responses to it, form a general field of effects on urban existence. The tendency of political leaders in the United States to exploit this field – to 'govern through crime' – is an independent threat to the social sustainability of our cities. This chapter explores that issue through a case study of Miami.

Miami offers a view of crime as it plays out among an array of other forces that are likely to become more central to cities throughout the United States (and other advanced post-industrial societies), including immigration, deindustrialization, and the hyper-extension of the news and entertainment industry.

Global City on the Edge

Miami, which celebrated its centenary in 1996, has been transformed in the last three decades from a declining centre for domestic tourism and retirement living, to a dynamic centre of international trade and global tourism. The engine of this transformation has been massive immigration, mainly from the Caribbean and Central America. The process began in the early 1960s with refugees from Fidel Castro's revolution in Cuba. This influx brought more than 100,000 Cubans, disproportionately middle- and upper-class individuals with considerable social capital (although much of their financial capital was abandoned in Cuba). 'Little Havana,' near downtown Miami, established itself as the centre of anti-Castro activities and a hub of small-scale commercial growth. In time the cultural and linguistic influence of the growing Cuban population began to attract Latin American business and tourism.

Immigration continued after a hiatus created by cold-war tensions, and more than 300,000 more Cubans entered the United States between 1965 and 1973 (Portes and Stepick 1993, 104). Although efforts were made by the American government to settle many of these refugees away from south Florida, a majority found their way back. In 1979 more than 80 per cent of all Cubans in the U.S. resided in the greater Miami area (Portes and Stepick 1993, 104). A third great wave of immigration took place in 1980, this time with astounding rapidity. In less than six months more than 100,000 additional Cubans entered Miami in a massive boatlift spurred by Fidel Castro's decision to open the port of Mariel in April of that year. The same summer saw a peak in the slower but steady influx of Haitians fleeing the Duvalier dictatorship and the hemisphere's worst economy. Despite aggressive efforts by the federal government to suppress this immigration throughout the 1980s (Taylor 1995), a 'Little Haiti' established itself in Miami, paralleling the growth of 'Little Havana' two decades earlier.

The initial effects of the 1980 wave (which continued on a much smaller scale throughout the 1980s) were largely negative. A major riot in the city's African-American community took place shortly after the influx.[1] A wave of highly publicized crimes followed the relocation of hundreds of young and desperate Cuban refugees to Miami Beach, which had a concentration of vulnerable retirees. The sense of danger was enhanced by Cuban propaganda that portrayed the Mariel refugees as consisting of criminals, mental patients, and deviants. Schools and other public services staggered under the weight of such a huge and comparatively poor immigrant population.

As Alejandro Portes and Alex Stepick (1993) describe in their brilliant study of Miami, the Mariel moment also reconfigured the city's political and economic circumstances. The Anglo (white, non-Hispanic) community had welcomed the economic stimulation of the 1960s and 1970s immigration waves, which left them firmly in control. Anglos felt far more threatened by the Mariel wave, which took place in the midst of a period of economic stagnation and was both poorer and more African in phenotype than were the earlier immigrants.[2] The backlash, sparked by the leading newspaper, included an English-only law adopted by the voters of Miami-Dade County (of which Miami is the seat and largest city),[3] and increased white-flight to Broward and Palm Beach counties, which lie north of Miami along the coast. Stung by this response, Miami's Cuban population, which had long focused on cold-war anti-Castro politics to the exclusion of local politics, became mobilized. Large numbers became citizens for the first time, and this increase in voters gave Cuban-American politicians a leading role in the city's governance.[4] The influx of Spanish-speaking immigrants (joined by Central Americans later in the 1980s) also provided a new working class to fuel the Cuban economic enclave.

Miami today belongs among the world's emerging 'global cities' (Sassen 1993). Its bilingual population has attracted major trading and investment companies focused on the Latin American market. Its large immigrant population provides the new labour for the various kinds of service economies global cities typically generate.[5] Tourism, traditionally drawing on the northeastern United States, now attracts both Latin Americans and Europeans in large numbers (as well as domestic tourists with a preference for the Miami's cultural diversity). This has revived declining entertainment areas, most famously Miami Beach. While generating enormous benefits, the processes of globalization have also left Miami with perhaps the most complex ethnic politics of any city in the nation. The traditional hierarchy, running from white Protestant native-born English speakers at the top, to African-Americans and non-Christian foreign-born non–English speakers at the bottom, has been transformed by both global capital investment and immigration into an even more complicated and volatile structure (Portes and Stepick 1993, 86).

The City of Miami proper had a population of about 350,000 at the time of the last census. The city spreads in a semicircle from where the Miami River opens into Biscayne Bay (see Figure 4.1). Traditional U.S. metropolitan areas have taken the shape of an older hub city surrounded by a ring of newer suburbs. In contrast, the Miami metropolitan area may be thought of as a set of suburb-like resort communities that were founded during the same period (1896–1930) and eventually fused together into a contiguous urban sprawl (Portes and Stepick 1993, 81).

In the 1950s a county-wide government structure was created by popular referendum for Miami–Dade County (the location of Miami) over vigorous opposition from most of the twenty-six separate municipalities that had incorporated since 1896. As a result, Miami–Dade County government controls many of the functions traditionally held by municipalities, including schools, building codes, road planning, and construction. In addition, like other counties, Miami–Dade provides police and fire service outside the larger municipalities. In the wake of the political changes brought on by Mariel, there has been a continuing struggle over governance structure as neighbourhoods of various class and ethnic composition seek to establish greater control by incorporating. Most recently, on 4 September, 1997, a proposition to disincorporate the city of Miami was defeated. The drive was prompted by a series of scandals involving corruption by highly placed city officials. Critics of the disincorporation proposition argued that the move was intended to dump Miami's large poor population into the county while allowing the city's wealthier neighbourhoods to incorporate as separate municipalities. Other critics saw it as an effort to attack the power of a Hispanic majority city, although Miami–Dade County itself now has a Hispanic majority.

Miami–Dade County is part of a larger Standard Metropolitan Statistical Area, along with Broward and Palm Beach counties to the north. But in popular consciousness there is a far more significant line between Miami–Dade County and its neighbours than might be true in other extended metropolitan areas. Miami–Dade's Hispanic majority sets it apart. Indeed, much of the growth of Broward and Palm Beach counties has come as a result of white-flight from Miami–Dade. Anglos made up just under a majority of Miami–Dade's population in 1980. By

Figure 4.1 Miami, Showing Areas of Predominantly Black and Spanish-origin
Population, 1990
Source: INRS–urbanisation, based on 1990 census maps supplied by Metro-
Dade Planning Department Research Division

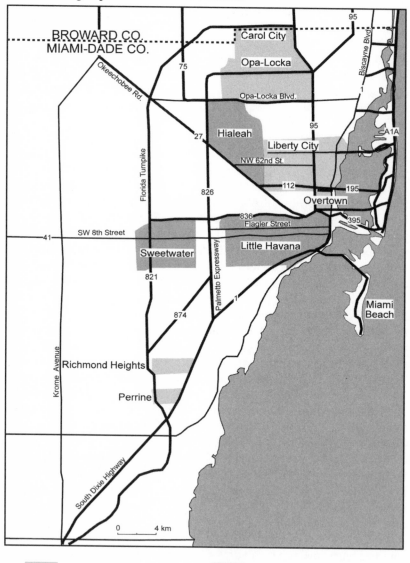

1990, they made up only slightly above 30 per cent of the county's population. Hispanics (consisting of any race, but mainly categorized as White) made up 36 per cent of Miami–Dade's population in 1980, and over 49 per cent by 1990. Blacks (consisting mainly of African Americans, but also Haitians, other Afro-Caribbeans, and Afro-Cubans) made up 17 per cent of the count in 1980, and just under 20 per cent in 1990 (Portes and Stepick 1993, 211).

Governing through Crime

When urban scholars a generation ago debated the question of 'who governs' cities, the principal alternatives were elected officials and business elites. Here, governing invokes a broader array of authorities both within and outside the formal boundaries of political institutions – not just the state, but employers, educators, helping professionals, parents, and even individuals. Michel Foucault's definition of power provides a useful reference point: 'To govern, in this sense, is to structure the possible field of action of others' (Foucault 1982, 220).

To speak of governing through crime may invoke the image of cities that are ruled with methods that approximate criminal assault, such as murderous death squads and disappearances. Regrettably, cities have existed and continue to exist in such conditions in parts of the world, but we should see such coercive standards as limiting cases rather than as typifying the relationship between crime and governance. Increasingly, authorities that seek to shape the conduct of urban populations do so in relationship to the problem of crime. This takes many forms, including: the population of offenders as exhibited in the correctional system; crime itself experienced directly or more commonly through the media; fear of crime; and popular identification with the experience of victimization. Each of these factors poses specific challenges to the sustainability of cities and the opportunities available for governing them. From this perspective it makes sense to speak of governing cities through crime when crime and our responses to it become the occasions and the institutional contexts in which we undertake to guide the conduct of urban life.

Correctional Populations

The most obvious way in which contemporary American society is governed through crime is the unprecedented growth of the population under correctional custody. In 1995, nearly 2.8 per cent of the adult resident population was in some form of custody (Bureau of Justice Statistics 1996). The expansion of correctional custody has been even more distinct in particular communities. In the mid-1990s more than 10 per cent of African-American males, and more than 30 per cent of all young African-American males, were in some form of custody (Mauer and Huling 1995).

National correctional statistics are not broken down by urban character of the offender, but it is well accepted that the urban population is overrepresented in correctional populations by a dramatic amount. A study of Baltimore and Washington, DC, in the late 1980s found nearly half of all young black men in the correctional system, or wanted by warrant, at a time when aggregate national figures stood at one in four. Nearly 1 per cent of the entire Miami–Dade County population (adults and children) was in the custody of the Florida Department of Corrections in 1995.[6]

In American urban poverty zones, an absolute majority of the young men are involved in the correctional system on any given day. From a formal legal perspective, this should provide a greater degree of regulatory control than would otherwise be available. Those in prison are removed from the community altogether. Even those under correctional supervision in the community usually lose most of their constitutional rights against police surveillance and arrest, and since many households in these communities include a correctional subject, this loss of rights is generalized to many others.[7] In practice, however, the growing correctional population signals a genuine crisis for the regulation of cities. Prisons ultimately return the vast majority of their inhabitants to the community. Once back in the neighbourhood, the ex-prisoner poses both a direct and an indirect challenge to sustainable neighbourhoods.

Directly, because the cognitive and behavioural skills inculcated by life in America's prisons only intensify the proclivity towards antisocial conduct that led to punishment in the first place (Abbott 1981; Silberman 1995). Indirectly, because the labelling effects of conviction and punishment have drastic consequences for the likelihood of future employment (Freeman 1996). Employment is the most significant source of regulation in the lives of most urban populations. In the United States in particular, because of the predominance of market relations, work also produces the income necessary for access to other sources of self-government, such as marriage and long-term residential stability (if not property ownership). As a result, correctional power tends to be self-undermining. Like some cancer drugs, it combats malignancy but only at the price of destroying the natural immunity of the body (Simon 1993). Not surprisingly, in many states more than half of those released from prison in recent years have returned to prison (Simon 1993).

The results for sustainable cities are visible to anyone who ventures into the poverty zones of cities like Miami. During the middle of the day, the streets are full of large numbers of young males with neither work nor schooling to occupy their time. For centuries such persons have provided the recruits for gang formation, opportunistic crime, and civil disorders. Miami has experienced all three in recent years.

Gangs have been a part of the urban scene in the United States since at least the early twentieth century, and probably well before (Thrasher 1927). Experts have long seen them as a breeding ground for future crime as well as a source of 'disorganization' in already troubled communities (Shaw 1929). Since the mid-1980s they have become associated with crime directly, especially illegal drug sales and the lethal gun play generated by that trade. Prison, ironically, has become a major recruiting ground for gangs and an intensification of their forms of solidarity. These new American urban gangs are being directly transferred through immigrants in cities such as Los Angeles and Miami to cities in countries such as El Salvador, Nicaragua, and Mexico.

Opportunistic street crime has emerged as a major problem in Miami since 1980. Mostly it takes the form of burglaries and armed robberies. These crimes are particularly burdensome to Miami as a city, which capitalizes heavily on tourism and those moving to improve their lifestyle. Many of Miami's most exciting entertainment districts are in close proximity to areas of poverty, including Miami Beach and Coconut Grove.

Urban uprisings are perhaps the single most dangerous threat that the formation of a large criminalized population poses to the sustainability of cities. After a large number of such events during the 1960s, American cities seemed to enjoy a reprieve from them during the 1970s and early 1980s. Some criminologists argued that the new and lethal gang formations described above were the new form of 'quiet riots.' But in the early 1990s the spectre of violent uprisings re-emerged. The Los Angeles riot of May 1992 was the most violent in American history.

Miami seemed to have missed the quiet phase altogether, suffering three major riots between 1980 and 1990 (Dunn and Stepick 1992).

As in the 1960s, recent urban riots have involved community responses to perceived assaults by law enforcement. Perhaps the most famous was the videotaped beating of Rodney King by Los Angeles police officers. It was the acquittal of those officers of state criminal charges in 1992 that set off the May 1992 uprising. Similar incidents lay behind all three of Miami's riots during the 1980s.

Crime

Putting people in prison or on probation is obviously a way of governing them – as is crime, in a less obvious way. Crime governs when people's decisions on where to go in the city to live, work, and consume are mediated by perceptions of crime risk. Crime governs when whole neighbourhoods are dominated by criminal organizations that establish norms of behaviour for others. Crime governs when schoolchildren, welfare beneficiaries, and public employees are regulated by the effort to prevent crime.

Contrary to what many contemporary observers believe, a pervasive sense of crime in cities is not new. Urban citizens in the eighteenth and nineteenth centuries experienced themselves 'as threatened by agglomerations of the criminal, vicious, and violent' (Silver 1967, 3). This was driven in part by an ideology among the elite classes incapable of differentiating the poor from the criminal. But it was also based on the real difficulties of managing conflict in rapidly growing cities undisciplined by industry and police. Historians now believe that European and North American cities experienced a secular decrease in violent crime from the middle of the nineteenth century on, as work discipline and professionalized police helped pacify the urban masses (Lane 1979; Monkonnen 1981). This pattern abruptly changed in the mid-1960s. Crime, and violent crime in particular, grew rapidly. While this growth levelled off in the 1970s, it has remained high.

Behind the grim image of violent crime-ridden America are different experiences. For the majority of Americans who now live in the post–Second World War urban neighbourhoods often called 'suburbs,' crime rates have declined since the 1970s. This decline has been quite significant for property crime, while violent crime remains as rare in these neighbourhoods as it is in Western Europe (Zimring 1997). In contrast, older inner city areas have endured continuing high levels of property crime and several cycles of escalating violent crime throughout the 1980s and early 1990s.[8]

In Miami this has recently taken the form of coding the city's freeway grid to mark areas implicitly as dangerous. In response to a series of tourist murders in the early 1990s, the city implemented a program designed to help tourists find their way from the airport to the seaside resorts without getting lost in the poverty areas in between. The program placed large solar symbols on the freeway exits appropriate for travel to the beach. Unfortunately, beaches lie at the end of virtually every Florida freeway, so that at some interchanges virtually all of the links are marked with the sun sign. The difficulties of the sun symbol reflect the political constraints on putting up the signs that would no doubt do the job – international distress symbols discouraging tourists from exiting the freeway into high-crime areas of the city. In effect, of course, the absence of a solar symbol does the same thing. The city is being physically coded for crime safety.

Miami has experienced a high rate of crime, even in comparison with other large cities. Miami–Dade County experienced a rate of more than 12,000 serious crimes per 100,000 residents in 1991, compared with 9,730 in Los Angeles County and 8,475 in Cook County (Chicago).[9] The consequences of these high crime levels for urban governability in the 1980s and 1990s have been disastrous. The reality and perception of criminal violence have marked these neighbourhoods as 'high-risk' zones with a resulting depressant effect on private investment of all kinds. This has, in turn, exacerbated the decline in employment, and with it the major source of social control for any community (Wilson 1996). The resulting stigma, however, has spread to whole cities, and even to their older suburbs. The image of violent street crimes helps paint urban life as inherently degrading and dangerous, and thus fuels a growing anti-urban bias in national politics. That bias, which has become dominant in U.S. politics since the 1980s, has led to a significant retreat in the concern of national and state governments for the fate of traditional urban areas. Even within metropolitan regions, the stigma of crime has helped fuel a growing movement by more affluent areas to seek separation from the larger frameworks of metropolitan government. Residents have also responded to the high levels of crime, many by leaving the city altogether. The retreat of much of the Anglo middle class to Broward and other areas to the north, and the growing movement to disaggregate wealthy neighbourhoods from Miami's county-government framework, have both taken their toll.[10]

Fear of Crime

Criminal victimization and penal supervision by the state may be highly concentrated on only part of the U.S. urban population. But in another dimension, fear of crime, things are far more equal. Most suburban districts of larger metropolitan areas have enjoyed declining property-crime rates and continuing low rates of violent crime throughout the 1980s and 1990s, but at the same time they experienced an escalating fear of crime. Playing on these fears has now become one of the dominant strategies of the media and political candidates. Choices about where to live, where to work, where to go to school, where to shop and play are made with crime perception in mind. Indeed, crime or its relative absence, increasingly marks the political imagination of urban space, once demarcated largely by such notions as race, ethnicity, and social function.

Urban leaders in the United States are increasingly aware of how fear of crime, in distinction to crime itself, can undermine sustainable cities. Fear of crime not only leads many residents to abandon central cities for outlying suburbs, but reduces the role that remaining residents play in their communities. Fearful of becoming victims, residents often abandon the convenience of local businesses for the perceived safety of suburban shopping malls. As a consequence, both homeowners and business owners are reluctant to sink more investment in properties whose value may be permanently limited by fear of crime.

Miami residents have, in fact, experienced somewhat higher rates of crime than have residents of many other cities, but fear of crime has outstripped its reality. The media promote crime fear by excessive and sensationalized accounts of local crimes. This has been especially true of television stations that compete with each other to bring the more violent incidents to the screen fastest. While most of these crimes involve assaults against family members or estranged lovers, the perception that violent crime is all around is nonetheless communicated. Miami's major newspaper, the *Miami Herald*, runs constant features about different aspects of crime in Miami. Recently, for example, a multipart series was published on guns and juveniles. The stories highlighted the large percentage of teenagers who claimed to have had possession of a firearm at some time or another. Only deep in the multicolumn story did the reader learn that the vast majority of these teens had handled weapons belonging to their parents, and in their homes.

Another recent series titled 'Crime and No Time' touted the allegedly liberal habits of Miami–Dade judges as a major problem in the county.

The Citizen as Victim

Finally, the priority of crime is reflected in the role it plays in defining the purposes and tasks of the state. As significant portions of the modern social-welfare state have been delegitimized and dismantled, fighting crime is one of the few things around which a solid consensus can be relied on for political initiatives of all sorts. As a result, crime victimization has taken on a new priority as a model of the relationship between citizen and state. In the short term this may provide political support for politicians who effectively manipulate the symbols of identification with crime victims (e.g., support for the death penalty). Mayor Alex Penelas, the first Cuban-American mayor of the whole of Miami–Dade County (a position just strengthened greatly by a major reform of county government), initiated his rule by launching a campaign of aggressive street stops and arrests directed at young males in the predominantly African-American 'Liberty City' community.[11]

At the same time, the transformation of the state into a policing body risks undermining the forms of participatory civic culture that effective government depends on. In an important study of regional governments in Italy, Robert Putnam (1993) and his colleagues discovered that those regions with the most ineffective governments were characterized by a growing demand for harsh and punitive crime-control policies. In such regions citizens looked to the state as an enforcer and a protector but did little to participate actively in making government effective.

Crime and the Crisis of Governance

In the short term, governing through crime may become a compelling way of increasing the legitimacy of various authorities struggling to control the city, but in the long run the increasing salience of crime endangers the social sustainability of cities. In the remainder of this chapter, we consider some of the factors that may be driving the increasing salience of crime as a locus of governing cities.

The priority of governing through crime might sensibly be thought to arise in response to a genuine increase in the experience of victimization. As suggested above, the long curve of declining violence in Western societies seems to have ended in the 1940s. But the steepest increases in crime, and violent crime in particular, came in the 1950s and 1960s. Crime rates since appear to have fluctuated within a relatively shallow range. In 1973 (the first year for which adequate victimization data are available), 123.6 victimizations occurred for every 100,000 Americans. In 1992 the figure was 91.7. Violent incidents occurred at the rate of 32.6 per 100,000 Americans in 1973, peaked in 1975 at 35.3, and declined to 32.1 in 1992 (Bureau of the Census 1996).

The demand for punishment, however, escalated in the midst of this flat period. Even a political lag would not explain why the demand has actually grown stronger throughout the last decade and half. In 1980, 69 per cent of a random sample of Americans agreed that too little was spent on fighting crime. Fourteen years later, after a massive and expensive prison-building boom, 75 per cent agreed (Bureau of Justice Statistics 1995, Table 2.27).

This gap may be explained by a variety of factors. Crimes reported to the police, unlike victimization, have shown an increase during the 1980s and early 1990s reflecting an increasingly aggressive law enforcement stance and perhaps greater willingness by the public to call the police. While criminologists tend to favour victimization data as a more accurate measure of underlying crime, the media and political discourse often focus on crime reported to the police. An even less accurate view is created by the preponderance of crime stories in the media. Crime journalism has definitely grown during the last two decades and may help to sustain the impression of an ever-growing problem with crime. This is especially true of violent crime, which the media always tend to favour in their coverage. But while media representation of crime is clearly a major factor in the politics of crime, it provides just as much of a question as an answer. In either event we need to understand why crime is such a compelling story about ourselves, and its quantitative increase alone will not explain that.

But even if crime rates do not seem to explain directly the dominance of crime-control strategies in governing cities, they do represent a stubborn indicator of the inability of governance institutions to achieve goals that they themselves have labelled as compelling. Having defined crime as the major threat to Americans, governments at all levels now find themselves discredited by the fact that, after billions in dollars of spending on crime-control measures, crime rates are close to what they were in the early 1970s. This has been particularly tough on city governments, which are most identified with the crime problem and have the fewest resources to respond to it.

This is especially true of the 'war on drugs' that American politicians declared in the early 1980s. No problem has proved less tractable (Gordon 1994). Nearly half of the increase in prison population between 1985 and the present is due to an increase in the severity of anti-drug laws (Donziger 1996; Miller 1996). This initiative has come largely from the federal government, but it has co-opted and coerced the state governments into committing extensive resources to fighting drugs as crime.

While largely insoluble with current techniques, the drug problem has managed to stigmatize America's large cities, which are regularly portrayed as the contagion centres from which drugs spread slowly towards the virtuous heartland of American life. Terms like 'crack houses' have become widely recognized symbols for America's urban plight. They conjure up images of abandoned homes and apartments in which acts of uncontrollable danger occur. Cities such as Miami, New York, and Los Angeles are regularly labelled drug-source cities in the media and court decisions.

Right-wing politicians in the United States who saw the drug issue as a way to stigmatize the permissive left initially deployed the rhetoric of the war on drugs. It is tempting to see the entire growth of governing through crime as a reflection of the political success of these conservative forces from the late 1970s through the early 1990s (at least) in the United States and other mature industrial societies. Conservatives might be thought (based on their rhetoric) to favour the criminal law as a tool of state governance, and highly punitive private norms as the preferred strategy in other settings for governance. From this perspective, the crime-and-violence surge of the 1960s can be seen as mobilizing support for conservative policies and vindicating the conservative critique of liberal governments as overly 'permissive.'

There is doubtless some link between the conservative ascendancy and the trend towards governing through crime. In a recent study of English-speaking societies, John Sutton (1997) found that a preponderance of 'right-wing' cabinet ministers in government was positively correlated with the growth of prison populations. But there are also reasons to doubt that governing through crime is fundamentally an accident of conservative political victories. For one thing, contemporary liberals also find themselves drawn towards punishment as a locus for governance. Laws and institutional rules punishing racist speech, domestic violence, sexual harassment, and pornography, for example, have become major agenda items for some liberals. Likewise, the election of a more liberal national administration in the United States in 1992 did little to slow the growth of governing through crime, while many recent conservative administrations, including that of Britain's Margaret Thatcher, chose not to emphasize crime control as a major strategy of governing. Indeed, twentieth-century conservatives often embraced non-criminal approaches to governance as an alternative to social instability (Gilbert 1972). It is indeed interesting that in a period of conservative ascendancy during which the right has articulated aspirations to govern through patriotism, work, and family, as well as crime, it is largely with respect to crime and punishment that there has been significant legislative success.[12]

Even if conservative ideology does not drive the trend towards governing through crime, conservatives in the United States and elsewhere have benefited politically from their ability to articulate more convincingly a tough anti-crime approach. Conservative politicians began in the 1960s to make the argument now shared by many of their fellow citizens that traditional and traditionally modernist[13] sources of social control were weakening. Liberal politicians, such as Bill Clinton in the United States and Tony Blair in Britain, have achieved success in part by affirming this belief that social control is breaking down, and that emphasizing crime and punishment is the most promising strategy for checking that.

Even during the ascendancy of conservative political parties in national politics, many city governments remained left of centre. Yet the social and economic forces affecting cities are more likely to be shaped by policies of strong national governments than by the far weaker and poorer local governments. Indeed, American cities have become showcases for the conservative critique of liberal government as places where crime and welfare both grow. More recently, cities in the United States have experienced the rise of a new set of 'tough on crime' mayors, many of them Republicans, who have explicitly made governing through crime their major emphasis.

A third element, the breakdown of the welfare state and related strategies for social management, may mediate the link between conservative governments and governing through crime. During the middle of the twentieth century, mature industrial nations enjoyed a period of affluence and stability associated with a variety of governance strategies focused on coordinating labour and business, assuring income, and providing mass access to education. Many scholars have examined the rise of these governance strategies and the new political technologies they deployed, including insurance, case work, and social statistics (Gilbert 1972; Donzelot 1979; Garland 1985; Harvey 1989; Rose 1990).

Lately we seem to be experiencing a crisis of these modes of governance. The United States and other advanced industrial societies have found themselves re-evaluating systems of collective risk distribution, such as welfare, public education, unemployment insurance, and workers' compensation. The failure of modest national health insurance in the United States in 1993 was a potent reminder of how muddled the basic narratives and rationalities supporting these governance modalities have become.[14]

Governing through crime, at its broadest, might be looked at as a response to this crisis, in two respects. First, it reaches back to real or imagined strategies for maintaining order in the past before governments shifted from the deterrence of the criminal law to welfare modes of governance. Second, it reaches forward towards new platforms to govern a social order that truly is undergoing remarkable demographic and economic change.[15] The former is the primary focus of conservative political discourse about crime, which advocates the reimposition of social discipline and the revalorization of traditional hierarchies. The latter has become the central focus of an emerging 'neo-liberal' political discourse, which sees the individual as a more efficient locus of responsibility than groups or the state (Rose 1996). The real strength of governing through crime may well be its ability to promise both simultaneously.

Cities were the great laboratories of the collectivist or welfare regime of government. It was primarily to stabilize the conditions of the urban working classes that forms of social insurance for work accidents and unemployment were first deployed during the early twentieth century. Indeed, city boundaries worked to link wealthy and poor into a common system of education, transportation, and security. It is no accident that the high point of welfare government in the United States corresponded to a time of tremendous emphasis on revitalizing cities, while the crisis of welfarism has corresponded to a growth in anti-urban sentiment. More materially, cities which became concentration zones for welfare clients of all sorts now are facing the task of managing these populations with little or no help from national governments.

If the city was the natural model of welfarist government and its rationales, the suburb is the clear home of both neo-conservative and neo-liberal alternatives. Suburban real estate has been sold with quite explicit appeals to those frightened by contemporary problems to return to the virtues of a more tradition-centred society (although they are often built over the real rural residues of such societies). Likewise, the very nature of urban life makes it difficult to refocus governance on individual choice. Not surprisingly the rise of neo-liberal strategies has corresponded to an open abandonment of strategies aimed at helping cities, such as public transportation, education, and municipal employment. Instead, the focus becomes one of helping to create incentives for people to exit troubled neighbourhoods, schools, and industries.

Governing through crime, however, is not an inevitable concomitant to the dismantling of the welfare state. Some countries that have successfully adopted such policies have done so without generating rising levels of crime and punishment, including Britain until recently, and Canada. But at least in the United States, where cultural and historical factors may give crime an added significance – as a site of governance – governing through crime may be a way of reinforcing this renewed imposition of disciplinary responsibility on individuals. The criminal law, with its emphasis on individual responsibility and accountability, is a perfect object lesson in the logics necessary for the new governance.

The symbolic politics of city and suburb have also increasingly been invested with a racial meaning. Cities are increasingly seen as the home of African Americans and other populations defined as disliked and distrusted by the white suburban plurality that dominates politics at the national level. Race and ethnic prejudice bring their own strong connection to crime. The problem of race has been intertwined in the practices of crime and punishment since the beginning of European settlement of North America. Today the real and imaginary links of violence (and street crime generally)[16] with young African-American men is helping to drive the imperative of governing through crime. Whether voters acknowledge it to pollsters or not, it is hard to ignore the continuities between the present situation and a traditional preference for governing predominantly African-American populations in distinct and distinctly less respectable ways. Indeed, the close proximity between the virtual disappearance of explicit white supremacist politics in the United States and the arrival of crime as the major issue of national elections is strongly suggestive of a substitution.

As American cities have experienced increasing concentrations of minority racial and ethnic groups, they have also been increasingly defined by crime. Indeed, where the presence of race was once used to demarcate the important boundaries of cities, crime now codes zones of access and danger.

Conclusion: Crime and the Future of Sustainable Cities

Urban experts have long recognized crime as one of the dominant challenges to sustainable cities. We must now recognize (at least in the United States) that crime has become a far more general framework through which a panoply of urban problems are defined and responded to. We are governing our cities through crime. This chapter has emphasized four dimensions of this governance framework.

First, an unprecedented portion of the urban population in the United States is now directly governed through the criminal justice system. Second, the extraordinary levels of victimization experienced by inner-city residents have increasingly come to define cities generally as dangerous and ungovernable. These communities have experienced a virtual collapse of social and economic organization as employers have moved out. Not only have the great industrial enterprises left, but many poverty sections of large cities, and some whole smaller cities, now exist without sit-down restaurants, movie theatres, or service providers. The institutions that remain, such as schools and churches, find themselves more and more caught up in responding to crime. Such school initiatives as integration and educational achievement have been pushed off the agenda by such issues as drug testing, metal detectors, curfews, and uniforms. In a very real sense, the organizing forces of these communities are either criminals, or organizations arrayed to fight crime. Third, fear of crime cuts across class and race boundaries. The new urban landscape (including the suburbs) is being shaped by this fear, which touches issues ranging from transportation siting to the design of residential and office spaces, and even to the organization of local government. Fourth, the rise of victims as an increasingly compelling magnet for political identification leads citizens to define their relationship to the state around the problem of crime.

Governing through crime in the broad sense used here is not the goal of any coherent political force or interest group in society. Rather, quite separate concerns and objectives drive each piece of this complex whole. By forcing them together, however awkwardly, I mean to call attention to the way in which they are forming a mutually reinforcing structure that no one would support and that endangers the future of cities that are not only livable but democratic.

The trend towards governing through crime poses a serious danger of undermining democracy in the United States and elsewhere through a number of interacting processes:

- The most direct danger is through disenfranchising large numbers of minority citizens from participation in the electoral process and, more important, from almost any hope of rejoining the fully legal economy. In both respects the concentration of these populations in our urban centres means that cities are both politically and economically weakened.
- The communities whose sons and fathers are disproportionately the subject of this incarceration must find themselves alienated from the institutions of justice and from the democratic will reflected in the laws that condemn so many of them. The United States has openly discussed this concern since the aftermath of the O.J. Simpson murder trial in Los Angeles. This primary alienation from official representations of virtue and justice inevitably diminishes the very power of the law to suppress crime. More generally, the resistance it gives rise to increases the cost of non-compliance in all institutions operating in cities, including schools, businesses, and government itself.
- Fear of crime encourages citizens with resources to abandon the forms of local government they once shared with poorer populations. These forms have long been key to democratic governance under the American constitution. This has been going on for a long time through suburbanization, but it has recently intensified through the creation of wholly private 'gated' communities, and the secession of middle-class neighbourhoods from existing city and county governments.[17] The emerging metropolitan form, with its combination of collapsed urban centres and sprawling suburban edge cities with their overlays of race and demonization, constitutes a direct challenge to the ideal of democratic nationhood.[18]
- Governing through crime generates a large and more powerful managerial apparatus that threatens to limit individual rights and the free and open access to public spaces long deemed essential to the reproduction of democratic will (Post 1995). This managerial apparatus is increasingly linked to a variety of community based networks of security (O'Malley 1991). While such links may introduce greater responsiveness, they may also expand the logic of governing through crime to other settings, including schools, families, and private associations.

Crime in the conventional sense is a threat to the urban future, but governing through crime is becoming an independent threat in so far as it dominates how we shape the urban agenda. We have focused here on cities in the United States and, by implication, in the advanced industrial world. The problem is potentially far more widespread. In many so-called third world societies, the crisis of governability in the cities, brought on by collapsing economies and corrupt governments, has led to intolerable levels of crime (Kaplan 1996). New fundamentalist governments promote themselves through their ability to organize the security of everyday life through a rigorous regulation of virtually all public activity. Indeed, some policy analysts now point to churches as the only institution that can help respond to the cycle of criminalization undermining cities in the United States (Bennet, DiIulio, and Walters 1996). While it may be successful in addressing crime, however, the rise of a new fundamentalism in multicultural societies poses a highly dangerous threat to democratic governance. The spectre of this threat should lead us to take a step back from pursuing policies that seem likely to create conditions under which democratic forms of governance are jettisoned in favour of social control at any cost.

This essay has concentrated on defining the problem rather than on possible solutions. Its central message, however, can perhaps be read to yield an optimistic last note. If, as we have argued, American cities are facing a crisis of governance rather than a crisis of crime and punishment, a rather different set of directions for change opens up (and one not yet littered by the corpses of failed policies). To produce socially sustainable cities, it is essential above all to replace failed institutions of governance with new ones. Reinventing government is hardly a novel thought today (Osborne and Gaebler 1992). Indeed, many of the powerful national politicians who have declined to rescue cities have become major proponents of reinventing government. Cities would do well not to wait for national initiatives to reach them.

Notes

1 The immediate cause was the acquittal of a white police officer who had killed a black motorcyclist, but contemporary observers acknowledged that the immigration crisis was a significant factor. Thousands of refugees awaiting processing were kept in a stadium and under a freeway, both sites proximate to the core of Miami's black community.

2 Cuba is multiracial society, which was traditionally stratified in terms of race with Europeans on top and Afro-Cubans on the bottom. The 1960s immigration wave was disproportionately European, while the Mariel wave included far more Afro-Cubans.

3 In 1997 voters changed the name from Dade County to reflect the international prestige of the name 'Miami,' which formerly applied only to the city proper.

4 Miami–Dade County government remained an Anglo stronghold until a federal court decision in 1992 forced the adoption of district-based elections for the county council, which is now dominated by Cuban-American representatives.

5 At the high end, this means business consulting and services. At the low end, this means house cleaners, nannies, and other personal-service workers.

6 Data from the Florida Department of Corrections. The figure does not include inmates in the county jail, or in various forms of juvenile custody. If one excluded the very young and the very old, and looked only at males, it would be a much higher percentage.

7 For example, a household that includes a member on parole or probation may have its common areas invaded by control agents without the requirement of a warrant supported by probable cause that such surveillance would normally require.

8 There has been a counter-trend since the mid-1990s. Some cities, most famously New York, have experienced record drops in homicides and aggravated (armed) assaults. Miami–Dade experienced more than a 10 per cent drop in serious crimes between 1995 and 1996.

9 Figures in Bureau of the Census (1995). Note that these comparisons are imprecise since the precise distribution of crime within the greater metropolitan areas is not adequately captured by simple county comparisons. Miami leaders have also pointed out that calculations of reported crime divided by census figures on population give a misleading impression because Miami's winter population of visitors greatly expands the pool of those available to be crime victims without being reflected in current population figures.

10 In Miami's case the strong ties that link middle-class and wealthy Hispanics to Miami with its reputation for Spanish-language dominance have covered this up.

11 Following the very successful lead of Mayor Rudolph Giuliani of New York City.

12 When we look more closely at strategies to govern through patriotism, or

the family, we find techniques of governing through crime, such as laws against flag burning and child sexual abuse. Indeed, when Senator Robert Dole, the presumptive Republican nominee for president in 1996, sought to articulate why women should support his candidacy, he listed his support for measures to make it easier to convict rapists and prosecute domestic violence (see Seelye 1996).

13 Ulrich Beck (1992) usefully suggests that modernity developed its own kind of traditional base, the urban and industrial life and culture, which is now waning.

14 Even where these governmental strategies remain strong, as in Germany, there is increasing pressure to change. See Klaus Friedrich 1996.

15 The broadest horizon is not necessarily the deepest. It is clear that other dimensions of late modern societies generally, such as renewed ethnic and racial polarization, also determine the attraction of a government through crime as well as the specific shape it takes in specific societies.

16 Polls suggest that many Americans view street crime in general as violent, even if the particular offence does not involve assaults or direct threats of bodily harm, e.g., burglary (Little Hoover Commission 1994, 61).

17 Several recent elections have been held in Miami–Dade County by cities seeking to incorporate themselves and thus gain the authority to form their own police. In California, the State Assembly approved a bill that will authorize the residents of the suburban San Fernando Valley to vote on secession from Los Angeles. In all these elections, crime has been the major issue.

18 The most powerful accounts of this emerging political landscape have come from Mike Davis (1990, 1998).

References

Abbott, Jack Henry. 1981. *In the Belly of the Beast: Letters from Prison.* New York: Vintage.

Beck, Ulrich. 1992. *Risk Society: Towards a New Modernity.* Translated by Mark Ritter. London: Sage.

Barry, Andrew, Thomas Osborne, and Nikolas Rose, eds. 1996. *Foucault and Political Reason: Liberalism, Neo-liberalism and Rationalities of Government.* Chicago: University of Chicago Press.

Bennett, William J., John J. DiIulio, and John P. Walters. 1996. *Body Count: Moral Poverty and How to Win America's War against Crime and Drugs.* New York: Simon and Schuster.

Bureau of the Census. 1995. *County and City Data Book 1994*. Washington, DC: U.S. Department of Commerce, Bureau of the Census.

– 1996. *Statistical Abstract of the United States, 1995*. Washington, DC: U.S. Department of Commerce, Bureau of the Census.

Bureau of Justice Statistics. 1995. *Sourcebook of Criminal Justice Statistics, 1994*. Washington, DC: U.S. Government Printing Office.

– 1996. *Sourcebook of Criminal Justice Statistics, 1995*. Washington, DC: U.S. Government Printing Office.

Chevalier, Louis. 1973. *Laboring Classes and Dangerous Classes in Paris during the First Half of the Nineteenth Century.* Princeton, NJ: Princeton University Press.

Davis, Mike. 1990. *City of Quartz: Excavating the Future in Los Angeles*. London: Verso.

– 1998. *Ecology of Fear: Los Angeles and the Imagination of Disaster*. New York: Metropolitan Books.

Donzelot, Jacques. 1979. *The Policing of Families*. Translated by Robert Hurley. New York: Pantheon.

Donziger, Steven R., ed. 1996. *The Real War on Crime: The Report of the National Criminal Justice Commission*. New York: HarperCollins.

Dunn, Marvin, and Alex Stepick III. 1992. 'Blacks in Miami.' *Miami Now: Immigration, Ethnicity, and Social Change*, ed. Guillermo J. Grenier and Alex Stepick III, 41–58. Gainesville: University Press of Florida.

Durkheim, Emile. 1933. *The Division of Labor in Society.* Translated by George Simpson. New York: Free Press.

Foucault, Michel. 1982. 'The Subject and Power.' In *Michel Foucault: Beyond Structuralism and Hermeneutics*, ed. Hubert L. Dreyfus and Paul Rabinow, 208–26. Chicago: University of Chicago Press.

Freeman, Richard. 1996. *Why Do So Many Young American Men Commit Crimes and What Might We Do about It*. Working Paper 5451. Cambridge, MA: National Bureau of Economic Research.

Friedrich, Klaus, 1996. 'The End of Germany's Economic Model.' *The New York Times* (national edition), 10 June, A19.

Garland, David. 1985. *Punishment and Welfare*. Brookfield, VT: Gower.

– 1996. 'The Limits of the Sovereign State: Strategies of Crime Control in Contemporary Society.' *British Journal of Criminology* 36/4: 445–71.

Gilbert James. 1972. *Designing the Industrial State: The Intellectual Pursuit of Collectivism in America, 1880–1940*. Chicago: Quadrangle.

Gordon, Diana R. 1994. *The Return of the Dangerous Classes: Drug Prohibition and Policy Politics*. New York: Norton.

Harvey, David. 1989. *The Condition of Postmodernity: An Enquiry into the Origins of Cultural Change*. New York: Blackwell.

Jameson, Fredric. 1992. *Postmodernism, or the Cultural Logic of Late Capitalism.* Durham, NC: Duke University Press.

Kaplan, Robert. 1996. *The Ends of the Earth: A Journey at the Dawn of the 21st Century.* New York: Random House.

Lane, Roger. 1975. *Policing the City: Boston, 1822–1885.* New York: Atheneum.

– 1979. *Violent Death in the City: Suicide, Accident, and Murder in Nineteenth-Century Philadelphia.* Cambridge, MA: Harvard University Press.

Leps, Marie-Christine. 1992. *Apprehending the Criminal: The Production of Deviance in 19th Century Discourse.* Durham, NC: Duke University Press.

Little Hoover Commission. 1994. *Putting Violence behind Bars: Redefining the Role of California's Prisons.* Sacramento: Little Hoover Commission.

Mauer, Marc, and Tracy Huling. 1995. *Young Black Men and the Criminal Justice System: Five Years Later.* Washington, DC: The Sentencing Project.

Miller, Jerome. 1996. *Search and Destroy: African-American Males in the Criminal Justice System.* Cambridge: Cambridge University Press.

Monkonnen, Eric H. 1981. 'A Disorderly People? Urban Order in the Nineteenth and Twentieth Centuries.' *Journal of American History* 68: 539–59.

– 1988. *America Becomes Urban: The Development of U.S. Cities and Towns, 1780–1980.* Berkeley: University of California Press.

O'Malley, Pat. 1991. 'Legal Networks and Domestic Security.' *Studies in Law, Politics, and Society* 11: 181–91.

Osborne, David, and Ted Gaebler. 1992. *Reinventing Government: How the Entrepreneurial Spirit Is Transforming the Public Sector.* Reading, MA: Addison-Wesley.

Park, Rober E., Ernest W. Burgess, and Roderick D. McKenzie. 1925. *The City.* Chicago: University of Chicago Press.

Portes, Alejandro, and Alex Stepick. 1993. *City on the Edge: The Transformation of Miami.* Berkeley: University of California Press.

Post, Robert C. 1995. *Constitutional Domains: Democracy, Community, Management.* Cambridge, MA: Harvard University Press.

Putnam, Robert D. 1993. *Making Democracy Work: Civic Traditions in Modern Italy.* Princeton, NJ: Princeton University Press.

Rose, Nikolas. 1990. *Governing the Soul: The Shaping of the Private Self.* London: Routledge.

– 1996. 'Governing "Advanced" Liberal Democracies.' In *Foucault and Political Reason: Liberalism, Neo-Liberalism and Rationalities of Government,* ed. Andrew Barry, Thomas Osborne and Nikolas Rose. Chicago: University of Chicago Press.

Sassen, Saskia. 1993. *The Global City: New York, London, Tokyo.* Princeton, NJ: Princeton University Press.

Seelye, Katherine Q. 1996. 'Dole says he has plan to win the votes of women.' *New York Times* (national ed.), 8 May, p. A1.

Shaw, Clifford. 1929. *Delinquency Areas: A Study of the Geographic Distribution of School Truants, Juvenile Delinquents, and Adult Offenders in Chicago.* Chicago: University of Chicago Press.

Silberman, Mathew. 1995. *A World of Violence: Corrections in America.* Belmont, CA: Wadsworth.

Silver, Allan. 1967. 'The Demand for Order in Civil Society: A Review of Some Themes in the History of Urban Crime, Police, and Riot.' In *The Police: Six Sociological Essays*, ed. David Bordua, 1–24. New York: Wiley.

Simon, Jonathan. 1993. *Poor Discipline: Parole and the Social Control of the Urban Underclass, 1890–1990.* Chicago: University of Chicago Press.

Sutton, John. 1997. 'Punishment, Politics and Social Policy: The Expansion of Remand and Sentenced Prison Populations in Four Common-Law Democracies, 1955–1985.' Paper presented at the 1997 Meetings of the American Sociological Association, Toronto, Canada, August.

Taylor, Margaret. 1995. 'Detained Aliens Challenging Conditions of Confinement and the Porous Border of the Plenary Power Doctrine.' *Hastings Constitutional Law Quarterly* 22: 1087–1158.

Thrasher, Frederick. 1927. *The Gang: A Study of 1,313 Delinquent Gangs in Chicago.* Chicago: University of Chicago Press.

Wilson, William Julius. 1996. *When Work Disappears: The World of the New Urban Poor.* New York: Knopf.

Zimring, Franklin. 1997. *Crime Is Not the Problem: Lethal Violence in America.* New York: Oxford University Press.

5 'A Third-World City in the First World': Social Exclusion, Racial Inequality, and Sustainable Development in Baltimore

MARC V. LEVINE

Despite periodic reports of an 'urban renaissance,' social and economic conditions have persistently deteriorated in U.S. cities since the 1960s. Particularly in the older, historically industrial cities of the northeast and Midwest, the grim litany of urban problems is familiar: high rates of crime and unemployment; concentrated neighbourhood poverty; deteriorating housing stock, schools, and social services; racial inequality; and the flight of the middle class to outlying suburbs. Across the country, suburban, 'Edge City' locations are supplanting central cities as regional economic hubs. By the mid-1990s, according to one study, thirty-four cities had declined beyond 'a critical "point of no return,"' past which central cities continue inexorably to slide downward economically, socially, and fiscally' (Rusk 1996, 21). For many major cities in the United States, the issue is not so much sustainability as survival.

No city better exemplifies this 'rough road to renaissance' (Teaford 1990) than Baltimore, a city whose 'Inner Harbor' downtown waterfront redevelopment has been widely heralded as a model of how older, industrial cities could remake decaying port districts into glittering tourist attractions. 'So successful has the Baltimore experience been that many of its concepts have been exported to other cities around the world,' wrote one analyst of the Baltimore tourism strategy (Craig-Smith 1995, 22). One envious mayor noted that 'Baltimore's quest to reinvent itself has made it one of the most inspiring stories on the East Coast' (Haner 1998a).

Yet, by the 1990s, few argued seriously that Baltimore had achieved anything approaching a genuine urban renaissance. There is 'rot beneath the glitter' of the waterfront rejuvenation, stated an influential report on the city's future in the late 1980s (Szanton 1986). In the 1970s and 1980s, Baltimore's boosterish mayor ceaselessly proclaimed it a 'Renaissance City.' However, by the 1990s, despite the bright lights of the Inner Harbor, a different Baltimore mayor noted that 'it is an unfortunate fact of life that we have in certain parts of our city health problems, housing problems, that resemble those in Third World countries' (Shane 1994). In 1994, the U.S. Agency for International Development (AID) designated Baltimore the first U.S. city to be targeted for assistance by AID's 'Lessons without Borders' program, which applies 'Third World' development techniques to American inner cities.

Once a self-styled 'Renaissance City,' Baltimore was now recognized as 'a Third World city in the First World' – such was the magnitude of the city's 'sustainability' crisis (Pietila 1996b). In reality, of course, there were 'three Baltimores.' One was the 'Renaissance City': the revived Inner Harbor and a waterfront 'Gold Coast' of luxury hotels and condominiums, high-rise offices, sports stadiums and tourist attractions. Just fifteen blocks away from the Inner Harbor, however, and extending to broad patches of the urban landscape, was another Baltimore, the 'Underclass City' of desolate neighbourhoods marked by social exclusion, high rates of crime and drug abuse, deepening ghetto poverty, and dilapidated or abandoned housing, where much of the city's predominantly black population lived. Finally, there was a third Baltimore: rapidly growing and prosperous suburbs, where jobs, businesses, and middle-class residents – first white, but eventually the black middle class as well – had migrated from the city since the 1950s. By the 1990s, per-capita income in the Baltimore City was only 64.3 per cent that of the suburbs, which were increasingly the engines of the metropolitan economy and places in which residents' daily lives and economic fortunes were increasingly disconnected from the central city.

This chapter traces the emergence of 'the three Baltimores' since the 1960s, focusing on the challenge to sustainable urban development posed by racial inequality, social exclusion, and metropolitan polarization. Baltimore's political leadership has been in the vanguard among U.S. cities over the past three decades in implementing various urban revitalization strategies: downtown waterfront redevelopment and tourism promotion; public–private partnerships for real-estate development; community 'action' and community development in impoverished neighbourhoods; and, more recently, regional planning and cooperation. Yet, despite the success of the Inner Harbor and praise for the Baltimore 'model,' the city's decline persists, and genuine renaissance remains elusive. In the face of fundamental changes in the structure of metropolitan economies, the Baltimore experience raises disturbing questions: Are cities like Baltimore truly 'past the point of no return,' and beyond the meliorative capacity of municipal policy? Is the 'model' of 'the three Baltimores' – a kind of metropolitan apartheid, U.S.–style – the balkanized metropolis of the future in the United States? Does *anything* work?

In the final analysis, this chapter concludes that without a pro-city regional development strategy to counter the polarizing effects of U.S.–style metropolitan fragmentation, Baltimore's future is not promising. Overcoming Baltimore's sustainability crisis will require a culture of socially just regionalism, a new social compact based on equitable and balanced development.

Baltimore: The Setting

Located along the east coast of the United States, about thirty-five miles northeast of Washington, DC, Baltimore was, through the 1950s, one of the country's leading port and industrial cities. The city's population reached a peak of 950,000 in 1950, making it the sixth-largest American city that year, and over 34 per cent of the city's labour force was employed in manufacturing. Although some suburbanization had occurred, the city of Baltimore was the economic and demographic hub of the region: three-quarters of the region's jobs and over 70 per cent of its population were located in the central city.

During the 1950s, however, Baltimore's social structure and economy changed, in ways that underlay the city's long-term sustainability crisis. First, the city began the painful transformation to a post-industrial economy. Between 1950 and 1970, Baltimore lost 46,000 manufacturing jobs, or a third of its industrial base. Deindustrialization has continued unabated since then, and between 1970 and 1995 Baltimore lost another 55,000 manufacturing jobs. All told, between 1950 and 1995, Baltimore lost 74.9 per cent of its industrial employment, and by 1995 only 8 percent of city jobs were in manufacturing. Industrial employment had provided entry-level job opportunities for relatively unskilled urban workers through mid-century and, as unionization raised the bargaining power of workers, these jobs also offered a blue-collar, middle-class standard of living. In Baltimore, however, those opportunities began shrinking considerably during the 1950s, and by 1995 Baltimore City had, to all intents and purposes, deindustrialized.

Second, Baltimore's great wave of suburbanization also began then. Since 1950, the city's population has declined continuously, falling to an estimated 657,000 by 1997, 30.8 per cent below its peak. While that shrinkage pales beside the demographic declines since 1950 in cities such as St Louis (59.0 per cent), Pittsburgh (48.3 per cent), Buffalo (46.6 per cent), and Detroit (45.9 per cent), it is steep and threatens the city's vitality. Residents (both black and white) flocked to the suburbs, where the population grew from 387,656 in 1950 to just over 1.8 million in 1997.

The combination of central-city population decline and the rapid growth of surrounding suburbs profoundly altered the demographic balance of the Baltimore metropolitan area. In 1950, the city contained 71 per cent of the region's population; by 1970, after the first great wave of suburbanization, that percentage had declined to 43.7 per cent. By 1997, after four and a half decades of continuing suburbanization, only 26 per cent of the Baltimore region's population lived in the city. Although Baltimore City is today not quite the proverbial 'hole in the doughnut,' suburbanization has reduced sharply the demographic importance of the city in the region.

Suburbanization also began eroding the city's economic base. Between 1954 and 1995, the city share of regional manufacturing employment dropped from 75 to 30 per cent. Similarly, as the new suburbanites desired shopping closer to their residences, the development of suburban malls drew retail trade from the city. Eighty per cent of the Baltimore region's retail sales took place in the city in 1954; by 1967, this proportion had fallen to 50 per cent, and it plummeted to 18 per cent in 1992 (Levine 1998). As a result, by the 1950s, there was an unmistakable deterioration of the downtown retail district and neighbourhood commercial strips.

Finally, Baltimore's racial composition began changing in the 1950s, intersecting with the processes of suburbanization and economic decline, to become an integral component of the 'urban crisis.' Baltimore was a major destination for the great migration of displaced, impoverished black sharecroppers from the rural South, and between 1950 and 1970 the city's black population almost doubled, growing by 195,000. Concomitantly, massive numbers of white Baltimoreans began an exodus to the suburbs. This combination of black migration and 'white flight' rapidly transformed Baltimore's racial composition (see table 5.1). Baltimore became a black majority city by the mid-1970s, and by 1997 the city's population was almost two-thirds black. Figure 5.1 illustrates the stunning extent of white flight from the city. In 1950,

Figure 5.1 White Flight in Baltimore: Percentage of the Region's White Population Living in Baltimore City, 1950–1997

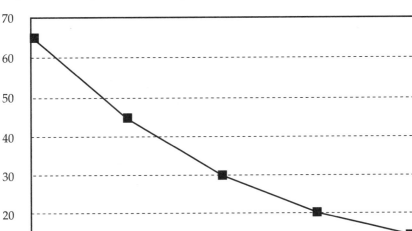

% of metro area whites living in city

Source: U.S. Bureau of the Census 1952, 1962, 1983, 1993, 1998

almost two-thirds of metropolitan Baltimore's white population lived in the city; by 1997, only 12.5 per cent of the region's whites – just one in eight – resided in Baltimore City. As a place to live and work, the city became more and more of a peripheral location in the daily lives of increasingly suburbanized white Baltimoreans.

By the late 1950s, the confluence of racial segregation, suburbaniza-tion, and economic decline had resulted in what urban planners called neighbourhood 'blight' and what sociologists recognized as the emer-gence of 'ghetto poverty.' By 1960, in all-black inner-city neighbour-hoods such as Upton, Sandtown–Winchester, and Greenmount West, over half the residents in some census tracts lived in poverty. In Balti-more as a whole, an estimated 30 per cent of the city's blacks lived in poverty in 1960, roughly triple the rate for whites. Unemployment, deteriorating housing, growing welfare dependency, and high rates of crime increasingly characterized inner-city neighbourhood life, and

Table 5.1 The Racial Composition of Baltimore's
Population, 1950–1997

Year	White	Black	Black %
1950	723,655	225,099	23.7
1960	610,608	325,589	34.6
1970	480,377	420,147	46.4
1980	345,080	431,153	54.8
1990	287,753	435,768	59.1
1997 (est.)	214,857	427,300	64.9

Source: U.S. Bureau of the Census 1952, 1962,
1972, 1983, 1993, 1998

the city's ghetto, once confined to relatively limited pockets in West Baltimore, now encompassed wider areas of the city.

Beginning in the mid-1950s, Baltimore's business and political leadership responded to these conditions with a series of initiatives. The Greater Baltimore Committee (GBC), a group of 100 leading business executives concerned principally about falling property values and the commercial erosion of downtown, spearheaded the 'Charles Center' urban renewal project, a $180-million, thirty-three-acre complex of offices, apartments and retail shops in the central business district. The city government also implemented several neighbourhood urban-renewal projects, focusing on improved housing, streetscapes, and recreational facilities in neighbourhoods such as Harlem Park and Upton. Throughout the 1960s, federal government's 'Great Society' programs provided millions of dollars to expand social services and support community development in the city's ghetto neighbourhoods.

On the whole, however, these programs did little to arrest the decline in Baltimore's neighbourhoods, nor did they significantly revive downtown commerce. In short, by the 1960s Baltimore was undeniably in the midst of a full-blown 'urban crisis.' The city's crime rate skyrocketed during the decade: by 1970, Baltimore had the highest rate of violent crime among the nation's fifteen largest Frostbelt cities and among the nation's highest homicide rates. Fear of crime, in turn, helped accelerate the exodus of the city's white middle class to the safety of racially homogeneous suburbs. Baltimore's racial turbulence of the 1960s spilled over into violence, with ghetto riots in 1968 following the assassination of Martin Luther King. As in cities across the United States, the riots in Baltimore represented a symbolic turning point, confirming the city's crisis and accelerating the secular trends of middle-class flight, urban disinvestment, and neighbourhood decay (Siegel 1997). By the end of a decade marked by racial turmoil and civil strife, municipal leaders openly evoked the spectre of a city on the verge of collapse and abandonment.

The Renaissance City

Improbably, out of these bleak conditions, Baltimore was able, in the 1970s and 1980s, to engineer a massive downtown redevelopment program and burnish a national image as a 'comeback city.' This 'Baltimore Renaissance,' as local promoters called it, was realized under the indefatigable and boosterish leadership of William Donald Schaefer, who served as mayor between 1971 and 1986. Schaefer hardly ignored the city's neighbourhoods, spending millions on various community-development projects in low-income, predominantly black neighbourhoods such as Upton and Park Heights. But the heart of his post-1960s strategy for rebuilding Baltimore was to recommercialize downtown, to reclaim it as 'middle-class territory' and make it attractive for investors, developers, and tourists. The geographic focal point for the 'renaissance' strategy was the Inner Harbor, a wasteland along the city's waterfront composed of ramshackle warehouses and decaying wharves (see figure 5.2). Schaefer's audacious aim was to transform this 'Skid Row' into a bustling 'carnival city' of tourist attractions (as well as offices and stores) that would lure visitors from the suburbs and beyond. In turn, a revitalized downtown, in conjunction with strategic investments in Baltimore's neighbourhoods, would be the engine reviving the city-wide economy, reattracting and retaining middle-class residents, and rejuvenating blighted neighbourhoods. In short, Baltimore would hitch its fortunes to property development and tourism.

Surmounting investor scepticism and fiscal constraints, Schaefer launched the Inner Harbor renaissance by creating a kind of Baltimore, Inc.: an urban redevelopment machine, fuelled with public dollars, that identified and packaged profit opportunities for developers. Public–private 'partnership' became the watchword of city policy, and Baltimore became a pioneer among U.S. cities in offering government incentives to entice development downtown. An elaborate network of 'quasi-public' corporations was established – critics dubbed it Schaefer's 'Shadow Government' – to lure developers to Baltimore by offering attractive financing, quickly and confidentially. Between 1976

Figure 5.2 Downtown Baltimore and Inner-City Neighbourhoods
Source: INRS–urbanisation

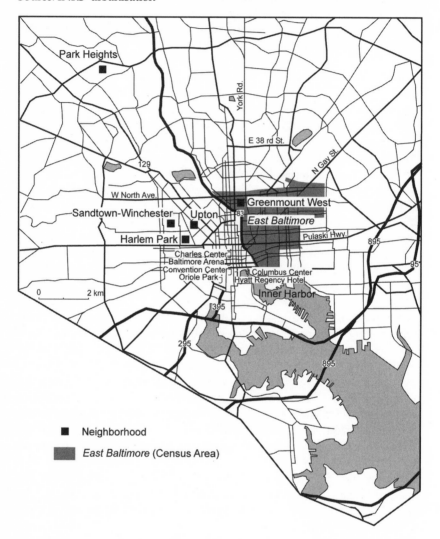

and 1986 – the key years in which Baltimore's downtown renaissance took flight – Schaefer's redevelopment machine leveraged over $800 million in private investment, almost half in downtown projects (Baltimore City Trustees and Loan Program 1986).

What kind of redevelopment did Baltimore, Inc. produce? First, the city made 'anchor' investments to create a Baltimore tourist industry. In 1979, Baltimore became a player in the national conventions business with the opening of a $52-million convention center, and in 1981 the city opened its National Aquarium, which became an instant visitor attraction, doubling expectations by drawing 1.6 million patrons in its first year of operation.

Second, city deal-making in tourism-related projects complemented these public investments. Desperate for a 'prestige' Inner Harbor hotel to lodge conventioneers and tourists and enhance the national image of Baltimore as a tourist destination, the city packaged $35 million in below-market-rate loans to attract a shimmering Hyatt–Regency Hotel, which opened in 1979. Over the next decade, the city would provide an average 30 per cent subsidy to every hotel built downtown (Matthews 1998). In 1980, the crowning investment of this phase of the 'renaissance' opened: the $22-million Rouse Corporation 'festival marketplace,' located on the harbour promenade and comprising two pavilions of shops, restaurants, and markets. Harborplace was an immediate commercial success and visitor magnet, and the national publicity accorded the development gave rise to the image of Baltimore as a 'renaissance city,' one which had 'broken out' of the downward spiral of declining 'rustbelt' cities.

The post-Harborplace Inner Harbor was a 'hot' redevelopment zone, and during the 1980s private investment surged. Baltimore's experience was not unique: cities across the United States experienced a speculative real-estate investment boom during the decade, as various Reagan-era federal tax policies enticed billions of dollars into downtown (and suburban) real estate (Fainstein 1994). 'Entrepreneurial' city governments, like Baltimore's, continued to offer various redevelopment subsidies, which further encouraged the real-estate 'bubble' of offices, hotels, and retail shops.

In this superheated speculative environment – critics called it the 'casino economy' – redevelopment dollars cascaded into the Inner Harbor. During the 1980s, the skyline around the waterfront became dotted with new office towers, as more than 3.5 million square feet of 'class A' office space was developed in and around the harbour. Fifteen hotels opened in the vicinity of the harbour between 1980 and 1989, more than tripling the number of hotel rooms available downtown. The convention and tourism business, which for all intents and purposes did not exist in Baltimore before 1980, took off, and by the end of the decade an estimated 7 million visitors, including almost 300,000 conventioneers, were coming to the Inner Harbor annually (Downtown Strategy Advisory Committee 1991). Luxury housing was built, and gentrified neighbourhoods around the harbour saw property values soar. All told, the once-decrepit Inner Harbor attracted a staggering $1.6 billion in development during the 1980s, almost 90 per cent of it private investment (a precise reversal of the ratios of public and private investment occurring in the 1970s) (Lally 1990). Downtown property-value assessments quadrupled during the decade. By the mid-1980s, speculative real-estate development began spreading to traditional working-class communities such as Fells Point and Canton, east and south of the downtown waterfront. City planners and developers began envisioning a Baltimore 'Gold Coast' of marinas, shoreline promenades, commercial establishments, and luxury housing, extending from the Inner Harbor for miles along the city waterfront.

However, by the end of the 1980s, this phase of the 'renaissance' foundered, with the bursting of the tax code–driven, speculative real-estate bubble. The 1986 federal tax reform act withdrew many of the real-estate tax shelters offered in 1981. This policy shift, combined with a massive international oversupply of downtown property built up during the 1980s speculative frenzy, brought redevelopment crashing to a halt from London's Canary Wharf to downtown Dallas (and Baltimore in between). In short, as swiftly as Baltimore rode the 1980s international real-estate boom to an Inner Harbor renaissance, the overbuilt downtown real-estate market crashed, and inflated property values collapsed. By the early 1990s, hotel and office construction had stopped, several high-profile commercial projects had failed, and dreams faded of a 'Gold Coast' of shoreline redevelopment beyond the Inner Harbor. Office vacancy rates downtown soared to 25 per cent, and by 1996 the total assessed value of downtown property had declined by over 40 per cent from its 1980s peak (Downtown Partnership 1998).

The early 1990s crash, however, did not mark the end of the 'Renaissance City.' In fact, by the mid-1990s, thanks to more than $1 billion in publicly financed sports stadiums, tourist attractions, and an expanded convention centre, the pace of redevelopment reaccelerated around the Inner Harbor and Gold Coast, and city leaders began proclaiming a 'second renaissance.' A new mayor was now at the helm, Kurt L. Schmoke, who took office in 1987 as Baltimore's first elected black mayor (in a city that had become, by then, almost 60 per cent black). Early in his tenure, Schmoke appeared anxious to tilt city priorities towards education and neighbourhood revitalization, stating that 'we must build upon the successes of our downtown redevelopment program and ensure that the benefits of growth reach the neighborhoods' (Levine 1987b, 134). The mayor launched several major neighbourhood initiatives, and underscored his commitment to improving public education by vowing to remake Baltimore into 'the city that reads.' After years of cuts, Schmoke actually increased real expenditures on schooling between 1987 and 1997.

However, by the early 1990s it was clear that the new mayor supported property development around the Inner Harbor as vigorously as had his predecessor. Under Schmoke's stewardship the city redoubled its commitment to Baltimore's 'carnival city' strategy, with massive public investments in tourism and entertainment facilities at the Inner Harbor:

- two sports stadiums ($500 million), for Baltimore's major league baseball and football teams;
- an expanded convention centre ($151 million), to attract larger conventions requiring more square feet of exhibition space;
- the Columbus Center ($147 million), a marine-biology facility designed as the Inner Harbor's next big tourist attraction;
- $85 million in subsidies for the Wyndham and Grand Hyatt hotels, to support the convention trade (and, in the case of the Wyndham, speculation that the mayor viewed it as a future site for a Baltimore casino).

These enormous public expenditures, along with an improving national economy, propelled a new wave of redevelopment along Baltimore's waterfront. A major entertainment complex, the $30-million 'Power Plant,' opened at the Inner Harbor in 1998, along with several restaurants and the entertainment staples of international urban tourism: Planet Hollywood and the Hard Rock Café. In shoreline neighbourhoods, old industrial sites re-emerged as office, entertainment, and housing projects. Beyond the waterfront, by 1998, an additional $1 billion in public and private investment was planned for downtown projects (Gunts 1998). In short, the downtown renaissance was no chimera. By the end of the 1990s, downtown property values were rising again, and deal-making was back in vogue.

Sustainable Development and the 'Renaissance City'

The rejuvenation of Baltimore's Inner Harbor is one of the great urban-redevelopment success stories of the past quarter-century. Beyond the stunning reconstruction of the waterfront district and billions of dollars in property development, downtown Baltimore has grown dramatically as an employment centre. Between 1970 and 1995, employment downtown grew by almost 80 per cent, far outstripping the growth rate in the downtowns of other frostbelt cities, such as Cleveland, Pittsburgh, Milwaukee, or St Louis. Indeed, all of Baltimore City's net job growth since the 1970s has been downtown; as a result, the share of city jobs located downtown increased from 12.3 per cent in 1970 to an estimated 25 per cent in 1997. Initially, white suburbanites garnered the lion's share of the new downtown jobs (Levine 1987a), but during the 1980s downtown growth began providing significant employment opportunities for the city's black community. Almost 60 per cent of the 27,000 jobs created downtown during the 1980s went to blacks. By 1990, 34.6 per cent of the downtown workforce was black, up significantly from 21.3 per cent in 1980 (U.S. Bureau of Transportation Statistics 1995).

Nevertheless, there remains considerable doubt as to whether the creation of a 'Renaissance City' at the Inner Harbor has made much of a dent in Baltimore's mounting social and economic distress, or whether the 'carnival city' strategy is generating socially sustainable development.

First, the Inner Harbor prosperity has remained primarily at the waterfront, not only barely touching the rest of the city, but hardly extending to the rest of downtown. Some planners fear a kind of 'Atlantic City' effect in Baltimore, with a layer of redevelopment extending along a 'Gold Coast' shoreline, but with continuing blight and decline just a few blocks inland. The traditional retail district, on the western edge of downtown, remains moribund, with vacant storefronts, dilapidated buildings, and seedy street life. The historical financial and business district, located just north of the Inner Harbor, continues to suffer from high office vacancy rates and to lose ground to the suburbs as an office centre. Several major firms left downtown for suburban locations in the 1990s. Indeed, by the late 1990s, downtown was looking less and less like a central business district and more like an urban 'theme park,' with investments in tourism and entertainment increasingly dominating the cityscape. As one prominent developer unabashedly put it: 'What we're helping create and solidify is the Inner Harbor as Disneyland, and it really can be one of the salvations to moving the city forward' (Gately 1997).

However, 'the Inner Harbor as Disneyland' has not yet proven to be a formula for sustainable urban regeneration. Although considerable residential development has occurred around the Inner Harbor, the waterfront increasingly resembles a 'tourist bubble': a district of hotels, convention centres, sports stadiums, entertainment, and restaurants, 'cordoned off' from the existing urban fabric and designed to 'cosset the affluent visitor while simultaneously warding off the threatening native' (Fainstein and Gladstone 1999, 26). Concomitantly, the late 1990s burst of commercial development all but obliterated the original vision of 'public space' at the Inner Harbor, and launched another speculative frenzy that threatens to overwhelm any city planning aimed at assuring maximum public benefit from waterfront redevelopment. As a *Baltimore Sun* (1998c) editorial put it: 'while Baltimore welcomes new development and the tax revenue and jobs it brings ... our downtown shoreline should not be allowed to deteriorate into a kitschy and overcommercialized tourist trap ...'

Second, there are serious questions regarding the social justice of the 'carnival city' strategy. Baltimore has succeeded beyond any city planner's dreams in creating a tourist mecca at the Inner Harbor. It is now the sixteenth-largest urban tourist destination in the country, and visitor spending pumps an estimated $1 billion into the city economy. Tourism-related jobs are now the primary source of downtown Baltimore's employment growth (Downtown Partnership 1998; Arney 1998). However, the quality of these jobs is dubious: they are not unionized, contain few fringe benefits or career ladders, are typically part-time, and pay about 60 per cent of the average city wage. Although hotel managers or convention planners earn handsome salaries, the vast majority of workers in Baltimore's tourism industry – waitresses, housekeepers, and kitchen workers – earn less than $15,000 a year. In 1994, concerned over social polarization in Baltimore's tourism labour market, community and labour organizations launched a campaign for a city 'Social Compact' in which city government would help pressure downtown hoteliers – the recipients of vast public subsidies – to pay a 'living wage' to their employees. Although the campaign pressured Mayor Schmoke into signing a limited ordinance, mandating 'living wages' for contractors doing work for the city, the hotels and restaurants of the Inner Harbor tourism enclave remain untouched by the law (Weisbrot and Sforza-Roderick 1996).

Third, the fiscal sustainability of the 'carnival city' strategy also appears problematic. Tourism is attractive to city policy makers, because it brings an infusion of 'outside' dollars into the local economy, supporting local retailers and increasing sales tax revenues. In an era of shrinking urban employment bases in the United States, tourism seems to be one industry in which cities have a 'competitive advantage.' However, Baltimore has invested over $2 billion in tourist facilities since the 1970s (in inflation-adjusted dollars), and provided millions more dollars in subsidies to private developers of hotels and entertainment complexes. As David Barringer points out, 'the carnival city model requires constant and expensive reinvention just to remain competitive' (1997, 29). Baltimore's investment in a convention centre, for example, required subsidies for hotels, ongoing expenditures for tourist attractions (to keep the conventioneers entertained), and, after a decade or so, further investments in expanded convention facilities (to keep up with newer facilities elsewhere), another round of publicly subsidized tourist attractions, and so forth. In view of this need to constantly – and expensively – 'reinvent' the carnival city, it is unclear, over the long run, whether the returns justify the investment, let alone whether Baltimore 'earns' enough from tourism to support expenditures for schooling, housing, or social services.[1]

All the available research, for example, concludes that public investments in sports stadiums are fiscal losers (Noll and Zimbalist 1997). And, while the evidence is mixed on convention centres (Fainstein and Stokes 1998), the high capital costs and operating expenses of these facilities, coupled with impending market saturation in North America (there have been more than thirty major urban convention-centre projects since 1985) makes such investments much riskier than perceived by cities such as Baltimore. The lagging bookings in 1999 and beyond for Baltimore's expanded convention facility is just one indicator of the uncertain fiscal return of such investments. In addition, the urban entertainment industry appears much shakier financially than the investor euphoria of the early 1990s would suggest. By the end of 1998, with their novelty fading, there were national reports of 'carnage' and 'collapse' in the market for so-called theme restaurants, the Planet

Hollywoods and Hard Rock Cafés whose opening heralded the Inner Harbor's 'second renaissance' (Bagli 1998).

Finally, the quality of the city's redevelopment deal-making since the 1970s exacerbated these fiscal and social-sustainability concerns. A 1992 analysis, for example, estimated that almost $60 million in city redevelopment loans since the 1970s had not been repaid (one-third of these to hotels), and found that 'City Hall has not even kept count of how much money was doled to developers during Baltimore's boom years, how much has been repaid, and how much has been lost' (Jacobson 1992). In the city's zeal to cut redevelopment deals, due diligence was often short-circuited, resulting in questionable and ultimately failed 'deals' in retail (the 'Fishmarket' and the 'Brokerage'), entertainment (the 'Power Plant' during the 1980s), and hotels. Moreover, in many cases, even if the projects turned out to be successful, deals were structured so that the city stood 'last in line' to receive any cash flow, despite having provided heavy 'up-front' subsidies to private developers. In some cases, such as the 1979 Hyatt hotel investment, the city did reap 'profit-sharing' benefits; yet, in other cases, such as Harborplace, the Omni Hotel, and the Tindeco Wharf apartments, deals were structured so that these profitable projects reported no net revenues subject to city profit-sharing. Publicly financed tourist attractions were also problematic. Although many attractions, such as the aquarium, were successful, others failed miserably. For example, the $147-million Columbus Center for marine biology, which opened in 1995, attracted one-quarter of the projected tourists and quickly went bankrupt, leaving taxpayers with a massive debt. State lawmakers admitted that the financial details and roseate visitor projections of the doomed project had never been adequately vetted (Murray 1998).

Indeed, rigorous cost-benefit analysis – including consideration of the 'opportunity costs' of 'carnival city' investments – has not been part of Baltimore redevelopment policy making. For example, a careful 1997 study of the economic impact of the city's two heralded 'Camden Yards' sports stadiums found, 'taking account of all of the measurable benefits of the ... investment (that is, job creation and tax imports),' that the stadiums run an annual 'best-case' fiscal deficit of $24 million (generating approximately $4 million in annual economic benefits to the Maryland economy, at an annual cost to taxpayers of approximately $28 million) (Hamilton and Kahn 1997, 271). Yet, public officials continued to tout the stadiums as a great economic-development success. The owner of Baltimore's new professional football team proclaimed stadiums more valuable to the city than 'thirty libraries,' an allusion to protests over the closing of neighbourhood branches of Baltimore's public library in the 1990s while the public financed his $260-million stadium (Pitts 1997). In a city of shuttered libraries and crumbling schools, public subsidies for luxury hotels and sports stadiums seemed far removed from socially just development.

The Underclass City

Whatever the successes and drawbacks of the 'Inner Harbor as Disney-land' strategy, one conclusion is undeniable: there was very little 'trickle down' redevelopment from the rejuvenated Inner Harbor to Baltimore's most distressed neighbourhoods. Since the 1950s, 'ghetto poverty' has relentlessly claimed vast sections of the city. Baltimore was once renowned as a city of vibrant, tightly knit neighbourhoods. But, by the 1990s, outside of the Inner Harbor and isolated pockets of neighbourhood stability, Baltimore increasingly resembled a patch-work of vacant lots, abandoned housing, and boarded-up stores. A 1997 survey found that an astonishing 40,000 housing units – around 15 per cent of city's stock – were either abandoned or boarded up (Haner and O'Donnell 1997). Neighbourhood commercial activity con-tinued to evaporate: even with the Inner Harbor boom, city-wide retail sales fell (in real dollars) by over 30 per cent between 1977 and 1992. The number of census tracts in which 40 per cent of the population was poor had doubled since 1960, and more than 100,000 Baltimoreans lived in these 'high-poverty' neighbourhoods in 1990.

The indicators of Baltimore's social distress were mind-boggling:

- *Drugs:* An estimated 9 per cent of the city's population in 1996 were drug addicts, and Baltimore led the nation in the rate of hospital emergency room episodes involving drugs (*Baltimore Sun* 1998a). During the 1980s, open-air drug markets proliferated in city neigh-bourhoods, and an explosion in crack-cocaine use ripped the fabric of neighbourhood life (Simon and Burns 1997).
- *Public health:* The city's infant mortality rate ranked third in the United States, according to a 1991 study, with the rate for blacks almost double that for whites (Evans 1991).
- *Crime:* Baltimore had, in 1995, the second-highest violent-crime rate of the nation's fifteen largest frostbelt cities, and the third-highest homicide rate among these cities. The city's neighbourhoods had

become something of an urban 'killing field,' as the murder rate qua-drupled between 1960 and 1995. A violent culture of guns and drugs has claimed 7,000 lives in Baltimore since 1970. In 1991, a survey found that, on an average day, 56 per cent of black men in the city between the ages of eighteen and thirty-five were involved with the criminal justice system: either in prison, on parole or probation, sought for arrest, or awaiting trial (West 1992).

* *Schooling:* Baltimore had, according to the U.S. census, the ninth-highest drop-out rate in the nation, with over one-fifth of the city's sixteen- to nineteen-year-olds either not completing high school or not enrolling in school. This was double the national average (*Baltimore Sun* 1992). Only 16 per cent of city third-graders scored satisfac-torily on standardized reading tests in 1998, compared with 44 per cent throughout the State of Maryland (Bowie 1998).

By the 1990s, Baltimore's inner city was ravaged by the simulta-neous presence of multiple social problems: drugs, poverty, jobless-ness, crime, family instability, physical blight. These difficulties are mutually reinforcing, and in distressed neighbourhoods 'each problem intensifies other problems and hampers their solution, making the whole worse than the sum of its parts' and overwhelming the commu-nity's problem-solving capacity (Committee for Economic Develop-ment 1995). Table 5.2 shows, on the key indicator of poverty, the shocking extent of social distress in the Baltimore's inner city. In ghetto neighbourhoods, the proportion of residents living below the poverty line is double the city average and quadruple the metropolitan-area rate.

William Julius Wilson has offered the most influential analysis of U.S. ghetto poverty, succinctly summarized in the title of his most recent book, *When Work Disappears: The World of the New Urban Poor* (1997). According to Wilson, while there is a discernible 'culture of poverty' in the inner city, the root of this culture and the social disarray of ghetto neighbourhoods is the erosion of job opportunities for inner-city residents, particularly for black males. The loss of entry-level man-ufacturing jobs, the rise of service employment requiring greater skills and education, and the displacement of industry from the central city to suburbs, has hit ghetto neighbourhoods with both a 'skills mis-match' and a 'spatial mismatch' in which job opportunities are educa-tionally or geographically inaccessible to most ghetto dwellers. As a result, large portions of the inner-city labour force are unattached to

Table 5.2 Inner-City Poverty, Baltimore, 1970–1990

Neighbourhood	(% of population living below official poverty line in selected Baltimore neighbourhoods)		
	1970	1980	1990
East Baltimore	27.8	38.8	39.9
Upton	46.4	51.8	49.0
Sandtown–Winchester	36.6	44.0	41.4
Lower Park Heights	21.7	31.3	31.2
Greenmount West	40.8	51.9	49.8
City average	18.0	22.4	21.2
Metro area	11.3	11.9	10.1

Source: U.S. Bureau of the Census 1972, 1983, 1993

the labour market, leading inexorably to the social isolation and erosion of stabilizing institutions that characterize inner-city life. Figure 5.3 shows the extent to which such 'labour-market exclusion' has become pervasive for males in Baltimore's major ghetto neighbourhoods. In 1960, over two-thirds of working-age males in these neighbourhoods were employed; by 1980, the majority of working-age males were either unemployed, not in school, or not in the labour market. For the city as a whole, the proportion of working-age black males holding jobs declined from 67.7 per cent in 1960 to 55.2 per cent in 1990.

Wilson also argues that the exodus of the urban black middle class to the suburbs – joining the white-flight that began in the 1950s – helped unravel the social fabric of the inner city (Wilson 1987). Baltimore provides one of the most vivid urban examples of this trend. In 1970, 85 per cent of metropolitan Baltimore's black families earning more than $35,000 a year (in 1990 dollars) lived in the city, their residential choices constrained by the region's rigid housing segregation; by 1990, only 56 per cent of the region's black middle-class families lived in the city. Suburban communities such as Lochearn, Woodmoor, Milford Mill, and Randallstown, just northwest of the city line, saw their black communities grow from 6 per cent of the population in 1970 to 65 per cent in 1990, a huge exodus of income and social capital from city neigh-

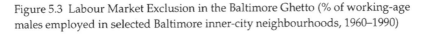

Figure 5.3 Labour Market Exclusion in the Baltimore Ghetto (% of working-age males employed in selected Baltimore inner-city neighbourhoods, 1960–1990)

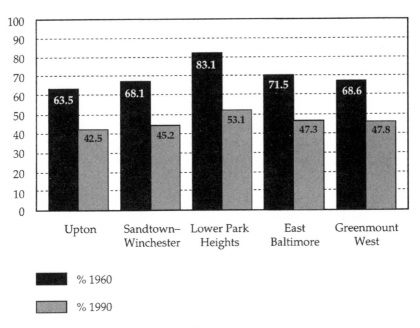

Source: U.S. Bureau of the Census 1962, 1993

bourhoods. Table 5.3 contrasts the 1990 income distribution among black households in Baltimore City and the 'Liberty Road Corridor' – the primary suburban destination for Baltimore's black families. As the table illustrates, the suburbanization of Baltimore's black middle class left behind a disproportionate concentration of low-income black households in the city. In ghetto neighbourhoods such as Sandtown–Winchester, Upton, and Greenmount West – with poverty rates approaching 50 per cent – this concentration of poverty and absence of a middle class has helped create the multifaceted social disarray of 'underclass' neighbourhoods.

It is abundantly clear that nothing approaching an urban 'renaissance' has taken place in Baltimore's inner city. The social sustainability of Baltimore's neighbourhoods, wracked by racial inequality and social exclusion, is very much in question. Like most U.S. cities, Balti-

Table 5.3 The Suburbanization of Baltimore's Black Middle
Class (distribution of black households, by income category,
Baltimore City and the Liberty Road Corridor, 1989)

| Annual household income ($) | % of households in each income category | |
	Liberty Road Corridor	Baltimore City
0–24,999	22.1	57.7
25,000–49,999	41.4	29.8
>50,000	36.5	12.6

Source: U.S. Bureau of the Census 1993

more has spent millions since the 1960s in 'community development'
programs to alleviate inner-city conditions. Since 1975, Baltimore has
spent an estimated $500 million in federal 'community-development
block-grant funds' in distressed neighbourhoods, and in 1994 the city
secured a $100-million federal 'Empowerment Zone' grant to build
homes and promote economic development in several inner-city
neighbourhoods. Millions more have been spent in city neighbourhoods on job training, social services, and housing programs. In addition, during the 1980s, Baltimore was among the first cities to
designate poor neighbourhoods as 'Enterprise Zones,' offering tax
incentives to lure businesses to the inner city.

Several major initiatives aimed at rebuilding inner-city neighbourhoods have been attempted over the past quarter-century. During the
1970s, Upton was the site of a major housing reconstruction program,
'the largest redevelopment project we've ever seen,' in the words of the
city's housing commissioner (Pietila 1996a). In the 1980s, the Park
Heights neighbourhood was touted as a model of how 'Enterprise
Zones' could revive inner-city economies. And during the 1990s, the
Schmoke administration launched two major 'community-building'
initiatives: in the depressed West Baltimore neighbourhood of Sandtown–Winchester, and in the East Baltimore neighbourhoods near the
epicentre of the 1968 riots.

Both of the Schmoke initiatives sensibly sought to combine physical
redevelopment with social renewal, mounting a 'comprehensive'
attack on the 'web of interwoven problems that can lock families out of

opportunity, permanently' (Walsh 1997, 12). Both initiatives were driven by the assumption that unless the city could 'curb crime, improve the schools, clean the streets, provide better health care, and fix other shoddy services,' new housing might temporarily improve the physical face of the neighbourhoods, but ultimately 'would not make much difference' (Schorr 1996, 321). In both initiatives, the city enlisted impressive partners: the Sandtown–Winchester project is piloted by the Enterprise Foundation, the non-profit arm of the same Rouse Corporation that developed Harborplace, while the East Baltimore project involves the world-class Johns Hopkins University medical centre (located in the heart of the eastside ghetto).

However, by the end of the 1990s, notwithstanding the fanfare surrounding these initiatives and some isolated indications of community improvements, there was little evidence that these inner-city neighbourhoods were truly on the road to revitalization. As one sympathetic observer put it: 'For all the inspiring activity it has catalyzed, Sandtown–Winchester has yet to reach the critical mass that would achieve "neighbourhood transformation ... rather than program-specific reform"' (Walsh 1997, 59–60). Another observer put the matter more ominously, noting a rise in vacant properties around Sandtown–Winchester and asking: 'What good will one rehabbed house do on a block that is otherwise ruined and abandoned?' (Pietila 1996a). Similarly, conditions in East Baltimore showed little discernible improvement (*Baltimore Sun* 1998b). In 1998, a highly publicized account of the existence of an open-air drug market ('Zombieland') operating in vacant rowhouses adjacent to an East Baltimore elementary school poignantly symbolized the continuing decay of this neighborhood (Haner 1998b).

In short, despite major city initiatives and the often heroic efforts of community activists, Baltimore's inner-city neighbourhoods remain in desperate condition. It is far too early to dismiss the latest initiatives as failures. After all, the Inner Harbor redevelopment did not reach critical mass until fifteen years into the project, at which point a meaningful private-investment market was created. In Baltimore's inner city – with depleted social capital, physical blight, and few legitimate jobs – transformation will take much longer. Community-building has shown promise in some neighbourhoods across the country (Kingsley, McNeely, and Gibson 1998); perhaps Baltimore's latest initiatives will begin showing more than isolated improvements.

On the whole, however, the record of community development in reclaiming neighbourhoods is not encouraging. Upton and Park

Heights, two that have received particular attention and significant public investments since the 1970s, continue to falter. Incredibly, despite the millions that have been spent on city neighbourhoods, the resources may not have been adequate, given the scope of ghetto problems. In addition, it may well be that community development is an inherently flawed strategy; as Nicholas Lemann has argued, the 'record of black success in America's cities since the 1960s has been almost entirely bound up with leaving the ghettos rather than improving them' (1991, 347). Michael Porter (1995) has advanced a 'market-oriented' version of the community development strategy, arguing that inner-city revitalization programs have failed because they have not sufficiently involved the private sector. According to Porter, inner cities have considerable 'competitive advantages' (cheap labour and land, central location, and unmet consumer markets) that would attract private reinvestment if cities nurtured a pro-business climate. But, while some national retailers have begun looking more closely at heretofore neglected inner-city markets (chiefly because of saturation in some suburban markets), there is scant evidence that the bombed-out cityscape and social disarray of ghetto strips such as 'Zombieland' are likely to entice major business investments away from the suburbs (Goozner 1998, 60). Indeed, all of the serious research on metropolitan labour markets concludes that employment and business growth are overwhelmingly concentrated in the suburbs, far away from inner-city turmoil (Kasarda 1993). There is little reason to believe that Porter's version of 'ghetto capitalism,' relying on market forces that have worked so devastatingly against inner cities over the past forty years, is likely to be any more successful than conventional community-development strategies in rebuilding neighbourhoods such as Upton, Sandtown–Winchester, or East Baltimore. Certainly, the failure of enterprise zones to revive neighbourhood economies is instructive, since they offered the same kinds of incentives – tax credits and regulatory relief – that Porter contends will activate the latent competitive advantages of the inner city. Baltimore is one of the sites for Porter's recently launched 'Initiative for a Competitive Inner City,' so there will soon be evidence on whether his version of market-based community development can revive the city's troubled neighbourhoods.

By the end of the 1990s, Baltimore's leadership was clearly frustrated by the intractability of inner-city problems and the disappointing results of virtually all reconstruction strategies. As a result, at City Hall and in corporate boardrooms, a 'new' strategy began taking shape:

demolition and relocation as the keys to the city's prosperity (Shields 1998). Of course, in the 1940s and 1950s, slum clearance was the American answer to urban blight; thus, the 'new' approach of solving Baltimore's problems by 'knocking down the parts of the city that are causing them' (Dilts 1998) represented a recrudescence of a once-discredited urban policy. Nevertheless, by the late 1990s, city leaders talked openly of 'planned shrinkage' for a depopulating city, in which the poor would be increasingly 'dispersed' to other jurisdictions, and abandoned buildings would be torn down. 'We must not allow our cities to become quarantine zones for the poor,' noted Mayor Schmoke, undoubtedly aware that, while Baltimore City contained 27 per cent of the region's population, it housed 67 per cent of metro Baltimore's poor (Shields 1998). During the 1990s, Baltimore began demolition of its notorious high-rise public-housing complexes, and the city was an eager participant in HUD's experimental 'Moving to Opportunity' (MTO) program, which helps the poor, through housing vouchers and relocation assistance, leave ghetto neighbourhoods for suburban locations closer to job growth. However, the MTO program generated considerable resistance in the suburbs, raising questions about the political feasibility of dispersal policy.

In sum, after four decades of decline, Baltimore's leaders faced the sobering prospect that 'neighborhood deterioration here ... has acquired such a pace and scope that the downward spiral may be unstoppable' (Pietila 1996a). A corrosive sense that 'nothing works' seemed to take hold in Baltimore, amid the growing belief that the sheer concentration of the ghetto poor rendered hopeless any neighbourhood revitalization strategies. By 1998, Baltimore's 'anti-poverty' strategy edged towards simply moving the poor out of the city and bulldozing blighted blocks, a tacit surrender to the formidable obstacles in the way of rebuilding inner-city neighbourhoods.

Suburbia and the Rise of 'Edge Cities'

Since the 1950s, efforts to rebuild downtown or revive Baltimore's neighbourhoods have foundered against a massive exodus of people, jobs, and businesses to sprawling suburbs on the outer fringes of the metropolitan area. The 'car culture,' with its inexorable sprawl-inducing effects, now dominates the Baltimore region, notwithstanding the construction since the mid-1970s of a $1.5-billion network of heavy- and light-rail mass transit radiating out of downtown. Initially, the suburbs were residential communities, which still revolved around the city as an economic hub. But, metro Baltimore's economic centre of gravity has now clearly shifted to outlying suburbs. In places such as Columbia, Towson, and Owings Mills, suburban clusters of offices and commerce have developed, 'Edge Cities' far removed from the central city and its litany of problems (see figure 5.4). This decentralization has resulted in a sharp metropolitan polarization, in which the destinies of rapidly growing, prosperous outer suburbs have become increasingly disconnected from a struggling central city. Unrelenting suburbanization inexorably draws more and more of the resources necessary for any hopes of an urban revival.

As in most U.S. metropolitan areas, the dimensions of Baltimore's suburban sprawl and economic deconcentration are astounding. As we saw earlier, the outflow of population from the city to the suburbs has been continuous since the 1950s, and shows no signs of abating. Sprawl has been particularly rapid since 1970, as the region's outer suburbs – in Howard, Harford, and Carroll counties – gained 360,000 residents (an increase of 153 per cent between 1970 and 1997), while the city lost almost 250,000 (a decline of 28 per cent). Growth has transformed these heretofore rural counties into sprawling suburban communities, with shopping malls, office parks, and low-density residential subdivisions gobbling up open spaces (Hedgpeth and Timberg 1997). For example, the 'country town' of Owings Mills, located 20 miles northwest of downtown Baltimore in a once-rural section of Baltimore County, has grown from the early 1980s to more than 40,000 residents today, with more than 5.5 million square feet of commercial space developed since the mid-1980s (Atwood 1998).

As noted earlier, the racial and income aspects of these shifts have deepened metropolitan social polarization. Between 1950 and 1997, Baltimore City's white population declined by over 70 per cent; during the 1990s alone, an estimated 73,000 whites (25 per cent of the total) left the city. This 'white flight' has made the city, in effect, a residential *terra incognita* for the region's white population. Since the 1970s, increasing numbers of the black middle class have also left the city. The upshot of this biracial flight of the middle class from Baltimore City has been a widening income disparity between the city and the suburbs. Per-capita income in Baltimore City shrank from just under 80 per cent of the suburban level to 64.3 per cent between 1970 and 1990, a rate of decline that ranked fourth worst among the fifteen largest frostbelt cities (Levine 1998).

Figure 5.4 The Greater Baltimore Region
Source: INRS–urbanisation

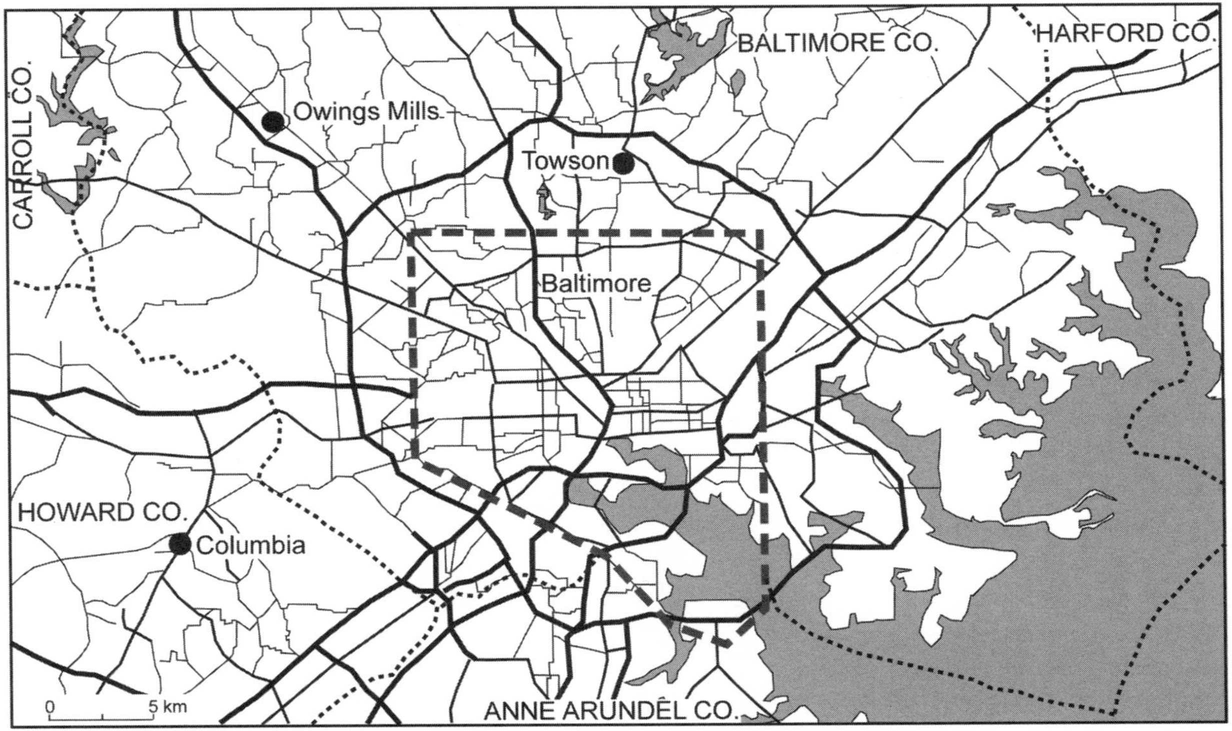

Suburban employment growth has followed these residential shifts, and business suburbanization has reduced the city's place as the economic core of the region. Advanced telecommunications technology makes it feasible for many firms to operate away from downtown locations, enabling them to take advantage of lower suburban land prices and office rents, as well as easier access to their workers, most of whom now live in the suburbs and commute by automobile. Thus, the share of metro Baltimore office space located in the suburbs has grown from 30 to 65 per cent since the early 1970s, and the disparity between downtown and suburban office vacancy rates in Baltimore is among the worst in the country (Downtown Partnership 1997, 4).

These economic changes are vividly illustrated in regional employment trends. Between 1960 and 1990, the proportion of workers in the Baltimore region commuting to jobs in the city fell from 60 per cent to 32 per cent. Put another way, by the 1990s, two-thirds of all metro-area workers commuted to jobs in the suburbs. Job creation in the service sector has exploded in the Baltimore suburbs, growing at a faster pace than in suburbs in most other frostbelt metropolises (Levine 1998). As table 5.4 makes clear, in all sectors of the economy, the city share of regional employment has shrunk considerably since 1970, with particularly dramatic growth in the proportion of jobs located in outer suburbs such as Howard County. Even in sectors such as finance and business services, which have historically clustered in urban downtowns, the city has lost ground to the suburbs. Economic deconcentration continued unabated during the 1990s: between 1990 and 1997, Baltimore city lost 65,000 jobs (13.7 per cent of its employment base), while suburban counties gained 124,000 jobs (an increase of 10.8 per cent).

Thus, for the vast majority of Baltimoreans in the 1990s, any connection to the central city is tenuous. Most of the region's residents now live, work, shop, and play in suburban enclaves and, for many, a 'tourist' trip to the Inner Harbor or the Camden Yards stadiums is their sole link to the urban core. As Robert Reich aptly put it, there has been a splintering in metropolitan America, a 'secession' of the 'fortunate' into 'exurban communities' where they can pool their resources with each other for optimal 'amenities,' while avoiding subsidizing anyone less fortunate (1991, 271). In 1997, a commissioner from Carroll County, on the outer fringes of metropolitan Baltimore, bluntly articulated this 'secessionist' ethos: 'If Baltimore dies, it dies,' he said. 'Maybe we will dig it up and make farmland out of it. Why should we bail Baltimore

Table 5.4 The Suburbanization of Baltimore's Jobs (% of employment located in various jurisdictions, 1969–1995)

Jurisdiction	All Sectors		Finance, Insurance, and Real Estate		Business Services	
	1969	1995	1969	1995	1969	1995
The City	61.5	31.6	78.9	39.1	82.4	27.9
All suburbs	38.5	68.2	21.1	60.9	17.6	72.1
Baltimore County	23.9	32.1	12.3	34.6	8.5	38.1
Howard County	1.6	10.5	0.6	10.4	0.8	12.2

Source: U.S. Bureau of the Census 1971, 1997

out or be drawn into its problems?' (*Baltimore Sun* 1997). Less malevolently, thousands of Baltimore-area residents and businesses opt for the suburbs because the degradation of urban life, combined with the conveniences of 'automobilized' suburbia, often makes the suburbs the only reasonable option, particularly for families with school-age children. This, of course, becomes part of a vicious circle in which flight to the suburbs depletes city neighbourhoods and tax bases, and exacerbates urban distress, promoting further departures and a new wave of urban decline.

Ultimately, as Baltimore's establishment has belatedly recognized over the past decade, regional policies are essential to cope with the consequences of suburban sprawl and urban decline. During the 1990s, the city's powerful Abell Foundation commissioned and aggressively publicized studies by (Peirce, with Johnson and Hall 1993), David Rusk (1996), and Myron Orfield (1997), the three leading U.S. 'apostles of regionalism.' All recommended regional approaches to Baltimore's problems. The city's influential daily newspaper, the *Sun*, has editorially become a vehement advocate of regionalism (*Baltimore Sun* 1998d). The Baltimore business establishment, through the same Greater Baltimore Committee that launched the Inner Harbor renaissance, has now embraced regionalism, issuing a 1997 manifesto that included, among other ideas, metropolitan 'tax-base sharing' to rectify city–suburb fiscal imbalances (Greater Baltimore Committee 1997). In 1997, perhaps a sign that 'regionalist' thinking was beginning to influence public policy, the State of Maryland passed a 'Smart Growth' law in which state expenditures for transportation and utilities would be channelled to 'growth corridors,' and state investments and incentives would be used to discourage sprawl and encourage urban development.

In short, there are the beginnings of a 'regionalist' policy response to urban decline and suburban sprawl in Baltimore. It remains to be seen how far such policies will go. Although there are signs of 'slow-growth' and 'anti-growth' sentiment in Baltimore's exurbs (Wheeler 1998), the bulk of suburban developers, homeowners, and public officials have genuine material interests in opposing plans for tax-base sharing, 'smart growth,' or other city-oriented regional strategies. Moreover, such regionalist strategies as dispersing the city's poor throughout the metropolitan area (Rusk 1996) have already generated predictable suburban opposition. Rhetoric about regional cooperation often elicits approval in the abstract, only to founder against formidable sociological and economic impediments: suburban homeowners fear that changes might raise their taxes, lower their property values, force them to subsidize the urban poor, or bring 'undesirables' into their neighbourhoods. In the final analysis, however, in view of the sad history of other approaches to urban revitalization, harnessing regional growth to city renewal may be Baltimore's last best chance to attack social exclusion and generate socially sustainable development.

Conclusion

Urbanists are fond of metaphors for summarizing the state of the city. Several seem to fit the U.S. city at century's end: the 'Abandoned City,' epitomized by the total collapse of cities like Detroit in the 1970s amid racial turmoil, social exclusion, and suburban separatism; the 'Fortress City,' to describe the architectural, sociological, and technological means by which metropolitan 'haves' seek security in an increasingly turbulent environment (Davis 1990; Kaplan 1998); and the 'Fantasy City' (Hannigan 1998), to describe the near-universal strategy of cities to resurrect themselves as tourist and entertainment centres.

Elements of all of these 'models' are part of Baltimore's recent history. To be sure, the Baltimore story is not one of unremitting crisis. Although the 'renaissance' proclaimed by city boosters in the 1970s and 1980s was limited, Baltimore was no Detroit; the city did not collapse. In fact, after hitting rock bottom in the 1970s, there were at least some signs in the 1980s of stabilization in Baltimore: per-capita income growth in the city ran ahead of that in most frostbelt cities, the city-wide poverty rate actually declined slightly, and employment growth downtown began providing jobs for the city's black community (Levine 1998).

However, none of the city's core difficulties had been successfully attacked, and by the 1990s the sense of decline in Baltimore was palpable. If not quite 'the Abandoned City,' Baltimore was close, with people, jobs, and businesses continuing to desert the city and with inner-city neighbourhoods on the verge of collapse. If not quite the 'Fortress City,' Baltimore nevertheless manifested all the signs of social 'secessionism' and balkanization, in a city where open-air drug markets and one of the nation's highest murder rates engendered fear and insecurity. By the end of the 1990s, after three decades of 'fantasy city' redevelopment strategies and heralded community-development initiatives, city policy makers seem to have run out of answers short of 'slum clearance' or 'planned shrinkage' to the problems of ghetto poverty and neighbourhood decay.

It may well be that Baltimore is past the 'point of no return,' and that decades of wrong-headed policies and unforgiving market forces have created an 'obsolete city.' Nevertheless, the new regionalism strategies espoused by the state government and the city's business elite do offer some grounds for optimism about the future. 'Smart Growth,' properly implemented, could reduce fiscal imbalances between city and suburb, encourage urban 'in-fill' development and discourage sprawl. Over time, a metropolitan marketplace structured by 'Smart Growth' instead of incentives for sprawl could change the dynamics of business location decisions and, to revisit Michael Porter's phrase, tap the 'competitive advantages of the inner city.' Even aggressively implemented, though, 'Smart Growth' is not a panacea for the multitude of problems facing Baltimore. But it might provide a substructure that would enable strategies such as downtown redevelopment and community-building to work better than they have in the past. Combined with massive investments in public schooling, serious crime control, and amelioration of the city labour market (through strategies such as job-link programs), Baltimore's new regionalism could make a difference.

There are imposing political obstacles to such a strategy and in the end a culture of socially just regionalism will need to be cultivated in Baltimore. As Norton Long put it, many years ago: 'The apostles of metropolitanism are coming to realize that the vision they are seeking is something more than a better means of moving traffic, an improvement in the plumbing, or even an increase in the competitive position of the local economy. It is the possibility of attaining a shared common goal of a better life' (1962, 183). Without such a common vision, the centre cannot hold, and Baltimore's possibilities for socially just, sustainable development will be grim indeed.

Note

1 For example, Baltimore did 'earn' approximately $25 million in repayments of loans provided the Hyatt–Regency project in 1979. But these earnings were recycled into other downtown investments: the expanded convention center and the Scarlett Place luxury condominiums (Jacobson 1992).

References

Arney, June. 1998. '13 million visited Baltimore in 1997.' *The Baltimore Sun*, 25 September.

Atwood, Liz. 1998. 'Owings Mills sees a growth spurt at 14.' *The Baltimore Sun*, 16 June.

Bagli, Charles V. 1998. 'Novelty gone, theme restaurants are tumbling.' *The New York Times*, 27 December.

Baltimore City Department of Planning. 1986. *The Baltimore Harbor*. Baltimore: Department of Planning.

Baltimore City Trustees and Loan Program. 1986. *Ten-Year Report*. Baltimore: City Trustees and Loan Program.

The Baltimore Sun. 1992. 'No cheers for being "No. 1".' 15 September.

– 1997. 'If Baltimore dies, it dies.' 21 March.

– 1998a. 'Baltimore leads in ER cases tied to drugs.' 22 March.

– 1998b. 'East Side renewal: Where is the action?' 3 May.

– 1998c. 'Inner Harbor requires our vigilance.' 19 July.

– 1998d. 'Regionalism that works.' 4–10 January.

Barringer, David. 1997. 'The New Urban Gamble.' *The American Prospect* 34 (September/October): 28–34.

Bowie Liz. 1998. 'New reading approach may be paying off.' *The Baltimore Sun*, 21 December.

Committee for Economic Development. 1995. *Rebuilding Inner-City Communities: A New Approach to the Nation's Urban Crisis*. Washington, DC: Committee for Economic Development.

Craig-Smith, Stephen J. 1995. 'The Role of Tourism in Inner-Harbor Redevelopment: A Multinational Perspective.' In *Recreation and Tourism as a Catalyst for Urban Waterfront Redevelopment: An International Survey*, ed. S.J. Craig-Smith and Michael Fagence, 15–36. Westport, CT: Praeger.

Davis, Mike. 1990. *City of Quartz: Excavating the Future in Los Angeles*. New York: Random House.

Dilts, James. 1998. 'City's west side plan endangers key buildings.' *The Baltimore Sun*, 17 December.

Downtown Partnership. 1997. *State of Downtown Baltimore Report*. Baltimore: Downtown Partnership of Baltimore.

– 1998. *State of Downtown Baltimore Report*. Baltimore: Downtown Partnership of Baltimore.

Downtown Strategy Advisory Committee. 1991. *The Renaissance Continues: Final Reports of the Technical Advisory Committees*. Baltimore: Department of Planning.

Evans, Martin C. 1991. 'Baltimore ranks 3rd in national for infant deaths.' *The Baltimore Sun*, 14 August.

Fainstein, Susan S. and David Gladstone. 1999. 'Evaluating Urban Tourism.' In *The Tourist City*, ed. Dennis R. Judd and Susan S. Fainstein, 1–30. New Haven, CT: Yale University Press.

Fainstein, Susan S., and Robert James Stokes. 1998. 'Spaces for Play: The Impacts of Entertainment Development on New York City.' *Economic Development Quarterly* 12/2: 150–65.

Fainstein, Susan. 1994. *The City Builders: Property, Politics, and Planning in London and New York*. Cambridge: Blackwell.

Gately, Gary. 1997. 'Revival pinned to Power Plant.' *The Baltimore Sun*, 1 July.

Goozner, Merrill. 1998. 'The Porter Prescription.' *The American Prospect* 38 (May/June): 56–65.

Greater Baltimore Committee. 1997. *One Region, One Future. A Report on Regionalism*. Baltimore: Greater Baltimore Committee.

Gunts, Edward. 1998. 'Wave of downtown plans rushes away from harbor.' *The Baltimore Sun*, 28 June.

Hamilton, Bruce W., and Peter Kahn. 1997. 'Baltimore's Camden Yards Ballparks.' In *Sports, Jobs, and Taxes*, ed. Roger Noll and Andrew Zimbalist, 245–81. Washington, DC: The Brookings Institution.

Haner, Jim. 1998a. 'Baltimore offers hope for St. Louis.' *The Baltimore Sun*, 6 October.

– 1998b. 'Drugs, decay, and despair hover around city school.' *The Baltimore Sun*, 4 October.

Haner, Jim, and John B. O'Donnell. 1997. 'City program's trail of rubble.' *The Baltimore Sun*, 6 April.

Hannigan, John. 1998. *Fantasy City: Pleasure and Profit in the Postmodern Metropolis.* London: Routledge.

Hedgpeth, Dana, and Craig Timberg. 1997. 'Sprawl transforms Howard Co. corridor.' *The Baltimore Sun,* 23 February.

Jacobson, Joan. 1992. 'City has lost $25 million in bad development loans.' *The Baltimore Sun,* 2 August.

Kaplan, Robert D. 1998. *An Empire Wilderness: Travels into America's Future.* New York: Random House.

Kasarda, John D. 1993. 'Cities as Places Where People Live and Work: Urban Change and Neighborhood Distress.' In *Interwoven Destinies: Cities and the Nation,* ed. Henry Cisneros, 81–124. New York: Norton.

Kingsley, G. Thomas, Joseph McNeely, and James O. Gibson. 1998. *Community Building Coming of Age.* Washington, DC: The Urban Institute.

Lally, Kathy. 1990. 'Capturing a City's imagination: Harborplace 10 years later.' *The Baltimore Sun,* 24 June.

Lemann, Nicholas. 1991. *The Promised Land: The Great Black Migration and How It Changed America.* New York: Knopf.

Levine, Marc V. 1987a. 'Downtown Redevelopment as an Urban Growth Strategy: A Critical Appraisal of the Baltimore Renaissance.' *Journal of Urban Affairs* 9/2: 103–23.

– 1987b. 'Economic Development in Baltimore: Some Additional Perspectives.' *Journal of Urban Affairs* 9/2: 133–8.

– 1998. *The Economic State of Milwaukee: The City and the Region.* Milwaukee: UWM Center for Economic Development.

Long, Norton E. 1962. *The Polity.* Chicago: Rand McNally.

Matthews, Robert Guy. 1998. 'Hotel foes rally against subsidy plan.' *The Baltimore Sun,* 12 March.

Murray, Shannon D. 1998. 'Columbus Center debt scrutinized by lawmakers.' *The Baltimore Sun,* 16 July.

Noll, Roger G., and Andrew Zimbalist, eds. 1997. *Sports, Jobs, and Taxes: The Economic Impact of Sports Teams and Stadiums.* Washington, DC: The Brookings Institution.

Orfield, Myron. 1997. *Baltimore Metropolitics.* Baltimore: Citizens' Planning and Housing Association.

Peirce, Neal R., Curtis Johnson, and John Stuart Hall. 1993. *Citistates: How Urban America Can Prosper in a Competitive World.* Washington, DC: Seven Locks Press.

Pietila, Antero. 1996a. 'Canute in Sandtown.' *The Baltimore Sun,* 16 February.

– 1996b. 'A Third World city in the First World.' *The Baltimore Sun,* 14 September.

Pitts, Leonard. 1997. 'Worth more than 30 libraries.' *The Milwaukee Journal-Sentinel*, 12 October.

Porter, Michael. 1995. 'The Competitive Advantage of the Inner City.' *Harvard Business Review*, 78/3 (May/June): 55–71.

Reich, Robert B. 1991. *The Work of Nations: Preparing Ourselves for Twenty-First Century Capitalism*. New York: Knopf.

Rusk, David. 1996. *Baltimore Unbound: A Strategy for Regional Renewal*. Baltimore: Johns Hopkins University Press.

Schorr, Lisbeth. 1996. *Common Purpose*. New York: Basic.

Shane, Scott. 1994. 'Baltimore to try Third World remedies.' *The Baltimore Sun*, 6 June.

Shields, Gerald. 1998. 'In Baltimore, renewal means moving the poor.' *The Baltimore Sun*, 27 October.

Siegel, Fred. 1997. *The Future Once Happened Here: New York, D.C., L.A. and the Fate of America's Big Cities*. New York: Free Press.

Simon, David, and Edward Burns. 1997. *The Corner: A Year in the Life of an Inner-City Neighborhood*. New York: Broadway.

Szanton, Peter L. 1986. *Baltimore 2000: A Choice of Futures*. Baltimore: Morris Goldseker Foundation.

Teaford, Jon C. 1990. *The Rough Road to Renaissance*. Baltimore: Johns Hopkins University Press.

U.S. Bureau of the Census. 1952. *Census of Population: Baltimore, Maryland*. Washington, DC: Government Printing Office.

– 1962. *Census of Population and Housing, 1960: Baltimore, Md.* Washington, DC: Government Printing Office.

– 1972. *1970 Census of Population and Housing: Baltimore, Md.* Washington, DC: Government Printing Office.

– 1983. *1980 Census of Population and Housing*. Washington, DC: Government Printing Office.

– 1993. *1990 Census of Population and Housing, Baltimore, Md.* Washington, DC: Government Printing Office.

– 1998. *Population Estimates Program*. Washington, DC: The Bureau.

U.S. Bureau of Transportation Statistics. 1995. *CTPP: Urban Package* (CD-ROM). Washington, DC: U.S. Department of Transportation.

U.S. Department of Commerce. 1971. *County Business Patterns, 1969: Maryland*. Washington, DC: Government Printing Office.

– 1997. *County Business Patterns, 1995: Maryland*. Washington, DC: Government Printing Office.

Walsh, Joan. 1997. *Stories of Renewal: Community Building and the Future of Urban America*. New York: Rockefeller Foundation.

Weisbrot, Mark, and Roderick Sforza. 1996. *Baltimore's Living Wage Law: An Analysis of the Fiscal and Economic Costs of Baltimore City Ordinance 442*. Washington, DC: Preamble Center for Public Policy.

West, Norris. 1992. 'Young city black men: 56 per cent in trouble.' *The Baltimore Sun*, 1 September.

Wheeler, Timothy. 1998. 'Growth issue is haunting incumbents.' *The Baltimore Sun*, 4 October.

Wilson, William Julius. 1987. *The Truly Disadvantaged: The Inner City, the Underclass, and Public Policy*. Chicago: University of Chicago Press.

– 1997. *When Work Disappears: The World of the New Urban Poor*. New York: Knopf.

6 Geneva: Does Wealth Ensure Social Sustainability?

ANTOINE S. BAILLY

Is it enough to be one of the world's wealthiest cities to be a socially sustainable city? Geneva would seem to offer an extraordinary success story, certainly in the sense defined by UNESCO's MOST program. The city has, to all outward appearances, created an urban environment that encourages social integration and harmony. Geneva has developed a clear sense of political and social identity. The city has been just as successful in nurturing an environment that fosters cultural and scientific creativity – examples being its university and research centres, such as the European Centre for Nuclear Research (CERN) – and in building an economic base linking research, services, and commerce, with banking and international affairs playing a prominent role. In sum, a safe city in a beautiful setting, Geneva is clearly a pleasant place to live by present-day urban standards. Despite its small size, it feels like an international city, with a reputation for its quality of life and its place in world affairs, founded to a large extent on the presence of the United Nations European headquarters.

A City Facing Changing Economic Conditions

The fragility of this positive view of Geneva became evident during the recent economic downturn. Geneva, not unlike Switzerland as a whole, faces new challenges, raising questions about its future development. Social sustainability has become an issue. Space is scarce and densities are very high, leading to traffic congestion and a dearth of vacant land for expansion; the area centred on the cities of Geneva and Lausanne is often called the 'Lemanic Metropolitan Area' (Bassand and Leresche 1991), named after Lac Léman ('Lake Geneva' in English), because of the

Table 6.1 Canton of Geneva: Selected Data, 1996

Land area	282 sq. km.
Population	400,000
Foreign-born population	37.9%
Employment	239,500
Income per capita (in U.S. dollars)	$36,488
Unemployment rate	6.8%
Automobiles registered	197,514

Source: Office Cantonal de la Statistique

density of its network of cities and villages. Another consequence of the lack of space is the high cost of living: in 1996 Geneva was ranked as the fourth most expensive metropolitan area in the world.

These factors, combined with the economic slowdown of the last decade, explain why population growth forecasts made in 1965 were never attained: instead of the 550,000 inhabitants projected for 1990, the canton had a population of just over 400,000 in 1996 (see table 6.1). Following a period of housing shortage, Geneva now has a situation of low demand for houses and apartments, with an occupancy rate of two persons per unit. A housing surplus is projected for at least the next twenty years, despite a sharp slowdown in residential construction, leading to the bankruptcy of several construction firms.

The 'Regio Genevensis' is not confined to the Canton of Geneva (Bailly 1992). Often considered a pioneer in transnational cooperation, Metropolitan Geneva, a Franco-Swiss initiative, includes the Swiss Canton of Geneva, parts of the neighbouring Canton of Vaud, as well as areas located in the French *départements* of Ain and Haute-Savoie (see table 6.2). The total population of Metropolitan Geneva in 1995 was 600,000. Even this figure is small in comparison with other European metropolitan areas, a factor that has not, however, prevented Geneva from being classified as one of Europe's major international cities (DATAR 1989; Bonneville et al. 1992).

According to the evaluation framework developed by Marc Bonneville and his colleagues (1992), using thirteen indicators, Geneva is classified in the same league as cities such as Amsterdam, Barcelona, and Frankfurt. The cities present, 'despite their differences in size, many similarities ... due to their internationalism.' Among the various criteria, the report notes the following:

Table 6.2   Geneva's Administrative Structure

---

1. Canton of Geneva: population 400,000
Comprising 45 municipalities, including the municipality of Geneva (population 175,000).

2. Metropolitan Geneva: population 600,000
Includes the Canton of Geneva, western municipalities of the Canton of Vaud, the municipalities on the Swiss border of the French *départements* of Ain (Pays de Gex) and Haute-Savoie.

3. Lemanic Metropolitan Area: population 800,000
Centred on the two cities of Geneva and Lausanne, this region covers the Canton of Geneva, the southern part of the Canton of Vaud, the Pays de Gex (Ain), and the northern part of Haute-Savoie. This is not an administrative unit but a geographical concept.

Source: The author

- the volume of airport traffic and the diversity of international destinations (Geneva airport received more than 6 million passengers);
- the importance of the foreign-born population (over 35 per cent in Geneva in 1995);
- the importance of employment in the financial sector (20,800, including 15,700 in foreign banks in 1994 in the Canton of Geneva);
- the number of upscale hotels catering to foreign visitors (of the 13,100 hotel beds registered in the Canton, 65 per cent are in four-star or five-star hotels).

Geneva is one of the most specialized metropolitan areas in Europe with respect to internationally oriented activities. The findings of the Bonneville et al. (1992) report are consistent with those of other recent studies. DATAR (1989) ranks Geneva behind Paris, London, and Milan, but on the same level as Amsterdam, Brussels, Frankfurt, and Barcelona. A study of cities in Central Europe (Messerli 1991) considers Geneva to be one of the 'macro-cities,' behind Paris and Frankfurt, but on a level with Brussels, Zurich, Munich, and Milan.

Economic Restructuring and the Spatial Division of Labour

A new metropolitan system is emerging, however, resulting in a functional redistribution of activities among cities. New forms of interenterprise organization are pushing firms towards Zurich. Geneva is losing its traditional manufacturing base. The city also stands to lose firms that supply business services to companies relocating outside Switzerland in response to the opportunities offered in the new integrated Europe.

These structural changes are not unique to Geneva. What is unique is the city's quality of life and its specialization in international activities. Does this specialization provide a better chance for the development of a socially sustainable city? Because of its past, the level of education of its population, and the quality of its cultural and natural environment, Geneva has many assets for the future as a socially sustainable city. However, new solutions must be found in the fight against the growth of a dual society.

The term 'deindustrialization' is often employed to describe the changes that are occurring in the economic structure of Metropolitan Geneva (Coffey and Bailly 1992). The secondary sector (manufacturing and construction) accounted for less than 19 per cent of total employment in 1995 in the Canton (down from 27.5 per cent in 1975), while the share for the tertiary, or service, sector now stands at 71.9 per cent.

The role of Geneva changed in the 1980s with the rise of more flexible forms of production and increasing European integration (Switzerland is not a member of the European Union). The results for the metropolitan area have been both an internal restructuring of industry and the departure of firms, looking for locations outside Switzerland within the European Union (EU). The canton has become more specialized: the more sophisticated and complex financial and commercial activities have often remained in the city, close to the centre, because of the continuing need for face-to-face contact; while other more standardized service activities have often moved to peripheral areas, taking advantage of lower land prices – the choice of a peripheral location being linked to the presence of communications infrastructure such as airports and motorways. However, this deconcentration now reaches into the neighbouring Canton of Vaud as well as the French *départements* of Ain and Haute-Savoie, and sometimes into places even further away, both in Switzerland and in France.

This spatial specialization of economic activity also tends to reinforce social and spatial divisions of labour. Many skilled Swiss workers and international employees have moved to France or to the Canton of Vaud, where living costs are generally lower. The flight of firms and people out of the Canton of Geneva is thus aggravated, with major consequences for the tax base of the canton and of local municipalities.

The consequences can also be felt in the housing and office rental markets; 250,000 square metres of office space were for rent in early 1996, as were 110 hectares of industrial land.

In sum, three main factors may be said to lie behind Geneva's current economic dilemma:

1 Skilled labour is expensive and often rare, in part due to Switzerland's strict immigration and residence laws (see below), in essence making the canton an increasingly less profitable location for many high-tech industries and high-level services.

2 Even where activities exist that might normally have located in Geneva because of the strong presence of international agencies and financial institutions, Geneva does not in fact possess – precisely because of its 'over'-specialization – the necessary diversity of high-level service firms to support such activities, compared, for example, with cities such as Zurich.

3 The Canton of Geneva, because of its small size, does not constitute a major market. In addition, the fact that Switzerland has chosen to remain outside the EU, meaning that the canton does not have free commercial access to surrounding European states and territories, only tends to exacerbate Geneva's isolation.

The Official Response: Geneva and Sustainable Urban Development

Aware of these difficulties, Geneva and French authorities published in September 1993 a White Paper on Metropolitan Geneva's future, setting out guidelines for sustainable urban development. Among the objectives identified, three are similar to the themes developed by the MOST research initiative on socially sustainable urban development:

• improved environmental quality, broadly defined to include natural and man-made environments, and covering such matters as parks, green belts, rural protection, and urban renewal;

• innovative and more efficient urban management across the entire urban region, including the creation of a Franco-Swiss Lemanic agency to promote common goals and policies;

• improved internal accessibility within the urban region, with a coherent transportation network integrating Swiss and French plans for motorways, trains, and bus services.

These proposals were also integrated into the 1997 draft plan for the Canton for 2015.[1]

With respect to the six policy areas identified by Mario Polèse and Richard Stren in the opening chapter of this volume, Geneva authorities have focused on land-use planning, transportation, and the environment. A Law on Territorial Planning (*Loi sur l'aménagement du territoire*), recently approved, governs urban planning decisions in the Canton. This planning framework, although it only covers the canton, attempts to take account of the strong interdependencies between the Canton of Geneva, that of Vaud, and neighbouring French *départements*. An informal council, the Conseil du Léman, has been created in order to allow for discussions at the Lemanic level. The Conseil du Léman is composed of representatives from the Cantons of Geneva and Vaud and the *départements* of Ain and Haute-Savoie.

The new regional-planning framework envisages major improvements in the transportation system, allowing for better access to the centre and to cities in France, as well to outlying areas of the Canton of Geneva (Kaufman and Giullietti 1996). One of the main issues at stake is the 'economic' balance between the Canton of Geneva and the international Lemanic metropolitan region. In this respect, one of the principal objectives is the creation of new development nodes in the canton and in France, such as Annemasse, and the construction of new TGV (high-speed train) stations in smaller cities (see figure 6.1). A multinodal region is planned for the year 2015. However, a local transportation network must link these nodes. A new tramway system and a regional railway network are being built to respond to these new developments: the area near the centre will be linked by buses and trams; the outer circle by regional trains. This new network should lead to the long-term integration of outlying towns and villages into the region. This translates the political will of local authorities to move from a fragmented to an integrated metropolis, a major shift from past thinking.

This high degree of 'hard' planning is a change from the period when Geneva's economy evolved largely on the basis of free-market forces, accompanied by much 'softer' planning and more informal regulations. In many cities, such an approach to urban development would have generated major equity concerns about, for example, housing provision for the poor and other excluded social groups, the provision of medical and social services, and the possible impact on crime and social divisions. In the Canton of Geneva, where average

Figure 6.1 Metropolitan Geneva
Source: Département des Travaux Publics et de l'Energie de Genève,
Projet 2015

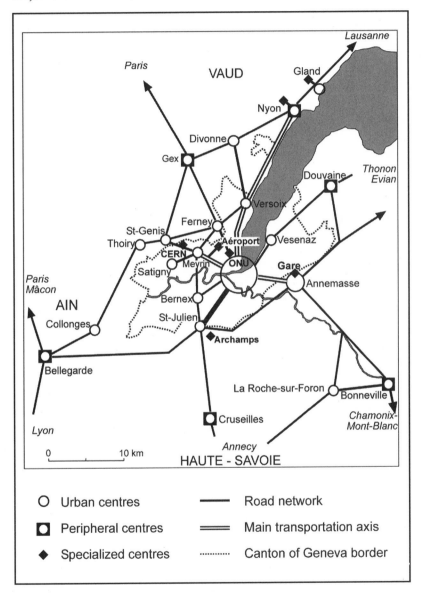

wages are considerably higher than in most cities in Europe, these equity concerns did not emerge until the late 1980s, when unemployment started to appear as a major issue. Before this, unemployment was almost unheard of in Geneva, as indeed in most of Switzerland. There are no real ghettos in the Canton of Geneva, which gives the impression of being an island of wealth and prosperity with one of the world's highest standards of living, with excellent public services and few visible social problems. For the visitor, the general impression remains one of overall well-being and social harmony.

In fact, the Canton of Geneva is today affected by serious social problems, with an unemployment rate standing at 6 per cent in 1999. Important social disparities are starting to show in what was previously regarded as a largely homogeneous (upper-middle-class) society. Figure 6.2, a schematic representation of Geneva's social areas, identifies various geographic zones:

- the so-called transition zones with their blue-collar populations, often of foreign origin or recently arrived from Swiss peripheral cantons such as the Valais;
- the zone of immigrant residences, where second-generation foreigners tend to concentrate, with medium-standard and moderately priced housing;
- the U.N. sector, with its office buildings and residences for high-ranking officials, followed by the wealthy Geneva suburbs to the northeast along the lake, often referred to as a restricted area since only the wealthiest can afford to live there;
- the satellite cities of mainly middle-class white-collar workers or new immigrants, depending on the social status of the satellite city and its location in the canton or in neighbouring France. Some of these cities are on the French side and are favoured by middle-class international employees seeking less expensive housing.

The French part of the Geneva region is also the place of residence of French cross-border commuters (numbering about 30,000 in 1995, and 26,000 in 1999) who work in the Canton of Geneva. It is important to note that this international (although infra-metropolitan) border allows cantonal authorities in Geneva to control this daily flow of 'foreign' workers in case of economic downturn. Since these commuters live outside Switzerland's borders, cantonal authorities have the option of not renewing their work permits. This also means that the

Figure 6.2 Geneva, 1997
Source: The author

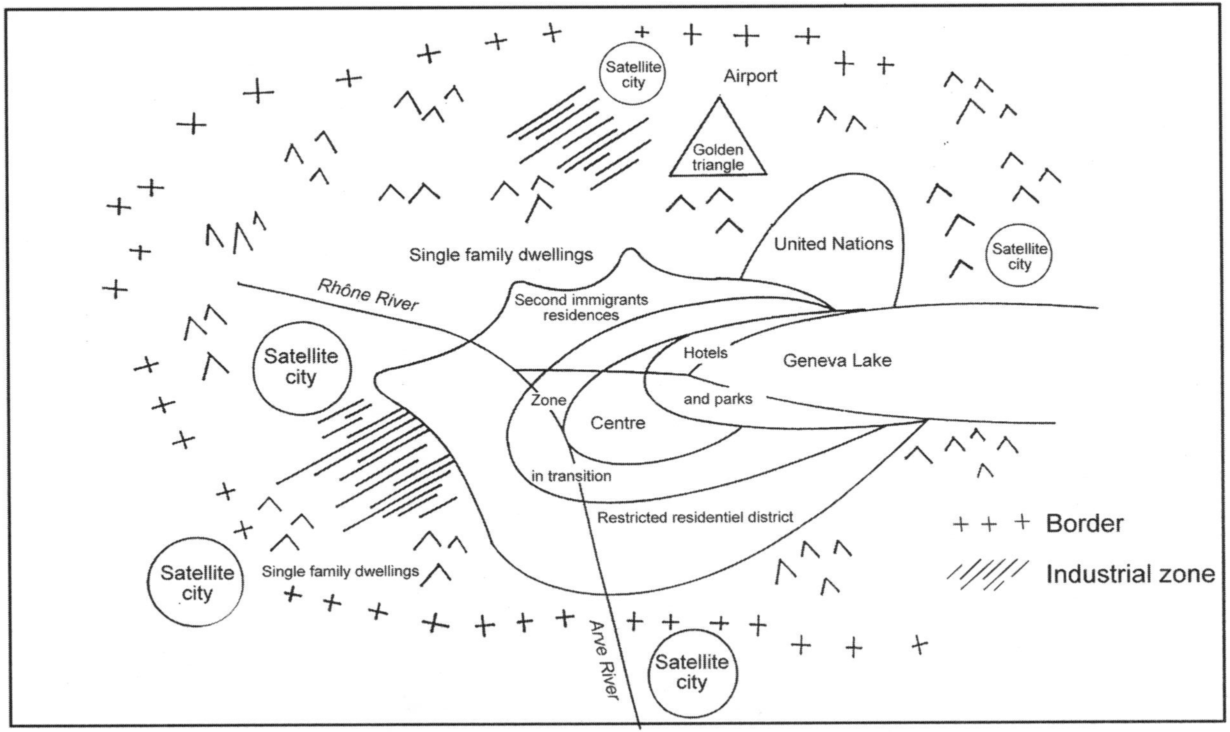

Satellite city

Satellite city

Satellite city

Satellite city

Satellite city

Airport

Golden triangle

United Nations

Geneva Lake

Hotels

and parks

Centre

Zone in transition

Restricted residentiel district

Second immigrants residences

Single family dwellings

Rhône River

Arve River

Single family dwellings

+ + + Border

////// Industrial zone

unemployment rate mentioned above is clearly an underestimate. Strict immigration and residency controls, and an even stricter citizenship policy, prevent these cross-border commuters from residing in the Canton of Geneva, obtaining long-term work permits, and eventually becoming Swiss citizens. The issue of cross-border mobility is one of the chief stumbling blocks in the negotiations between Switzerland and the EU. Were Switzerland to join the EU, citizens of other EU countries would be able to work freely and settle in Geneva, eliminating the current legal and bureaucratic barriers (discussed below), considerably modifying the urban dynamics of Swiss Geneva, which would then move from a closed to an open system.

Exclusion, Geneva-Style

In the Geneva case, issues of immigration, residence permits, work permits, and citizenship lie at the heart of Geneva's singular form of social and economic regulation. Various classes of foreign workers exist, in addition to the cross-border commuters from France. Foreigners wishing to live and work in Switzerland must obtain an 'A' permit (seasonal: maximum of nine months) or a 'B' permit linked to specific employment. 'A' permits must be renewed outside Switzerland. After various years of residence, some foreigners may obtain a 'C' permit (allowing an extended stay), the number of years required for eligibility varying according to the applicant's country of origin. In sum, cross-border work permits as well as 'A' and 'B' permits are temporary in nature, giving Geneva authorities a degree of discretion and flexibility in the management of labour flows unlike that of most local authorities.

It is thus not surprising that economic downturn brought a fall in the number of foreign workers, although the foreign population still makes up some 38 per cent of the total population. Most foreign workers are not counted in Swiss unemployment figures. When their employment ceases, they leave Switzerland following the non-renewal of their work and residence permits. Restrictions on the right to reside are also a way to exclude certain foreigners from Swiss social benefits; once foreigners with 'A' or 'B' permits lose their jobs, they lose their rights to such benefits. Geneva's apparent social cohesion and harmony may, in other words, be in part explained by a managed system of social exclusion via work permits, residence permits, controlled commuter flows, and restrictions on citizenship.

The proximity of an international border is a key element in this managed system of social exclusion. Switzerland's strict immigration laws apply also to the French living in the French suburbs of Metropolitan Geneva. Geneva is unique in being separated from its natural suburbs by an international boundary, allowing authorities to practise 'influx controls' into the central city. These controls of labour flows are reinforced by a strict system of land-use planning, raising housing costs, which discourages the settlement of less wealthy populations. Housing prices in central Geneva are three to four times those in neighbouring France, pushing part of the population towards the French suburbs or into the neighbouring Canton of Vaud. Market forces thus tend to reinforce the spatial impact of the regulatory framework.

To become a true *Genevois* with full civic rights can take time, sometimes even for Swiss from other cantons (called *Confédérés*) who comprise 30 per cent of Geneva's population. However, for other Swiss wishing to settle in Geneva, residence and work permits are as a rule granted automatically. Nor are there any restrictions on their right to vote. Rather, more informal rules and practices, especially in major economic sectors such as private banking, produce de facto social exclusion. Geneva's success in banking is in part attributable to rigid social rules that concentrate financial power in the hands of a few Geneva families (often Calvinist). A dual society has been the tradition for centuries; on one side a closed *Genevois* society, on the other, Swiss *Confédérés* and foreigners working for the prosperity of Geneva.

One may ask whether this model is still sustainable. How can the city's international reputation and prosperity be maintained without power being more equitably distributed? The social and physical borders that allow the exclusion of certain groups are becoming barriers to effective metropolitan integration. Geneva has, in many areas, priced itself out of the market. Geneva increasingly runs the risk of becoming a high-cost economy closed in by economic and social borders. Many cities in the rest of Europe now offer equivalent monetary and social stability, but with lower labour costs and free access to the vast market of the EU.

Geneva's Policy Response: An International Centre in the Grip of Change[2]

In light of the challenges outlined above, Geneva civil society has made deliberate attempts to keep its high quality of life and attract new economic activities. An example is the marketing campaign 'Genève gagne' ('Geneva wins,' but which can also be translated as 'Geneva earns'), launched by the Chamber of Commerce of the canton. The campaign aims to develop a new image for Geneva as a dynamic city, based on its history, its culture, and its environment. Influential individuals and interest groups such as private banks are piloting the project, demonstrating, it can be hoped, that the business community is indeed preparing for the future and is playing an effective role in attracting new firms and new international organizations. Some concrete results can already be seen in the area of communications and environmental activities (Hocké 1996).

Geneva's new policy orientation can also be seen in its visible efforts to stay international in reaction to the growing challenges to its traditional role as a major international centre. The case of Kurt Waldheim who, during his tenure as U.N. secretary general, attempted to move some of the organization's offices to Vienna, provides an obvious indication of Geneva's vulnerability to political decisions beyond its control.

Since 1990 many cities have challenged Geneva, attempting to attract U.N. agencies and the offices of various NGOs. The head offices of international agencies in the areas of biodiversity and climatic change have for example recently gone to cities such as Bonn and Montreal. Geneva has managed to keep the World Trade Organization, the successor to GATT (General Agreement on Tariffs and Trade). But Geneva's bargaining power may be diminishing; Switzerland is, after all, not a major player in the international jostling for U.N. agencies, certainly not compared with nations such as Germany, Japan, France and the United States. A similar trend is discernible for multinational companies despite the weight of organizations such as Dupont and Reuters that have as their European headquarters in Geneva. A number of multinationals have moved their head offices to cities within the EU: the Battelle Institute moved to Frankfurt; the First City Bank of Boston moved its European head office to Luxembourg; and, following a long search, Euronews finally located in Lyon. What was taken for granted in the 1970s is no longer certain. Geneva must increasingly fight to hold on to its international position. The consequences for Geneva's local economy are clearly visible: the hotel and restaurant business is declining and many luxury shops are closing. Even Geneva's airport is showing a decline in the number of direct international flights, due to the location of Swissair's hub in Zurich's Kloten Airport. Notwithstanding Geneva's 'golden triangle' (the upscale area close to the airport, containing head offices and hotels), the central location of its airport in Europe, and its continuing reputation as an international centre (for expositions, conferences, and so on), many new ventures are choosing to settle partly or entirely in neighbouring France.

This flight of economic activity is a reflection of the dilemma, noted earlier, facing a small metropolitan area trapped in a 'closed' nation. In the referendum of 6 December 1992, the Swiss electorate rejected the proposed integration of Switzerland into the European Economic Community (now the EU). As Europe integrates, with perhaps a common currency, the dilemma facing Geneva will grow stronger. Many firms, looking to the EU market, will seek out more attractive locations. In addition, many specialized services and offices are increasingly attracted to the nation's main economic centre, Zurich. In sum, the picture is one of increased competition for international activities, but where Geneva still may enjoy comparative advantages, and a probable decline in economic activities serving the European market due to the restructuring of European management and production systems.

The 1995 federal census gives some indications of employment trends: full-time employment dropped between 1991 and 1995 from 190,000 to 173,000 – a loss of 17,000 jobs, although the drop in part-time employment was less severe. The number of unemployed in Geneva was close to 16,000, but this figure is an underestimation for the reasons given earlier. The biggest job decline was in the manufacturing sector (see table 6.3): employment fell by 34.8 per cent in printing and publishing, 23.3 per cent in the chemical industry, and 28.4 per cent in machinery manufacturing. At the same time, other areas are expanding: education by 10.6 per cent, and postal and telecommunications services by 8.4 per cent; and the so-called luxury sector, specifically the watch-making industry, saw a 28.3 per cent employment growth during the 1991–5 period. Since 1985, health and social services have been the fastest-growing sectors, reflecting the emergence of a city specializing in high-quality services. But, with the reorganization of the banking sector, and the decline in wholesale trade and in hotels and restaurants, the general trend is towards a fall in employment and a rise in uncertainty about the future.

New Challenges for International Geneva

It is in this context that the authorities of the Canton of Geneva have reaffirmed their financial commitment to maintaining Geneva's role as

Table 6.3 Employment Change in the Canton of Geneva, 1985–1995
(Selected Industries)

	1985	1991	1995	% change 1991–5
Printing	3,323	3,254	2,123	−34.8
Chemicals	3,015	3,070	2,355	−23.3
Machinery	2,903	2,863	2,049	−28.4
Wholesale trade	15,415	16,246	12,524	−22.9
Business services	19,043	22,904	23,580	3.0
Post, telecomm.	4,414	5,118	5,548	8.4
Education	13,391	14,556	16,098	10.6
Watchmaking	4,689	4,815	6,178	28.3

Source: Office Cantonal de la Statistique

an international centre. Promoting socially sustainable development is at the forefront of this commitment. Intergovernmental and non-governmental organizations which contribute to the protection of the environment, life, and human rights, and to promoting peace and communication – organizations working in areas such as humanitarian aid, health, the environment, telecommunications, and world trade – will receive financial support from the Canton of Geneva and as well as from the federal government.

To improve the aesthetic quality of the presence of international organizations, an international competition has been launched for the redevelopment of the Place des Nations, close to the original site of the U.N. In this manner, the canton hopes to express the new spirit of Geneva, promoting the city as an international centre with a high quality of urban life. However, Geneva voters in a 1998 referendum rejected the project, essentially for fiscal and economic reasons. Voters apparently preferred to maintain the site as is, with parks and green spaces, rather than to develop it. The Canton of Geneva is also attempting to improve the integration of foreigners working in U.N. agencies and international NGOs. Immigration laws for their families have been made more flexible: work permits are now given to family members without forcing them to go through the old process of obtaining 'A' and 'B' permits.

Challenges and Responses: A Summary

Let us summarize the challenges that Geneva must confront if it is to maintain its international status. Following each point, we briefly state the actions which are being proposed in response (LEA 1995):

- To better Geneva's position with the aim of developing its image in the light of growing international competition. To improve its effectiveness in dealing with international agencies and their employees. *Response:* Launching of the 'Genève gagne' campaign; granting of financial aid to NGOs locating in Geneva, including the provision of free buildings; development of an integrated high-tech communications network linking international organizations to each other and to the main conference centre.

- To increase the competitiveness of the Geneva airport and of the city's telecommunications services. *Response:* Investments in telecommunications planning introducing the most modern links. A fibre-optic network has been built linking most buildings with international networks. Geneva hosts 'Telecom,' the biggest telecommunications exposition in the world, and is the European headquarters of communications firms such as Reuters. The airport has been put under new private management.

- To improve the management of the international Franco-Swiss Geneva metropolitan region. *Response:* Establishment of the Conseil du Léman to create a regional cross-border planning framework providing for the development of linked development poles in France and Switzerland (see above).

- To improve cultural and social development in the city with the aim of creating a better quality of urban life. *Response:* Creation of a museum of modern art; subsidies for numerous cultural events such as music festivals, *fêtes de Genève*, and so on.

- To improve environmental quality. *Response:* A Green-Blue Plan (see box) that will preserve agricultural land and provide a network of natural spaces, including river valleys and lakefronts, as a transition zone between built-up and agricultural areas. Also, Geneva is attempting to position itself as an important research centre in environmental sciences, both by attracting related NGOs and institutions, and by developing the University of Geneva as a centre of excellence in environmental research.

The Geneva Green–Blue Plan

Geneva is well known for its lakeside parks. Used mainly by tourists, they offer flowerbeds, botanical gardens, a museum, and the famous clock in front of the water-geyser. After a complete inventory of the natural environment carried out between 1992 and 1994, another park concept is being developed for Geneva's population: The Green–Blue Plan, using the valleys of the Rhône and the Arve as well as smaller rivers and streams flowing into Lake Geneva. Starting in the Alps and the Jura mountains, the valleys penetrate the agricultural belt (with an area in the Canton of Geneva of 8,400 hectares), then the urban milieu. The plan is seen as an integrated green network, including a pedestrian plan, rehabilitation work under the name *au fil du Rhône*, and a protection plan for the banks of the Arve. Conceived by Geneva and French authorities, the plan has the dual purpose of protecting biodiversity and allowing human activities such as walking, biking, water sports, and group sports where the natural environment permits.

Conclusion: Geneva's Dilemma – To Be Closed or Open

After many years of exceptionally high living standards and an enviable quality of life in what is essentially a protected urban environment, Geneva today finds itself on the horns of a dilemma. How can Geneva conserve its quality of life founded on a tradition of partial closure (especially of labour flows) while at the same time opening itself up to an increasingly integrated world economy? How Geneva resolves that dilemma will largely determine its future as a socially sustainable city. The political and economic boundaries which surround the city (Canton), which allowed it to practise a form of 'social protectionism' and to ensure the development of a high wage economy, are increasingly being undermined by international agreements that facilitate the arrival of outsiders. Will these newcomers threaten the social stability of the canton? Or, on the contrary, will they serve to strengthen the city's attractiveness, as in the past, as an international centre open to the outside world?

Caught between 'local' and 'global,' Geneva no longer has much choice if it does not wish to be marginalized in relation to the French suburbs that surround it and especially in relation to the rest of Europe, which is continuing to integrate. The city cannot afford to remain cut off from the rest of Europe, its natural market. Given a new perspective of openness to its European neighbours and to the international economy, the Canton of Geneva can no longer be seen as an isolated urban entity, but rather as part of a larger urban community transcending international boundaries, and which must develop a common regional planning framework. Rather than attempting to concentrate all high-order (prestigious) activities in the central Canton of Geneva, a more multinodal form of development must be fostered, allowing for the parallel development of the French and non-Geneva (Swiss) parts of the metropolis. The residential structure of the metropolis is also changing and becoming more integrated (more transnational) as commuters choose to live in the French parts of the metropolis. Working-class suburbs have developed in some French communities (such as Annemasse) while other French Alpine communities have attracted single-family homes and secondary residences.

Only an international governance framework for the entire metropolitan area can come to grips with the development problems of such a complex metropolis. The urban-governance issues are well known but must here be resolved in a transnational setting: planning, management and financing of common infrastructure, especially transportation; watershed management; pollution and environmental protection; not to mention the difficult issues of financial equity and common representative (democratic) structures. Such is Geneva's dilemma and its challenge. Geneva will never again be that small, closed, city restricted to an international elite, but will increasingly have to adapt to the reality of being part of a larger transnational and open metropolis whose mode of governance reflects the complexities of a globalizing world.

Notes

1 Project 2015 is 'a plan that offers a concerted approach to reforms in various fields, in addition to more conventional areas. This outward reach, the first of its kind in Switzerland and perhaps Europe as well, reflects a novel and genuinely multidisciplinary conception for prospective action' (Hocké 1996).
2 This section draws heavily on Hocké 1996.

References

Bailly, Antoine S. 1992. 'Genève: Maillage spatial et relations transfrontalières.' *Revue Géographique de l'Est* 3: 217–31.

Bassand, Michel, and Jean-Philippe Leresche. 1991. *La Métropole lémanique et la Suisse romande*. Research report no. 92. Lausanne: Institut de Recherche sur l'Environnement Construit.

Bonneville, Marc, M.A. Buisson, N. Commerçon, and N. Rousier. 1992. *Villes européennes et internationalisation*. Recherches en sciences humaines no. 9. Lyon: Université de Lyon.

Coffey, William, and Antoine S. Bailly. 1992. 'Producer Services and Flexible Production: An Exploratory Analysis.' *Urban Studies* 29/2: 857–68.

DATAR. 1989 [Délégation à l'Aménagement du Territoire et à l'Action Régionale]. *Les Villes européennes*. Paris: Délégation à l'Aménagement du Territoire et à l'Action Régionale, la Documentation Française.

Hocké, Jean-Pierre. 1996. 'Geneva: An International Centre in the Grip of Change.' Paper prepared for the Colloquium on Socially Sustainable Cities, Geneva, 8–10 October.

Kaufmann, Renée, and Mirko Giulietti. 1996. 'Access Networks and Urban Polarization in Geneva.' Paper prepared for the Colloquium on Socially Sustainable Cities, Geneva, 8–10 October.

LEA [Laboratoire d'Économie Appliquée]. 1995. *Genève à la croisée des chemins*. Geneva: University of Geneva, LEA.

Messerli, Paul. 1991. 'Die Schweiz und Europa.' *Geographische Rundschau* 9: 494–502.

7 Room to Manoeuvre: Governance, the Post-industrial Economy, and Housing Provision in Rotterdam

FRANS M. DIELEMAN and
ROBERT C. KLOOSTERMAN

Social Sustainability and the Post-industrial City

The phenomenon of globalization, the growing integration of the world into a global economy and a worldwide financial system, is now seen by many scholars as one of the major structural trends of our epoch (Dieleman and Hamnett 1994; Daniels and Lever 1996). For the welfare states of the Western world, the emergence of the global economy coincides, and is interrelated in a complex way, with a transition from an industrial to a post-industrial society, the advent of which is first and foremost characterized by shifts in the economic base consisting of a sharp erosion of employment in manufacturing together with a rapid expansion of services, most notably financial and producer services. This transition has manifested itself in advanced urban economies in particular, where many long-established manufacturing industries collapsed in the 1970s and 1980s, while sectors related to the knowledge- and information-intensive post-industrial society expanded rapidly.

It is often argued that the post-industrial city is, inevitably, more polarized than its industrial predecessor (Sassen 1991; Fainstein, Gordon, and Harloe 1992). The contraction of manufacturing and the expansion of producer and consumer services in the cities of the Western world seem to have reduced the number of jobs that pay middle incomes, while at the same time the distribution of the rising service sector is more bimodal, with concentrations of jobs at both the high-paid and the low-paid ends. Marc Levine (1992), Chris Hamnett (1994), and Robert Kloosterman (1996) have questioned this allegedly deterministic nature of the post-industrial transition. They have argued that the impact of the joint processes of manufacturing decline and service-sector increase is contingent on the national institutional framework (such as the type of welfare provision and other forms of state intervention) and on the specific make-up of the city (its economic base, history, population composition, and city politics, for example). Changes in the structure of employment in different cities may therefore have differing consequences for the distribution of earnings, in particular, and social polarization, in general. This view thus emphasizes the role of both the national and the local government in influencing the outcomes of the post-industrial transition.

A strongly socially polarized city, with a significant part of the population permanently caught in a web of poverty and living in distinct, deprived areas, contradicts the ideal of a truly open, democratic city in which citizens are able to participate on an equal basis, at least in principle. With polarization, social sustainability, in a narrow sense, becomes a matter of social control and policing. Social sustainability in a broader sense, however, implies much more than just peacekeeping and precluding the outbreak of violence; it entails attacking the very roots of the social and spatial divide. How can a national and a local government act in an age of globalization to prevent the rise of a polarized, and thus socially unsustainable, city?

This chapter examines processes of economic restructuring and polarization in Rotterdam. In the Dutch context, housing policy plays a pivotal role in influencing social and, even more, spatial outcomes of economic restructuring on a local level. Housing policy has recently changed rather drastically, however, and we explore here the consequences of this shift. The Rotterdam case thus serves as an illustration of how welfare-state arrangements and local governance can contribute to social sustainability in an advanced economy.

Rotterdam: A Gateway in a Global Economy

The Rotterdam economy is still dominated by the port and port-related activities (see figure 7.1). In terms of total throughput, the port of Rotterdam is still the largest in the world – in 1995 just larger than Singapore and well ahead of Shanghai (Meijer 1994; Kreukels and Wever 1996). Its economic importance transcends by far its municipal boundaries. No fewer than 295,000 jobs are estimated to relate to the port, a figure which amounts to 6 per cent of all jobs in the country, whereas

Figure 7.1 The Rotterdam Metropolitan Region
Source: The authors

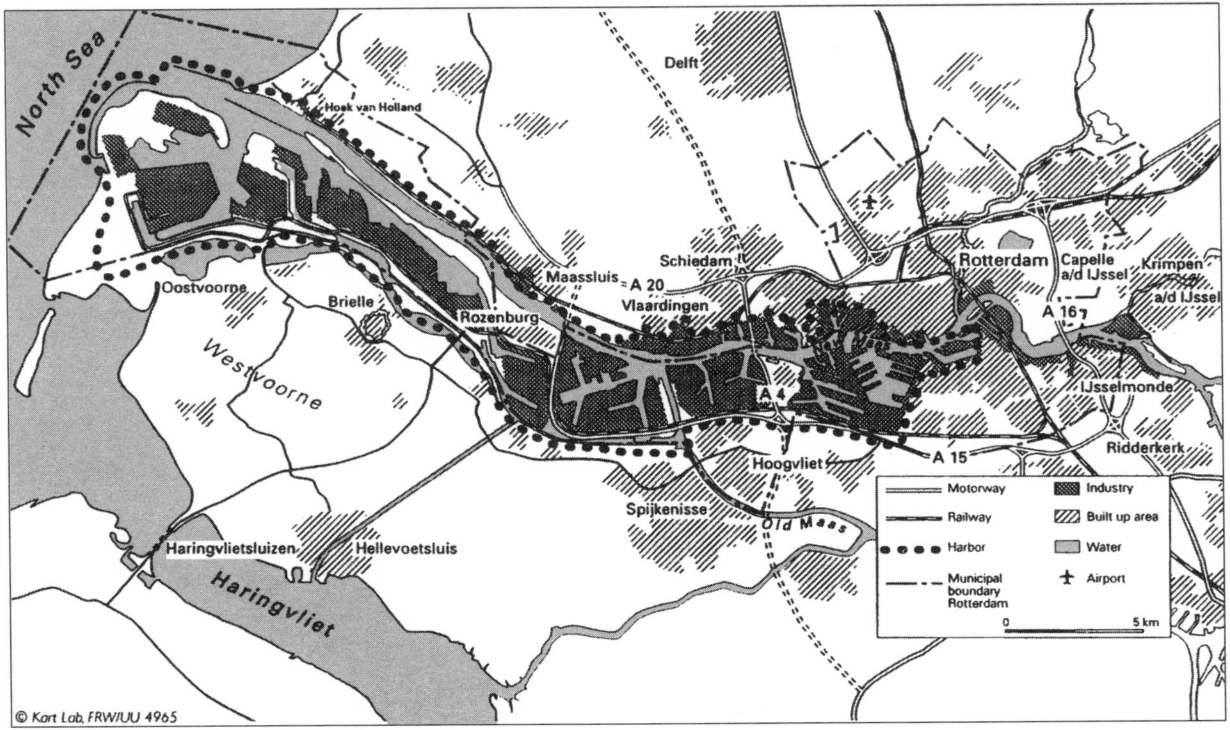

total added value in the port of Rotterdam stands at 50 billion Dutch florins (Dfl.), or 10 per cent of national added value (Wever 1996; Schoenmaker and Doe 1997). The port of Rotterdam is, accordingly, an essential component of the Dutch economy.

The success of the port of Rotterdam is to a large extent, but not exclusively, a matter of location. Both the municipal government and the port authority contributed significantly to strengthening the position of the port by investing large sums in infrastructural facilities. This permitted the development of a large industrial complex (especially petrochemical plants) between the city proper and the North Sea, and both the port and manufacturing activities prospered in the 1950s and 1960s.

However, as a linchpin of the emerging global economy, mainport Rotterdam was also exposed to world market forces and matters took a different turn in subsequent decades as far-reaching processes of economic restructuring manifested themselves very clearly. First, long-established industries, notably shipbuilding, nearly vanished as they could no longer compete with low-wage producers. Second, labour productivity in port activities increased rapidly, mainly due to the worldwide processes of containerization which shrank the demand for labour in this important sector of the Rotterdam economy. Third, as ships became larger, port activities moved westwards, away from the city of Rotterdam. Port-related activities are now spread over such a wide region that Rotterdam itself is not automatically their beneficiary (Kreukels and Wever 1996).

These developments have significantly affected the Rotterdam labour market. The direct impact of the combined processes of deindustrialization and rising levels of labour productivity falls under two headings: there has been a decrease in the level of aggregate demand for labour in Rotterdam in the 1980s; and a significant shift in the composition of the demand for labour away from manufacturing to the service sector.

Change at the Aggregate Level and in the Composition of
Demand for Labour

Although employment statistics differ as to exact numbers, it is obvious that the decline in the number of jobs in Rotterdam started in the 1970s (SCP 1996b, 81) and continued in the first half of the 1980s. Only when the Dutch economy started booming after 1985 did job growth in

Table 7.1 Sectoral Composition in the Central City
of Rotterdam, 1980 and 1992 (% of total employed)

	1980	1992
Manufacturing[a]	24.5	19.8
Trade, hotel[b]	15.7	14.2
Transport	17.5	15.2
Producer services	14.0	18.6
Public services	28.4	32.2

Source: Kloosterman 1996
[a]Including construction
[b]Including catering

Rotterdam resume, albeit very modestly, and with insufficient strength to compensate for the losses that had occurred. In 1980, the total number of jobs stood at 280,000; twelve years later the figure was 273,000.[1] In this respect, Rotterdam differs not only from the Netherlands as a whole, but also from its rival and counterpart Amsterdam (Kloosterman 1996). As a port city strongly oriented towards manufacturing, Rotterdam was evidently hard hit by economic restructuring after 1973. Moreover, when the central city lost 8 per cent of its total jobs between 1973 and 1983, the ring around Rotterdam (the greater metropolitan area without the central city) showed an employment growth of 6 per cent (SCP 1996b, 81). Compared with the Netherlands as a whole, with Amsterdam, and with its own adjacent metropolitan area, the central city of Rotterdam was doing badly.

The process of economic restructuring also affected the sectoral composition of jobs. Table 7.1 shows, at a relatively high level of aggregation, the changes between 1980 and 1992: deindustrialization is very clearly manifested in a decline in the total share of employment, from almost a quarter of the labour force to a fifth. Remarkably, the share of trade, hotel, and other personal services also declined, albeit slightly. In marked contrast to national trends and those in Amsterdam, these services – an integral part of the evolving post-industrial employment structure – stagnated in Rotterdam, explaining in part the decline in the total number of jobs.

Transport services, the sector most closely related to the port, also shed jobs. Notwithstanding the rise in throughput of the port, the increase in labour productivity in transport activities, and the relocation of part of them to elsewhere in the region, have resulted in a decline of employment in the city itself. Producer services and public services were the only two sectors which showed growth in absolute terms and whose shares, subsequently, increased (see table 7.1). Neither producer nor public services are directly dependent on local consumer spending power. It seems, therefore, that the job growth that has taken place in Rotterdam was fuelled by firms and taxpayers' money and not by its own residents.

So far, the post-industrial transition in Rotterdam has been a very mixed blessing. Total employment in the central city has stagnated – a combination of deindustrialization, labour-shedding in transport services, and a lagging of local spending power in personal services. Against this backdrop of socio-economic restructuring, the local government has to try to dampen the impact of these changes in order to preserve the social fabric of Rotterdam.

Urban Governance and the National Administrative System

Local urban policy in advanced capitalist welfare states cannot be properly understood without reference to the national administrative framework in which these local political entities are embedded; indeed, they are strongly intertwined, and the scope of municipal governance is, therefore, dependent in part on the division of responsibilities. One of the most striking features of the Dutch administrative system is the dominant role of the central government and the ensuing specific relationship between national and local levels in the Netherlands.

The potential scope of city government is also determined by the (historically contingent) local political geography – more precisely, the geography of daily urban activity systems. As in many advanced economies, in the Netherlands these transcend by far the (political) boundaries of the central urban municipality, often hindering the governance of urban regions at the local level, and leading to experiments with wider regional authorities, as is the case in the Rotterdam region.

The Netherlands has three levels of public administration: the national, the provincial, and the municipal. Historically, the system was quite decentralized, with strong provinces and municipalities (Spit 1993). But as a consequence of the growth of the welfare state in the twentieth century, the constitutional and financial autonomy of these was increasingly curtailed, and eventually largely superseded by policy set at the national level. The decline of local autonomy in local taxation began as early as 1865, and with each subsequent step the

Table 7.2 Proportionate Sources of Municipal Resources, 1932–1994
(% of total revenues)

Revenue sources	1932	1953	1980	1994
Municipalities fund incl.				
discretionary grants	25	53	32	30
Special purpose grants	25	30	62	56
Own resources and taxes	50	17	6	14
Total	100	100	100	100

Source: Estimates by the authors

financial system became ever more centrally directed. In 1929 the Municipalities Fund, financed from the national tax base, was established to compensate for the loss of the local tax base. This fund is still operating, and municipalities receive resources from it on the basis of their size (mainly the number of inhabitants and dwellings) and their specific needs (for example, where health and educational provisions are disproportionate to the size of the municipality). The allocation of money from the Municipalities Fund accounts for 30 to 40 per cent of municipal resources, and Special Purpose Grants generate more than 50 per cent, as shown in table 7.2.[2] These funds are used to finance a wide range of municipal activities, including health care, education, social housing, and unemployment benefits. Table 7.2 also shows that, with the expansion of the welfare-state in the Netherlands since the early 1950s, the Special Purpose Grants gradually became the main source of municipal finance. One of their salient features is the power of the central government in their allocation, determining both their amount and how they are to be used (WRR 1990), and the data for 1994 show the effect on the grants of national budget cuts for welfare-state expenditures in the 1980s and 1990s. The importance of the Special Purpose Grants for municipal budgets has declined somewhat, while the local tax base has become more significant, in part because of higher local property taxes, but also as a result of the higher fees for government services provided locally (sanitation, garbage collection, and so on).

This characteristically Dutch system has two important advantages. First, municipal resources are not heavily dependent on the local economy and the wealth or poverty of the local residents. Second, municipalities within the same urban region do not have to compete very strongly for the local tax base, which makes cooperation between them easier than is often the case under more locally financed systems. Thus, the Dutch system helps, to a certain extent, to minimize differences in both financial resources and the quality of service provision among municipalities within the same region. This centralized financial system has also made possible the creation of an extensive social-housing stock in cities, without having to rely on the local financial and political situation; in addition, it has allowed the undertaking of extensive urban-renewal schemes, heavily subsidized from the national tax base (see the discussion on housing provision later in this chapter).

The Dutch system has also, however, some major disadvantages that are currently an issue of public debate (see Spit [1993] for a discussion). Curtailing local financial autonomy clearly limits the scope of urban governments to respond to changes in the local economy and to a rise in unemployment. Adjusting the local educational system, for example, or implementing initiatives to increase local employment, are hard to bring about by financially and politically constrained city councils. This lack of discretion also hampers local governments when they want to coordinate initiatives in different policy domains at the local level. Even more important – and most hotly debated (WRR 1990) – it makes local governments less responsive to the needs and opinions of the local business community and to the preferences of local residents in, for example, housing. Ton Kreukels and Egbert Wever (1996) argue that the close cooperation between the local business community and the Rotterdam city government, which was instrumental in the 1950s and 1960s in the extensive investment in infrastructure, weakened in the 1970s and 1980s partly because of the increased independence of the local government from the local tax base. In the course of the 1980s, when the provisions of the national welfare state were curtailed, interest in public–private cooperation at the local level re-emerged.

As have other countries, the Netherlands has struggled for decades with the problem that urban activities outgrow municipal boundaries. Annexation of surrounding municipalities by the central urban municipality is, of course, a way out, but has often proved hard to realize. Two alternatives have therefore been tried: voluntary cooperation between municipalities in urban regions, in the form of regional authorities; and the establishment of urban provinces covering daily activity systems. A well-known drawback to the first solution lies in its voluntary nature itself, and related to this its lack of political legitimacy. Regional urban authorities are usually not directly elected and therefore have little political power; they also entail the creation of an extra layer of government within the three-tier system, which reduces overall effectiveness. In the recent past we have seen the demise of such a regional authority in the Rotterdam region (Openbaar Lichaam Rijnmond), for exactly these reasons.

In 1994, the Ministry of the Interior proposed an alternative plan: the division of the Netherlands into thirty new regions, replacing the twelve existing provinces. The plan included a metropolitan province of Rotterdam. In order to reduce the inequalities in size, number of inhabitants, and, thus, political power, between the city of Rotterdam and the smaller municipalities, the plan also proposed to subdivide Rotterdam into smaller municipalities. There was, however, much popular opposition to the subdivision – local chauvinism turned out to be much stronger than many suspected – and a 1995 referendum produced a vote of no less than 86 per cent against the new province and the splitting-up of the central municipality. This seemed to have brought the debate about new, more regional forms of urban government to a stalemate for a number of years.

In the spring of 1997, however, the national government decided to submit a new proposal for a metropolitan province of Rotterdam, consisting of the undivided municipality of Rotterdam and seventeen surrounding suburban municipalities. This was accepted by the national parliament and was planned to take effect in the year 2000, after a direct election for its representative body in 1999. The debate on the division of administrative and financial responsibilities between the new metropolitan government and the existing municipalities had not been settled by this new plan. The city of Rotterdam kept on arguing for more power for the new provincial government than was foreseen, whereas the surrounding municipalities wanted to limit it. The delegation of responsibilities from the existing municipalities to the new provincial government created so many political problems that in a later stage the national parliament decided to abolish the plan for a new metropolitan province of Rotterdam.

The existing administrative system, with its decentralized funding, although clearly advantageous in some respects, does not make city councils responsive to local needs, nor does it provide them with enough scope to devise their own local policies. Moreover, as daily

Table 7.3 Unemployment in Rotterdam: Central City and the Greater
Metropolitan Area without the Central City (the Rest), 1981–1994

	(% of total labour force)					
	1981	1983	1985	1990	1992	1994
Central city	8	13	12	12	11	14
The Rest	4	7	6	5	6	6

Source: SCP 1996b, 85

urban activity systems transcend municipal boundaries to an ever
greater extent, local governments are increasingly confronted with spatially limited parts of problems, which cannot be tackled properly at
the level of a municipality. Central cities such as Amsterdam and Rotterdam are facing a marked spatial articulation of problems that are
part and parcel of a much larger metropolitan area. Traffic congestion
and unemployment, for instance, manifest themselves most clearly in
these central cities, but are generated at higher spatial levels (Kloosterman 1994a). Local governments are therefore not well placed to cope
with these cross-border problems. The plan for a new province around
Rotterdam is intended to deal with this flaw.

The Social Impact of Economic Restructuring

Unemployment in Rotterdam, as in other large Dutch cities (Kloosterman 1994a; SCP 1996b) has risen considerably since 1981 (see table 7.3).
Again, as with the trends in job growth, these developments in the central city of Rotterdam have been at odds with trends both at the
national level and in the directly surrounding area.[3] In 1994, the rate of
unemployment in the central city of Rotterdam was more than twice as
high as that in the rest of the greater Rotterdam metropolitan area. In a
sense, then, the core city was saddled with the unemployment generated on a metropolitan level, thereby undermining the sustainability of
the social fabric of Rotterdam itself.

This pattern of (very) high unemployment in the central city has also
been found for Amsterdam (Kloosterman 1994a). In both central cities,
the emergence of a complex mismatch between the composition of
demand for and supply of labour in the 1980s can be seen as the root

cause of this spatially concentrated unemployment problem. This mismatch hinges on two conditions.

The first one relates to changes in the supply of labour in the central city which, because of suburbanization, has lost many of its (lower- and upper-) middle-class households since 1960. To some extent, the houses that they vacated have been filled by migrants from Turkey, Morocco, Surinam, the Antilles, and other less-developed countries.[4]

The second condition relates to changes in the demand for labour. As the urban economy moves towards a post-industrial orientation, jobs in the service sector as a whole grow. These are either high-skilled and high-paid or low-paid and, in many cases, part-time. Only a relatively small minority of the migrants qualify for the former. Consequently, they queue in the lower segments of the labour market. Due to the recession of the early 1980s, labour supply, especially in the lower segments, far outstripped demand. Employers were then in a perfect position to choose from a large pool of applicants. This happened at a time when ever more (indigenous) women entered the labour market. For years, the Netherlands had one of the lowest rates of female labour participation of all the advanced economies. This changed about 1985, when the rate of job growth for women was the highest in all the OECD member states (Kloosterman 1994b). On average well educated, with Dutch as their first language, in many cases willing to work part-time and traditionally well represented in the service sector, women were able to profit strongly from the job growth in the service sector. As a result, the share of commuters living outside the central cities but working within them rose considerably in the first half of the 1980s. In Rotterdam, commuters amounted to 35 per cent of the total workforce; in 1985 this had risen to no less than 48 per cent (SCP 1996b, 88).

As a result of these two developments, unemployment in the two largest Dutch cities soared in the 1980s and has stayed high ever since (Kloosterman 1994a). A considerable part of the population of both cities is now more or less permanently excluded from the formal labour market (Esping-Andersen 1991; 1996; SCP 1996a, 1996b). This strongly articulated insider–outsider cleavage in Dutch central cities seems to be the spatial expression of an emerging social divide within the corporatist welfare state with, on one side, those who are included in the formal labour market and, on the other, those who are not actively part of this (Burgers and Kloosterman 1996). Among the latter, immigrants are strongly overrepresented; unemployment rates, especially among

Table 7.4 Percentage Distribution of
Jobs by Wage Class in the Central
City of Rotterdam, 1980 and 1992

	Low	Middle	High
1980	25.0	50.0	25.0
1992	29.2	44.3	26.5

Source: Calculated from data supplied by Central Bureau for Statistics
(CBS) 1994

Turks and Moroccans, are staggeringly high (about 40 per cent [SCP 1996a]). Although unemployed, they are not totally excluded as the corporatist welfare state also provides relatively high benefits. In the central city of Rotterdam, these two sides of the coin of the Dutch welfare system are manifestly present.

The unemployed outsiders are, of course, not evenly spread over the city but are concentrated in certain neighbourhoods where relatively cheap housing is available. This means that the insider–outsider divide has a distinctly spatial expression not only at the level of cities, but also within cities. In marked contrast to, for instance, the United States, the state – either at the national or at the local level – has not abandoned these neighbourhoods. The level of provision in terms of housing, education, police, and public transport is therefore still relatively decent (Burgers and Kloosterman 1996). In this sense, the corporatist Dutch welfare state with its centralized funding has avoided the emergence of anything like ghettos in the Dutch cities, even though the processes of exclusion driven by labour-market trends have been funnelled to very specific areas of these cities.

Post-industrial social divisions in Rotterdam are not confined to the insider–outsider cleavage; as a result of economic restructuring, notable shifts in the employment structure have also occurred. Table 7.4 shows the overall changes in the wage distribution of jobs in the central city. For this kind of calculation, Bennett Harrison and Barry Bluestone (1988) – who have made an important contribution to the debate of 'the declining middle' – have devised a specific method. For a chosen base year, the earnings distribution is divided into a low (first 25 per cent), a middle (next 50 per cent), and a high (top 25 per cent) segment. The two

Table 7.5 Changes in the Number of Jobs by Wage Class and Sector,
Central City of Rotterdam, 1980–1992

	Low	Middle	High	Total
Manufacturing[a]	−2,600	−14,200	2,400	−14,400
Trade, hotel[b]	3,100	−7,400	−900	−5,200
Transport	−1,200	−9,600	3,300	−7,500
Producer services	3,600	4,300	3,700	11,600
Public services	6,200	6,300	−4,200	8,300
Total	9,100	−20,600	4,300	−7,200

Source: Calculated from data supplied by Central Bureau for Statistics
(CBS) 1994
[a]Including construction
[b]Including catering

cut-off points, expressed in money wages, are then transferred (after correcting for the rate of inflation) to another year. Subsequently, the shifts among the three wage segments can be calculated in terms of numbers of wage earners. Accordingly, a rise in the number of wage earners in the bottom and the top segments, in combination with a decline in the middle segment, indicates a trend towards polarization.

As can be seen in table 7.4, the central city of Rotterdam clearly displays a trend towards polarization. The middle has declined from 50 per cent to 44.3 per cent, whereas both the higher and, especially, the lower ends have gained. In table 7.5, the same method is used to trace the shifts within specific sectors of the Rotterdam economy.

Deindustrialization has clearly had a dramatic impact on the central city of Rotterdam – a total manufacturing job loss of 14,400 between 1988 and 1992. Broken down into wage categories, this loss was made up of a decline in the middle segment of 14,200 and in the lowest segment of 2,600, and an increase of 2,400 in the number of high-paid jobs. Consequently, deindustrialization has meant not only a severe loss of jobs, but also a marked tendency towards upgrading. The number of high-paid jobs in the transport sector in the central city, for instance, was clearly on the rise in this period, a tendency probably related to Rotterdam's role as a global transportation hub. International competition seems to have reduced manpower while at the same time boosting labour productivity.

The private sector in the central city of Rotterdam has created a surplus of 2,900 jobs in the lowest wage class, a very large net loss of 26,900 jobs in the middle-paid segment, and a growth of 8,500 high-paid jobs (Kloosterman 1996). The private sector has thus shown a strong tendency towards polarization (which was, however, to a large extent blunted by the trends in the public services). Even with this move to polarization, lower-end job growth has been insufficient to deal with the supply of labour in the central city. Many low-paid jobs have been taken up by part-time female workers. Employers tend to prefer indigenous workers for service jobs that require direct client contact because of their fluency in the Dutch language (and sometimes also because of sheer discrimination), whereas immigrants who are living on welfare would stand to lose income by accepting a part-time job (cf. Kloosterman 1994a, 1994b). At the higher end of the market, the gains have probably mainly benefited commuters.

Although Rotterdam as a port has done quite well in terms of throughput, the outcomes for the labour market have been, to say the least, less than beneficent. Demand for labour in the central city not only declined, but also changed in composition. Both the quantitative and the qualitative changes have been detrimental to a large part of the Rotterdam population. The decline of manufacturing and the concomitant rise of jobs in low-paid services that require mostly part-time labour, and high-paid services that require mostly high educational qualifications, have left many of the growing, mainly low-skilled, immigrant population behind. As a consequence, increasing numbers have become (long-term) unemployed.

The high unemployment prompted the city government to develop specific local policies to enhance the labour-market position of its inhabitants. When it became clear that unemployment would not fall on its own, even though the Dutch economic model showed its resilience by generating strong job growth (Visser and Hemerÿck 1997), the city council initiated a number of policies to combat the emerging dualism of the city. Besides the rather conventional measures on the demand side (trying to lure firms to Rotterdam) and the supply side (training schemes for the unemployed), the city council embarked on an ambitious program that tries directly to link the unemployed with jobs on a neighbourhood level. This innovation, called the 'Social Renewal Program,' involved schemes for direct job creation related in part to community tasks in deprived neighbourhoods (for example, as street cleaners, concierges, and the like), by using welfare money for wages (the initiative was later adopted by the Dutch government to be implemented on a national level). Neighbourhoods are, it transpired, not very useful spatial entities to conduct labour-market policies when daily urban-activity systems transcend city boundaries. More ambitious employment programs should cover (at least) cities, and the national government, headed by the social-democratic prime minister Kok, has even gone beyond this in its first term, 1994–8; it has launched a huge program of job creation for the unemployed, with the four largest cities (Amsterdam, Rotterdam, The Hague, and Utrecht) as the main targets to combat social exclusion.

Housing Provision and Residential Segregation

A serious decline in the labour-market position of a considerable part of the Rotterdam population has, of course, consequences in other domains as well. In general, such changes in the labour market and in the related trends of income polarization also affect housing conditions in cities. In the course of the 1980s, a 'new poverty' emerged in many cities of Western Europe, creating neighbourhoods of extreme deprivation (e.g., Wacquant 1993; Faist and Häussermann 1996). Such marked forms of poverty and geographical concentrations of deprivation have been avoided in Rotterdam to a significant extent, as a result of the existence of an extremely large social-housing stock of relatively good quality, although the management and financing of this stock is no longer strongly supported by the national government.

In the nineteenth century, the provision of housing in the Netherlands was left, for the most part, to market forces. The large influx of population from the rural areas into cities in the first stage of the industrial era between 1870 and 1915 created considerable housing shortage and very poor shelter conditions. In 1901 the first Housing Act tried to remedy this situation. It was aimed mainly at combating unhealthy sanitary conditions and at a more planned expansion of residential neighbourhoods, but it also provided for the establishment of non-profit housing associations that could be subsidized by the national government to construct new housing. In the wake of the First World War, a small wave of construction of new housing by newly founded non-profit organizations occurred. But it was only after the Second World War that this sector became an important provider of housing. Private rental housing predominated well into the 1950s in the Netherlands, particularly in the cities.

Because of the large housing shortages resulting from the war, in the 1950s the national government embarked on a program of mass-production of social housing unequalled even in other countries in Northwestern Europe (Dieleman 1994). This political support for the expansion of non-profit housing remained in place under governments of a different nature for four decades. This can be explained only in the context of the specific nature of the Dutch welfare state, and the place of housing provision in it. Support for social housing, provided at low rents, was often part of social contracts between the national government and the labour unions and the business community. The provision of social housing at low cost was linked to moderate wage demands intended to give the Netherlands a competitive edge in this respect, and to keep inflation low. At the same time, rents were also controlled and kept low in the private rental sector, which made investment in this sector unprofitable, and good maintenance of dwellings difficult. As a result, social housing and homeownership quickly became the dominant housing sectors.

Cities, especially the largest cities like Rotterdam, were able to exploit the generous and continuing support of the national government for the construction of social housing. Because the allocation of subsidies for construction in this sector was linked to the size of the existing housing stock, and population growth in the cities was lower than elsewhere, urban governments were able to pursue a policy of new construction almost exclusively in the non-profit rental sector. Even in the late 1970s and 1980s, when the demand for owner-occupation was growing rapidly, the Labour party–dominated city councils could ignore this demand for owner-occupied housing and keep on building social housing in large quantities with the help of national subsidies. This sector currently contains over 50 per cent of all housing in the cities of Rotterdam and Amsterdam.

The large cities could pursue a comparable policy in urban renewal. In the 1970s the national government embarked on a major program of renovating the older parts of the urban housing stock, mainly private rental housing. The city of Rotterdam developed an extensive program of buying housing from private owners, renovating it with funds from the national tax base, and subsequently making it part of the public rental stock. Large residential neighbourhoods directly adjacent to the city-centre went through this process. By 1995 a total of 70,000 dwellings in Rotterdam had been renovated with national subsidies (*Volkshuisvestingsplan* 1995).

Table 7.6 Housing Stock of the Central City of Rotterdam and the
Rest of the Metropolitan Region, by Tenure and Price, 1993–1994

	Rotterdam city (%)	Rest of metropolitan region (%)	Total metropolitan region (%)
Rental			
<fl. 590/month	61	28	46
fl. 590–790/month	14	19	16
>fl. 790/month	7	9	8
Owner-occupied			
<fl. 145,000	7	9	8
fl. 145,000–195,000	4	15	9
>fl. 195,000	7	20	13
Total	100	100	100
N =	269.25	219.05	488.3

Source: Knippers, van der Zanden, and Bartels 1996

As a result of these policies during the 1950–90 period, the present supply of housing in the central city of Rotterdam is predominantly in the non-profit sector (see table 7.6). Many of these dwellings are available at moderate rents, even after more than a decade of major increases pursued by the national government since 1980 (Dieleman 1996). In 1993–4 rental dwellings of up to 790 guilders per month were intended for households with low or moderate incomes. And the small stock of owner-occupied housing is also moderately priced, in part because of the subsidized construction of low-cost owner-occupied housing in the 1970s and 1980s, and also because part of this stock is in small apartments; units at up to 195,000 guilders are accessible to households with median incomes.

The composition of the housing stock in the rest of the greater metropolitan region (the seventeen municipalities) is strikingly different from that of the central city. The majority of the stock is also in the rental sector, but it is newer on average and more expensive to rent. The cheaper rental stock (less than Dfl. 590 per month) in this part of the metropolitan region is concentrated mainly in the older cities of Schiedam and Vlaardingen and the new towns of Capelle and Spijkernisse (see figure 7.1). Most of the more attractive owner-occupied housing is in the latter two and the more suburban municipalities.

Various authors have argued that the very large rental stock of relatively good quality and moderate price in the large cities of the Netherlands has a number of major advantages (Dieleman 1994; Hamnett 1994; Murie and Musterd 1996). There is ample opportunity for the population of unemployed and minimum-wage households to find decent housing at a reasonable price. Unemployment and low income are therefore not automatically translated into poor housing situations, let alone homelessness. The large non-profit-housing sector built up over a period of consistent support for this part of the welfare state has helped to cushion the impact of the post-industrial transition.

Immigrants in Rotterdam have certainly benefited from this large supply. The access rules for the non-profit-housing stock do not hamper immigrant entry into this sector, and the large majority now lives in the social-housing sector of moderate quality and price, and a sizeable group lives in the renovated parts of the older housing stock, which has now become part of the non-profit rental-housing sector (Knippers, van der Zanden, and Bartels 1996).

Because the social rented stock in Dutch cities is so large, it also houses many households with median and even higher incomes. This has been argued to be instrumental in avoiding the extreme forms of residential segregation by income and country of origin which have now become quite common in European cities, and often stigmatize rather than help those living in social housing (Meusen and Van Kempen 1995; Murie and Musterd 1996). But if one looks at the spatial concentration of the immigrant population in Rotterdam in the mid-1990s, this viewpoint is debatable. Taking all the ethnic minorities as one group, and ignoring the large variety in country of origin, language, and religion, the concentration of the immigrant population in some census tracts (*subbuurt*, very small areas) in the city of Rotterdam is quite high (see figure 7.2). And the segregation index of the immigrant population and the indigenous Dutch population, 0.43 at the neighbourhood level (*wijk*, with an average of 10,000 inhabitants), is not very high if compared with that of other cities in North America, but still at the same level as in other West European cities (SCP 1995). So the large social-housing stock in Rotterdam certainly seems to help in the provision of reasonable-cost, decent housing for the immigrant population even though they have borne the brunt of the post-

Figure 7.2 Distribution of Immigrant Population in Rotterdam, 1995
Source: Knippers, van der Zanden, and Bartels 1996

industrial economy in terms of high structural unemployment. This
state-led protection against market forces has not, however, safe-
guarded them from spatial residential segregation.

There are also major problems attached to Dutch housing policy in
general and to that of Rotterdam in particular, which relate to our earlier discussion of the Dutch administrative and financial system.

First, the housing policy of Rotterdam with, until 1990, its heavy
emphasis on social-housing provision, illustrates how unresponsive
policy can become to shifts in the general and local housing preferences of residents. Housing policy in Rotterdam did not respond to

these local preferences because it could rely heavily on national subsidies. The growing demand for owner-occupied housing could thus be ignored, the result being a large difference in the composition of the housing stock in the city compared to the suburban region (see table 7.6). One consequence of this contrast was, of course, that many middle-and higher-income households moved out of the city to buy housing elsewhere. So the housing policy of the city of Rotterdam is partly to blame for the income differences that now exist between those living in the city and those living elsewhere in the metropolitan region, and also for the huge influx of higher-income commuters.

One of the main objectives of the current housing plan for the city of Rotterdam for the period 1995–8 (*Volkshuisvestingsplan* 1995) is to redress these spatial contrasts in the composition of the housing stock, by building more expensive housing in the central city and a good number of affordable rental dwellings in the surrounding municipalities. The last objective is hard to realize now that national subsidies for the construction of such housing have largely been abolished, and the creation of a provincial government in the Rotterdam region is no longer a serious option.

The second, and even more important, disadvantage of the heavy reliance of local housing policy on the national budget is the vulnerability of local practices to changes in national subsidy regimes. This became manifest when major changes in national housing policy were implemented in the 1990s: large cities, Amsterdam and Rotterdam in particular, were forced to change their own housing policies.

The national changes were mainly triggered by two factors that eroded political support for extensive government intervention in housing at the national level (Dieleman 1996). One was the necessity to cut back on government expenditure in the 1980s as economic and unemployment problems mounted. The huge financial obligations for the housing sector accumulated by the national government in the early 1980s really had to be cut back in the early 1990s. A second factor was the parliamentary enquiry into (mal)practice in connection with subsidies for new construction of affordable housing in the mid-1980s. This damaged the image of social housing as a sector preferable to private rental housing.

A memorandum articulating this new direction in national housing policy was approved by parliament in 1989. The aims of that new policy can be summarized as follows: (1) independence of the housing corporations from the national budget, and decentralization of responsibility for housing provision to the municipal level; (2) more reliance on market forces and reduction of public expenditure for housing – this could be accomplished by increasing rents towards market level, and abolishing subsidies for new construction and for urban renewal; (3) targeting of support for the provision of housing to a smaller group of households at the bottom of the income scale; and (4) promotion of home ownership.

Rents had already been allowed to increase above the level of inflation since the early 1980s. Between 1993 and 1995, drastic measures were taken to disentangle the national government's financial interests in the social-housing sector (Priemus 1996), putting an end to bricks-and-mortar subsidies for social housing, and shifting the task of supervising the non-profit housing associations from the national government to the municipalities. The system of means-tested housing allowances to individual households was kept in place. This is important for a city like Rotterdam, with so many low-income households and such a large rental sector, a point we will return to below.

For the city of Rotterdam, these changes in national housing policy have inevitably had major implications. The local government has become dependent for the provision of affordable housing on the housing associations operating in the city and the metropolitan region. It has to come to terms with this new reality and the first steps have been taken to align the housing policy of the city government with the capacities and practices of the housing associations. The housing plan for the city for the 1995–8 period thus depends heavily on the agreement reached between the city and the associations.

The national government has taken measures to bolster the position of the associations as providers of social housing. Over the 1980s, rents were raised close to market level to make the housing associations less dependent on national subsidies. Two funds were created to help the associations cover their larger financial risks, after the abolition of budgetary support from the national tax base (Priemus 1995): the Social House-Building Guarantee Fund facilitates the raising of loans on the capital markets for new construction of housing in the non-profit sector; and the Central Housing Fund has been created to provide financial support for weak housing associations.

So, even with the changes in housing policy at the national level, the very large social housing sector in Rotterdam is still very much in place as the major provider of affordable housing. The housing associations in the city have agreed to keep a stock of 174,000 dwellings accessible to low- and middle-income households. There are also agreements on the number of new dwellings to be constructed in the social rented sector in the coming years and on the renovation of the older stock. But these agreements are good intentions, to a large extent dependent on the economic and financial conditions that will prevail in the coming decade. Even now, in the favourable environment of low inflation, low mortgage rates, and better economic prospects in the Netherlands, some effects of the change in national housing policy are already evident in the housing situation in Rotterdam.

The level of new construction, as foreseen in the 1995–8 housing plan, is lower than in the previous period. And much of the new construction will be in the more expensive parts of the housing market, and therefore not directly accessible to households of median and low income. These households will become more dependent on the existing older housing stock, and on the good management of this stock by the housing associations. The policy of raising rents above inflation levels, moreover, is creating an affordability problem in the rental sector, even in a city with a relatively cheap rental housing stock. The shelter portion of household income in the rental sector has risen substantially since 1990 (*Volkshuisvestingsplan* 1995). The national system of housing allowances to individual households, which has been kept in place as a provision of the welfare state, therefore continues to be of major importance for the city and its inhabitants. No fewer than 63,000 households in Rotterdam qualified for this national subsidy in the mid-1990s – 23 per cent of all households and 29 per cent of all renters. On an annual basis these households received a total of 118 million guilders in housing allowances from the national government.

Conclusions

As one of the largest ports in the world, Rotterdam plays a key role in the new global economy. As a port it has been very successful, as indicated by an almost continuous rise in throughput. The success of Rotterdam is symbolized by a forest of cranes, countless piers, impressive petrochemical plants, and huge stores of containers lining the canals all the way from the city to the North Sea. This is, however, only one side of the picture. In the central city itself, economic change has not been only beneficial. Unemployment has been continuously high for the past fifteen years or so. Even strong phases of economic growth, as in the second half of the 1980s and during the current boom that started in 1994, do not significantly reduce unemployment in Rotterdam. Unemployment, as with nearly all social phenomena, is neither evenly spread among the population nor evenly distributed spatially; it hits immigrants especially hard, and it is very high in certain neighbourhoods in the central city. The emerging polarization in this advanced urban economy tends to undermine the social cohesion of Rotterdam. Being a strategic part of the global economic machine by itself, evidently, does not guarantee a socially sustainable city.

Rotterdam is not only an integral part of countless economic networks spanning the globe, it is also a large city in the Netherlands. Like other advanced European economies, the Netherlands has a very extensive welfare state with a high level of active state intervention in socio-economic affairs (Katzenstein 1985). Two important postwar welfare-state policies have, over the years, strongly contributed to the social sustainability of the Netherlands. The first was the construction of a very extensive system of relatively generous and easily accessible social benefits; unemployment or disability did not automatically result in a financially deprived existence. The second was housing policy, by providing a large stock of not-for-profit housing at low rents and by embarking upon a massive program of urban renewal in the 1970s and 1980s; good-quality housing, therefore, became affordable even for low-income groups.

Notwithstanding the (mostly) well-meant intentions of the designers of these policies (mainly Christian- and social-democrats), unintended and even perverse consequences manifested themselves, especially in larger cities, when, in the 1970s, the Dutch economy got into trouble. The cyclical downswing that followed the first oil crisis was only a harbinger of a more structural transition to a post-industrial economy. This transition was particularly strongly articulated in central cities, where deindustrialization, the rise of new services, and the presence of a large number (from the viewpoint of the labour market) of vulnerable immigrants came together. One of the results of this combination was the emergence of structural unemployment in central cities such as Amsterdam and Rotterdam. The high level of social benefits proved to be an obstacle to job growth at the lower end of the labour market, and immigrants had great difficulty in finding entry-level jobs. Housing policy geared towards affordable housing for low-income groups also turned out to have a negative side-effect. By concentrating on those groups, the social mix of Rotterdam in particular tilted towards them, while higher-income groups were almost forced to move outwards. Residential segregation of immigrants reached considerable heights and, as unemployment increasingly came to be concentrated among immigrants, it also acquired an ever more marked spatial expression.

Under the current system of strong centralization, the city council has had only limited scope for redressing this downward spiral. Employment policies are hard to implement on a local level, and housing policies were first and foremost a national matter. However, confronted with a socially, ethnically, and spatially divided city in the making, threatening the very social sustainability of the city in the long term, the city of Rotterdam responded actively, thereby questioning existing policies with respect to the labour market, housing, and the relationship between local and national administrative levels.

In the labour market, Rotterdam pioneered the use of social benefits to create jobs for the long-term unemployed. This policy was eventually adopted by the national government. In addition, the city council of Rotterdam (and those of other large cities) increasingly acknowledged the disadvantages of the one-sided structure of their housing stock. There is debate currently on how parts of the rental stock could be converted into owner-occupied housing, and more emphasis is put on this latter sector in new construction. In the longer term this shift in housing policy might bring back some more middle- and higher-income households into the city of Rotterdam and create a more mixed socio-economic structure of the city's population.

Recently, the Dutch model has drawn attention from almost everywhere. Strong job growth and fiscal stability are now going hand-in-hand. The Dutch welfare state – although, in some respects, it took a long time to adjust to the post-industrial transition – is successful once again. Globalization clearly does not necessarily mean the adoption of neo-liberal *laissez-faire* policies. Developments at the local level of cities like Rotterdam, however, do not warrant unblemished optimism. Partly as a result of unintended consequences of long-standing welfare policies that have only recently been changed, Rotterdam still faces the emergence of a dual city. The solutions for combating this process are, properly, sought within the broad tradition of the Dutch welfare state by redirecting and adjusting existing labour-market and housing policies. Local government can play only a limited role in this by initiating new policies and influencing the national government to adopt them in a more comprehensive way. The referendum that voted down the proposal for breaking up the city, showed the attachment of the people to their city as a local community with its distinct local down-to earth culture, its pride in new buildings and its famous football club Feijenoord. This local sense of togetherness and identity can constitute a sound base for collective action and, more specifically, local governance to combat social exclusion and thus contribute to social sustainability in Rotterdam.

Notes

1 These data are based on the so-called *Statistiek Werkzame Personen/ Loononderzoek* (Labour Force Survey/Wage Survey); cf. Kloosterman (1996).
2 Compared with other Northwestern European countries, this strong financial reliance of the municipalities on the national tax base is quite exceptional. To give some examples, in Germany 57 per cent of local government income is generated from local revenues, in Belgium this stands at 42 per cent, in Britain at 40 per cent, in Sweden at 67 per cent, and in Switzerland at 88 per cent.
3 Before 1970, unemployment rates in Dutch central cities were in the same league as the national average (Kloosterman 1994a).
4 The immigrant population of the city is increasing rapidly; in 1986 it amounted to 16 per cent of the population, while in 1994 immigrants made up 24 per cent of central-city residents, with the Surinamese, Antillians/ Arubans, Turks, and Moroccans being the largest groups.

References

Burgers, J., and Robert C. Kloosterman. 1996. *Dutch Comfort: Postindustrial Transition and Social Exclusion in Spangen, Rotterdam*. Utrecht: Department of General Social Sciences, University of Utrecht.
Buursink, J., G. Mik, and W. Ostendorf, eds. 1990. *Geografisch Tijdschrift* 3. (Theme issue on Rotterdam.)
Daniels, P.W., and William F. Lever, eds. 1996. *The Global Economy in Transition*. Harlow: Addison-Wesley Longman.
Dieleman, Frans M. 1994. 'Social Rented Housing: Valuable Asset or Unsustainable Burden?' *Urban Studies* 31/3: 447–64.
– 1996. 'The Quiet Revolution in Dutch Housing Policy.' *Tijdschrift voor Economische en Sociale Geografie* 87/3: 275–83.
Dieleman, Frans M., and Chris Hamnett. 1994. 'Globalisation, Regulation and the Urban System: Editors' Introduction to the Special Issue.' *Urban Studies* 31/3: 357–64.

Dieleman, Frans M., and Sako Musterd, eds. 1992. *The Randstad: A Research and Policy Laboratory.* Dordrecht: Kluwer.

Esping-Andersen, Gösta. 1991. 'Mobility Regimes and Class Formation.' In *Changing Classes: Stratification and Mobility in Post-Industrial Societies,* ed. Gösta Esping-Andersen, 225–42. Newbury Park, CA: Sage.

Esping-Andersen, Gösta. 1996. 'Welfare States without Work: The Impasse of Labour Shedding and Familianism in Continental Social Policy.' In *Welfare States in Transition: National Adaptations in Global Economies,* ed. Gösta Esping-Andersen, 66–87. London: Sage.

Fainstein, Susan, Ian Gordon, and Michael Harloe, eds. 1992. *Divided Cities: London and New York in the Contemporary World.* Oxford: Blackwell.

Faist, Thomas, and Hartmut Häussermann. 1996. 'Immigration, Social Citizenship and Housing in Germany.' *International Journal of Urban and Regional Research* 20/1: 83–98.

Hamnett, Chris. 1994. 'Social Polarisation in Global Cities: Theory and Evidence.' *Urban Studies* 31/3: 401–24.

Harrison, Bennett, and Barry Bluestone. 1988. *The Great U-Turn: Corporate Restructuring and the Polarization of America.* New York: Basic.

Katzenstein, Peter J. 1985. *Small States in World Markets: Industrial Policy in Europe.* Ithaca, NY: Cornell University Press.

Kloosterman, Robert C. 1994a. 'Amsterdamned: The Rise of Unemployment in Amsterdam in the 1980s.' *Urban Studies* 31/8: 1325–44.

– 1994b. 'Three Worlds of Welfare Capitalism? The Welfare State and the Post-industrial Trajectory in the Netherlands after 1980.' *West European Politics* 17/4: 166–89.

– 1996. 'Double Dutch: Polarisation Trends in Amsterdam and Rotterdam after 1980.' *Regional Studies* 30/5: 467–76.

Knippers, K.M., W.H.M. van der Zanden, and R.J.G. Bartels. 1996. *Tussenkeuze en concessie: Het zoekproces van migranten op de Rotterdamse woningmarkt.* Rotterdam: Centrum voor Onderzoek en Statistik.

Kreukels, A.M.J., and E. Wever. 1996. 'Dealing with Competition: The Port of Rotterdam.' *Tijdschrift voor economische en Sociale Geografie* 87/4: 293–310.

Levine, Marc V. 1992. 'The Changing Face of Urban Capitalism.' *Urban Affairs Quarterly* 28(1): 171–80.

Meijer, H. 1994. *Rotterdam Delta.* Utrecht/The Haag: Information and Documentation Centre for the Geography of the Netherlands.

Meusen, H., and R. Van Kempen. 1995. 'Towards Residual Housing? A Comparison of Britain and the Netherlands.' *Netherlands Journal of Housing and Built Environment* 10: 239–58.

Murie, Alan, and Sako Musterd. 1996. 'Social Segregation, Housing Tenure and Social Change in Dutch Cities in the Late 1980s.' *Urban Studies* 33/3: 495–516.

Priemus, Hugo. 1995. 'How to Abolish Social Housing? The Dutch Case.' *International Journal of Urban and Regional Research* 19/1: 145–55.

Sassen, Saskia. 1991. *The Global City: New York, London and Tokyo*. Princeton, NJ: Princeton University Press.

Schoenmaker V., and A.J. Doe. 1997. 'From Landlord to Mainportmanager: The Port of Rotterdam.' In *North Sea Ports in Transition: Rising the Tide?*, ed. T. Kreukels and E. Wever, 33–43. Assen: Van Gorcum.

SCP [Sociaal Cultureel Planbureau]. 1995. *Rapportage Minderheden 1995*. Rijswijk: Sociaal Cultureel Planbureau.

– 1996a. *Rapportage Minderheden 1996*. Rijswijk: Sociaal Cultureel Planbureau.

– 1996b. *Sociaal en Cultureel Rapport 1996*. Rijswijk: Sociaal Cultureel Planbureau.

Spit, T.J.M. 1993. *De Bestuurlijke kaart achter de Ruimtelijke Ordening*. Onderwijsbundel B3VAK Basisdoctoraal Sociale Geografie-Planologie 1995–1996.

Thrift, Nigel. 1994. 'Globalisation, Regulation, Urbanisation: The Case of The Netherlands.' *Urban Studies* 31/3: 365–80.

Visser, J., and A. Hemerÿck. 1997. *'A Dutch Miracle': Job Growth, Welfare Reform and the Revival of Corporatism in the Netherlands*. Amsterdam: Amsterdam University Press.

Volkshuisvestingsplan. 1995. Rotterdam: Gemeente Rotterdam.

Wacquant, Loïc J.D. 1993. 'Urban Outcasts: Stigmata and Division in Black American Ghetto and the French Urban Periphery.' *International Journal of Urban and Regional Research* 17: 366–83.

Wever, E. 1996. *The Port of Rotterdam: Gateway to Europe*. Utrecht: Faculty of Geographical Sciences, Utrecht University.

WWR [Wetenschappelijke Raad voor het Regeringsbelied]. 1990. *Van de stad en de rand, Rapporten aan de regering*. The Hague: Sdu Uitgevers.

8 São Paulo and the Challenges for Social Sustainability: The Case of an Urban Housing Policy

ANA AMÉLIA DA SILVA

The challenges confronting the management of Brazil's large cities are closely linked to the country's complex and difficult struggle for democracy. After more than twenty years of military government, the so-called democratic issue is still present in Brazil as an enigma in the social fabric, weaving in paradox, ambiguity, and uncertainty – perhaps we could use the terms 'antinomy' or 'disjunction' to express a sense of conflict, doubt, and contradiction. To understand the democratic issue we have to understand the difficulties it has encountered and the absence of 'bridges,' which seem to collapse before they can offer passage to important changes or democratic solutions (Silva 1996).

Over the past fifty years, Brazil has undergone a process of industrialization; has established a large consumer society; has urbanized to the point where three-quarters of its population live in cities; has developed sophisticated service, commercial, and financial sectors; and has blazed trails of economic growth that have opened continental frontiers.

At the same time, during the long transition from a military regime to the formal democracy established in the mid-1980s, Brazil witnessed the organization of new social movements around demands for rights. Numerous studies (for example, Kowarick 1988; Sader 1988; Paoli 1995) have examined the emergence of these since the late 1970s: a new workers' movement, baptized a 'new unionism,' which became the cradle of a major political party, the PT, or Partido dos Trabalhadores (Workers Party); the creation of important union federations, among which the independent national Força Sindical (Union Force) and the Central Unica dos Trabalhadores (the United Workers Federation) stand out; popular movements involving the landless and urban homeless who demanded basic rights of urban survival (housing, transportation, health care, education, basic sanitation, and so on); and various other movements such as those of the rural landless, women, blacks, and other minorities struggling for better living and working conditions.

However, if Brazil is known today for its brutal social, political, and cultural crises, which seem to swallow up its strengths once celebrated in 'prose and verse,' such as the 'country of the future,' or the 'country of the economic miracle' (the slogan so dear to the military during the dictatorship), it is because its growth has been and continues to be strongly marked by exclusion and injustice in the social arena – with poverty, unemployment, underemployment, and violence being the most visible – and by the difficulty of inserting the rights of citizenship into the social practices of the broad majority of the population.

International and national organizations have furnished impressive data that reveal the growth in inequality and social exclusion in Brazil – recently exacerbated by the adverse effects of an economy of increasingly global dimensions. With its 156 million inhabitants, Brazil has shocking levels of poverty, despite its giant economy: almost 42 million people live in poverty, comparable to levels in the poorest nations of Africa with the lowest rankings of the Human Development Index (U.N. Development Programme 1995, 1996). Brazil's social inequalities are revealed in its concentration of wealth, one of the greatest in the world: 65 per cent of the national income is concentrated in the hands of the richest fifth of the population, while the share of the poorest half is just 12 per cent. A profusion of reports produced by official agencies in partnership with NGOs and other citizen groups have established new and challenging frontiers that separate the 'new pariahs'[1] from the minority at the top of the social pyramid, whose privileges offer examples of the divisions, fragmentations, and differences that delineate Brazil's social inequality.

Certainly, the reality of social crisis, although intersected by many different economic, social, and cultural matrices, is not exclusive to Brazil. The 'world's misery,' to use Pierre Bourdieu's (1993) expression, feeds discrimination and segregation in many countries. However, what appears to characterize Brazil at the end of this century and millennium is that, for the majority of its population, citizenship is becoming increasingly precarious and vulnerable without ever having been established in an inclusive way. Unlike in advanced countries, especially those of Europe and North America, social practice in Brazil has no experience of universality of the rights of citizenship – civil, political, and social – such as those studied by T.H. Marshall (1967).[2]

This disjuncture between poverty and social inequality, on the one hand, and 'restricted citizenship,' on the other, gains its sharpest expression in the study of Brazilian cities, which contain 79 per cent of the total population. A new conflictual order has developed around this disjuncture, especially during the last two decades, when popular movements inscribed social rights in the new constitution of 1988, thus setting the stage for giving more power over social policies to municipalities (large and small) such as São Paulo.

The broad objective of this chapter is to reflect upon some challenges to the social sustainability of Brazilian cities. It analyses some elements of a 'social interest' housing policy, implemented by the democratic municipal administration of 1989–92 in Brazil's largest city, São Paulo. It will argue that the handling of the 'social question,' as it concerns poverty, inequality, and citizenship, depends in part on the ability of local governments to establish public policies and norms of democratic regulation capable of broadening the rights of citizenship for the vast majority of the excluded. If this does not resolve all the challenges and dilemmas for the construction of democracy in the country, our presumption is that it can at least point to the construction of some bridges that offer important democratic passages, involving the broad participation of citizens in the management of their urban destinies.

Brazil: Scenes of Restricted Citizenship

Recalling Brazil's entry into the modern age at the end of the nineteenth century and the beginning of the twentieth allows us to perceive how social relations and an authoritarian political culture were forged from a peculiar combination of bourgeois liberal ideas of European and North American origin, and the arbitrariness and violence that sprang from Brazil's long and painful experience with slavery. Brazil was one of the last countries in the Western world to end slavery, doing so only in 1888. The discourses of the dominant elite during this period of transition to a republican and capitalist order show how the promised modern ideal of liberty was accompanied by the paternalistic practices of favouritism, tutelage, and patronage, and by privileges that had been dominant in the social relations of slavery. Not without reason, the classic studies, such as that of Roberto Schwarz (1988), have identified a 'dislocation or decentring' of the bourgeois liberal ideal, using the metaphor 'ideas out of their place.' Schwarz refers principally to the fact that the dominant elites of the period operated a 'partial and selective ideological filtering' of the meaning of liberty, distancing it from ideas of democracy and equality. In fact, the meaning of liberty in the Brazilian case was restricted to property; *citoyens* were the 'master-citizens' (Adorno 1988), and there were very few of them in a society in which the majority came to be composed of recently liberated ex-slaves, workers of the new industrial order, women, blacks, and poor immigrants.

Not giving recognition to the intense heterogeneity and diversity that marked its social classes, Brazilian society codified its social inequalities, structuring them as social exclusion in which prejudice, stigma, and discrimination were added to deprivation of material needs, and inscribing social injustice as the principal unresolved question – as it remains today. It was in the period of the 'Old' Republic (1890–1930) that the bourgeois imagination coined the expression 'dangerous classes,' including within them the growing working class and all those in the so-called informal sector: workers in services and commerce, people in certain lower professions, residents of *cortiços* (a type of slum tenement), abandoned children, and so on. Whether workers or not, they were all stigmatized as bandits, vagrants, and criminals, for they did not fit the idea of the 'civilized' bourgeois family (Chalhoub 1996). Michael Hall and Paulo Sergio Pinheiro (1986), among others, call attention to the intense degree of police violence in the cities of Rio de Janeiro and São Paulo in the early decades of the twentieth century, and their handling of social conflicts in the world of labour relations, extending to the repression of popular demonstrations for survival. This history can explain, to a substantial degree, the strategy of police violence in the large Brazilian cities today.

Maria Célia Paoli (1989) traces the threads in the fabric of difficulties with which Brazilian society in the first Republican period faced the introduction of public spaces of 'democratic recognition, representation, and negotiation: ... workers during this early industrial and urban period appear as true pariahs ... as "rootless outcasts" or "vagrant plebes" ... In the symbolic society's *mise-en-scène* the common people and urban workers are not presented as entitled to being subjects of republican legal equality, but precisely as people conceived as outside effective constitutional or legal guarantees' (Paoli 1992, 149).[3]

When the state entered the scene in 1930, with the start of the Vargas era,[4] social rights (a minimum wage, social security, regulation of the workday and of the work of women and children; and social policies for housing, health care, education, and other matters) appeared entirely under the tutelage and control of the state, in what became known as 'regulated citizenship' (Santos 1979).

Once again, Paoli's studies record important aspects of this situation. All the subsequent labour and union legislation had its foundation in the workers' strikes, tenant leagues, and social conflicts, and the campaigns against terrible living and working conditions conducted in a vigorous workers' press. These collective actions reached the entire social fabric in the years of the 'First' Republic, following the revolution of 1930. In an authoritarian, centralizing, and normatizing manner, however, the state did not recognize the poor and working classes as subjects with rights who could participate in the public sphere, where they could negotiate, exercise control, and create new rights. 'Regulated citizenship' meant that only those in the formal labour markets could claim rights or benefit from social policies. The right to strike was 'born prohibited' (meaning that union leaders and militant workers were banned, persecuted, or murdered), the unions remained tied to the power of the state (this became known as 'corporatist unionism'), and the poor and working classes were left to the imperatives of simple survival. State regulation of social rights was only for those in the formal labour market – identified by an official labour card – and conferred the status of a restricted, not universal, citizenship, leaving the whole range of 'informal' and poor workers outside (Paoli 1989, 57).[5]

We have traced the roots of citizenship in Brazilian society because it offers two important considerations for our discussion of social sustainability. First, it is important to note that 'restricted citizenship' was not limited to the world of labour relations. Historical studies of the cities of São Paulo and Rio de Janeiro point to the many ways in which the concept of the dangerous classes extended to urban space. This was visible in the implementation of an *urban social apartheid*[6] through measures that controlled the poor neighbourhoods, placing 'each one in their place' (Rolnik 1981) and outside the status of citizenship. The idea of 'social reform' – of individuals, groups, and social classes – based on theories of the 'hygienization' and medicalization of 'indocile' bodies and minds (Foucault 1987),[7] was most visible in the way in which it contained the dangerous classes in their own territories, and prohibited their appearance in the public spheres of the bourgeois order. Poor and working-class housing, at the time principally *cortiços*, were the focus of the 'sanitizing' and 'hygienic' activities, when they were not completely removed or destroyed by the urban reforms and legislation of the elite (Chalhoub 1986).[8] It is common even today for images from famous speeches of the beginning of this century to be repeated; one observation, made by Washington Luiz, president of the Republic from 1926 to 1930, became notorious: 'the social question is a police question.' These notions frequently still work – even if they are more sophisticated and couched in 'modern' terms – to stigmatize and criminalize those who live in *favelas* and *cortiços*, and the homeless and landless, both rural and urban.

The second, and linked, consideration indicates the immense difficulties confronting Brazilian society in building public spaces of dialogue, negotiation, and representation that can broaden the rights of citizenship, decrease social inequality, and improve the quality of life. The economic and political situation of the 1990s appears to have given rise to a new conflict within the complex relations between civil society and a state increasingly torn by structural adjustment, the restructuring of production, the 'flexibilization' of labour relations and of rights, and deregulation. In other words, the articulation of the country with the dictates of the global financial market is consolidated at the expense of social rights and marked by the fragility or absence of social programs capable of confronting the 'social question.' This situation is expressed in the dismantling of policies and the privatization of essential services, such as health care, education, housing, and sanitation; in the attempts at the 'deconstitutionalization' of basic rights, won at great cost in the struggles of the late 1970s and inscribed by the social movements in the Constitution of 1988; and in the marginalization of the legitimacy of proposed social policies by means of discourse that depoliticizes and disqualifies their collective action and, even worse, by the denial of democratic practices of dialogue and negotiation. In this way, the 'decency' of a less unequal life ('decent' housing, work, and nutrition being included in basic and elementary rights) is always 'being petitioned,' whether in the demands put forward by important social actors, or in the proposals for alternative policies for the administration and social sustainability of the cities.

São Paulo and the Dark Side of Social Sustainability

The municipality of São Paulo is a 'global' city; with its 10 million residents, it is one of the world's largest. The metropolitan region – the so-called Greater São Paulo (which includes an additional 38 municipalities) – contains a population of 16 million in a continuous urban area of 1,500 square kilometres (see figure 8.1).

This urban space contains 'two cities.' São Paulo is abandoning its previous role as an important industrial centre in favour of developing increasingly large and more sophisticated markets of consumption, services, and commerce. The city is also home to the national and international headquarters of Brazil's most important financial groups and companies, as well as to a significant part (some 25 per cent) of the country's wealthier population, in addition to important universities, cultural institutions, and research and technology centres. As a commentator in the nation's largest paper, the *Folha de São Paulo*, indicated, 'to walk along certain avenues such as Berrini or Paulista, and look up at the (post) modern, mirrored, clean, marvellous buildings ... is like being in Tokyo!' (Gonçalves 1996).

However, when the gaze shifts from the skyscrapers to the 'feet' of the city, São Paulo reflects a very different picture, of poverty, misery, and vulnerability – the world of social exclusion, with its intensity of material needs, unemployment, underemployment, violence, and precarious labour relations and living conditions. Increasingly sophisticated comparative studies have measured these conditions. One of them has examined the 'lines of poverty' in Greater São Paulo, based on four variables: employment/unemployment, education, housing, and income (SEADE 1995). Dividing families into socio-economic groups that range from those who claim no 'material needs' to those who combine all four needs, the research not only shows the impoverishment of the entire metropolitan region, but details that group of people considered to live in extreme poverty; the number of families living in poverty within a short period, 1990 to 1994, grew by 42.2 per cent (an increase of 640,000 families), and in 1994 these families included 2.3 million people living in absolute poverty.[9]

A large part of this population – not only the poorest – appears in the unemployment data and in other indicators that reveal precarious conditions to be one of the effects of the structural economic adjustments that have hit the labour market, causing impoverishment and insecurity. Between 1990 and 1994 the percentage of salaried industrial workers in the São Paulo metropolitan region who had no official labour card jumped from 6.8 to 10.2 per cent (Telles 1995), and these workers are excluded from social-security benefits, unemployment insurance, and union benefits. An increasing number of people are

Figure 8.1 The Metropolitan Region of São Paulo
Source: Empresa Metropolitana de Planejamento da Grande São Paulo

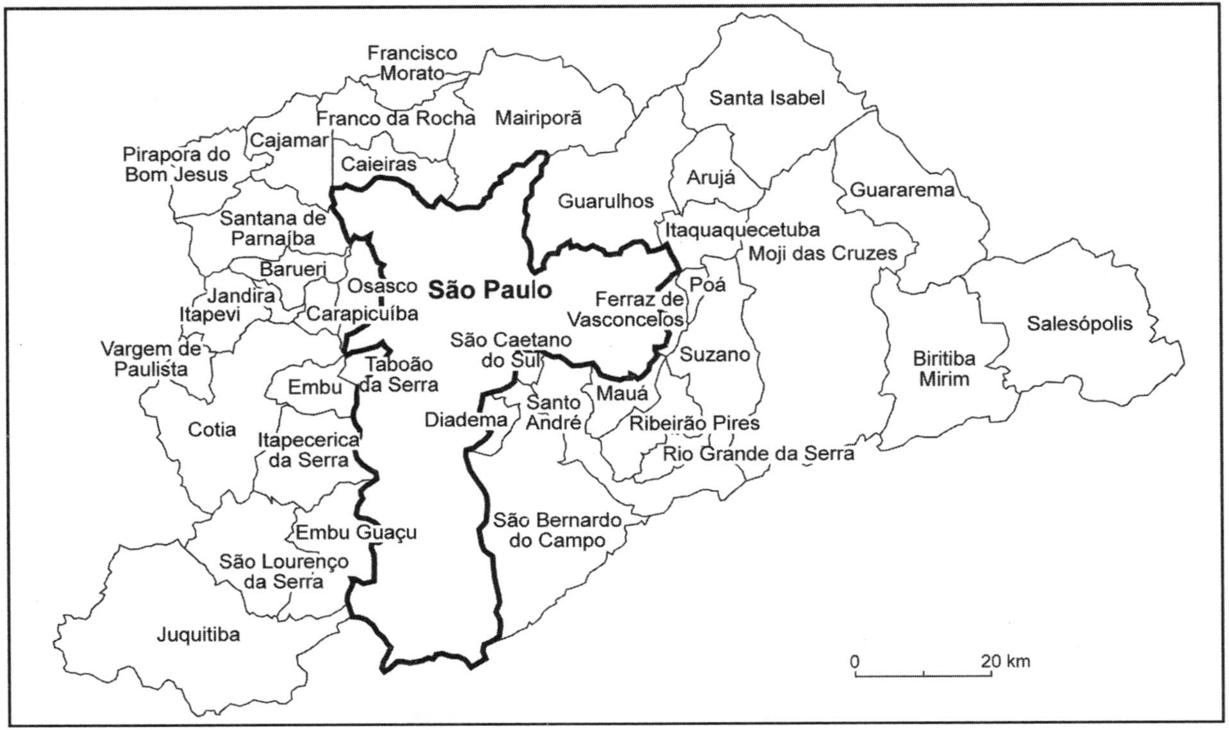

thrown out of the protective web of basic rights, including nutrition, health care, employment, and housing.

Unemployment and underemployment directly reflect what is conventionally called the 'clandestine city' within São Paulo, where the population does not have access to urban rights such as property ownership and building permits, and where people live in areas of risk, in irregular and illegal subdivisions. Those who live in the 'legal' city, in contrast, have access to urban rights, and thus to the support of urban legislation. If before the 1990s the clandestine city was concentrated in the peripheral areas, distant from the central city, nowadays the increasing amount of precarious housing has spread all over the city, including its inner areas. The magnitude of this phenomenon is large, casting many into the cruel and precarious world of illegality. In 1993, data from the São Paulo municipal government indicated that 2 million people lived in *favelas*, 1.5 million in slum tenements, and 50,000 were homeless – the 'new nomads' of the city (FIPE 1993; SEMPLA 1995). The slum tenements and *favelas* are added to the images found in the national and international news of street vendors, abandoned children, beggars at traffic lights, homeless people sleeping beneath highways and, recently, being burned alive. While for some people these images do not cause indignation, for others they depict the dualistic nature of São Paulo: 'São Paulo is a first-world city in the fifth world' (Souto and Kayano 1996; see figures 8.2 and 8.3).

We can also speak of a recent increase in violence and criminality in the poorest areas, although not of an automatic relationship between poverty and criminality – to claim that would be to support those who consider the homeless and residents of *favelas* to be criminals. Nevertheless, violence and criminality are rooted in deprivation and precarious living conditions, and make the risky life of the socially excluded even more difficult. For instance, the district of Jardim Paulista, which includes the richest street of São Paulo – Avenida Paulista – experienced only 3 murders from January to April 1997. This contrasts with Jardim Angela, one of the poorest areas of the city, where there were 136 murders during the same period (*O Estado de São Paulo* 1997). It is in these areas (since the poor do not have access to the judicial system or to education and health care, and have no guaranteed basic rights) that private justice, the taking of justice into one's own hands, opens the door to the death squads or hired killers known as *justiceiros*.

Violence presents other dimensions as well. São Paulo is the city in

Figure 8.2 São Paulo's Two Cities: The Face of Commerce
Source: Apoena Loloian

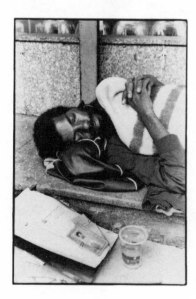

Figure 8.3 São Paulo's Two Cities: The Face of Homelessness
Source: Apoena Loloian

which the police force is known as one of the most arbitrary and violent in the world. According to Teresa Caldeira, in 1992 'the Military Police of São Paulo killed 1,470 civilians, including 11 prisoners in the House of Detention. In the same year, the Los Angeles police killed 25 civilians and those in New York City, 24' (Caldeira 1997, 158). Corruption, torture, murder, summary executions, and all the scenes of explicit violence contribute to the spectacle of barbarity exercised by a police force that is the product of the military dictatorship, and whose crimes are not judged in common courts and are thus committed with impunity.[10]

In this case, violence has to be understood as a shift from the traditional form of segregation which separated the centre from the periphery. The violence has led to the construction of real and symbolic walls which grow out of fear and insecurity, but also out of prejudice; Caldeira (1992) points to a São Paulo increasingly dominated by fear and based on stereotyping of the 'poor classes as the dangerous classes.' The middle and upper classes choose to live in private, fortified, and exclusionary enclaves, producing a new form of urban segregation. These residential areas share the city's space with the poor neighbourhoods, but have sophisticated security systems, private guards, high gates, closed-circuit television, and all the electronic gadgetry needed to keep strangers out. This increases social distance, segregation, and isolation. Thus, 'São Paulo today is a city of walls.' Security, comfort, isolation, and status, according to Caldeira, sharpen even more strongly the discourses that disqualify people who live in *favelas* and slum tenements, the homeless and street children.

The greater challenge for local management of cities such as São Paulo lies in the repositioning of perverse forms of social relations that arise from segregation and hierarchy in urban space, and which today are not restricted to the old dichotomy between central and peripheral areas. These forms of social relations are at the root of social exclusion and the alarming increase in private violence in the large cities. At the same time they can block the creation of public spheres by strengthening stigmas, prejudices, and differences. Associated with fear, isolation, and insecurity are elements that impede the construction of a collective life dedicated to the public management of the common good. So it is important, in terms of political approaches for the cities, to point to experiences that open horizons to cope with the disjunction between poverty and inequality, on the one hand, and citizenship, on the other.

Development of an Urban Housing Policy

The new federal constitution of 1988 was enacted under pressure from organized civil society, within which various social actors transformed their demands into basic rights, to be inscribed in the constitution. Although much has already been written about this constitutional 'moment,' it would be useful to reiterate its multiple and complex meanings. New relationships were established between organized civil society and the legal institutional world through new developments, such as the legitimation of mechanisms for public representation of different interests; new processes of dialogue and negotiation; an emphasis on mediation and participatory democracy; a new legal order for collective and individual rights; and new demands to broaden civil participation in the development of social policies and laws. At the same time, however, it is possible to identify tensions, contradictions, and differences that place the 'popular energies' in confrontation with what remains of the 'old' conservative and authoritarian order. This old order attempted to isolate the new, when in fact it was well able to defeat many of the proposals of the popular forces (such as agrarian reform, which the strength of the rural landowners' lobby kept out of the Constitution).

In pointing to a new stage of conflict, we emphasize the complex scenario that developed after the enactment of Constitution of 1988 and that included the creation of new rights, some of which were immediately subsumed in a perverse process of reversal and removal, while others entered the 'dead letter' of the law, as they were never normatized.

In this context, the National Forum of Struggle for Urban Reform was born. The forum organized urban social movements, especially housing groups, NGOs, unions, human rights groups, and academic research centres that worked with the urban question. A new 'place' in organized civil society declared basic and elementary rights for urban life. Two fundamental principles guided the Urban Reform Forum. The first was that the social function of the city and of urban property should be guaranteed by what became known as 'urban rights' and various legal-political instruments; these included the normalization of property ownership; the expropriation of unused urban land; mechanisms to avoid real-estate speculation; the guarantee of possession or ownership of urban land; tax mechanisms to redistribute wealth; investments in housing in the 'social interest' for the city's poor; and the creation of social interest zones that could then receive heavy investments in infrastructure and social facilities. The second guiding principle was the democratic management of cities, by which citizenship was understood as the broad participation of the city's residents in defining their destinies (Urban Reform Forum 1992).

The urban-reform agenda was permeated by tension and hostility, particularly over the social function of urban property (the right to housing and ownership of urban land), which placed civil society in conflict, mainly with speculative real-estate capital. Nevertheless, it is important to emphasize that the new legal order opened up by the Constitution of 1988, which included 'urban rights' being understood as important social and political rights, constituted a principal space for the publicizing of conflicts around the management of cities. This in turn opened up other spheres for dispute and dialogue between social movements and local public administrators: the state constitutions and the municipal charters (a kind of cities' constitution that all municipalities had to proclaim) in 1989 and 1990, respectively, and the new spaces of participation created by municipal governments.

The Emergence of Democratic Local Government

This was the context for the emergence, in 1989, of democratic local governments in some of the largest and most important cities of the country, including São Paulo. Relying on the greater autonomy and decentralization offered by some elements of the new constitution, these local governments could implement innovative policies, introducing a new concept of social, political, and cultural governance. They reversed previous approaches to the 'social question,' opening new channels for dialogue and negotiation with organized sectors of civil society and implementing more universal social policies in an effort to extend the rights of citizenship to those previously excluded.

It was in this context also that Luiza Erundina of the Workers Party was elected to govern São Paulo from 1989 to 1992. The new mayor faced sharp conflict over demands to introduce social policies in the field of housing. The failure of the state regulatory system to implement social policies for the poor and other vulnerable groups became more evident. Earlier public policies had been marked by their stopgap and dysfunctional nature, resulting in the continuation of the long traditions of patronage, hand-outs, corruption, and clientelism; in general they were more effective at adding privileges to the range of private financial and speculative interests than they were at guaranteeing social rights, particularly given the precarious progress of these in Brazilian political culture.

This was the case with housing policies for low-income populations. From its creation in 1964 during the military dictatorship to its termination in 1986, the Sistema Financeiro Habitacional (SFH; Housing Finance System), administered by the Banco Nacional de Habitação (National Housing Bank), directed 70 per cent of its resources to the middle class and, as a consequence, stimulated speculation around large private-sector housing projects. The poor population continued to be excluded from decent housing, even at the end of the 1970s, when large amounts of public funds were directed to unemployment insurance and housing investments through the Fundo de Garantia por Tempo de Serviço (FGTS; Fund Guaranteed by Time of Employment). In São Paulo, from the 1950s to the 1980s, local administrations were subservient to the interests of large builders and were repressively engaged in violent evictions. Starting at the end of the 1970s and the beginning of the 1980s, they sought to confront the numerous and growing collective occupations of land by housing movements (in *favelas* and *cortiços*, and of the urban landless), at the same time as broad social movements, the 'new unionism' and new parties increasingly occupied the political arena, as we have discussed.

In a similar manner to the struggle of the rural landless movement, the invasion and occupation of urban lands – a common practice in all the nation's large cities – appears as the only, and thus a legitimate, way to gain access to housing. Public or private lands are invaded because of people's inability to pay high rents and, especially, because housing policies for the poor are precarious. This explains why the right to possess land is so important and why it encourages the mobilization of *favela* residents.

The Social Interest Housing Policy

When she became mayor of São Paulo, Luiza Erundina confronted the land invasions and sought to open dialogue with social movements and citizens' groups that were demanding partnership in the administration of public issues. In light of the depth and range of housing problems emerging in the city, the municipal government established a housing policy known as 'social interest,' giving priority in housing and urban planning to the needs of the poor and vulnerable people in the 'clandestine city.' This social policy was oriented to finance the renewal of *favelas*, the revitalization and reform of the *cortiços* in the central areas of the city, and the construction of housing projects in new districts and poor neighbourhoods. These projects were characterized by the involvement of residents through collective self-help groups known as *mutirões*, in which residents contributed their own labour. The traditional relationship between the government and recipients of government aid took on a new dimension – self-management of the projects and, more important, self-management of the public investment. Public resources and decision-making powers were transferred to legally organized community associations and/or housing co-operatives through a special municipal fund. In this way, the associations came to administer the production process, organize the worksite, prepare infrastructure and housing projects, and have a wide range of decision-making power, including the hiring of labour and technical assistance, such as architects, social workers, lawyers, and accountants. Together with these professionals, the housing groups discussed and defined all phases of construction, community services, internal regulations, payment methods, regulations for administrative work, and so on.

This innovative housing policy was most important for the manner in which it encouraged both tremendous consensus and great dissent, which helped characterize the municipal administration as a whole. An important initial aspect was the extreme diversity within the housing policy, which covered a range of different programs and subprograms, including those for *favelas* and *cortiços*, the construction of housing projects, regularization of property rights, legal assistance, and resources for the acquisition of urban land. The programs required the redefinition and regularization of road systems, water, sewerage, drainage, slope retention, opening of access, paving, and so on, according to the physical demands of the sites. Above all, the interventions attempted – not always successfully – to develop collective responsibility and to stimulate the awareness of citizenship with an environmental perspective, including interactions with the city.

Another immediate result was the high quality of housing built and its lack of standardization. This included architectural projects that were highly diversified and sophisticated, the use of innovative technologies and great flexibility in the construction of houses with an average floor space of 60 square metres, in contrast with the usual standard of housing for the poor of 20 square metres. The lower cost of this housing, compared to that built by the large private firms, is always emphasized as an important factor; the community associations received financing of some $6,000 for each housing unit. The return on this investment was defined after the completion of construction, according to family income and size.

These policies implied a new partnership between local government and the organized citizen housing movements, and explained the advance in collective struggle around the right to housing. Encouraged by the São Paulo experience, housing movements, NGOs, union movements, human rights groups, and various others stimulated a participatory process at the national level and without precedent in the country; this was the first popular initiative for legislation in the federal Congress in November 1991 – the creation of a national fund for popular housing. This proposal was generated in the midst of an intense debate among citizens' groups about the role of public funds destined for social development; this was the case of the Brazilian version of unemployment insurance and housing investments, the FGTS, mentioned above. The debate involved criticisms of the improper and often corrupt use of these public resources. At stake was the struggle for the restoration of the public function of state funds for social development because, as Francisco de Oliveira (1993, 78) revealed, in 'incomplete' welfare states such as Brazil, 'the funds are controlled by the state but the logic of the state is private.'

We will not go into the details of the national low-cost-housing fund, but mention it only to emphasize the 'democratic invention' that it inspired – a type of revival of the São Paulo experience in self-management processes. The idea of co-responsibility in the management of public programs is expressed in one article of the proposed legislation, which determined that the fund should have 'four-party' management, with representatives of the federal Congress and the federal government, the construction sector, building unions, and housing movements, assisted by NGOs and other citizen groups. Despite the limitations of the proposal, other negotiating forums were opened, and the social movements were able to use these for discussion about public funds for a low-income housing policy for the entire country, together with state housing and urban-development agencies, representatives of building companies, and other bodies.

Certainly, there were problems with the 'social interest' housing policy. One of the most visible was the issue of size. By the end of its administration in 1992 the Erundina government had built some

40,000 low-income houses or apartments (the next government halted some of these projects, as we will discuss below). Eleven thousand of these units were constructed under a system of self-management. This construction record was the target of criticism that served to illustrate the negative and petty nature of the opposition in the face of the enormous problems and precariousness of the housing situation.[11] Nevertheless, concerning the gravity of the housing problem in São Paulo, Lucio Kowarick and André Singer (1993, 208) argue that 'to build 40,000 houses is equivalent to building a city for some 200,000 people,' and while previous governments reached some 6,000 families through programs of urban development and improvements in *favelas*, by the end of the Erundina administration 41,000 families had benefited from government housing projects.

Another challenge confronting the local government over the program for the *favelas* was the non-approval of municipal legislation linked to the housing policy. In addition to the policy of urbanization of *favelas* through self-management that we are analysing here, the São Paulo government intended to concede the right to ownership of land at the 1,200 *favelas* located on public land.

In 1992, just before the end of the Erundina administration, the municipal housing legislation was put to a second vote in the city council, losing by only one vote. The position of council members – the majority in opposition to the government – revealed their prejudice and their refusal to recognize the *favela* residents as subjects with legitimate interests who had a right to housing and deserved to become owners of the property they occupied, and thus to escape from the world of exclusion; their position was entirely contrary to the notion of sharing resources, which would allow excluded groups to manage their own habitat – a habitat disputed by real-estate, financial, and other interests.

Another issue, mentioned by residents, professionals, and housing movement representatives, is indicative of the conflicts, tensions, and divisions within some of the construction projects (Silva 1996). This is the problem of hierarchical and authoritarian relations among residents, leaders, builders, technical professionals, and assistants; between 'those who know more' and 'those who know less,' between those who take care of the finances and those who carry out the construction. In yet other projects, discriminatory attitudes to the work of women were apparent. At the root of many of these divisions lay a vision of the centralization of power that militated against broader social work which would overcome the immediacy and individualism of the mere provision of houses, without concern for the collective project. Participants in the movements point to the persistence of the fragile tradition of democracy, revealing the dilemmas and difficulties of new forms of negotiation and representation under which the public dimension frequently could not be included in a collective work experiment.

With the 1992 mayoral elections came a change in administrations:[12] that of Luiza Erundina was followed by one from a different party – the conservative 'right-wing' government of Paulo Maluf (1993–6), from Partido Progressista Brasileiro (PPB). In addition to cutting the channels of communication and negotiation with the housing movements, Maluf halted the self-management experiment in almost all the projects. The excuse, as in this comment by the Municipal Housing Secretary quoted in the newspaper *Folha de São Paulo* on 4 February 1996, was that 'the residents do not have enough experience to manage resources, which were being wasted.' With the clear goal of benefit to the large private building companies, the Maluf government initiated the financing of new highways, tunnels, and other large and costly construction projects aimed at private transportation and housing for the city's elite. Only at the end of 1995 did the construction of low-income housing begin in the controversial 'Project Singapore,' which built high-rise apartment houses in *favelas*. This produced a kind of urban 'façade,' a 'slum wall' along the highways at the edge of the city. The *favelas* sprawled out behind the project, with their shacks without water, electricity, or sewerage. Only a few residents received the new apartments, and newspaper articles reported on the poor conditions in them: cracks, leaks, and non-functioning sewerage. Comparing those who moved to the new apartments with those who remained behind in the *favelas*, Maluf announced what we could call a new division of social classes in the Singapore projects: 'very soon, Singapore will create castes of slum-dwellers within the same *favela*' (*Folha de São Paulo* 13 October 1996).

On finishing his term at the end of 1996, Maluf had built only 3,800 low-cost housing units. On the eve of the election, a columnist commented upon a declaration issued by a group of some forty-five architects and planners known as the 'Urbanists for São Paulo,' which offered some comparative data: 'From [1993 to 1996] 3,800 families received housing at a cost of R$204 million [Brazilian reals].' The article presents estimates by the Economic Research Foundation Institute of

the University of São Paulo, that 450,000 families live in *favelas*; it concludes that, 'at the pace of the Singapore project, the eradication of the
favelas would take 409 years to provide *less indecent* housing to the
entire *favela* population in São Paulo' (emphasis added). The article
also mentions a comparison with a highway complex that includes a
large tunnel built by Maluf (the large majority of the city's population
– which is poor – does not use these tunnels, in which public transportation is prohibited; they are reserved for people with cars): 'the South-
west-Centre Corridor, which includes the tunnel running under the
Ibirapuera Park, cost US$1.28 billion, to serve some 50,000 people ...
With these resources it would be possible to build, at international
prices, 20 kilometres of subway which would serve 450,000 people per
day or nine times more than the corridor' (Rossi 1996).

It is important to emphasize that in a massive political marketing
strategy, works such as the Singapore project were presented by the
media as projects offering the status of citizenship, although they did
not even offer the right to ownership or possession of the apartments.
This was a case of 'virtual citizenship.' According to Pinheiro (1996),
this reinforces the 'consecration of the simulacrum' which the 'virtual
projects' of Maluf control by 'addressing the citizens as "mere political
consumers" and not as bearers of rights and responsibilities in a new
modernized version of right-wing populism' (Pinheiro 1996). In October 1996, the population of São Paulo elected Maluf's ally to succeed
him; this administration is now mired in a major corruption scandal
over the improper use of public funds and has little likelihood of
bringing forward policies that address the 'social question.'

Conclusions

The scene we have described is disillusioning in that it points to the
return of the practices of patronage and authoritarianism so deeply
rooted in Brazilian political culture. Nevertheless, it is important to
emphasize the positive aspects of the housing policy analysed here.
First, it was one of the innovative experiments selected by the Brazilian
government for presentation at Habitat II in 1996, as one of Brazil's
'best practices.' In addition, various important experiments were
developed by other democratic governments in Brazilian cities that
demonstrated the possibility of opening up new fields for dialogue on
the administration of cities, new spaces for negotiation of social policies and norms, and new fields of popular representation guided by a

'culture of the rights of citizenship' – understood as a life with dignity and social justice on the plane of public policy.[13]

In this way, in spite of its conflicts, difficulties, and tensions, the housing policy we have discussed points out an important issue for the democratic sustainability of cities. By highlighting the construction of 'decent' housing (as described by residents, professionals, and community leaders) through a diversity of programs, standards, and plans that were discussed and negotiated with those involved, the policy revealed the importance of the sharing of responsibilities for the administration of public policies. By opening new spaces for dialogue, negotiation, and participation, it showed how the government of a large city such as São Paulo could develop public policies aimed at the poorest and most excluded. In spite of the problems that accompanied this social experiment, we can affirm that the awareness of 'the right to have rights' (Arendt 1981; Lefort 1988) could find in the economic and political scene of the 1990s 'bridges' that offer exits or passages to spaces where poverty and inequality could be articulated with citizenship.

The municipal administration in partnership with the network of social actors has generated the democratic norm, a process stimulated by the legal 'images' of a new order and of social rights. The process triggered 'democratic inventions' at the level of new forms of legality, as well as other experiments in municipal administration. We are not dealing with implemented norms or standards, because in São Paulo the proposed legislation to allow *favela* residents possession of their land was not approved; rather, we are concerned with norms reinvented in the democratic field in which some 'passages' can be seen within the scope of 'social' law. With this we wish to maintain that local public policies – such as the plan to organize the *favelas* by means of self-management or co-management and the proposed legislation for ownership – was negotiated and agreed upon by housing movements and other important social actors. Moreover, it was negotiated in its form as a 'social law' which, as François Ewald (1986, 46) indicated, 'seeks to be an instrument of intervention to compensate or correct inequalities, ... a law of positive discrimination.' In this sense it is important to emphasize that, if today we still witness the brutal evictions of the urban homeless and landless, we also witness a new perception of public and social responsibility that some judges and lawyers have raised in their rulings, thereby increasing awareness of the conflicts between the right to housing and the right to landownership.

Another question concerning 'democratic construction' in the context of local public policies can be raised: to what degree can 'urban rights' be translated as basic social rights in the face of this devastating wave of destitution of rights? A review of documents produced by the Urban Reform Forum, published in NGO newspapers, revealed the contempt with which the federal government has cut these spaces of dialogue and negotiation, at the same time as it is cutting support for social policies and social programs, exemplified by the trend to privatization of health and education in the entire country. Thus these actors, without giving up the space of policy debate, have severely criticized the generality with which proposed legislation or policies presented by the government treat the principles that broaden the active exercise of citizenship: the lack of availability of investments for housing, infrastructure, and development; the cuts in important social spending; and, most of all, the lack of dedication and non-adoption of proposed legislation which has been widely discussed and approved by different members of civil society – business, unions, social movements, and NGOs. These criticisms point to the lack of political will to deal with social policies that would allow the integration of broad contingents of the excluded. This would imply confronting the question of landownership to make the right to land and housing effective by regulating – a decade after the approval of the constitution – the social function of property.

If all of this has not led to greater participation by important social actors at the national level, it nevertheless points to the fact that innovative public policies implemented by local democratic governments can create a public space where the rights to citizenship can be extended to those situated on the 'borders' of Brazilian society.

Notes

1 The term 'new pariahs' refers to those suffering stigmatization arising from new forms of poverty and social inequality; more important, 'pariah' is used by Hannah Arendt to refer to those deprived of the singular experience of participation in public space through a word or action which would allow them a share in rights and a common sense of belonging (Arendt 1981).

2 For a critical sociological view of Marshall's work see Bryan Turner 1992 and 1993.

3 Important variables that measure life expectancy, educational level, income of residents, and so on, show that blacks and those of mixed race (47 per cent of the national population) have higher levels of illiteracy, have greater difficulty entering a university, and suffer discrimination in the labour market. Beyond the general data on unemployment, underemployment, and precarious working conditions, data about the 'feminization' of poverty (an enormous contingent of poor and 'single' women are today their families' providers) reveal that women are still paid less than men; if they are women and black, the discrimination is sharper (U.N. Development Programme 1996).

4 The presidency of Getúlio Vargas (1930–54), including his dictatorial coup in 1937.

5 'This meant that the employer's dominant power – to exploit the workers' productivity, to establish discipline through brutality, to extend the working day or to intensify production, to calculate wages, to pay 'persons' and not exactly workers, to dismiss whomever and whenever they liked and so on – was exercised in the same traditional arbitrary and personal way as it had for the then-free workers in the previous slave system. Labour relations were still governed by private verbal agreements slightly "adjusted" to the novelty of the feeble liberalism of the new republican order. Thus, to work outside a legal contract and guarantee was a common practice for more than 40 years and which – as an informal situation – persisted far beyond the subsequent regulation of labour relations' (Paoli 1992, 148).

6 The role of legislation in urban exclusion is brilliantly described in Raquel Rolnik's (1995) doctoral thesis. There are many studies that deal with the concept of urban social apartheid; among others, the work of Sidney Chalhoub (1986, 1996), Rolnik (1995), Sérgio Adorno (1990), Maria Auxiliadora De Decca (1987), and Maria Célia Paoli (1991).

7 Michel Foucault's work has had a major influence on Brazilian studies of the 'new' social history, especially his *Discipline and Punish* ([*Vigiar e Punir*] 1987), which gave rise to many analyses that explain the urban social apartheid influenced by the ideology of 'hygienization' of the cities, as a means of controlling social conflict in urban spaces.

8 '[T]hey excluded those involved in the so-called informal economy (like street peddlers, temporary labour, outdoor factories, and home workers) as well as unemployed people and women and children, for whom excessively expensive legal protection produced unemployment, except when they accepted work "outside the law" (which they did); not to mention rural workers, who were to obtain their rights many years later. These people were in fact thrown into "modern" illegality and thus subject to

moral suspicion, repression, and vigilance, since they failed to become "legal" established workers' (Paoli 1992, 152).

9 These are families who cannot meet the costs of basic food on their low incomes. The majority of the family members are of school age, or are out of school but illiterate. For some families, unemployment leaves them in a more vulnerable relationship with the formal labour market. (The unemployment rate among the poorest families grew from 18.1 per cent in 1990 to 24.6 per cent in 1994.) The great majority of these families receive from one to three minimum salaries per month (from US$110 to US$350). They have 'informal' jobs, which are temporary and insecure, compounding the problem of low salaries (SEADE 1995).

10 The most recent example of these was the videotape shown on national and international television (CNN) of police in greater São Paulo beating, killing, and torturing people who were stopped on the street – the case of *favela Naval* in Diadema, a poor city of the metropolitan area, in April 1997.

11 At the time there was said to be a deficit of 1 million residences in São Paulo. Recent data from the Brazilian Institute of Geography and Statistics are considered more realistic; they indicate a deficit for all of Brazil of some 6.4 million residences, concentrated mostly in the cities of the north and northeast. But this is a polemical question that demands more reliable data in view of the growing precariousness of housing in São Paulo.

12 Under the Brazilian constitution, a mayor can serve only one four-year term.

13 As an example we can cite the participatory budget process implemented in the southern city of Porto Alegre; this is now recognized nationally and internationally, and has been reproduced in other Brazilian cities. Other examples are of social-policy practices of popular councils that are not limited to the organized movements but involve common citizens as well in alternative economic projects; forums for negotiations between unions, the government, business, and popular movements; policies such as the guaranteed minimum income at the local level; the People's Bank, and new versions of the Grameen Bank of Bangladesh, which offer investments and financing for the poorest of the poor.

References

Adorno, Sérgio. 1988. *Os aprendizes do poder – o bacharelismo liberal na política brasileira*. Rio de Janeiro: Paz e Terra.

– 1990. 'A gestão filantrópica da pobreza.' *São Paulo em Perspectiva* (São Paulo, SEADE) 4/2 (April/June): 9–17.

Arendt, Hannah. 1981. *A condição humana*. Rio de Janeiro: Forense.

Bourdieu, Pierre. 1993. *La misère du monde*. Paris: Seuil.

Caldeira, Teresa. 1992. 'City of Walls: Crime, Segregation and Citzenship in São Paulo.' PhD dissertation in Anthropology, University of California at Berkeley.

– 1997. 'Enclaves fortificados: a nova segregação urbana.' *Novos Estudos* (São Paulo, CEBRAP) 47: 155–76.

Chalhoub, Sidney. 1986. *Trabalho, lar e botequim – o cotidiano dos trabalhadores no Rio de Janeiro*. São Paulo: Brasiliense.

– 1996. *Cidade febril – cortiços e epidemias na Corte imperial*. São Paulo: Companhia das Letras.

De Decca, Maria Auxiliadora. 1987. *A vida fora das fábricas – cotidiano operário em São Paulo (1920–1934)*. Rio de Janeiro: Paz e Terra.

Ewald, François. 1986. *L'état providence*. Paris: Grasset.

FIPE [Fundação Instituto de Pesquisas Econômicas da Universidade de São Paulo]. 1993. *Favelas e Cortiços na Cidade de São Paulo*. São Paulo: FIPE.

Forum Nacional de Reforma Urbana. 1992. *Carta de Princípios*. São Paulo: Forum Nacional de Reforma Urbana.

Foucault, Michel. 1987. *Vigiar e Punir* [*Discipline and Punish*], 5th ed. Rio de Janeiro: Vozes.

Gonçalves, M.A. 1996. 'O olhar fora do lugar.' *Folha de São Paulo*, 17 November.

Hall, Michael, and Paulo Sergio Pinheiro. 1986. *On Widening the Scope of Latin American Working-Class History: Some General Considerations and a Brazilian Case Study*. São Paulo: IFCH/UNICAMP.

Kowarick, Lucio. 1988. *As lutas sociais e a cidade*. Rio de Janeiro: Paz e Terra/ UNRISD.

Kowarick, Lucio, and André Singer. 1993. 'A experiência do PT na Prefeitura de São Paulo.' *Novos Estudos* 35(March): 195–216.

Lefort, Claude. 1988. *Democracy and Political Theory*. Cambridge: Polity Press/ Basil Blackwell.

Marshall, T.H. 1967. *Cidadania, classe social e status*. Rio de Janeiro: Zahar. (First published in English, as *Class, Citizenship and Social Development*. New York: Doubleday, 1964.)

O Estado de São Paulo. 1997. [News item], 10 April: A-11.

de Oliveira, Francisco. 1993. 'A metamorfose do arribaça.' *Novos Estudos* 27(July): 67–92.

Paoli, Maria Célia. 1989. 'Trabalhadores e cidadania: experiência do mundo público na história do Brasil moderno.' *Estudos Avançados* (São Paulo, USP) 3/7: 4–66.

- 1991. 'São Paulo operária e suas imagens, 1900–1940.' *Espaço e Debates* (São Paulo, NERU) 11/33: 27–41.
- 1992. 'Citzenship and Inequalities: The Making of a Public Space in Brazilian Experience.' *Social and Legal Studies* 1: 134–59.
- 1995. 'Movimentos Sociais no Brasil: em busca de um estatuto político.' In *Movimentos Sociais e Democracia no Brasil*, ed. M. Hellman, 24–55. São Paulo: Marco Zero.
Pinheiro, Paulo Sergio. 1996. 'A consagração do simulacro.' *Folha de São Paulo*, 27 October: 1–3.
Rolnik, Raquel. 1981. 'Cada um no seu lugar.' Master's dissertation, Faculty of Architecture and Urban Planning, University of São Paulo.
- 1995. 'The City and the Law.' PhD dissertation, New York University.
Rossi, C. 1996. 'Cingapura, ano 409.' *Folha de São Paulo*, 24 September: 1–2.
Sader, Eder. 1988. *Quando novos personagens entraram em cena – experiências e lutas dos trabalhadores na Grande São Paulo*. Rio de Janeiro: Paz e Terra.
Santos, Wanderley Guilherme. 1979. *Cidadania e Justiça*. Rio de Janeiro: Campus.
Schwarz, Roberto. 1988. *Ao vencedor as batatas*, 3d ed. São Paulo: Duas Cidades.
SEADE [Sistema Estadual de Análise de Dados e Estatística]. 1995. *Report of Quality of Life*. São Paulo: SEADE.
SEMPLA. [Secretaria Municipal de Planejamento]. 1995. *Dossiê São Paulo*. São Paulo: SEMPLA.
da Silva, Ana Amelia. 1996. 'Cidadania, Conflitos e Agendas Sociais – das favelas urbanizadas aos fóruns internacionais.' Doctoral dissertation in Sociology, University of São Paulo.
Souto, A.L.S., and J. Kayano. 1996. *São Paulo – a cidade e seu governo: o olhar do cidadão*. São Paulo: POLIS.
Telles, Vera. 1996. 'Questão social: afinal, do que se trata?' *São Paulo em Perspectiva* (São Paulo, SEADE) 10/4: 85–95.
Turner, Bryan S. 1992. 'Outline of a Theory of Citzenship.' In *Dimensions of Radical Democracy*, ed. C. Mouffe, 33–62. London: Verso.
- 1993. *Citizenship and Social Theory*. London: Sage.
U.N. Development Programme. 1995. *Human Development Report*. New York: United Nations Development Programme.
- 1996. *Human Development Report*. New York: United Nations Development Programme.

9 Downtown San Salvador: Housing, Public Spaces, and Economic Transformation

MARIO LUNGO

The current state of development of central San Salvador is in many ways paradoxical.[1] While, on the one hand, its commercial dynamism negates any suggestion of economic decline, on the other hand, El Salvador's capital city presents a patent case of spatial segregation and social exclusion with a clear social and spatial division between the old city-centre and high-income areas (see figure 9.1).

Important changes have occurred in central San Salvador's economy. In a movement that began in the 1950s, becoming more pronounced in later decades and especially since the late 1960s, bank headquarters, specialized business services, and the most prestigious department stores have moved out of the old historical core and relocated to the city's west side (see figure 9.4). In addition, the construction of luxury hotels and modern shopping centres was accompanied by the relocation of high-income families to the west-side area, this latter movement having started in the 1930s and continuing into recent years.

A significant number of consumer-oriented small and medium-sized businesses remain, however, in the downtown area. The suggestion that downtown San Salvador needs to be economically revitalized is therefore not entirely correct. Such a negative diagnostic rests on a mistaken supposition that confuses physical deterioration, spatial segregation, and social exclusion with economic decline. We must equally reject the idea that it is possible for downtown San Salvador to return to the way it was before the middle of this century. The old historical centre has changed. Rather than economic revitalization per se, the real challenge is to initiate a process that will combine physical reconstruction with the restoration of public spaces and residential functions, taking advantage of the commercial dynamism of the city-centre. Such a policy would be instrumental in contributing to the reversal of the processes of spatial segregation and social exclusion.

In this sense, rather than concentrating on the rehabilitation of old buildings, as in the historical centres of numerous Latin American cities, the aim is to promote an integrated recovery plan. This will include remedial work on streets and public transportation where respect for the historical urban design is essential (Salazar 1996), in addition to the restoration of the few remaining buildings of historical value in the city's central area.

The profound transformations that have occurred in central San Salvador, however, raise two questions:

1/ Has the social differentiation that now exists between downtown and high-income west-side areas produced an irreversibly 'divided city,' given the prevailing degree of spatial segregation and levels of social exclusion?
2/ Does this process of sociospatial separation necessarily preclude the possibility of socially sustainable development in the case of San Salvador?

The response to these questions is crucial to the city's future, as well as to the challenges faced by urban policy makers and all downtown inhabitants. It will require a new form of urban governance that is democratic, participatory, and flexible. In metaphorical terms, the challenge is to construct 'permanent urban bridges' by way of local policies and institutions that make the central area an urban space that is increasingly integrative and inclusive, reducing inequality and social exclusion, and promoting socially sustainable development:

> For the management of a city to be successful, its policies need to be conducive to social sustainability. Social sustainability for a city is defined as development that is compatible with the harmonious evolution of civil society, fostering an environment conducive to the compatible cohabitation of culturally and socially diverse groups while at the same time encouraging social integration, with improvements in the quality of life for all segments of the population. (Polèse and Stren 1995, 8)

The fight against spatial segregation and exclusion, especially crucial in the old historical centre, given its present state, is fundamental in the case of San Salvador. This will require an increase in the number of local residents, and the restoration of public spaces (plazas and parks), and their uses. This will not be easy for downtown San Salvador; its current state can almost be equated with an 'urban apartheid space,' shunned by large sectors of the more well-off population, and as such must indeed be seen as an obstacle to socially sustainable development.

The Historical Development of Downtown San Salvador

The physical and social deterioration, and the profound changes in downtown San Salvador's economy, were accentuated by the rapid urbanization experienced in the nation over the last four decades. In recent years, moreover, economic restructuring, globalization, and regional integration have assigned a new role to the city in the Central American region (Lungo 1993).

Founded more than 450 years ago, San Salvador was consolidated at the beginning of the twentieth century and became the country's main economic and political-administrative urban centre. This took place in the context of the surging rise of the agro-export development model largely based on the production and commercialization of coffee (Browning 1975; Lindo 1990). Firms manufacturing liquor, ground coffee, beverages, soaps, and other consumer items, as well as import–export brokers, banks, and insurance companies, all appeared during the first four decades of this century (Martin 1981; Lungo and Baires 1988).

Most of this activity was initially concentrated in downtown San Salvador, bringing changes in land-use patterns. Between the end of the nineteenth and the middle of the twentieth century, the modern symbols of a capital city were put in place: the national palace, the national theatre, the cathedral, high buildings of up to eight storeys, bank headquarters, hotels, and service agencies, all compactly surrounded the main central plazas.

This evolution corresponded, although at a more modest scale, to similar urban-development models in other Latin American cities, where the construction of luxury homes in certain central areas coincided with the emergence of housing sectors for poor ('popular') groups, in turn creating a perceived 'social problem' (Arango 1989). High-income residents of downtown San Salvador began to leave, moving to the city's west side in the 1930s, completely abandoning the area by the 1950s. The low-income population started to inhabit the abandoned high-income residences in the 1930s, giving rise to a new type of housing that became common in the central areas of many Latin American cities: the *mesones*, or large houses subdivided into small rooms, each of which is occupied by a family. As a result of these changes, sociospatial segregation became manifest.

Nevertheless, the city's centre remained a public and socially integrated space and meeting place for different social groups until after the middle of this century. It continued as the site of bank headquarters, of specialized business services, of most governmental institutions, and of the few luxury hotels and restaurants then in existence, and also as the location of the casinos and social clubs of the rich that shared the central space with the offices of labour unions and artisans' associations. In those days, one still spoke of 'going downtown,' mostly at night for festive occasions and weekends. The city's festivals during the first week of August were especially popular, organized with the participation of society's wealthiest women (Rodriguez 1997). The city-centre acted, in sum, as a public space in which people of various social origins coexisted and crossed paths.

Since the 1950s, the gradual exodus of high-income downtown residents has been followed by the main economic functions. The majority of the city's population made a deliberate attempt to avoid downtown and merely to 'pass through the centre,' a place now characterized by urban violence, as is the case for many other Latin American central cities: 'Without a doubt, in opposition to the security of private space – the house – the violence of the public space – the street – is one of the principal daily characteristics of the metropolis of industrialized underdevelopment: public space in the metropolis constitutes the negation of the citizenry ...' (Kowarick 1991, 92).

The transformation of the city centre accelerated drastically during the 1960s in the era of the economic policy of import substitution and the creation of the Central American Common Market. The dynamics of the urban economy changed; new industrial zones were established, the financial system broadened, and the business-service sector grew. As a result there was a rapid expansion of new residential developments, demanding drastic modifications to roadways, the public transportation system, and other infrastructure (see figure 9.1).

These were the years of rapid growth and the formation of the San Salvador Metropolitan Area as a planning entity, culminating in an ambitious urban development plan, known as 'Metroplan 80' (CONA-PLAN 1969). The plan stressed the role of the San Salvador urban area within its own local environment, as well as within the broader eco-

Figure 9.1 San Salvador City-Centre and the Current High-Income Zones
Source: SIT-OPAMSS

High Income Zone

Historic Centre

1 km

nomic space of the Central American region. The plan allocated subordinate status to the city's centre. In spite of the low level of implementation of Metroplan 80, this nonetheless contributed to the tendency in subsequent years of giving only minimal attention to the centre's specific problems and generally neglecting its pivotal position within the city.

This evolution received a strong impetus from the earthquake of 10 October 1986, which destroyed a significant number of buildings in downtown San Salvador. As the headquarters of the major banks, insurance companies, and financial institutions fled downtown for the west side, the central area came largely to be occupied by 'informal' economic activities, informal street vendors, small artisans, and the like. The exodus of the financial institutions from the centre and the rise of new commercial centres in the west during the 1980s has been documented in a recent study (Lungo and Baires 1995).

The profound transformation and deterioration of central San Salvador continues to this day, and has given rise to numerous discussions and ideas for downtown revitalization. The debate, however, has been limited to physical restoration and road improvements, as presented, for example, in the urban development plan (*Plan de Desarrollo del Area Metropolitana de San Salvador* [PLAMADUR 1996]) and the transportation plan currently being drawn up for the metropolitan area. It is important, within the context of socially sustainable development, to introduce issues such as social networks and social capital (Portes 1998) that relate to informal economic activities and their links with social exclusion and sociospatial segregation, the lack of local urban policies and the new type of urban management that it is necessary to promote.[2] It is also necessary, more specifically, to restore the residential function and public spaces in the downtown.

Both the restoration and renovation of residential uses in the centre as well as the renovation of public spaces (parks, plazas, and streets) must explicitly seek to mix different social groups. There are no significant racial or ethnic divisions (or conflicts) in San Salvador, but the deep economic and social divisions within the Salvadoran population remains a major factor behind the high level of spatial segregation and social exclusion.

Land Use and the Disappearance of Public Spaces in the Centre

PLAMADUR's 'Plan for the Revitalization of the Historic Centre' has

Table 9.1 Characteristics of Central San Salvador

	City centre	Consolidated centre
Number of blocks in zone	59	130
Buildings of historical value	350	134
Land use (% of total area)		
Commerce	83.0	66.0
Education/recreation	3.0	10.0
Housing	0.2	11.0
Other	13.8	13.0

Source: PLAMADUR 1996

defined two zones in the central area: the 'City Centre' and the 'Consolidated Centre,' shown in figure 9.2, in addition to the 'Central Commercial District,' defined by the San Salvador Metropolitan Area Planning Office (OPAMSS) at the end of the 1980s.

The PLAMADUR preliminary analysis identifies different characteristics for the 'city-centre' and the 'consolidated centre,' as shown in table 9.1. The city-centre presents the greater level of physical transformation as it has the highest number of empty lots (Lungo and Oporto 1998) and buildings destroyed by the 1986 earthquake, while the consolidated centre is more compact, although it has a lower density of buildings (structures averaging one to two storeys).

Although commercial use is clearly predominant in the city-centre, giving it a monofunctional character that reinforces spatial segregation and social exclusion, the consolidated centre features an important number of educational activities (secondary schools and universities). A significant number of government institutions are included in both zones; the north side of the consolidated centre in particular contains the institutional complex known as the 'Government Centre,' which houses various ministries, the legislative assembly, and the headquarters of autonomous agencies. This general institutional and physical environment should in principle be conducive to the restoration of lost residential functions and recuperation of public spaces.

Another study (ISAM/Konrad Adenauer Stiftung 1994) noted that recreational space made up only 1.9 per cent of the total area, which demonstrates the shortage of public spaces in the downtown area. Such spaces are often occupied by sidewalk vendors and shops, an

Figure 9.2 Downtown San Salvador
Source: SIT-OPAMSS

integral part of the processes of change in the downtown urban economy, a result both of the concentration of public transportation routes and the saturation of the Central Market facilities, but also of the absence of a clear urban development policy for downtown (see box).

- There are streets in downtown San Salvador where up to 636 buses an hour run.
- 54 per cent of sidewalk and roadway space is occupied by street vendors.
- Only one-third of street vendors are from San Salvador County.
- 89 per cent of buildings are occupied by stores or warehouses.

OPAMSS 1995 data reveal that, for the entire municipality of San Salvador, only 2.12 per cent of the land was used for green spaces (VMVDU 1996). If the public spaces in the downtown have historically been few in number, their disappearance has accelerated over the last decades, a trend that clearly runs counter to what we have termed socially sustainable development.

Residential Functions

A clearer understanding of the loss of residential functions in the downtown area can be gained through analysing its demographic growth in relation to the San Salvador metropolitan area and the municipality. As table 9.2 shows, the municipality's total population more than doubled between 1950 and 1992, and its density tripled. However, the demographic weight of the municipality within the metropolitan area declined from 80 per cent to 40 per cent.

What these data fail to reveal is that most of the growth occurred in the municipality's westside area. PLAMADUR has calculated that only 13,000 people live at present in downtown San Salvador, even though the area's carrying capacity is in excess of 60,000.

In spite of the lack of studies on the social composition of the downtown population, a significant number of older persons living alone and street children living alone or in groups can be identified. PLA-MADUR has estimated from 1992 census data that 48 per cent of the population is over twenty-five years of age, 53 per cent has had primary education (nine years), and 14 per cent has completed secondary

Table 9.2 San Salvador: Population Growth, 1950–1992

	1950	1961	1971	1992
San Salvador Metro. Area (SSMA)				
total population	213,363	352,299	564,967	1,494,000
Municipality of San Salvador				
total population	171,270	255,744	338,154	442,664
popt'n. as % of SSMA	80	73	60	40
growth rate	–	49	32	31
density (pop'n/km^2)	2,371	3,540	4,680	6,127

Source: National Census

school (twelve years). The available information is clearly insufficient for drawing definite conclusions. However, the abandonment of the residential function is revealed by the estimated number of downtown San Salvador's remaining inhabitants, who now make up only 3 per cent of the municipality's population.

This population decline is also related to the almost non-existent investment in new housing in the central area of the city, be it by the state or by the private sector. Gradually, the old homes in the centre have deteriorated and have been converted into *mesones*, commercial spaces, and small offices. At the same time, many old residences have been abandoned, left unattended, part of the generalized process of urban degradation which still continues (Lungo forthcoming).

In 1947 it was estimated that *mesones* constituted 40 per cent of total housing in those municipalities which today make up the San Salvador metropolitan area, a figure reaching 58 per cent in 1975 (FUNDASAL 1976). Exact information on the current number of *mesones* in the central area is unavailable, but a recent study (FUNDASAL 1995) showed that the importance of *mesones* among the various housing categories in the metropolitan area had declined since 1971 (see table 9.3). Furthermore, the destruction of a good number of *mesones* in the 1986 earthquake reduced the downtown population even further. The 1986 earthquake information shown in table 9.4 reveals the heavy loss of *mesones*.

PLAMADUR's recent estimates, based on the 1992 census, indicated the existence of 4,300 dwelling units in the centre of San Salvador, occupied by an average of 3.5 persons. Four per cent of the units were empty.

Table 9.3 San Salvador Metropolitan Area: Types of Urban Housing

Housing type	1971 (%)	1977 (%)	1986 (%)	1993 (%)
Slums	8.9	9.0	11.8	11.4
Mesones	31.7	27.8	9.9	7.8
Unregulated settlements	19.3	15.8	16.5	16.1
Other	40.1	47.4	61.8	64.7

Source: FUNDASAL 1995

Table 9.4 San Salvador Central Area: Number of Rooms in
Mesones Before and After the 1986 Earthquake

	Before		After	
	Rooms	Population	Rooms	Population
Central Area*	9,903	54,474	2,643	11,890

Source: Lungo 1988 (from official statistics)
*Includes various neighbourhoods which are not part of the
PLAMADUR limits

Of the downtown inhabitants included in the census, 50 per cent
lived in independent houses, 20 per cent in apartments, and 20 per cent
in mesones. These figures, while approximate, indicate that about 2,600
individuals live in mesones in the city's centre. A comparison with the
number estimated for the principal neighbourhoods of San Salvador
affected by the 1986 earthquake would indicate that the meson is
important on the fringes of the city's centre, especially in the southeast
area.

This finding is significant for the adjacent zones of the south and
east where the majority of the municipality's slums are also concentrated (FUNDASAL 1995; see figure 9.3). Many of the individuals who
work in the centre probably live in these areas. With respect to forms of
housing tenancy, the PLAMADUR study indicates that, of the almost
half of the population which participated in the census, 44 per cent
were renters; of this figure, 41 per cent were renters of mesones, and 35
per cent of independent houses. Housing tenancy is an important element of urban social sustainability related to one's sense of belonging

Figure 9.3 San Salvador Metropolitan Area: Location of Slums and Illegal Settlements
Source: SIT-OPAMSS

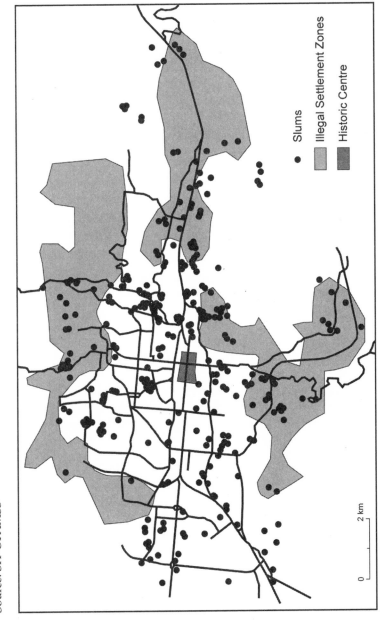

Slums

Illegal Settlement Zones

Historic Centre

0   2 km

to the area one lives in, not only as a passing resident but also as a stakeholder. Access to home ownership and a new rental law are particularly vital, and any plan for downtown residential revival must address this issue.

The Changing Economic Profile of the Central Area

The importance of downtown San Salvador for the city's economy is directly related to the presence of commercial, financial, and service activities, especially since there has never been any significant concentration of manufacturing industry in the downtown area (see figure 9.4). The exodus since the 1960s of bank headquarters, insurance companies, and financial institutions, as well as of stores serving high-income populations, has had numerous negative consequences.

These trends do not, however, necessarily imply a decline in the economic vitality of downtown, but rather a profound transformation in the mix of activities (see table 9.5) resulting in a downtown economy characterized by the following:

- services mainly oriented towards consumers and final demand;
- the predominance of small and micro-enterprises;
- the predominance of the informal labour market.

These changes have in turn affected the demand for housing and public space, and have also involved a restructuring of local urban stakeholders.

The changes in the downtown San Salvador economy have occurred within a context of a highly informalized metropolitan economy. Although the data presented in table 9.6 are for the metropolitan area, including the municipality, PLAMADUR has estimated that 54 per cent of employees in the central area work in the informal sector. It is likely that the number of employees in commerce and informal service activities is even higher in the downtown area. According to estimates by the municipality, the Central Market alone generates around 20,000 jobs, most of them in the informal sector.

The downtown area also has a high level of urban poverty and violence. The metropolitan area's poverty rate is around 40 per cent (of total families), with 30 per cent of that number being headed by women. In addition, the high levels of violence have a major effect on commercial activities in the downtown area. An opinion survey con-

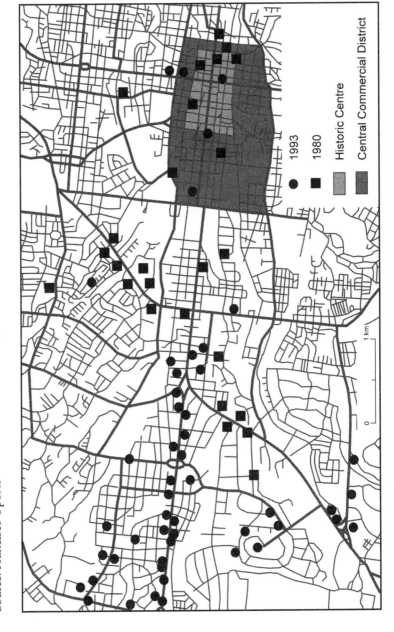

Figure 9.4 San Salvador: Location of Commercial and Service Establishments, 1980 and 1993
Source: Francisco Oporto

Table 9.5 Municipality of San Salvador:
Employment of Residents, 1992

Sector	% of employed residents
Services	52.39
Commerce	22.39
Industry	17.95
Construction	5.97
Agriculture	1.30

Source: 1992 census

Table 9.6 San Salvador Metropolitan Area: Distribution (%) of Employment in the Informal Economy, 1988–9 and 1994

	1988–9	1994
By industrial sector		
Manufacturing	21.3	24.9
Construction	5.8	6.0
Commerce	42.1	39.0
Transport/communications	6.6	6.2
Finances	0.4	0.2
Services	12.9	13.5
By occupational class		
Managers	6.1	8.0
Owners	55.3	56.2
Relative without remuneration	9.2	12.0
Permanent salaried	11.1	11.0
Temporary salaried	18.4	11.6

Source: Briones 1996

ducted by the Chamber of Commerce and a downtown university shows that the most significant problems in this respect are, in order of importance: delinquency, traffic congestion, juvenile gangs, the lack of parking space, street vendors, and deficiencies in the collection of solid waste (CCIES/Universidad Tecnológica 1995).

Spatial Segregation and Social Exclusion

Brief analysis of the city's spatial development clearly reveals spatial segregation and social inequality. This is particularly true when looking at the differences between the western and southwestern zones, on the one hand, and the downtown area and eastern and northeastern zones, on the other. But closer examination also reveals the existence of poverty 'pockets' in the higher-income zones along the city's ravines.

Downtown San Salvador is characterized as an area of generalized physical degradation, which also contains small pockets of extreme poverty, especially in the south and southeast, where the majority of the municipality of San Salvador's small-scale slums can be found. These divisions are accompanied by inequalities in the provision of infrastructure and social services, although the differences are less noticeable for infrastructure.

While San Salvador is a spatially segregated city that has pockets of poverty in certain distinct areas, the downtown area could be described as one concentrated pocket of poverty in the middle of the city.

The spatial segregation observed in large cities of developing nations has often served as a basis for a dualistic interpretation of the city. However, this rather unidimensional interpretation of urban duality has been widely criticized (Balbo 1991) as residential segregation is only one of the factors contributing to urban social exclusion, albeit an important one. A recent study attempting to measure social exclusion in three Central American nations defined exclusion as 'the mechanisms by which persons and groups are rejected from participation in exchanges, practices and constituent rights of social integration and, therefore, of an identity' (author's translation [FLACSO/ UNDP 1995, 25]). These mechanisms include exclusion from information and decision-making processes, exclusion from access to services, and exclusion resulting from the various mechanisms that promote segregation: social norms, prohibitions, controls which are illegal and/or tolerated. However, the FLACSO/ UNDP (1995) study failed to incorporate the territorial dimension totally. Particularly in the case of large cities, spatial segregation as well as localized urban poverty should be included as indicators of social exclusion (Rolnik and Cymbalista 1997).

The concept of exclusion, a concept which goes beyond the simple measurement of poverty or of spatial segregation, also allows us to introduce another element – social vulnerability, which has demonstrated its usefulness in recent studies as a means of depicting the complexity of urban processes (Moser 1996).

A study currently in progress (Sabatini 1997) presents an interesting attempt to broaden the concept of segregation. Starting from the premise that the social segregation of space is a common trait of Western cities, especially in Latin America, even more so than the presence of poverty, the study suggests that the segregation of urban space involves three major dimensions: (1) differences in the welfare levels (of populations) of different zones; (2) geographic divisions among residential areas; (3) subjective social segregation.

While the first dimension relates to poverty and the second to spatial segregation, the third refers to an aspect of urban reality that is absent from most analyses – the self-perception of the city's inhabitants. These three dimensions can indeed constitute a template for describing urban social exclusion, as illustrated by the case of downtown San Salvador. First, downtown shows a higher poverty rate than other zones of the city. Second, as a result of the generalized degradation process of its physical environment, it is a spatially identifiable and delineated area, related also to the loss of residential functions and the near-absence of public spaces. Third, the majority of the capital's inhabitants subjectively view it as a stigmatized zone, a disreputable area to live, and an unsafe place to go.

In sum, this is a manifest case of urban social exclusion, originating in the changes in the functions and economy of downtown, as well as in the westward movement of the most socially mobile residents and activities. Downtown San Salvador has been excluded de facto by the flight of residents and activities, and by public neglect. Combating the tendency to 'demonize' downtown San Salvador and to depict it as a place to avoid will not be an easy task. Bringing about its restoration, and at the same time respecting the transformations that have taken place, are fundamental challenges if we wish to reverse social exclusion and contribute to the socially sustainable development of the whole city.

A word about crime. Although urban violence is by no means restricted to central San Salvador, an unfortunate attribute shared with the entire metropolitan area (Lungo and Baires 1994), we feel that downtown warrants special attention in this respect, with special targeted programs. Such programs should not be limited to police action and surveillance, but should also include social, political, and cultural responses, especially aimed at the young. The recuperation of public spaces, to be used by all, would go a long way in achieving this goal and as such would become a powerful tool in building a socially inclusive environment.

Devising New Downtown Development Policies

Within this context, actions taken and proposals made to rescue downtown San Salvador have until now remained extremely limited and scattered. Emphasis has been largely placed on the restoration and conservation of some historical monuments and buildings. While valid, such actions are limited. There has been a lack of much-needed political will on the part of various stakeholders to rescue the downtown area; this is especially true of the central government and the San Salvador municipal government. Only recently has there been any discussion of the revitalization of the city's historical centre. Following from PLAMADUR's Central City Rescue Plan, the municipality of San Salvador has created an office with the same objective, relating it to the city's 450th anniversary. Another contributing factor to the debate has been a major and much publicized seminar funded by the Spanish government and promoted by the National Council of Culture (CONCULTURA). An important conclusion of this seminar was the decision to include social integration henceforth as an element of the current physical restoration program of historical buildings. Physical restoration alone, the seminar concluded, would be ineffective.

Above all, the overriding problem of the development of both the metropolitan area and downtown San Salvador is weak, uncoordinated, and overcentralized urban management. Urban development and planning remain primarily the preserve of the central government, with municipal government and civil society playing only a minor role in the decision process. This situation is compounded by the existence of numerous and frequently contradictory laws and by-laws, an extremely fragmented institutional framework, and few effective regulatory instruments. The issue of urban governance, seen as the state–civil society relationship (McCarney, Halfani, and Rodriguez 1995), equally arises as one of the most important challenges for the future development of the metropolitan area and of downtown San Salvador.

The information in table 9.7 raises the issue of the consequences for the downtown area's development of the weaknesses and contradictions in the administrative-regulatory environment. Among the most

Table 9.7 The Problems of Urban Management

Component	Administrative management level	Problems
Urban legislation	National and metropolitan	General, contradictory, and obsolete
Institutional framework	National and metropolitan	Sectoral, contradictory, and centralized functions
Regulatory instruments	Metropolitan	General and weak application
Economic instruments	National	Unplanned and contradictory

negative consequences is clearly the lack of a specific development plan and of adequate public-policy instruments for implementation. In part because of this, the current application of urban regulations and by-laws is highly inadequate. The Historical Centre Rescue Plan included in PLAMADUR, and the Special Plan for the Rescue of the Historic Centre that is currently being developed, present an opportunity to build a new institutional arrangement for governing downtown San Salvador's development, involving comprehensive discussions among stakeholders. The majority of buildings of historical value are privately owned, while publicly owned land in the area is minimal. The state and the private sector must therefore arrive at a process of consensus and combined action that takes into account existing social capital and the emergence of downtown interest groups as well as attempting to recover a positive sense of downtown identity as a fundamental element of socially sustainable urban management.

Urban management, broadly defined, remains the chief problem, demanding significant changes entailing coordinated actions at three levels: legislation; institutional reform; and new flexible, broad-ranging, urban public-policy instruments. Isolated actions focusing only on new by-laws, institutional restructuring, or separate plans and programs is destined to fail. In our opinion, urban management could serve as a useful pretext to build new relationships among the state, municipal governments, and civil society. These relationships, subsumed here under the heading 'urban governance,' centred on the management of future urban development, appear as a fundamental element of urban social sustainability.

Finally, we need up-to-date research and analysis of the changing spatial distribution of economic activity in the urban region in relation to changing housing patterns and the use of public spaces. Such information could make a significant contribution to the policy debate surrounding the role of downtown San Salvador and to the promotion of urban-development strategies that are socially sustainable. This evolving social and spatial portrait of the urban region would be designed from the policy perspective of a more inclusive, participatory, and self-sustainable model of society, one that promotes integration and reduces the prevailing level of social exclusion.

Notes

1 Central, or downtown, San Salvador is defined here as the general area identified on figure 9.2, and which includes the old city-centre and historical core.
2 We include at least four processes in the definition of 'urban management': planning; regulation; administration; and investment, both public and private. The combination of these processes with the participation of the state and civil society should contribute to building new urban-governance relations. In this respect, urban management is different from a more traditional urban-government approach.

References

Arango, Silvia. 1989. *Historia de la arquitectura colombiana*. Santa Fe de Bogotá: Universidad Nacional de Colombia.

Balbo, Marcello. 1991. *Frammentazione della città e planificazione urbana nel Terzo Mondo*. Venice: Istituto Universitario di Architettura di Venezia.

Browning, David. 1975. *El Salvador. La tierra y el hombre*. San Salvador: Ministerio de Educación.

CCIES [Cámara de Comercio e Industria de El Salvador]/Universidad Tecnológica. 1995. *Survey on Salvador Downtown Main Problems*. San Salvador: CCIES/Universidad Tecnológica.

Consejo Nacional de Planificación y Coordinación Económica. 1969. *Metroplan 80*. San Salvador: Consejo Nacional de Planificación y Coordinación Económica.

FLACSO [Facultad Latinoamericana de Ciencias Sociales]/UNDP. 1995. *Análi-*

sis de la exclusión social a nivel departamental: Los casos de Costa Rica, El Salvador y Guatemala. San José: FLACSO.

FUNDASAL [Salvadorean Foundation for Development and Low-Cost Housing]. 1976. *La vivienda popular urbana en El Salvador*. San Salvador: FUNDASAL.

– 1995. 'Estadísticas básicas de los asentamientos populares urbanos del AMSS.' *Documentos de Estudio* 15. San Salvador: FUNDASAL.

ISAM [Instituto Salvadoreño de Administración Municipal]/ Konrad Adenauer Stiftung. 1994. *La problemática urbana: los casos de las zonas comerciales de San Salvador y Nueva San Salvador*. San Salvador: ISAM/KAS.

Kowarick, Lúcio. 1991. 'Ciudad y ciudadanía. Metrópolis del subdesarrolo industrializado.' *Nueva Sociedad* 114 (July/August): 84–93.

Lindo, Héctor. 1990. *Weak Foundations: The Economy of El Salvador in the Nineteenth Century, 1821–1898*. Berkeley: University of California Press.

Lungo, Mario. 1988. 'San Salvador: el hábitat popular después del terremoto,' *Medio Ambiente y Urbanizacion* 24: 46–53.

– 1993. 'Las ciudades y la globalización. Una mirada desde Centroamérica y el Caribe.' *Urbana* 14/15: 47–58.

– Forthcoming. 'San Salvador: ¿es posible vivir en el centro?' In *La vivienda en las áreas centrales de las ciudades latinoamericanas*. San Salvador: CYTED (Programa de Ciencia y Tecnología para el Desarrollo).

Lungo, Mario, and Sonia Baires. 1988. 'Población y economía en la consolidación de la capital salvadoreña: 1880–1930.' In *La estructuración de las capitales centroamericanas*, ed. Rodrigo Fernández and Mario Lungo, 131–59. San José: EDUCA (Editorial Universitaria Centroamericana).

– 1994. 'La delincuencia en San Salvador después de la guerra: ¿Cuales causas? ¿Cuales planes para su control?' In *Ciudad y violencias en América Latina*, ed. Mario Lungo and Sonia Baires, 265–73. Quito: Programa de Gestión Urbana.

– 1995. 'El sector servicios en el Area Metropolitana de San Salvador. Factores de su transformación y localización.' Paper presented to the International Seminar on Urban Management, Montreal, Canada, 11–13 August.

Lungo, Mario, and Francisco Oporto. 1998. *Vacant Land in Downtown San Salvador*. Research report. Cambridge, MA: Lincoln Institute of Land Policy.

Martin, Percy. 1981. *El Salvador*. San Salvador: UCA Editores.

McCarney, Patricia, Mohamed Halfani, and Alfredo Rodriguez. 1995. 'Towards an Understanding of Governance. The Emergence of an Idea and its Implications for Urban Research in Developing Countries.' In *Urban Research in the Developing World: Vol. 4, Perspectives on the City*, ed. Richard Stren and Judith

Kjellberg Bell, 91–141. Toronto: Centre for Urban and Community Studies, University of Toronto.

Moser, Caroline. 1996. *Confronting Crisis: A Comparative Study of Household Responses to Poverty and Vulnerability in Four Urban Poor Communities*. Environmentally Sustainable Development Studies, Monograph Series no. 8. Washington, DC: The World Bank.

PLAMADUR [Plan Maestro de Desarrollo Urbano]. 1996. *Plan de Rescate del Centro Ciudad, versión preliminar*. San Salvador: PLAMADUR.

Polèse, Mario, and Richard Stren. 1995. 'Understanding the New Socio-Cultural Dynamics of Cities: Building a Knowledge-Base for Urban Management in the Twenty-first Century.' Paper prepared for the Workshop on Socially Sustainable Cities, INRS-urbanisation, Montreal and Centre for Urban and Community Studies, Toronto, 15–18 October.

Portes, Alejandro. 1998. 'Social Capital: Its Origins and Applications in Modern Sociology.' *Annual Review of Sociology* 24: 1–24.

Rodríguez, América. 1997. 'Perfil socio-cultural del Centro Histórico de San Salvador.' Unpublished research. San Salvador: CONCULTURA (Consejo Nacional de Cultura).

Rolnik, Raquel, and Renato Cymbalista. 1997. *Instrumentos urbanisticos contra a exclusão social*. São Paulo: POLIS.

Sabatini, Francisco. 1997. 'Liberalización de los mercados de suelo y segregación social en las ciudades latinoamericanas: el caso de Santiago de Chile.' Paper presented at Twentieth Latin American Studies Association International Congress, Guadalajara, Mexico.

Salazar, Flora. 1996. 'Estructuración urbana del Centro de San Salvador.' *Realidad* 52 (July/August): 573–85.

VMVDU [ViceMinisterio de Vivienda y Desarrollo Urbano]. 1966. *Indicadores urbanos y de vivienda de las tres principales de El Salvador*. San Salvador: VMVDU.

10 Social Transformation in a Post-colonial City: The Case of Nairobi

DIANA LEE-SMITH and DAVINDER LAMBA

During its short history of 100 years, Nairobi has experienced two major social transformations and appears to be undergoing a third, which is the subject of this chapter. By 'social transformation' is meant a fundamental and relatively abrupt change in social structure and organization, as opposed to social changes that are both gradual and less extensive. As this chapter will show, none of these social transformations has so far been conducive to social sustainability, in the sense of fostering social integration of culturally diverse groups, with improvements in the quality of life for all segments of the population (Polèse and Stren 1995, 8). The question is raised whether the current social transformation, which is treated as ongoing, can lead to greater social sustainability through better governance, or whether Nairobi will become a victim of forces of social disintegration.

The first transformation occurred with the founding of the colonial city in a border area between different ethnic groups and the imposition of British law and social norms that set out to exclude the local population. The second transformation occurred with independence in 1963 and the creation of a multi-ethnic African state. Although the new social order was ostensibly a parliamentary democracy, in reality it was characterized by a pyramidal state power structure centralized in an executive presidency that controlled, and continues to control, local government. The policy of social exclusion also continued, but based on income rather than on ethnicity.

The third transformation is identified with the national transition to multiparty democracy in 1992. Although the transition to democracy cannot be said to be either successful or complete, society has to some extent already been transformed through free speech and the emergence of a multitude of actors jostling for position and creating new political spaces.

Each social transformation can be located at a defining moment in time, although the actual social processes leading to a different social order took place, or are taking place, over more extended periods. The purpose of this study is to analyse the social processes at work in the ongoing production of a new social order by defining the actors and their interactions.

Nairobi's third transformation is characterized by civil-society activism for social reform on a broad front, including civic reform. For some, the focus of reform is on social inclusiveness, particularly of the urban poor. The national movement for political and social reform is centred in Nairobi, where both the grievances and the potential for social movements are greatest. This was also the case for the movements of the 1940s and 1950s that were the precursors of independence.

We examine here the social transformations of Nairobi, including the mechanics of social and spatial exclusion, first historically and then sectorally in relation to land, food, and transport. We then present the various civic and national actors involved in the city's third, and ongoing, social transformation, suggesting that what is required for social sustainability is some form of accommodation between these competing interests in a new system of governance. Governance here implies cooperation between governmental and non-governmental actors.

The major social transformations that have occurred in the past and are taking place currently in Nairobi can be explained theoretically in a number of ways. For example, the replacement of the colonial by the post-colonial city fits Manuel Castells's theory of urban social change, and the various interests currently vying for power in Nairobi can be described in terms of urban social movements. This theory of urban politics can explain how the categories of actors are situated in relation to each other, but may not help in teasing out empirically how they deal with each other (Castells 1983, 291–327; Fainstein and Hirst 1995, 185; Pickvance 1995, 262–3). Regime theory, which addresses the mechanics of power, has up to now only been applied in the North and to relatively stable regimes of government and non-government forces that cooperate to further their goals. However, there are aspects of regime theory that deal with the creation of political space by competing interests, and these may be useful in understanding Nairobi's situation (Judge, Stoker, and Wolman 1995; Stoker 1995, 54–61).

It is not at all clear whether the actors engaged in the governance crisis of Nairobi's third social transformation will develop a cooperative regime or whether their current conflicts will increase. This is the question raised in the conclusion of this chapter, which asks how the powerful forces engaged in the city can deal with each other.

Nairobi's History: From Ethnic to Economic Exclusion

The Colonial City

It has been said that the defining moment in Nairobi's history came in June 1899, when the Kenya–Uganda railroad, connecting the Indian Ocean coastline with Lake Victoria, made Nairobi an important point on the imperial map (Lamba 1994). Before that, the area, known to the local Maasai people as 'Enkare Nairobi' – 'the place of cold waters' – was home to the Kikuyu, Kamba, and Maasai peoples. Nairobi lies at the junction of highland forest and savannah grassland; the Kikuyu people, in the highlands to the north and west of Nairobi, and the Kamba peoples, to the east, practised agriculture and mixed farming, while the Maasai, living on the grasslands, practised nomadic pastoralism (Hirst 1994, 14–20).

The first social transformation of Nairobi began in 1896 with a small European camp that served as a depot for the caravan trade between Uganda and the coast. The caravan route had been established by Arab traders earlier, leading to the spread of Islamic culture and religion in the surrounding areas (Ghaidan 1975). The European camp became a town when the railhead reached there in 1899 and construction halted while engineers worked out how to climb the escarpment of the Rift Valley. The camp grew rapidly, with a Township Committee and regulations in 1900, and a population of 11,000 by 1906. A municipal council was established in 1919 and, when Kenya was changed from a protectorate to a colony in 1920, Nairobi became the capital (White, Silberman, and Anderson 1948, 17; Lee-Smith 1989, 279; Lamba 1994, 3–4).

It was the regulations, laws, and social mores of the British Crown and settlers that dominated the environs of Nairobi, at the expense of the local population who were required to conform to these regulations and laws. Africans were legally prevented from owning freehold property in the city until the 1920s, when the British government prohibited separation of the races. Thereafter the settlers prevented such ownership through zoning and social pressures. Segregation was extended to education and cultural amenities through European, Asian, and 'native' schools; commercial areas; and cultural and religious facilities (White, Silberman, and Anderson 1948, 17; Hirst 1994, 51–65).

In 1926, Nairobi's population of almost 30,000 consisted of over 60 per cent Africans and 30 per cent Indians, with less than 10 per cent being European (2,665 persons), although the Europeans owned almost all the land (Hirst 1994, 77). Meanwhile the tropical highland climate around Nairobi attracted settlers from Europe, particularly Britain, who turned its lush countryside into the private farms of the 'White Highlands' – the 3 million hectares reserved exclusively for European settlement. Many Kikuyu became squatters on these large farms. It was this extensive land alienation which led to the Mau Mau, or Kenya Land Freedom Army, guerrilla struggle of the 1950s which presaged formal independence in 1963, when Kenya became a republic (Kanogo 1987).

The Municipal Council of Nairobi elected its first mayor in 1923, but refused to permit Asian representation until forced to do so by the governor. The first Asian respresentatives came into conflict with their European counterparts over discrimination in providing services and the payment of rates. Both African and Asian communities engaged in civic organizations to resist social exclusion in the 1920s and worked in solidarity, even though they were subjected to divide-and-rule tactics by the Europeans (Patel 1997, 106–27; White, Silberman, and Anderson 1948, 17).

Sanitation was initially provided by pit latrines and septic tanks, while piped water had first been provided by the railways, with the municipality buying the undertaking from them in 1931 (Hirst 1994, 69, 78). Electric power was developed by an independent company, East Africa Power and Lighting, set up in 1923 (Hirst 1994, 80–1). During the 1930s plans were made for the expansion of the water supply from the original Nairobi dam and for the building of a sewage system, while the municipality also took over managing public health from the colonial government. The Nairobi Master Plan of 1948 projected physical, social, and economic development for the coming twenty-five years, including minimally serviced housing for African workers (White, Silberman, and Anderson 1948; Hirst 1994, 82–102).

Development of the city centre proceeded rapidly in the 1940s and 1950s, as did the growth of racially segregated residential areas. Despite the creation of the Nairobi African Advisory Council in 1946, with representatives from African housing locations who nominated two councillors to Nairobi City Council (NCC), disaffection was increasing in these areas due to the poor living conditions and lack of civil and political rights. Africans were systematically being excluded from city life at the time Nairobi received its city charter in 1950, and their complaints were also growing (Hirst 1994, 111–12).

The detentions, curfew, and repression of the African population that accompanied the State of Emergency declared in 1952 to combat the rural guerrilla war only exacerbated the disaffection of the urban population. Although by 1957 there were eight provincially elected African representatives on the Kenya Legislative Council (LEGCO), there were still only three nominated African councillors in the NCC, compared with thirty elected by the Europeans and Asians (Hirst 1994, 118). Things began to change as independence approached. By 1959 the NCC agreed that four African councillors could be elected by about 13 per cent of the African population, those who were deemed to be property owners; and Nairobi's first African mayor, Charles Rubia, took office in 1962 (Werlin 1974; Lee-Smith 1989; Hirst 1994, 129).

The Post-colonial City

The coming of political independence in 1963 can be described as the second social transformation of Nairobi, when political control of the nation passed from the British Crown to the Republic of Kenya, with a parliamentary system of government, and the NCC likewise became a forum for local representatives elected by residents of the various neighbourhoods. This transformation was similar in social terms to the end of apartheid in South Africa, in that racial divisions no longer had a formal basis, and central and local state power was held by representatives of the African majority population.

However, three-quarters of the new city councillors had no previous experience of local government while at the same time the council was loaded with extensive new responsibilities, it had to provide services to everybody, while the boundaries of the city were extended to encompass six times the geographical area. Municipal finance emerged as a major problem due to the contradictions between social expectations, physical expansion, and the limited financial independence of the city council from central government. In 1973, the situation further worsened with the abolition of Graduated Personal Tax (GPT) which had been the council's main source of revenue (Lee-Smith and Memon 1988).

As in other African countries, the removal of colonial restrictions on freedom of movement at independence meant a rapid increase in rural–urban migration. Efforts were made to address the needs of the growing population, but these were largely ineffective, faltering when it came to policy implementation, with the result that the 'self-help city' grew like a balloon (Hake 1977; Lee-Smith 1989, 281).

As a result, Nairobi still reflects its segregationist heritage with regard to planning, amenities, and administration. The middle-class residential areas in which Europeans and Asians previously lived separately from one another now house a racial mix and have both extended and densified. The old 'native' housing areas are still there, and the city has extended further to the east, with new housing and unauthorized settlements. The populations here are predominantly African and low-income.

It is generally recognized that there is a class division between Wa-Benzi (Mercedes-Benz) people, those living in suburban estates and driving expensive cars, and the toiling Jua Kali (hot sun) or dispossessed class. This entirely African dispossessed class is in fact made up of numerous ethnic groups, commonly labelled 'tribes' in Kenya. Members of most such groups are found among both the poor and the rich, making for a complicated matrix of ethnic and class divisions in Nairobi's society that is reflected in its politics.

The approximately fifty ethnic groups of Kenya, each with its own language, can be broadly distinguished as the nomadic pastoral peoples (including the Somali, Oromo, Maasai, and the various Kalenjin peoples) and the settled agricultural peoples (including the Kikuyu, Kamba, Luhya, and Luo) (Were and Wilson 1972). It was the numerically dominant agricultural ethnic groups who formed the bulk of the Nairobi population both before and after independence, and among them the Kikuyu have tended to predominate due to their historical proximity to the city, as shown in figure 10.1. They constituted one-third of its population in 1989 (Kenya 1994, 6–3).

Politicians from among the agricultural peoples dominated the central government after independence, Kenya's first president, Jomo Kenyatta, being a Kikuyu. He was succeeded in 1978 by Daniel Arap Moi, a Kalenjin, and members of the pastoral peoples have gained increasing political and economic power since then. Both national leaders represented the Kenya African National Union (KANU), which took power at independence. KANU ruled what was in effect a single-party state from 1961. This was legalized as one-party rule for the decade from 1982 to the end of 1991.

Figure 10.1 Proportion of Major Ethnic Groups in Nairobi
Source: Mazingira Institute, based on 1989 population census

Mazingira Institute, Data based on 1989 Population Census

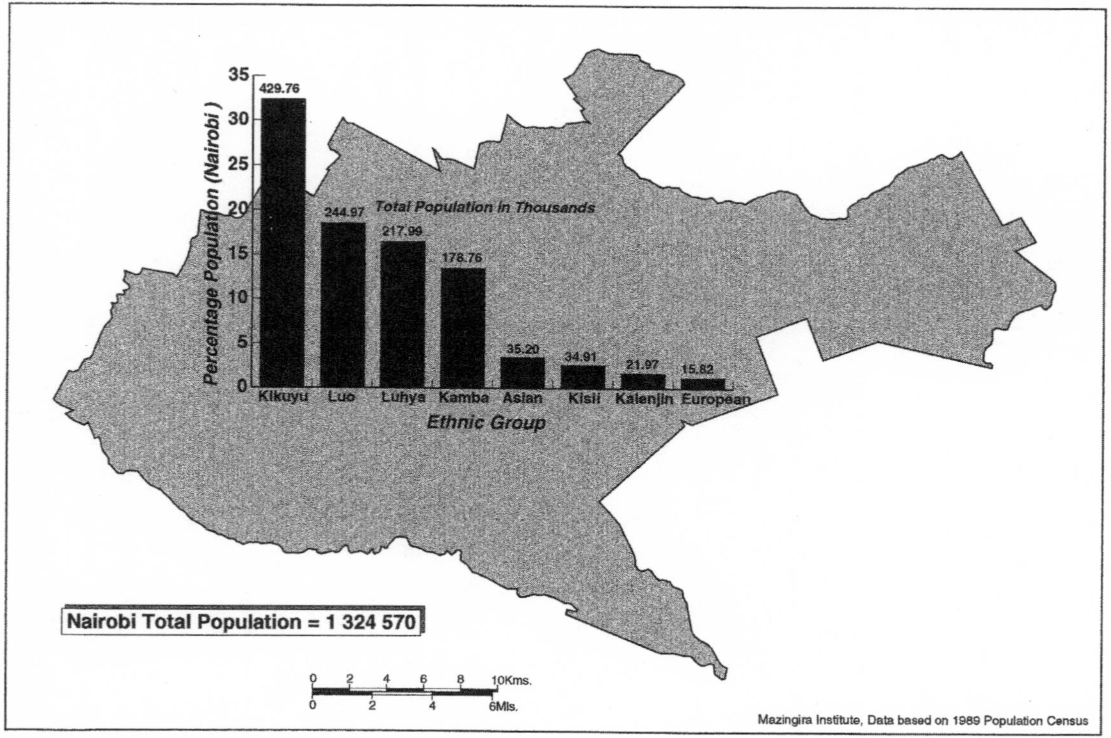

The Asian minority, which by 1989 constituted only 3 per cent of the city's population, owned large amounts of land in Nairobi and controlled some 80 per cent of Kenya's commerce at independence (Hirst 1994, 134–5; Kenya 1994, 6–3). Although the balance has shifted towards African landownership, Asians still have a substantial stake in commerce and industry. However, this community is as diverse as the Africans, comprising numerous sects of two major religions, Islam and Hinduism, as well as cultures of diverse origins whose members tend to intermarry less often than do the African groups. There are also differences between the Asian majority of small owners and the poor artisans, factory employees, and construction workers, while a tiny but visible elite is involved in big business.

Europeans are an even smaller minority, totalling 16,000, or only 1 per cent of the city's population in 1989 (Kenya 1994, 6–3). Fewer than 2,000 of these were at that time Kenyan citizens, mainly descendants of the white settler community. Less prominent in the economic profile of Kenya than the Asians, they nevertheless retain sizable tracts of land and have developed business partnerships with transnational companies and agribusiness.

As the capital, Nairobi received most of the largest industrial, commercial, and social-infrastructural investments in the country. The Nairobi Stock Exchange, launched in 1989, is the fourth-largest in Africa. These investments have made Nairobi the most important city in the East Africa region in terms of manufacturing, transshipment, servicing of agricultural machinery and motor vehicles, advanced medical facilities, and regional and international airline connections. Besides this, the city is a major tourist destination as well as housing representatives of major financial institutions and international agencies, including two United Nations agency headquarters.

Tensions between central and local government reflect the struggle for control over the resources of the wealthiest area of the country. Central government has maintained control of the city's administration, and various revenue-generating sources have been removed from the council by the central government, which also has to approve any measure increasing those still under local jurisdiction. Until 1983, when the City Council was dissolved due to 'gross mismanagement and poor delivery of services,' the city was largely dependent on the government for grants to supplement its own meager resources (Bubba and Lamba 1991).

On dissolution, the elected NCC was replaced by Nairobi City Com-

mission, composed of commissioners appointed by central government, but the change in name did not spell the expected magic, nor did
it root out the newly manifest trend of a self-seeking and corruptible
staff. Instead, there was continuous infighting among officials, with the
period between 1983 and 1991 seeing five chairpersons of the commission come and go. And although the number of commissioners was
increased from three to twenty-six in 1988 (compared with fifty councillors previously), subsequent commissions were plagued with the
threat of dissolution every other year, much to the chagrin of the city's
residents, whose lot grew continually worse.

Nairobi in the 1990s

The third social transformation of Nairobi is considered to have begun
with national multiparty elections in 1992. These followed a year of
intense political activity after the removal of the clause of the Constitution making Kenya a one-party state. This constitutional change was
itself the result of great political activity, mostly centred in Nairobi.

The NCC was re-established and its elections took place at the same
time as the national elections. The national elections were won by the
previous ruling party (KANU). This win was attributed to government
control of the media and public administration, as well as to the fragmented opposition and some vote-rigging. Nevertheless, urban support for the opposition was massive, especially in Nairobi (Throup and
Hornsby 1998).

Most of the representatives who were elected, as opposed to being
nominated, by central government were from the opposition parties.
These parties are supported, among others, by the Kikuyu people, who
form the single largest ethnic group in the city. Central government,
dominated by the minority pastoral Kalenjin people since 1978, continued to exercise political control through councillors nominated by the
minister (Stren, Halfani, and Malombe 1994).

Through a combination of coercion and manipulation, central government virtually paralysed the operations of the city government in
the period 1993–7. This was nowhere so evident as in the condemna-
tion of the Nairobi Action Plan emerging from the 1993 Nairobi City
Convention, preventing it from being implemented. This first-ever
mass-based consultation with the city fathers embodied professional
engagement and popular zeal (Karuga 1993).

After five years, elections were again held in December 1997; three-

Table 10.1 Nairobi City Councillors by Political Party, Ethnicity and Gender, 1998

	Elected		Nominated	Total	
	No.	%	No.	No.	%
Political Party					
Kenya African National Union	14	25.9	4	18	25.4
Democratic Party	28	51.9	9	37	52.1
National Development Party	5	9.3	2	7	9.9
Social Democratic Party	3	5.5	1	4	5.6
Other	4	7.4	1	5	7.0
Ethnicity					
Kikuyu	35	64.8	8	43	60.6
Luo	10	18.5	3	13	18.3
Kamba	2	3.7	—	2	2.8
Other	7	13.0	6	13	18.3
Gender					
Men	52	96.3	10	62	87.3
Women	2	3.7	7	9	12.7
Total	54	100.0	17	71	100.0

Source: The authors
Note: The Nairobi provincial commissioner is an ex-officio member of NCC and is not
included in the total.

quarters of the elected councillors were from opposition parties and
almost two-thirds were Kikuyu (see table 10.1). Proportional control by
political parties of the seventeen nominated seats was also won
through intense public and political pressure in January 1998.

Sectoral Aspects of Social Transformation

Land

The availability of land, both for housing and as a means of livelihood
or a place to work, is the most basic resource in a city. It is through
restricting access to it that the Nairobi authorities have practised social
exclusion, racially in the colonial city and economically in the post-
colonial city. The servicing of land is another dimension of social exclusion that was practised in both eras of Nairobi's development, through
the failure to extend services to areas inhabited by the excluded group.

This dates back to the earliest days, when in 1901 African housing inside the boundary was banned, except in a small area in the east. People therefore settled outside the boundaries, and these are some of today's informal settlements. African housing areas that grew up inside the boundary were demolished and residents evicted. 'Native' workers' housing, built by the railways with single-room accommodation for men only, was located near the industrial area and the railway sidings. In 1919 an official African housing area was designated, but people had to build the housing themselves and no services were provided. More such areas were designated later. And whereas Europeans were given freehold titles to land, Africans were only allowed usufruct rights, meaning they could not buy or sell the property (White, Silberman, and Anderson 1948, 14–19; Hirst 1994, 49–63).

The first city-council housing for Africans was built in 1921, as a barracks-type dormitory for returning soldiers. More working-class African housing estates continued to be built up to the time of independence, along the railway line to the east of the town-centre. Demand was calculated in bed spaces for workers, with 28,000 in 1946 and about 70,000 in 1957, although supply did not meet this demand. Unauthorized settlements continued to be demolished, and peripheral settlements to grow. Among these were Dagoretti, a Kikuyu reserve, and Kibera, a community of Sudanese soldiers allowed to settle on Crown land in 1912. These same areas house substantial numbers of Nairobi residents today, and are still largely unserviced (Lamba 1994, 21; Hirst 1994, 60–5).

Access to the urban area was strictly controlled through a pass system whereby only employed Africans were recognized, especially during the State of Emergency in the 1950s. Employers were mainly European, although there were increasing numbers of large and small Asian entrepreneurs, and Asians had their designated area, which was both commercial and residential. Licensed hawkers were also permitted into the urban area; these were mainly women who sold in the markets operated by the city council.

After independence, policy intentions to house Nairobi's population were not implemented. A United Nations study in 1964, followed by a government sessional paper on housing in 1966–7, outlined an approach to providing serviced sites to meet the growing urban population's need for affordable housing, but by the late 1970s only 6,000 units had been built, falling far short of demand (Lee-Smith and Memon 1988). The National Housing Corporation, established in 1967, built only high-cost housing, and the same applied to NCC council housing (Lee-Smith 1989, 281). As a result, the amount of informal housing grew at an even faster rate. Mathare Valley grew in the late 1960s and early 1970s to house about 100,000 people, and similar, smaller settlements developed all over the city. In 1971 it was estimated that one-third of the city's population was living in unauthorized housing, and in 1972 the International Labour Organisation stated that 30,000 jobs in the city were not officially counted and thus constituted what they called an 'informal sector' (ILO 1972; Hake 1977; Lee-Smith 1989, 281).

Figure 10.2 shows the population densities in Nairobi in diagrammatic form. The figures, which are approximate due to rounding, are based on projections from the 1989 census. Although the average density is 2,200 people per square kilometre, densities are up to 40,000–50,000 per square kilometre in some informal settlements, as shown in the boxes on the map. Fifty-five per cent of the population lives on 5.8 per cent of the residential land in Nairobi. Furthermore, these densely settled informal areas are virtually denied access to services (Lamba 1994, 3–6; Alder 1995, 86).

Evictions occurred in the late 1960s and early 1970s, and again in late 1978, when many people were driven out of informal settlements in middle-income neighbourhoods and the city-centre and dumped in Korogocho, to the east of Mathare Valley (Hirst 1994, 146–7; Lee-Smith 1990). Thus the pattern of social exclusion in the eastern unserviced areas was repeated with a vengeance by the post-colonial city authorities.

And yet the authorities are involved in the creation and management of the informal settlements, through the local chiefs and district administration. People are settled on public land by the administration, and representatives of the administration sit on their local committees. Because of the informal nature of the settlements, the process has become corrupted, with officials requiring bribes – *kitu kidogo*, meaning 'something small' – for each plot.

This creates its own form of business; unscrupulous people buy public land from these officials and become slumlords, building wooden or mud-and-wattle structures that are then rented out to the poor as housing or business premises or both. In one settlement it was found that 87 per cent of residents were tenants. The landlords range from politicians to local residents (Lee-Smith 1990). The chiefs, supported by the village committees, the administration police, and youth gangs

Figure 10.2 The Seven Most Crowded and Poorest Areas (Sub-Locations) in Nairobi
Source: Mazingira Institute, based on 1996 population census

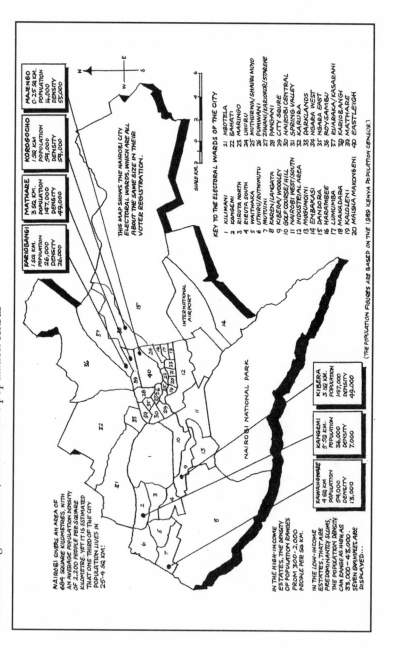

attached to the ruling political party, act as enforcers. A similar system operates for informal-sector business premises, locally known as 'kiosks,' found mostly on public land, especially road reserves.

As political pressure for reform and multiparty democracy mounted in the 1990s, forced evictions of people from their homes and places of work have become even more prevalent, but they have also been met with more resistance, in terms of both physical confrontation and organization. In 1990, around 10,000 people were affected by violent demolitions of homes and informal businesses in the city-centre and periphery, and these were accompanied by running street battles (Mazingira Institute 1991, 10–11).

Further violent evictions of residents and informal-sector businesses have occurred in 1994, 1995, and 1996, affecting tens of thousands of people (Mazingira Institute 1995, 3; 1996a, 3; 1996b, 2–3; 1997a, 3–4). Many evictions are precipitated by the phenomenon of 'land grabbing,' whereby the 'private developer' connives with city authorities or provincial administration to clear plots, most of which are in fact on public land. This mode of acquiring public land has come to be associated with political manipulation by the ruling party in its attempt to buy off political opponents.

The slum dwellers are increasingly taking matters into their own hands, battling those who attempt to encroach on their land, destroy their shelters, and put up fencing or permanent structures. At the same time, they are getting legal support from NGOs and organizing themselves into an advocacy organization, Muungano wa Wanavijiji Maskini, with a membership from eighty-six communities in Nairobi and its environs. A recent meeting of the organization was held at the City Stadium to accommodate the attendance (Mazingira Institute 1997b, 4; Muungano Wa Wanavijiji 1997).

Mob justice got the upper hand in the Soweto slum, located in the upper-income neighbourhood of Spring Valley, in December 1996 and January 1997, when three security guards from a team sent to demolish the slum were lynched (Mazingira Institute 1997a, 3–4). A number of cases have been taken to court, including Soweto, where the squatters are suing a businessman for possession of the land. So far, however, there have been no court rulings in favour of low-income people, judgments always being in favour of the business people (Mazingira Institute 1995, 1996b).

The community-based organizations are supported by NGOs such as a community legal-support unit, and by Operation Firimbi (Whis-

Figure 10.3 A scene of forced eviction in Nairobi. Five thousand homes were destroyed when the Nairobi City Commission demolished shanties in Kangemi in 1991. Source: *Daily Nation*

tle), a campaign run by the Mazingira Institute, which offers advocacy, documentation, advice, and support on cases of public land-grabbing (Mazingira 1996b, 3; 1997a, 2–3). The Kenya Federation of Jua Kali Associations and the Hawkers and Vendors Association are other organizations formed to protect the interests of informal-sector businesses.

Middle-income neighbourhoods have also taken the initiative to organize associations that can deliver services or lobby with the authorities on behalf of their members. For example, the 'Karengata' association in an upper-income area has asserted its right to collect rates, the Westlands Association is setting up a system of networks and task groups to be inclusive of different interests and to negotiate with the NCC (Westlands Association 1998). These and numerous other residents' associations met to form a coalition in mid-1998.

Food

Nairobi's early food supply came largely from its surroundings. Vegetable gardens and livestock were available from the start; it was mainly Kikuyu women, who were already engaged in small-scale local trade of their surplus produce in their own and adjoining communities, who brought supplies to the railway camp and later to the town. By 1914 there were about 2,000 hawkers selling all kinds of goods, although their numbers were later reduced through controls on the type of goods sold, mainly restricting hawking to fruit and vegetables (Mitullah 1992). In the same period, Somali families were allowed to graze herds for slaughter in the environs of the town (Hirst 1994, 69).

This pattern is typical of urban food supply in Africa, where indigenous markets and food networks adapted to provisioning the new colonial towns. Since they were dominated by women, these networks led to women's characteristic role within the urban informal sector. The difference in Nairobi was in the degree of development of settler agriculture, whose producers had political power as opposed to the indigenous suppliers (Guyer 1987).

The British settlers established experimental gardens and set up provisioning farms in what are now residential suburbs close to the city, including livestock farms for meat and dairy products. By 1909, these were supplying customers with beef, milk, butter, cream, and a variety of cheeses. Although the colonial government pushed for the development of cash crops, the diversity of food production remained, though the exclusion of African producers applied to both food and cash crops, with the exception of the vegetable and fruit hawkers who formed the embryonic informal sector (Hirst 1994, 69).

The social changes accompanying independence in 1963 brought benefits to African farmers in the environs of the city, and local elites developed out of the windfall inheritance of large farms and control over the government machinery of regulation and marketing (Heyer, Maitha, and Senga 1976, 4–5). Small-scale African producers also benefited, most notably from the absence of restrictions rather than from the machinery of government support (Heyer, Maitha, and Senga 1976, 187–218).

However, access to food and food security for the urban population is more tied to income and the capacity to buy food than to its availability. Thus, the social transformation of the 1960s brought about greater problems of access to food for the populations of the informal city than for their counterparts in rural areas. The urban poor began to emerge as vulnerable in terms of nutrition in the 1970s.

One of the strategies by which the urban poor feed themselves is urban agriculture, a phenomenon that was not documented until the 1980s. Then, it was found that 20 per cent of Nairobi's households engaged in urban crop production and 7 per cent kept livestock in the city, while even more engaged in farming on their rural land. Access to urban land for food production emerged as a critical issue for those urban residents whose incomes did not enable them to buy enough food (Lee-Smith et al. 1987; Lee-Smith and Lamba 1991; Egziabher et al. 1994).

But the appearance of rural activities such as the growing of maize and beans on roadsides, and chickens and goats in urban neighbourhoods, upset official notions of the image of the city and were met with harassment by city officials (Freeman 1991). Also, the haphazard spread of unplanned activities, including informal housing and businesses, tends to quickly replace urban agriculture as a land use. This means that the food security of the poorest is increasingly threatened by urban densification. Among the poorest, those who lack access to rural land are the most threatened, and this includes many female-headed households, who lack the right to inherit rural land according to custom (Lee-Smith 1997; RELMA/PROP/Mazingira 1998).

The history of Nairobi's food supply and its problems thus reflect the social transformations identified and their characteristic patterns of social exclusion. Since those most affected by the lack of land for producing urban food are the poorest and least articulate members of

Nairobi's society, urban farming is not one of the organized sectors of civil society that makes its presence felt in Nairobi's third social transformation. The need to address urban agriculture as an important aspect of food security is only just beginning to be recognized and articulated (RELMA/PROP/Mazingira 1998).

Transport

The story of Nairobi's public transport also reflects the social transformations it has gone through. The bus company established under the colonial city government was a subsidiary of a multinational that was given a legal monopoly, which still exists on paper. After independence, local pirate taxis (*matatus*) were supported by presidential decree, giving encouragement to the growth of small-scale entrepreneurs, but confining them to the informal sector of operation and thus creating chaos on the roads as different interests in the city competed for power, economic benefits, and planning control. In the 1990s, overt conflicts between *matatu* operators, police, the public, and government administration are a microcosm of the political forces at work in the city.

In the colonial city, there were plans for buses as early as 1932, but public support was insufficient and costs too high. Yet, two years later, the Kenya Bus Service (KBS) began operation as a private concern, part of the British multinational United Transport Overseas (UTO). Its arrangements with the Municipal Council included its legal monopoly over public transport, which has been rendered meaningless over time, and a 25 per cent city stake in the company (Lee-Smith 1989, 279–85).

The service expanded steadily from its original 2 buses in 1934 to 140 in 1968. However, neither the bus service nor the planning of movement in the city in general was ever geared towards the needs of the majority African population. Most workers were unable to afford bus fares and consequently walked to work. They also could not afford bicycles. Yet there was no provision for footpaths in the planning or building of roads in Nairobi, in total disregard for people's needs and safety. Roads were planned for the use of motor vehicles used by the settlers, with drains at the side and seldom any space for walking.

President Kenyatta's decree of 1973 recognizing *matatus* was a response to their popularity, both in meeting people's needs for a more flexible and adaptive form of public transport and as a form of self-employment and employment for the urban workforce. For the first decade of independence before the decree they had operated completely illegally. After another decade, the Traffic (Amendment) Act of 1984 increased recognition of the *matatus*, but they have never been fully incorporated into city planning and continue to suffer harassment by police. In 1982 they paid three times as much in bribes to policemen as the public revenue they generated (Kapila, Manundu, and Lamba 1982; Lee-Smith 1989).

The Matatu Vehicle Owners Association became a powerful force in civil society, and government attempted to suppress it at various times after the change from Kikuyu to Kalenjin leadership at the national level in 1978. The size of vehicle fleets expanded in the 1980s and the predominantly Kikuyu owners and operators became more powerful political players as the movement for political reform mounted in the 1990s.

In 1982, KBS buses were used for 27 per cent of all trips, *matatus* for 23 per cent, private cars 22 per cent, bicycles or scooters 4 per cent, while 24 per cent of trips were on foot because of the high cost of transport (Lee-Smith 1989, 285–6). In 1991, although the bus company's fleet had expanded to 300 vehicles, its market share had declined. Its competitors were the Nyayo Bus Corporation, a parastatal, and the *matatus*. While the *matatus* had overtaken the KBS, with 57 per cent market share in public transport compared to 40 per cent, the Nyayo Bus Corporation only had 3 per cent and later collapsed (Godard and Teurnier 1992).

As a result of the political conflicts over control of city hall in 1990s, public infrastructure, including roads, has been poorly maintained, with some roads in the city becoming impassable. *Matatu* operators have raised fares and staged strikes in protest, with passengers refusing to pay the high fares. *Matatu* operators have also staged protests over police harassment and extortion by youth wingers from the ruling political party, KANU, while the provincial commissioner of Nairobi has exhorted the police to crack down on them.

Because of police corruption and increasing lawlessness in the city, as well as lack of planning and maintenance, the general public suffers with long and hazardous journeys to work. The large numbers of pedestrians who walk many kilometres a day due to low incomes still lack footpaths, not to mention bicycle paths, demonstrating that the NCC has not emerged from the heritage of colonial planning.

A Governance Crisis: Nairobi's Third Social Transformation

Who Governs?

A system of governance that involves all the key players in government and civil society is essential to resolve the current conflicts and contradictions in Nairobi. As this historical and cross-sectoral synopsis has shown, the conflicts and contradictions are rooted in a system that militates against social sustainability by excluding what is now the majority of the population of the city from civic recognition and by pitting diverse groups against one another. This has led to a crisis of governance.

Nairobi's institutions are currently locked in a destructive battle for power that is eroding the capacity of its citizens to manage the undoubted wealth concentrated in the city for the common good. The city's history of exclusion has structured the way institutions operate as much as, or more than, it has structured physical space. Moreover, this social exclusion of well over half Nairobi's citizens on the basis of wealth is now much more extensive than social exclusion in the colonial city, which was based on race, simply because of the growth in the city's size. Nairobi's population rose from 0.5 million in 1969 to 1.35 million in 1989, to 2 million in 1997, by which time social exclusion was affecting over a million citizens (Lamba 1994, 4; Kenya 1996, 25).

The actors engaged in the struggle are not limited to those represented in the inherited formal institutions, even in the way they have been adapted over time. They also include, apart from formal business and labour institutions which are typical of governance regimes anywhere, informal-sector bodies and enterprises and a large corpus of non-governmental civic action groups. Even these, however, hardly begin to represent the interests of Nairobi's socially excluded population.

Figure 10.4 illustrates the complexity of the formal institutions of central and local government as they relate to the territory of Nairobi; the constituencies of the eight members of parliament (MPs) cover the geographical areas of the wards of the fifty-five elected city councillors, as shown on the diagram. The city councillors ostensibly govern as a legislature on behalf of their constituents through the council administration, but their powers are in fact limited by the control central government has over the appointments of heads of departments, as well as other controls stipulated in the Local Government Act of 1984.

Perhaps even more important, the government structure of Nairobi

Figure 10.4 Who Governs Nairobi: Central or Local Government Structures?
Source: Mazingira Institute

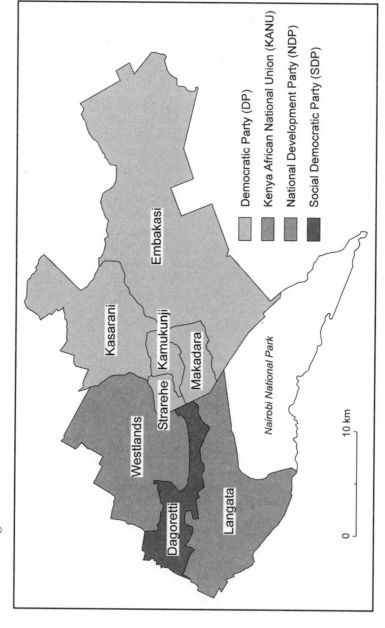

Democratic Party (DP)

Kenya African National Union (KANU)

National Development Party (NDP)

Social Democratic Party (SDP)

Embakasi

Kasarani

Kamukunji

Makadara

Strarehe

Westlands

Dagoretti

Langata

Nairobi National Park

0   10 km

is overlaid with the alternative institutional framework of the Office of the President, the provincial administration. This administrative apparatus has a hierarchical structure headed by a provincial commissioner (PC) appointed by the president, with district commissioners, district officers, chiefs, and sub-chiefs answerable to him. It is an administrative structure inherited from colonial times, and was challenged in 1997 by the civil society reform movement. Subsequently, the powers of chiefs in particular were curtailed by amendments to the Chief's Authority Act, as agreed by the Inter-Parties Parliamentary Group (IPPG) just prior to the December 1997 elections.

More extensive reductions in the powers of the provincial administration advocated by the civil-society reform movement and, to a lesser extent, by the IPPG were, however, resisted and members of the administration openly worked for a KANU victory in the December elections. The victory of KANU in national elections and the victory of the opposition (mainly the Democratic party) in most Nairobi constituencies as well as the council elections, has further provoked the president into placing a high-profile hard-line PC, Joseph Kaguthi, in Nairobi. Conflicts between the provincial adminstration and various interest groups in the city have escalated during 1998, even though the mayor and council have a stated policy of cooperation with central government.

The ability of residents in the informal slum areas to organize to address their needs has been greatly restricted. Until late 1991, the KANU offices in each area worked with village committees of community elders and the district administration, but with the advent of multipartyism those links were weakened. The administrative structure, however, remained in place; efforts to develop local-governance structures in one informal slum area under the government's own Social Dimensions of Development Programme were broken up by the chief with police reinforcement in May 1997 (NGOs Council 1997). The repeal of the Public Order Act in December 1997 as part of the IPPG reforms removed the legal prohibition on meetings of ten or more persons without permission of the local chief, although the provincial administration continues to break up meetings of its choice on the pretext that 'notification,' which is now required, has not been correctly issued.

Sectoral groups have in the past been subjected to similar controls. The Matatu Vehicle Owners Association was banned after it achieved some degree of public profile in organizing and representing its members interests (Lee-Smith 1989, 300). The Civil Servants Union was likewise proscribed, as have been various NGOs. However, during the pressure for reforms in the mid-1990s, numerous groups have reasserted themselves, and the prospects for organizing formal- and informal-sector interest groups to represent their members' interests are improving as the pressure for social reforms continues.

Kenya's machinery of government has not always acted as an agent of law and order. Rather the reverse, as the provincial and district administration personnel have been instrumental in structuring Nairobi's informal settlements, as already described, and in administering these areas of social exclusion outside the legal framework of the formal city. The divide between city- and central-government officialdom is certainly not clear-cut in this respect, with many, if not most, city officials colluding in these activities, which also conveniently provide them with income in the form of bribes.

The socially excluded groups in Nairobi rely for most of their services on assistance from NGOs. Religious organizations also play an important role in support for these communities. The number and range of such support activities has increased rapidly in recent years although data are limited (Bubba and Lamba 1991; Lee-Smith and Stren 1992; Lamba 1994; Alder 1995; KHRC 1996).

The range of actors engaged in Nairobi's haphazard governance is thus not only broad, but also uncoordinated by any mechanisms of negotiation, and is to a large extent unknown, or at least undocumented. In summary, these actors may be classified as follows:

- elected representatives or politicians: city councillors and MPs;
- employed officials of the NCC, including professionals, supervisory staff, labourers, and enforcement staff;
- provincial administration officers: the provincial commissioner, district commissioners, district officers, chiefs and subchiefs, and administration police;
- formal-sector business enterprises and their representative bodies;
- informal-sector business enterprises and their representative bodies;
- NGOs;
- religious organizations;
- citizen groups, either residential or sectoral.

Explaining the Pressure for Change

The political and civil society pressures for reform in Kenya have mounted throughout the 1990s, with the emphasis on political reform, first for the abolition of the one-party state, and subsequently for a 'level political playing field' through constitutional changes. However, public support for constitutional reform is powered by underlying social grievances and is particularly strong in urban areas, and Nairobi in particular, where the majority of those affected by social exclusion live. Moreover, the religious and non-governmental organizations, which have been involved in social-reform activities such as poverty alleviation for much longer, and have recently become more active in advocacy work, play a leading role in the constitutional reform movement.

Pressures for urban reform were already expressed in the preparations for the 1992 multiparty elections, when several political parties combined to articulate a post-election platform (PEAP, the Post Election Action Programme) that incorporated several sectors affecting Nairobi, including housing and other aspects of social exclusion (Friedrich-Naumann-Stiftung 1992). However, the common platform was submerged in the scramble for power through mainly ethnic allegiances and alliances in the run-up to the elections. Such reforms were next articulated in the Nairobi City Convention mentioned above, which included inputs from a wide spectrum of urban interests as compared with the PEAP document, which comprised expert advice to politicians (Karuga 1993). Again, the program, which included halting of demolitions, extension of services to informal settlements, and reform of building codes, was submerged in political in-fighting in the NCC, manipulated by central government. The director of the German foundation that supported both initiatives financially was deported.

The movement for constitutional reform, which developed a high political profile during 1997, focuses on the process of constitution-making and who has power over that. Opposition politicians within the movement see it largely as a way of increasing their chances of electoral victory through legal and administrative reforms. Civil society actors, including NGOs, religious organizations, and community-based groups, have a range of concerns that include urban issues, and these are articulated in the many detailed resolutions emerging from the four national convention assemblies held in 1997 and 1998 (NCEC 1997a, 1997b, 1997c, 1998).

Apart from this national forum, and the initiatives of Muungano wa Wanavijiji, Operation Firimbi, and the residents' associations mentioned above, the potential participants in a system of governance that would make for a more socially sustainable city are not engaged in any form of either negotiation or setting of goals that might contribute

towards such a system. All that exists in the late 1990s is some movement towards formation of more community-based and sectoral civic
organizations that might have the potential at some stage in the future
of defining their different interests and achieving strategic goals.

This makes it difficult to apply theories and models of urban politics
to analyse what is happening in Nairobi; the governing authorities are
fragmented and in conflict, and the social movements are inchoate.
Many different theories could explain the relationships between the
various actors, but not many can explain the details of how they deal
with each other. It is tentatively suggested that the lens of regime theory may be useful in examining how new coalitions might emerge
from the array of formal and informal interest groups currently jostling
within the Nairobi political arena (Stoker 1995).

There are aspects of regime theory which deal with power as a
means of gaining a capacity to act and accomplish goals, rather than as
control and resistance – 'power to' rather than 'power over.' It also
addresses power relations in socially complex systems and thus provides the opportunity of exploring empirically how different actors
open up political spaces for themselves, even though it has never been
applied in a situation like Nairobi's (Stoker 1995, 59, 69–70). It may
thus help to explain how the excluded groups in Nairobi can further
their goals in relation both to the existing power structure of urban politics and to the way in which powerful interests currently enjoy sys-
temic advantage (Stoker 1995, 57). Some such explanation is needed of
how the actors engaged in the governance crisis of Nairobi's third
social transformation can deal with each other.

Conclusion: Cooperation or Conflict?

In order for Nairobi's excluded majority to participate in the city's governance, the current social transformation must work its way through
towards greater democracy. We have explained how this is already
happening in the form of pressure for social reform, although the
nature of a new system of governance and how it will be established is
not clear. Such a system needs to be based in the dispossessed neighbourhoods and to reinvigorate the NCC from below. But it is not easy
to see how this will happen.

The PEAP and the Nairobi City Convention documents called for
neighbourhood associations that have formal recognition and a
defined relationship to local government. Muungano wa Wanavijiji as

a mass movement has representation from eighty-six Nairobi communities that are articulating their demands. These include the election of chiefs by residents as opposed to their appointment by the state. How are these demands going to work themselves out in relation to the existing structures of laws and administration, including the state apparatus and the NCC, which have their own conflicts based on competition for political control?

The Operation Firimbi campaign, run by the Mazingira Institute against the grabbing of public land by individuals for private use, encourages residents with grievances to organize local chapters and to campaign within the confines of the law, which is explained in public-information materials. But violations of the law backed by the authorities are so blatant that numerous communities have resorted to pulling down illegal structures and fences. Meanwhile, attacks on informal settlements and kiosks in the city have escalated. These are carried out by city and administration police, hired security guards, or gangs of youths, although the political leadership, at both national and city levels, frequently denies responsibility, claiming that the enforcers are simply upholding the law.

A Nairobi NGO official recently quoted a judgment of the Zimbabwe Court of Appeal: 'Law in a developing country cannot afford to remain static. It must undoubtedly be stable, but at the same time if it is to be a living force it must be dynamic and accommodating to change. If it fails to respond to fluid economic and social norms and values and altering views of justice and is not based on human necessities and experiences rather than philosophical notions, it will one day be cast aside by the people because it will have ceased to serve any useful purpose' (Weru 1998). This sums up the need for judicial as well as administrative reform, but the case of Nairobi is special in that those entrusted with upholding the law are as much or more prone to breaking it than are members of the general public. In this anarchic situation, it appears that a trend towards violent confrontation is more likely than that of a negotiated coalition of interests.

For a governing regime that incorporates a sufficient range of interests in the city to emerge in this context demands a considerable balancing act of the powerful forces at work. There is an opportunity for the high- and middle-income neighbourhoods to chart the course for a more inclusive system of governance, which could possibly provide a model for the excluded neighbourhoods. However, this will depend, first, on the model being socially inclusive in its own neighbourhoods, and, second, upon agreement by the NCC and government that such a model is acceptable. Should this occur, social forces within the city could have opened up the required political space for a new balance of power and greater social inclusiveness. A more democratic system of local governance would have the potential for social sustainability through the inclusion and distribution of benefits to various groups. But it will first be necessary for central government to move from its present position of intransigence to accommodate more interests in the city.

Notes

1 The authors are grateful to Dr Zinnat Bader Jaffer for material contributed to an earlier version of this paper.

References

Alder, Graham. 1995. 'Tackling Poverty in Nairobi's Informal Settlements: Developing an Institutional Strategy.' *Environment and Urbanization* 7/2: 85–107.

Bubba, Ndinda, and Davinder Lamba. 1991. 'Urban Management in Kenya.' *Environment and Urbanization* 3/1: 37–59.

Castells, Manuel. 1993. *The City and the Grassroots*. Berkeley and Los Angeles: University of California Press.

Egziabher, Axumite G., Daniel G. Maxwell, Diana Lee-Smith, Pyar Ali Memon, Luc J.A. Mugeot, and Camillus J. Sawio. 1994. *Cities Feeding People: An Examination of Urban Agriculture in East Africa*. Ottawa: International Development Research Centre.

Fainstein, Susan, and Clifford Hirst. 1995. 'Urban Social Movements.' In *Theories of Urban Politics*, ed. David Judge, Gerry Stoker, and Harold Wolman, 181–204. London: Sage.

Freeman, Donald B. 1991. *A City of Farmers: Informal Urban Agriculture in the Open Spaces of Nairobi, Kenya*. Montreal and Kingston: McGill-Queen's University Press.

Friedrich-Naumann-Stiftung. 1992. *Blueprint for a New Kenya: Post Election Action Programme*. Nairobi: Friedrich-Naumann-Stiftung.

Ghaidan, Usam. 1975. *Lamu: A Study of the Swahili Town*. Nairobi, Kampala and Dar es Salaam: East African Literature Bureau.

Godard, X., and P. Teurnier. 1992. *Les transports urbains en Afrique à l'heure de l'ajustement*. Paris: L'Institut National de Recherches sur les Transports et leur Sécurité (INRETS).

Guyer, Jane I., ed. 1987. *Feeding African Cities*. Manchester and New York: Manchester University Press, Studies in Regional Social History for the International African Institute.

Hake, Andrew. 1977. *African Metropolis*. Brighton: Sussex University Press.

Heyer, Judith, J.K. Maitha, and W.M. Senga, eds. 1976. *Agricultural Development in Kenya: An Economic Assessment*. Nairobi: Oxford University Press.

Hirst, Terry, with Davinder Lamba. 1994. *The Struggle for Nairobi*. Nairobi: Mazingira Institute.

ILO [International Labour Organisation]. 1972. *Employment, Incomes and Equality: A Strategy for Increasing Productive Employment in Kenya*. Geneva: ILO.

Judge, David, Gerry Stoker, and Harold Wolman, eds. 1995. *Theories of Urban Politics*. London: Sage.

Kapila, Sunita, Mutsembi Manundu, and Davinder Lamba. 1982. *The Matatu Mode of Public Transport in Metropolitan Nairobi*. Nairobi: Mazingira Institute.

Kanogo, Tabitha. 1987. *Squatters and the Roots of Mau Mau*. Nairobi: East African Educational Publishers.

Karuga, James, ed. 1993. *Action towards a Better Nairobi: Report and Recommendations of the Nairobi City Convention: 'The Nairobi We Want.'* City Hall, 27–9 July. Nairobi: Nairobi City Council.

Kenya, Republic of. 1994. *Kenya Population Census 1989*, vol. 1. Nairobi: Central Bureau of Statistics.

– 1996. *Kenya Population Census 1989: Analytical Report. Vol. VII: Population Projections*. Nairobi: Central Bureau of Statistics.

KHRC [Kenya Human Rights Commission]. 1996. *Behind the Curtain: A Study on Squatters, Slums and Slum Dwellers*. Nairobi: KHRC Land Rights Program.

Lamba, Davinder. 1994. *Nairobi's Environment: A Review of Conditions and Issues*. Nairobi: Mazingira Institute.

Lee-Smith, Diana. 1989. 'Urban Management in Nairobi: A Case Study of the Matatu Mode of Public Transport.' In *African Cities in Crisis: Managing Rapid Urban Growth*, ed. Richard E. Stren and Rodney R. White, 276–304. Boulder, CO: Westview.

– 1990. 'Squatter Landlords in Nairobi: A Case Study of Korogocho.' In *Housing Africa's Urban Poor*, ed. Philip Amis and Peter Lloyd, 175–87. Manchester and New York: Manchester University Press for the International African Institute.

– 1997. '"My House Is My Husband": A Kenyan Study of Women's Access to

Land and Housing.' Lund, Sweden: University of Lund, Department of Architecture and Development Studies, PhD Thesis 8.

Lee-Smith, Diana, and Davinder Lamba. 1991. 'The Potential of Urban Farming in Africa.' *Ecodecision* 3: 37–40.

Lee-Smith, Diana, Mutsembi Manundu, Davinder Lamba, and P. Kuria Gathuru. 1987. *Urban Food Production and the Cooking Fuel Situation in Urban Kenya*. Nairobi: Mazingira Institute. (Main research report and six town reports [Isiolo, Kakamega, Kisumu, Kitui, Mombasa, and Nairobi] giving results of a 1985 national survey.)

Lee-Smith, Diana, and Pyarali Memon. 1988. *Institution Development for Delivery of Low-Income Housing: An Evaluation of Dandora Community Development Project*. Monograph no. 1. Nairobi: Mazingira Institute.

Lee-Smith, Diana, and Richard Stren. 1991. 'New Perspectives on African Urban Management.' *Environment and Urbanization* 3/1: 23–36.

Mazingira Institute. 1991. *Settlements Information Network Africa (SINA)*. No. 24. Nairobi: Mazingira Institute.

– 1995. *SINA*. No. 34. Nairobi: Mazingira Institute.

– 1996a. *SINA* No. 36. Nairobi: Mazingira Institute.

– 1996b. *SINA* No. 37. Nairobi: Mazingira Institute.

– 1997a. *SINA* No. 38. Nairobi: Mazingira Institute.

– 1997b. *SINA* No. 39. Nairobi: Mazingira Institute.

Mitullah, Winnie. 1992. 'Hawking as a Survival Strategy for the Urban Poor in Nairobi: The Case of Women.' *Environment and Urbanization* 3/2: 13–22.

Muungano Wa Wanavijiji. 1997. 'Manifesto on Land Security and Permanent Shelter for the Urban Poor.' Nairobi.

NCEC [National Convention Executive Council]. 1997a. National Convention Assembly First Plenary Session. Limuru, 3–6 April. Declaration, Resolutions and Committee Reports.

– 1997b. National Convention Assembly Second Plenary Session. Limuru-Ufungamano 2, 25–8 August. Declaration and Resolutions.

– 1997c. National Convention Assembly Third Plenary Session. Limuru-Ufungamano 3, 27–9 October. Resolutions.

– 1998. National Convention Assembly Fourth Plenary Session, Limuru-Ufungamano 4, 26–8 February. Resolutions.

NGOs Council. 1997. 'Report of the Disbanded Urban SDD Programme Pilot Workshop on Community Participation and Conscientisation at the Grassroots Level held on May 13, 1997 at Korogocho Community Centre, Nairobi.' Mimeo.

Patel, Zarina. 1997. *Challenge to Colonialism: The Struggle of Alibhai Mulla Jeevanjee for Equal Rights in Kenya*. Nairobi: Publishers Distribution Services.

Pickvance, Christopher. 1995. 'Marxist Theories of Urban Politics.' In *Theories of Urban Politics*, ed. David Judge, Gerry Stoker, and Harold Wolman, 253–75. London: Sage.

Polèse, Mario, and Richard Stren. 1995. 'Understanding the New Socio-Cultural Dynamics of Cities: Building a Knowledge-base for Urban Management in the Twenty-first Century.' Paper prepared for Workshop on Socially Sustainable Cities, INRS-Urbanisation, Montreal, and Centre for Urban and Community Studies, Toronto, 15–18 October.

RELMA/PROP/Mazingira [Regional Land Management/Programme on Population and Development, Lund University/Mazingira Institute]. 1998. *Urban Food Production: A Survival Strategy of Urban Households*. Report of a Workshop on East and Southern Africa in Nairobi, Kenya, 3–5 May. Nairobi: RELMA, PROP, and Mazingira Institute.

Stoker, Gerry. 1995. 'Regime Theory and Urban Politics.' In *Theories of Urban Politics*, ed. David Judge, Gerry Stoker, and Harold Wolman, 54–71. London: Sage.

Stren, Richard, Mohamed Halfani, and Joyce Malombe. 1994. 'Coping with Urbanization and Urban Policy.' In *Beyond Capitalism vs. Socialism in Kenya and Tanzania*, ed. Joel D. Barkan, 175–200. Boulder, CO: Lynne Reiner.

Throup, David, and Charles Hornsby. 1998. *Multi-Party Politics in Kenya*. Nairobi: East African Educational Publishers.

Were, Gideon, and Derek A. Wilson. 1972. *East Africa through a Thousand Years, AD 1000 to the Present Day*. Ibadan: Evans Bros.

Werlin, Herbert. 1974. *Governing an African City: A Study of Nairobi*. New York and London: Africana.

Weru, Jane. 1998. Memo to Murtaza Jaffer on Nairobi land court cases. Facsimile. 21 May.

Westlands Association. 1998. 'Nairobi.' Flyer.

White, Thornton L.W., L. Silberman, and P.R. Anderson. 1948. *Nairobi: Master Plan for a Colonial Capital*. London: HMSO.

11 Cape Town: Seeking Social Sustainability in a Fast-Growing City

JOHN ABBOTT

On 1 July 1997, a new structure of local government was formally insti-
tuted in Cape Town, bringing to an end over a century of institutional-
ized racial segregation. The new structure replaces a complex system
of multilevel and segregated racial area authorities (see figure 11.1),
each having a racial classification that defined the group permitted to
live permanently within it – a racially defined zoning policy that
resulted in what is known as the 'apartheid city.'[1] The new structure
consists of a metropolitan council and six local councils (see figure
11.2). In accordance with government policy, the boundaries of the new
council were drawn to provide an equitable racial mix, and to ensure a
more even distribution of financial resources, providing thereby a basis
for the integration of the apartheid city. Such a restructuring, however,
can only provide the political framework for change; it cannot, of itself,
change the economic, social, and spatial realities.

Each major city in South Africa has experienced the urbanization
process in a different way, affected by factors such as migration trends,
levels of industrialization, and the effectiveness of application of the
1950 Group Areas Act which established the racially segregated zones.
Under apartheid, Cape Town was classified as a 'coloured labour preference area,' and the influx of people classified as 'black' was tightly
controlled. As a result, Cape Town is the only city in South Africa
where black Africans do not form a majority of the population. This
situation affects social sustainability in several ways. First, the city
experiences two distinct types of poverty. Among coloured people, the
areas of poverty tend to be in poorly maintained public-housing areas,
where many people live in tenements; here, the problems would be
similar to those associated with urban poverty in the North – high

school drop-out rates, gang warfare, and drugs. In the black areas, the poverty is that of the South – low levels of income and informal housing, and high informal-sector economic activity. To all of this must be added the spatial imbalance which is the major legacy of apartheid, as illustrated in figure 11.3.

In addressing these urban imbalances and inequalities, the primary concern at all levels of government has been to integrate the apartheid city. This in turn involves a heavy emphasis on physical interventions and spatial restructuring. Mario Polèse and Richard Stren (1995, 9) point out the importance of reducing spatial fragmentation in order to achieve social sustainability. Any discussion of social sustainability must take into account the spatial structure of the city, particularly in South Africa, where this has played a major role in shaping social conditions. It is important, therefore, to understand the extent to which physical intervention and spatial determinism can help to change those social conditions and, as a consequence, affect social sustainability.

Background: Cape Town since 1982

The recent social history of Cape Town can be divided into three phases. The first began in 1982, with the national change from a unicameral to a tricameral parliament,[2] which gave racial groups[3] classified as 'white,' 'coloured,' and 'Indian' separate 'parliaments' to handle their own affairs. One of the three, the House of Delegates, represented the coloured people and had its primary population centre in Greater Cape Town. Acting within its limited powers, the House of Delegates' major focus of activity was on housing and infrastructure. This led to a major social-housing initiative which resulted in the construction of 20,000 homes, albeit within the framework of the Group Areas Act, and therefore segregated.

For black African people the situation in 1982 was different. They continued to be excluded from any form of decision making at the national level, while locally they were grouped into new 'Black Local Authorities' (BLAs). In Cape Town, five BLAs were formed, of which three were within the boundary of the city as it existed at that time (see figure 11.1).

Prior to 1982, only three black townships within the city boundary (Langa, Nyanga, and Guguletu) had formal legal status, and access to them was tightly controlled, this control being a central feature of the Apartheid State. However, as David Dewar, T. Rosmarin, and Vanessa

Figure 11.1 Cape Town: The Apartheid City
Source: Cape Metropolitan Council

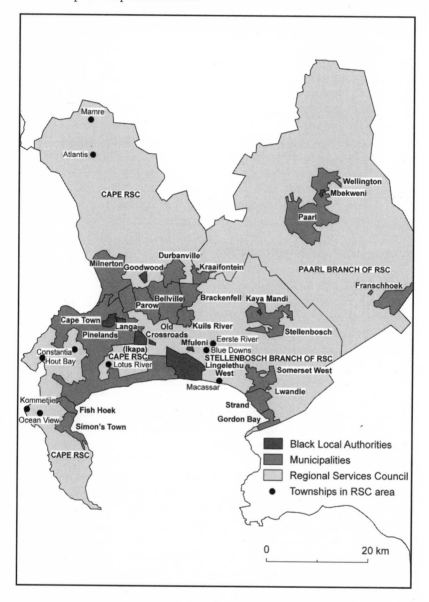

Figure 11.2 Cape Town Metropolitan and Local Authority Boundaries
(After 1 July 1997)
Source: Cape Metropolitan Council

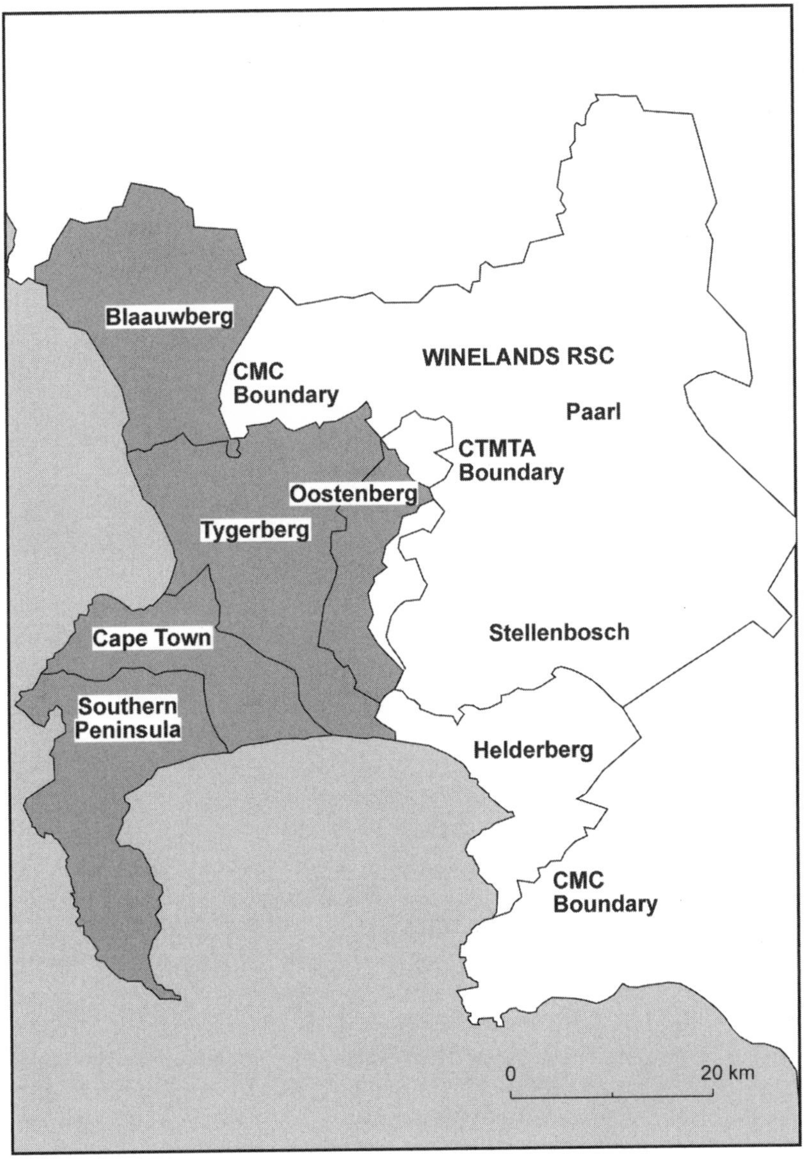

Figure 11.3 Racially Based Development, Cape Town
Source: CMC 1996, p. 18

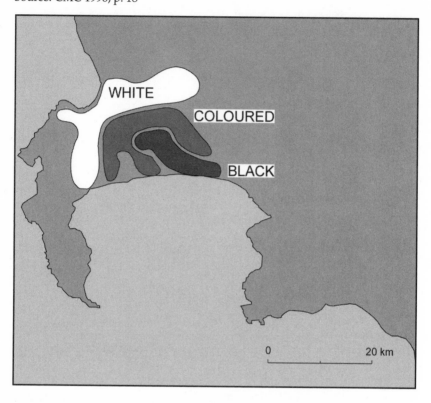

Watson point out, three factors made it particularly effective for Cape
Town. The first was the labour preference policy described earlier. 'The
second factor, linked to the first, was the cessation of the construction
of family housing for Africans in Cape Town' (Dewar, Rosmarin, and
Watson 1991, 14). The third factor was the absence of homeland boundaries close to Cape Town. This situation meant that migrants to Cape
Town had to find accommodation, either legally or illegally, within the
boundaries of the metropolitan area, thereby increasing pressure on
the city's only 'informal' area, Old Crossroads. In an attempt to remove
this last remaining 'black spot,' the South African government established the new area of Khayalitsha, which, however, simply filled with
new migrants, while Crossroads became a battleground of warlords
fighting for control. The period from 1982 to 1990 therefore saw the

black population increase threefold, as well as a shift from predominantly formal housing to predominantly informal housing.

The second phase of Cape Town's social history began in 1990, with the unbanning of the African National Congress (ANC) and the first discussions on local-government reform. Although the exact nature of the future local authority structure was then unclear, three features of the urban landscape were obvious. The first was the lack of access to economic opportunity for many of the coloured and black apartheid townships. The second was the fact that racially defined BLAs, which were in a state of financial and administrative chaos, would not survive the approaching political transition. Finally, the influx of black people from the rural areas of the Eastern Cape was continuing, and the absence of housing was leading to the growth of informal settlements, a situation that needed to be dealt with. The result was a series of initiatives around physical and spatial intervention, aimed at redressing these specific problem areas.

Cape Town is now entering a third phase, initiated by the election of democratic local authorities in October 1996 and the adoption of formal responsibilities by these new authorities in July 1997. For the first time in South Africa's history, all tiers of government are now democratically elected. This means that the power structure has changed from one controlled by white politicians to a more mixed elite system. Organizationally, the city has adopted a two-tier structure of metropolitan and local government, within which both the Cape Metropolitan Council (CMC) and the Cape Town Municipality (CTM) have created specific departments focusing on social or community development. In both cases the extent of the lack of meaningful social data is now obvious. At the same time, there is an emerging recognition that redressing the inequities of apartheid through specific physical interventions does not necessarily redress social inequalities. Hence a distinction should be drawn between, on the one hand, the need to deal with the integration of the apartheid city and the creation of a framework of social justice and, on the other, the need to address the specific issue of social sustainability in its own right. This will require a shift in emphasis and a change in the nature of current intervention strategies.

The Current Development Focus in Cape Town

The period between 1990 and 1995 represented a period of intense debate within local-government circles on how best to deal with South

Africa's apartheid cities. In Cape Town, four areas of strategic intervention emerged from the local-government restructuring process as central themes. The first two, spatial planning and transportation, gave rise in turn to two initiatives: first, the Metropolitan Spatial Development Framework (MSDF) with the associated implementation of the Wetton–Lansdowne Development Corridor; and, second, the Cape Town Transport Strategy, started by the City Council of Cape Town, but now being implemented by the Metropolitan Transport Directorate of the CMC.

The third area of strategic intervention was that of housing. Here, the primary area of focus was the integrated Serviced Land Project (iSLP), intended to house residents of the informal settlements on serviced land. The fourth area, associated with the upgrading of physical infrastructure in the formal black townships of the apartheid era, is not discussed in this chapter since, although it does contribute to the long-term social sustainability of the city, it deals primarily with a small, well-defined target group and has specific objectives. The chapter examines instead the first three of these initiatives, as they have much wider effects and more complex cross-linkages with one another.

The Metropolitan Spatial Development Framework (MSDF)

The concept of the MSDF grew from the need for long-term and developmentally oriented planning in the Cape Town Metropolitan Functional Region (Cape Metropolitan Council [CMC] 1996, viii).[4] It originated in 1991, when it became evident that local government would need to be completely restructured and a serious attempt made to integrate the different fragments of what then constituted the apartheid city. The process leading to the development of the framework was intended to be an inclusive one, and involved workshops with a number of key actors from government, business, labour, NGOs and civic organizations.

Conceptually, the basis of MSDF is

a vision of a well-managed, integrated metropolitan region in which development is intensified and compacted, and sprawl contained. It contains a series of spatial principles and policies that guide:
(a) Where physical development should and should not occur (or occur within constraints); and
(b) The desired form this growth should take. (CMC 1996, 5)

This vision is then translated into a series of development principles, goals, and guidelines, the evaluation criteria for which state that

> a central aim in the restructuring of the CMR [Cape Metropolitan Region] is to reduce the high life costs for the disadvantaged – not just the price of goods and services – but the costs of achieving routine daily tasks and goals. Such costs include the time and travel distances necessary to buy goods and the responsibilities and uncertainties of daily activities such as feeding a family. The objective is to improve this situation through an enhanced physical and social environment which offers necessary opportunities and a greater sense of personal and community control over the arrangements and processes of daily life. (CMC 1996, 32)

Finally, the document states that

> the experience of rapidly urbanizing cities indicates that the challenges of urbanization require more than a narrow focus on physical or spatial planning. Holistic, integrated and strategic planning is needed to ensure the coordinated provision and management of assets, services, facilities and infrastructure. (CMC 1996, 30)

This approach should provide a strong basis for integrated social development. Several key elements are mentioned – namely, resource management, community participation, and the interrelationship between spatial planning and economic and social policy. Unfortunately this integrated vision is not carried through into practice. The technical report (the detailed concept plan which acts as a reference report) itself states that

> the main purpose of the MSDF is to provide a framework to guide the form and location of physical development in the CMR at a metropolitan scale. This is essential in order to provide the context within which communities and private sector activity (formal, informal and international) can grow and expand. Growth and development are vital in order to address the historical legacy of under-development and deprivation that has contributed to leaving our cities and towns spatially (and socially) divided, highly inefficient, reliant on subsidies (particularly for public transport) and, in some areas, environmentally disastrous. Unless a concerted effort is made to alter and improve land-use and transport patterns, communities and the private sector will be unable to respond to all development opportunities. (CMC 1996, 3)

Hence, the primary objective of the MSDF is spatial planning, and is founded in the historical Eurocentric view that physical planning remains the primary determinant of urban form for cities in the South. To this end, MSDF identified four basic metropolitan structuring elements (CMC 1996, 4):

- urban nodes;
- activity corridors;
- a metropolitan open space system (MOSS); and
- an urban edge.

Of these four sets of spatial interventions, it is the elements of nodes and corridors that are given immediate priority. The MSDF identifies three 'mature metropolitan nodes' and then designates a fourth, the Philippi Centre, as a proposed metropolitan node (see figure 11.4). The MSDF argues that

> the development of a metropolitan node at the Philippi Centre is seen to be an advantage for the metropolitan region as a whole because [among other reasons] it forms the fourth, and final link, in a transportation system linking the Cape Town CBD, Bellville CBD and Claremont/Wynberg CBD. Given the huge daily flows of people from the Metro South East, the development of employment opportunities in this area would reduce the pressure on the public transport network. (CMC 1996, 36)

The Cape Town Municipality has accepted this concept as the basis for integrated spatial development within their area, and is implementing it through the Wetton–Lansdowne Development Corridor Project.

The Wetton–Lansdowne Corridor

The Wetton–Lansdowne Development Corridor comprises a 13.3-kilometre stretch of road between Wynberg and Philippi (see figure 11.4). It is the first major development to arise from the MSDF, and will contribute significantly to a coherent and integrated city structure, by linking the apartheid-zoned black and coloured areas, which were previously underserviced, with commercial and industrial centres in formerly white areas. The aim of the program is to stimulate the development of a major corridor and, to achieve the goals, it is considered essential to direct and prioritize initiatives in order to (among other aims):

Figure 11.4 Metropolitan Corridors and Nodes, Cape Metropolitan Region
Source: CMC 1996, p. 46

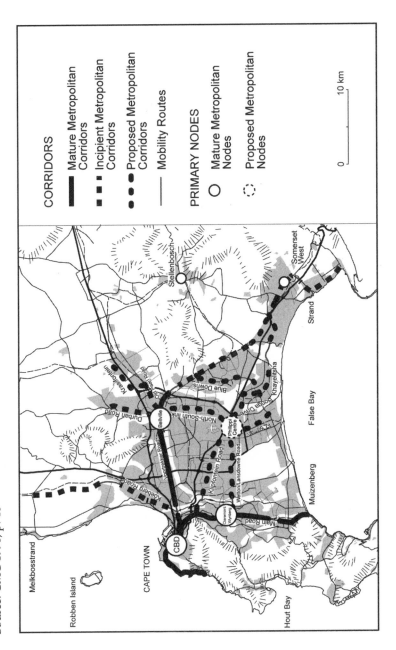

- ensure the integration of the study area with the greater city;
- ensure efficient urban form and an appropriate land-use mix;
- ensure that development takes place at the desired densities in order to sustain economic development and the proposed public transport system (Cape Town Municipality [CTM] 1997).

In pursuing the concept of a development corridor, the municipality has moved away from the 'Curitiba model'[5] originally envisaged by the CMC. Instead of high-density corridors, with dedicated high-speed transport lanes, it is emphasizing a mixed-use corridor that is similar in many ways to the city's existing corridors.

There is a great deal of logic to this approach. It is highly unlikely that the Curitiba model would work in Cape Town, given the limited regulatory power of local government in South Africa. On the other hand, a mixed-use corridor along this route does provide access to many areas that under apartheid were spatially isolated from the major urban nodes. This in turn contributes to the integration of the area into the greater city and begins to redress the imbalances in quantity and quality of services and facilities. At the same time, both the MSDF and the Wetton–Lansdowne Corridor project demonstrate that spatial planning is inextricably linked to transport planning. Thus the success of the former is dependent, to a large degree, on the success of the latter.

Moving Ahead: Developing a Transport Strategy for Cape Town

In the past, the production and annual updating of a metropolitan transport plan was a relatively mechanical exercise. It fulfilled a statutory requirement for the release of government funds for planning and implementation of metropolitan transport projects, to be approved by the provincial government, provided only that it 'integrates infrastructure, land-use, public transport, goods movement, traffic and travel demand management plans and programs' (CMC 1997, 1–1).

In 1994, the then-Metropolitan Transport Planning Branch of the City of Cape Town initiated a process called 'Moving Ahead,' intended to be a more holistic approach to transport planning in order 'to provide a transportation framework for the development of the Cape Metropolitan Region towards a more integrated and efficient urban environment, offering a better future for all the residents of the metropolitan area' (CMC 1997, 1–1).

As with many policy documents, Moving Ahead contains policy statements and strategic objectives that are politically and socially appealing, with an emphasis on economic and financial efficiency (CMC 1997, 2–1). From a social perspective the primary statement is that the goal of the transport policy should be 'meeting the basic needs of all transport users at affordable, acceptable and equitable levels of service' (CMC 1997, 2–5). The important issue to be debated is the extent to which these statements translate into practice. In this case,

> the principles of Moving Ahead ... are based on the following three premises:
> There will be a significant degree of spatial restructuring ... where there will be a much better match between people and jobs in all areas;
> This restructuring will occur primarily through integrated spatial development initiatives at major activity nodes and along activity corridors;
> An important role will be played by the containment of urban sprawl within a statutorily defined 'urban edge.' (CMC 1997, 4–1)

The transport plan assumes that these changes will happen, then looks at the resulting changes in terms of their spatial distribution, and then builds a transport strategy on the basis of these assumptions. It is thus an essentially reactive, rather than a proactive, policy.

The plan covers all modes of motorized transport. However, its main focus is on road transport and, within that specialized modal form, on commuter traffic. This bias is surprising for two reasons. First, because the wide spread in the objectives of car travel is clearly recognized by the following statement: 'It is a well known fact, both locally and internationally, that commuter trips (journeys to work) constitute only about 20–25 per cent of the total travel market in metropolitan areas. The majority of travel therefore takes place outside commuter peaks and consists primarily of commercial, business, and recreational trip purposes' (CMC 1997, 5–2). Second, at the national-government level, 'it is a national strategic objective to promote the use of public transport over private transport with the goal of achieving a ratio of 80:20 between public transport and private car usage' (CMC 1997, 5–14).

The current modal split for the journey to work in metropolitan Cape Town is 49:44:7 (public:private:walk/other). The Provincial Green Paper on the Western Cape Transport Policy proposes that 'a suitable target for the year 2005 is 54:34:12, [with] any reduction in the target for 'walk/other' being reflected in an increased share by public transport' (CMC 1997, 5–14, quoting PAWC 1996, 45–6). This policy is broadly supported by 'Moving Ahead,' which argues that the government's goal is unrealistic. Interestingly, 'Moving Ahead' suggests that achieving the '80 per cent public transport target can only be reached by focussing future transport policies and investments primarily in the direction of the middle and higher income groups ... [which] will almost certainly be unaffordable and politically unacceptable' (CMC 1997, 5–15).

To whom this would be unacceptable is not clear. In any case, the argument itself is a spurious one. The transport strategy which emerges from the document focuses primarily on road improvements for commuters, even though the same document shows that 88 per cent of road commuters are from those same upper- and middle-income groups (CMC 1997, 5–13). The more important, but unstated, point, is that a move towards public transport would require the introduction of financial penalties for road commuters. This contrasts with the policy as it is currently formulated, which proposes major additional expenditure for those same groups at little or no direct cost to themselves.

Spatial Restructuring and Social Sustainability

Over the past five years, Cape Town has undergone political restructuring, has developed a new spatial development framework, and has an emerging transport policy. All these initiatives are crucial in laying the foundations for social sustainability in the city. The question is to what extent they can achieve that objective. In this regard Cape Town, and South African cities generally, have a difficult task. Apartheid had a major impact upon the spatial structure of cities, which led in turn to gross inefficiencies in their spatial economies (Cameron 1995, 1). The World Bank argues that the correction of these urban spatial distortions through appropriate spatial and transport strategies 'will be particularly significant in the design of programs of economic growth and poverty alleviation' (Cameron 1995, p. 2, quoting the World Bank 1991).

The reality is that the spatial restructuring process has two distinct objectives. The first is to integrate the apartheid city. This is an objective in its own right, and initiatives such as the MSDF and the Wetton–Lansdowne project provide the mechanism for its achievement. The second objective is economic and social development. Both the MSDF and Wetton–Lansdowne have stated economic and social objectives;

Table 11.1 Contribution of Economic Sectors to GGP,
Cape Town Metropolitan Region, 1992

Sector	% contribution to GGP
Informal sector	28
Social services	22
Manufacturing	19
Commerce	11
Construction	7
Financial services	5
Agriculture & fishing	4
Transport & communications	4

Source: WESGRO 1992

they appear to rely, however, on two key assumptions to achieve these. The first assumes that spatial planning is the primary determinant of urban form; the second, that the linkage among spatial, economic, and social development will take the following form:

Spatial restructuring → Economic development → Social development

These are both questionable assumptions. On the one hand, international experience indicates that physical planning has been singularly unsuccessful in its attempts to determine the urban form of cities in the South. On the other hand, the assumed linkage is neither obvious nor automatic, particularly now that South Africa has entered the global economy and Cape Town must compete for capital at an international level. As Bill Cameron (1997) points out, the assumptions upon which the spatial-development scenarios of both the MSDF and 'Moving Ahead' are based 'are not so much predictions as "desired visions" of future urban form. [As such] they appear to be largely underpinned by physical planning notions in which accessibility, or proximity of people to activities, is the dominant logic.' The result, Cameron argues, is that 'the economic-spatial predictions are unconvincing. Political and market factors will be paramount in governing spatial development in the metropolitan region' (1997, 18–19). To this could be added the ongoing influx of poor people and the growth of informal settlements.

    The second area of concern relates to the potential for increased marginalization of the urban poor that could follow from the implementation of this framework, if the specific needs of this group are not taken into account. The MSDF states that 'a central aim in the restructuring of the CMR is to reduce the high life-costs for the disadvantaged' (CMC 1996, 32). Yet there is no clear strategy on how this is to be done, other than through spatial restructuring and improved access to formal job opportunities. However, as the U.N. Centre for Human Settlements (UNCHS) points out, 'governments often react to what appear to be spatial inequalities with spatial programmes when it is the inequality in the distribution of income or of government resources that underlies these inequalities, [whereas] the cost to the government ... may have been far more effectively spent in working with the low-income population there in developing their livelihood opportunities and in improving infrastructure and service provision' (UNCHS 1996, 107).

A brief examination of some basic data will give an indication of the broad social and economic conditions in Cape Town. According to interim 1996 census figures, the Western Cape as a whole has an urban population of 3.7 million (CSS 1997). Subtracting from this figure the population of the smaller towns, it would appear that Cape Town has a total population in the order of 2.4 million. The economically active population is estimated at 1.15 million; of these, approximately 736,000, or 64 per cent, are in formal employment (table 11.1 shows the contribution to Gross Geographic Product [GGP] of formal and informal-sector economic activity in the CMR). Of the 414,000 people who are unemployed or working in the informal sector, almost 50 per cent are black residents (WESGRO 1992).

Given a total black population of approximately 540,000, this means that the unemployment rate among the economically active black African population in Cape Town is in excess of 50 per cent. The majority of the black population leave school with only a Standard 6 education (reached at the age of fourteen) or lower, while fewer than 40 per cent of the economically active population have a secondary school qualification higher than Standard 4 (usually attained by age twelve) (Palmer Development Group 1990). Only 31 per cent of the CMR's residents are adequately housed; the majority of the population, or 69 per cent, are evenly divided into those who are homeless (living in informal or squatter settlements), and those who are poorly housed (including in site and service areas) (WESGRO 1992).

This situation is central to the debate on social sustainability. The World Bank sees the consequences of spatial and transportation strategies as being of particular significance in the design of programs for poverty alleviation. Yet it is not clear how this will occur. As discussed earlier, both the spatial-restructuring and transport-policy documents rely on a tenuous linkage among spatial restructuring, economic development, and social development, and even there the issue of poverty alleviation is not discussed as an issue in its own right.

The social indicators outlined above provide a different interpretation, appearing to indicate that spatial planning is only one component of a more complex development process, consistent with the UNCHS argument mentioned above. If this is the case, it raises serious concerns about the ability of spatial interventions to improve social conditions directly. However, before arguing this point too strongly, it is important to explore the extent to which the spatial intervention does in fact tie in with other development initiatives, which are aimed specifically at the urban poor. Here, the only initiative of major importance is centred on housing provision. The section that follows describes this initiative, and then relates it to the spatial and transportation strategies before drawing final conclusions.

Housing and Social Sustainability in Cape Town

Forty-nine per cent of all South African families have an income in Rand (R) of less than R1,000 per month (equivalent to US$220 at 1997 exchange rates) (Department of Housing 1997). This is clearly a major constraint on the extension of homeownership. To address this problem the government has pursued a policy of providing a capital subsidy towards the cost of physical infrastructure and housing (Department of Housing 1994). At present the subsidy can only be granted to families who have tenure, a policy which results, effectively, in new or greenfield developments.

The capital subsidy scheme used in South Africa is based upon construction being financed by the end user, who receives a subsidy on transfer of the property. The concept was piloted by the Independent Development Trust, following the allocation of R750 million for housing in the 1990 Budget. This concept was developed by the de Loor Task Group on Housing and adopted by the ANC government when it came to power in 1994. Essentially, the subsidy comprises a once-only capital grant of up to R15,000 for families with a monthly household income of less than R800. The subsidy operates on a declining scale, descending to R5,000 for those families earning between R2,501 and R3,500 per month.

The Integrated Serviced Land Project

By 1990, the influx of people into a restricted Cape Town housing market had led to the creation and growth of increasing numbers of squatter settlements and backyard shacks. The result was that, by May 1991, 'there were some 56,000 families without rights to serviced land, but living in and adjacent to the formal townships of Langa, Nyanga and Guguletu' (Cape Provincial Administration 1992, 2). Using the concept of the capital subsidy described above, the SLP (Serviced Land Project, later renamed the 'integrated Serviced Land Project,' or iSLP) was established in 1991 to develop a managed land-settlement policy.

The SLP identified four different implementation 'techniques' for housing inhabitants of informal settlements: site and service, managed land settlement, 'roll-over' upgrading, and 'in-situ' upgrading (Cape Provincial Administration 1993, 2).[6] In practice, however, in the early years the project concentrated on the first of these and has only recently begun to work on roll-over upgrading (which is used to complement, rather than replace, site and service schemes).

The reason for this choice was based upon the project's perceptions of 'acceptable' densities. Informal settlements in Cape Town do not achieve the levels of density experienced in Latin American cities, and densities are also extremely variable, ranging from 40 to 120 dwelling units per hectare (du/ha). While the SLP recognized that in-situ upgrading can achieve densities of up to 110 du/ha, the final recommendation was that 'a minimum initial density of 30 du/ha should be achieved in all residential development projects except where precluded by servitudes that cannot be amended or physical barriers that cannot be relocated, and that where possible, every endeavour should be made to achieve densities of 40 du/ha' (Cape Provincial Administration 1993, 4).

The result was that the vast majority of families were moved to site-and-service schemes located on inhospitable sites on the periphery of the city, where they were provided with box-like dwellings measuring approximately 20 square metres. Although 'public participation in planning processes and the ability to make choices are important cornerstones of the Serviced Land Project' (Cape Provincial Administration 1992, 6), this has not happened in practice. Discussions with community members in affected areas indicate that there is no choice. On the contrary, people are warned that if they do not move to a site and service scheme they will lose their right to a housing subsidy (personal communication 1997).

The results of the iSLP are mixed. Unlike other capital subsidy schemes elsewhere in the world, indications are that the iSLP has managed to target the very poor (those earning less than R800 per month). The process itself, however, has not been particularly effective. Under this scheme, approximately 6,000 families have been relocated over five years to the periphery of Cape Town, at a cost of over R750 million. In the same period the population of those same settlements has continued to grow, with an increase of 25 per cent in 1994–6 alone.[7] Coupled with the destruction of social cohesion, the loss of social capital and the loss of economic opportunity associated with this process of relocation, there must be serious doubts about the negative impact of this program on social sustainability in Cape Town.

From a Housing Policy to a Shelter Strategy

If housing provision is to benefit the poor, the housing developments must be situated close to the major areas of work opportunity, and must create socially cohesive neighbourhoods. A 1993 study set out to ascertain the various ways in which the 'compaction' of Cape Town could be achieved, including the promotion of higher densities (Behrens 1993). The study's review of international experience indicated that the greatest potential for significantly more compact urban form lies in the form of high-density infill development of well-located, vacant, or underused land parcels. This was seen as being more effective than densification in areas of low residential and population density, which was seen to be a much slower process (Behrens 1993).

A second study focused specifically on low-income residents in the city. Its purpose was to 'establish whether or not higher density infill developments will offer significant costs or savings over the current pattern of peripheralised [sic] development for lower income groups, and determine how it will be possible to provide affordable shelter on well-located public land' (Development Action Group 1993, 2).

The study identified five portions of 'well-located'[8] public land, with a total area available for development in excess of 1,200 hectares. Having identified the land, the report then made two important points on its use. The first was that higher-density infill developments would not be significantly more expensive, and in some cases would offer savings, when compared with the current pattern of peripheral development. The second conclusion was that, because of the cost of formal housing, the provision of such housing on well-located sites would still exclude approximately 80 per cent of black households (Development Action Group 1993, 118).

To address the latter problem, the study recommended subsidizing the land for low-income housing. However, this recommendation failed to take account of economic realities. Although the local authority paid lip-service to the concept of low-income housing close to the city, this was overridden by economic pressure. Of the first three (and most important) sites on the list, one was allocated to the Olympic bid committee, and the second is being sold piecemeal to commercial development. Only in the third is there a small allocation for low-income families. This was achieved through the formalization of a land invasion, and resulted in the housing of 1,000 families. Thus the experience in Cape Town to date indicates that the use of a spatial planning approach will not succeed in achieving the redistribution of housing to the urban poor.

From these findings, the report identified four options: a significant increase in the subsidy; providing serviced sites without dwellings; granting recognition to (and thereby, to a degree, encouraging) land invasion; or subletting backyard shacks or rooms. Dealing with land invasions was considered politically unacceptable at that time. Hence the focus was upon the last option – the informal rental market. This in turn resulted in a major study which is still taking place (see Gilbert et al. 1997).

In the intervening period, the number of land invasions in Cape Town has grown significantly. Current research indicates that, depending upon how boundaries are classified, there are 62 informal settlements within the Cape Town Metropolitan area, comprising 60,200 shacks (see note 7). In addition, a significant number of shacks are situated within the backyards of formal dwellings. Further, the number of shacks within the metropolitan boundary increased by 23 per cent between mid-1994 and mid-1996.

The iSLP classified those people living in informal settlements as 'the homeless population' (Cape Provincial Administration 1992, 2). This is consistent with the view that informal settlements are a 'problem.' Current international thinking recognizes that, on the contrary, these settlements can be seen as the beginning of a solution to the crisis of cities in the South.[9] In line with this thinking, the Urban Management Research Group at the University of Cape Town has been adapting and developing Brazilian-based methodology for the in-situ upgrading of informal settlements. This research indicates that such upgrading can provide a viable alternative to relocation which would be of immense benefit to the urban poor and would contribute significantly towards a meaningful policy of social sustainability in Cape Town (Abbott, Huchzermeyer, and Martinez 1997).

Measuring Social Sustainability

The living conditions of the urban poor were of little interest to the previous, apartheid, government. As a result the only data to have been collected tend to be limited in scope and sector-based. Both levels of local government have recognized this constraint. The CMC has established a Directorate of Economic and Community Development, and the CTM a Directorate of Community Development, with the different titles reflecting the different emphases of the two tiers of local government. Both acknowledge the dearth of social information and are attempting to rectify the situation. In the interim, however, the various initiatives described above continue without these data, making the measurement of social sustainability extremely difficult.

In comparison with other cities in the South, Cape Town is relatively affluent. It has a higher-than-average mean per-capita income, and is perceived to have a lower level of urban poverty. It is this perception that has led to the focus among professionals on Curitiba as a development model. However, the perception is misplaced. Over one-third of Cape Town's population still either work in the informal sector or are unemployed. Over one fifth of all families live in shacks, while a further third live in overcrowded, substandard accommodation. Hence, Cape Town is much more typical of cities in the South than many professionals recognize. The misconception is due partly to the way in which the apartheid city 'hid' poverty in areas that were not easily seen or recognized, and partly by the dearth of social data, which has masked the true situation. Coupled with these factors is the dual nature of urban poverty, which was mentioned in the introductory section. Without a means of measuring social sustainability, it is difficult to see how the various developmental initiatives currently under way and described here can meet the ambitious economic and social objectives that they define for themselves.

Towards Social Sustainability for Cape Town

Four conceptual 'themes' emerge from the analysis of the current process of change in Cape Town, when viewed from the perspective of social sustainability. The first of these is the strong emphasis on physical planning and physical intervention as the primary instrument of change in the city. This intervention is crucial, and should not be underestimated. Under apartheid, Cape Town was divided into three racial groupings, each with its own designated areas. However, as mentioned earlier, virtually all the economic activity was situated in areas classified as 'white.' Breaking down these artificial barriers is essential if the city is to move towards social sustainability. The creation of spatial linkages, such as the Landsdowne–Wetton Development Corridor, is crucial in this regard. This type of development, however, while it improves access to formal employment opportunities, does not necessarily lead to social equity.

Based upon the limited social and economic data available, what appears to be happening in Cape Town is a polarizing of society – the second theme. On one side are those with education and skills, who are finding increasing opportunities in the formal employment sector. On the other side are those with neither, who are living in the informal city and the informal economy, and whose social and economic conditions appear to be deteriorating. Spatial restructuring does very little to aid this group, yet this is the fastest growing sector of the population. With its net growth rate of 23 per cent over two years, meeting the needs of this sector is an essential component of any attempt to achieve social sustainability.

This leads us to the third theme, which is the failure to use transport to influence structural change. The introduction of an effective and efficient public transport system is central to the success of the MSDF and, more critically, as a basis for long-term social sustainability. Unfortunately the current transport policy gives public transport a very low priority, as indicated by the minimalist approach to changing the private-vehicle share of the market. There is an overriding focus on commuter traffic, even though the low ratio of commuter trips to total trips is acknowledged.

Coupled with this is 'a strong anti-rail bias among transportation professionals, the majority of whom come from a background in roads, [illustrated by various] scathing comments about "the undesirability of a return to the railway city era of urban development"' (Cameron 1997, 11). As Cameron points out, these are 'irresponsible in that they create negative attitudes towards rail and oversimpify the situation' (1997, 11).

This point reflects the lack of any attempt to address the transport needs of the urban poor. Effective transport planning could play a major role in integrating the urban poor into the formal city. It is essential in addressing the needs of women, many of whom work in the informal sector. Meeting the needs of children, in improving home-school linkages, for example, would have a major long-term benefit. There is also a need to understand how different modes of transport are used by different sectors of the population over the entire day. And finally, there is the need to improve the public transport system for the poorer sections of the population. Yet none of these issues has been considered. Instead, the city is developing a transport plan which concerns itself solely with middle-class commuters, one which is geared primarily to maintaining their privileges, presumably on the basis that the transport needs of this group are most critical to international competitiveness.

The fourth theme which emerges from this study is the inappropriateness of the current housing delivery process. As Polèse and Stren point out,

> control over patterns of land and housing is a central function of urban-based management systems almost everywhere in the world. The manner in which housing and land markets function is a very important determinant of the capacity of households to choose where to live, and therefore their ability to build up tangible future assets and make a commitment to the urban area in question. Successful policies in this field will have a strong relationship with the integration of imigrant groups into city life, with the development of a viable approach for environmental sustainability, and with the maintenance of viable neighbourhood life. (Polèse and Stren 1995, 14)

The strategy of moving from non-tenured sites virtually all of the city's estimated 56,000 families who lack rights to serviced land has not worked. While only a small proportion of these families have been moved to site-and-service schemes, the number of families living on non-tenured sites has doubled. Neither has the move taken into account the importance of social networks and of social capital. Similarly, there has been no attempt to evaluate the living expenses of people in these new areas, compared to their expenses in the informal settlements.

Conclusions

This analysis has highlighted the danger of focusing on these physical interventions in isolation from their direct social impact. It argues that there is a strong need to create direct linkages which seek to identify and define the impact of (and preferably the relationship between) the physical intervention and the social improvement. It is in moving to this next phase that the challenge, and the hope, for a sustainable future for Cape Town lies.

To make that transition the city needs to learn from the experiences of other countries, in both the North and the South, for Cape Town spans this divide perhaps more evenly than any other city in the world. The thrust of the MSDF, and the Development Corridor Project associated with it, seeks to improve social conditions through improved access to employment opportunities. But this is of benefit only to those with skills to trade. The experience of the North points to high unemployment among the young, who never have the opportunity to enter the job market. This is happening on an increasing scale among the coloured community. The experience of the South points to the growing informal sector that is excluded from the formal city and increasingly marginalized. This, too, is happening in Cape Town, among the black population.

These are the challenges that Cape Town must face in its search for social sustainability. This means moving forward with some of the current initiatives, but also modifying them and bringing in others. The planning focus is still too Eurocentric. The informal sector contributes 28 per cent of the area's GGP (see table 11.1). This sector needs to be encouraged, but it also needs to be researched. In particular there is a need to identify the linkages between the informal sector and the informal settlements. How much do these settlements contribute to the sector? How important is the role of social capital in these areas? How can they be upgraded, with minimum relocations, in a way which builds local capacity, encourages individual growth, and enhances self-respect? And how can they be integrated more fully into the formal city?

A different set of issues arises in connection with high unemployment among Cape Town's youth. Major expenditure on school buildings in the new area of Mitchells Plain (at the time a coloured area) during the 1980s did not improve the education of the population to any significant extent, nor did the provision of community halls prevent the development of the social problems now emerging on the

Cape Flats. A new urban development node at Philippi may offer major benefits. These will be of little value, however, if they are not being integrated into a framework of social sustainability.

In conclusion, this paper has argued that the strategic interventions currently being initiated in Cape Town are directed towards a specific objective – the integration of the Apartheid City. They are not directed specifically at the achievement of social sustainability. Economic and social development are secondary objectives, but it is extremely unlikely that these will be achieved. The interventions need to be refocused if they are to address the issue of social sustainability in a meaningful way. Social objectives need to be defined, and social indicators identified which measure these objectives. Only then can Cape Town say that it is working towards social sustainability as a goal in its own right.

Notes

1 Richard Tomlinson, quoting PLANACT (1990), defines the apartheid city in the following way: 'The *apartheid* city has four components:

i. A spatial system that allocates populations in urban space according to their colour ...

ii. An urban management system predicated on the notion that towns and cities can be compartmentalised into separate units presided over by separate local governments, with their own fiscal, legal, administrative and representative systems.

iii. A system of urban service provision that provides land, infrastructural services, transport and community facilities in a way that severely disadvantages the urban poor and subisdises the white ratepayer with surpluses generated from black consumption.

iv. A housing delivery system that subsidises whites and relegates the black majority to either homelessness or rental status with no security of tenure. (Tomlinson 1994, 5).

For a more detailed explanation of this concept see Lemon 1991.

2 Derek Japha and Marie Huchzermeyer 1995, p. 5, point out that 'there is as yet no comprehensive history of the housing policies and practices that created townships [in South Africa].' However, their own publication does provide something of a history of black township development, both prior

to and during this period. A further useful, albeit more specific, case study is to be found in Awotono et al. 1995.

3 The South African apartheid system classified people according to their racial origins. A total of four distinct racial groups was defined. The first was 'white' and was reserved for people of European origin. The second was 'African,' often referred to as 'black.' This referred to the indigenous population of the country. The third was 'coloured.' This referred to all people of mixed race, people of Hottentot background, or people descended from the early Malay slaves. The fourth group was 'Indian' and referred to people whose origins lay in the Indian subcontinent.

4 The Cape Metropolitan Area and the Winelands Region form one functional region referred to as the Cape Metropolitan Region (CMR).

5 The Curitiba model is a specific approach to integrated land-use and transportation planning, based upon the concept of development corridors and a road-based public transport system. The name stems from the town in Brazil where the model was developed. According to P. Vithlani, these corridors promote an extension of 'downtown functions' (i.e., good service and residential facilities, with many cultural activities in close proximity) achieved by developing a mixed-use land concept (Vithlani 1997, 1). Development in the corridor zone is strictly regulated and the average height of buldings is set at 25 storeys, with the first two floors being for service and commercial activity. This means that the corridors support an average of 600 dwelling units per hectare. The maximum walking distance to a bus stop is 3 minutes, and the maximum waiting time for a bus is 10 minutes.

6 In a South African context, the term 'rollover' upgrading refers to the condition whereby shacks are first removed from a site, after which the site is graded, set out and pegged, and provided with services. Some of the shack dwellers are then allowed to move back on to newly established sites, but this is usually a much smaller number than originally occupied the site. Those less favoured are moved to a new site, generally on the periphery of the city. The term 'in-situ upgrading' refers to the situation where the site is provided with infrastructure while the people stay where they are. There is an absolute minimum of relocation, and those who have to be moved are relocated as close to the existing site as possible.

7 This figure is drawn from a longitudinal study of shack growth in Cape Town, obtained by a count of shacks over a two-year period. This work is being carried out under a research project in progress.

8 The term 'well located' is used in the document to refer to land that is situated within or close to areas where industrial and commercial activi-

ties are concentrated, not simply land surrounding the Cape Town city-centre.

9 In Belo Horizonte, Brazil, the Uniao dos Trabalhadores da Perifia (Union of Peri-Urban Workers) coined the slogan that *favelas* is not a problem: it is a solution' (AVSI 1995, 4).

References

Abbott, John, Marie Huchzermeyer, and I. Martinez. 1997. 'Methodologies for Integrating GIS with Social Processes: The Need for Appropriate Informal Settlement Upgrading.' Paper prepared for iKUSASA/CONSAS 97 international conference, Durban, South Africa, 24–8 August.

AVSI [Associazione Volontari per il Servizio Internationale]. 1995. 'Alvorado Programme: Providing Security of Tenure for the Poor.' Informal paper prepared by AVSI, Belo Horizonte, Brazil, for presentation to the Dubai International Conference on Best Practice for Habitat II, November.

Awotono, A., D. Japha, I. Prinsloo, L. Le Grange, M. Huchzermeyer, D. Boberg, and M. Briggs. 1995. *Townships in Cape Town: Case Study Area Profiles*. ODA Research Scheme no. R6266 – The Integration and Urbanisation of Existing Townships in the Republic of South Africa, Working Paper 9. Newcastle: Centre for Architectural Research and Development Overseas (CARDO), Department of Architecture, University of Newcastle.

Behrens, R. 1993. 'Higher Density Development: A Review of Policy Measures, Restrictive Regulations and Residential Trends in Greater Cape Town.' Unpublished project report. Urban Problems Research Group and Development Action Group, Cape Town.

Cameron, J.W.M. 1995. 'Urban Restructuring and Development: Proposals for a Multi-departmental Integrated Urban Restructuring Strategy.' Draft report prepared for the South African Department of Transport, October.

– 1997. 'Transportation Assessment.' A component of the Strategic Environmental Assessment for the Cape Town Olympic Bid. Unpublished document, Cape Town Olympic Bid Committee, May.

Cape Metropolitan Council [CMC]. 1996. *Metropolitan Spatial Development Framework: A Guide for Spatial Development in the Cape Metropolitan Functional Region*. Technical report. Cape Town: CMC.

– 1997. *1997–1998 Interim Metropolitan Transport Plan*. ('Moving Ahead': Cape Metropolitan Transport Plan). Cape Town: CMC.

Cape Provincial Administration. 1992. 'Serviced Land Project: An Overview.' Report 4 of the Serviced Land Project. Cape Town.

- 1993. *Illustrated Guidelines on Densities, Planning Principles and Levels of Service.* Report 3 of the Serviced Land Project. Cape Town.

Cape Town Municipality [CTM]. 1997. 'The Wetton–Lansdowne Development Corridor Programme: Project Overview.' Unpublished document. Cape Town.

Central Statistical Service, Republic of South Africa. 1997. *Preliminary Estimates of the Size of the Population of South Africa.* Project no. 113/1997, June 1997. Pretoria: Central Statistical Service.

Department of Housing, Republic of South Africa. 1994. *White Paper: A New Housing Policy and Strategy for South Africa.* Government Gazette, Vol. 354, no. 16178. Pretoria: Government Printer.

- 1997. *Housing the Nation: Doing Justice to Delivery.* Unpublished report prepared by the Ministry of Housing, January.

Development Action Group. 1993. *Well Located Housing: Key Issues in the Provision of Affordable Higher-Density Shelter on State-Owned Land in Metropolitan Cape Town.* Research report. Cape Town: Development Action Group.

Dewar, David, T. Rosmarin, and Vanessa Watson. 1991. *Movement Patterns of the African Population in Cape Town: Some Policy Implications.* Working Paper no. 44 (Occasional Paper no. 31). Cape Town: Urban Problems Research Unit, University of Cape Town.

Gilbert, Alan, Alan Mabin, Malcolm McCarthy, and Vanessa Watson. 1997. 'Low-Income Rental Housing: Are South African Cities Different?' *Environment and Urbanization* 9/1: 133–47.

iSLP [integrated Serviced Land Project]. 1998. 'iSLP Quota Allocation Table.' Unpublished document, iSLP, Cape Provincial Administration.

Japha, Derek, and Marie Huchzermeyer. 1995. *The History of the Development of Townships in Cape Town, 1920–1992.* ODA Research Scheme no. R6266 – The Integration and Urbanisation of Existing Townships in the Republic of South Africa. Working Paper 2. Newcastle: Centre for Architectural Research and Development Overseas (CARDO), Department of Architecture, University of Newcastle.

Lemon, Anthony. 1991. 'The Apartheid City.' In *Homes Apart*, ed. Anthony Lemon, 1–25. Bloomingtom and Indianapolis: Indiana University Press.

Minter, S. 1997. 'Integrating Transport and Land Use: Lessons from the North and South.' Draft Working Paper, February. Cape Town: Urban Problems Research Unit, University of Cape Town.

Palmer Development Group. 1990. 'Education in South Africa.' Unpublished commissioned report to provide Science Park background information.

PAWC [Provincial Administration of the Western Cape]. 1996. *Provincial Green*

Paper on Western Cape Transport Policy. Cape Town: Department of Transport and Public Works, PAWC.

PLANACT. 1990. *Annual Report 1989/90.* Yeoville [Johannesburg]: PLANACT.

Polèse, M., and R. Stren. 1995. 'Understanding the New Socio-Cultural Dynamics of Cities: Building a Knowledge-base for Urban Management in the Twenty-first Century.' Paper prepared for a workshop on Socially Sustainable Cities, Montreal and Toronto, 15–18 October.

Tomlinson, Richard. 1994. *Urban Development Planning: Lessons for the Economic Reconstruction of South Africa's Cities.* London and New Jersey: Zed Books.

UNCHS [United Nations Centre for Human Settlements. Habitat]. 1996. *An Urbanizing World: Global Report on Human Settlements 1996.* Oxford: Oxford University Press.

Vithlani, P. 1997. 'Integrated Public Transport: Transition of the Curitiba model to Cape Town.' Unpublished document. Urban Problems Research Unit, University of Cape Town.

WESGRO. 1992. *South Africa's Leading Edge? A Guide to the Western Cape Economy.* Cape Town: WESGRO.

Wilkinson, P. 1997. 'Housing Policy in South Africa: Retrospect and Prospects, Housing in the 21st Century: Looking Forward.' Paper presented to the international conference of the International Sociological Association, Research Committee 43: Housing and the Built Environment, Alexandria, VA, 11–14 June.

12 Learning from Each Other: Policy Choices and the Social Sustainability of Cities

MARIO POLÈSE

What Is New?

The ten cities examined in this volume all exhibit spatial segregation and social segmentation in varying degrees, whether based on class, ethnicity, or language. The reader may well ask, What is really new? Throughout history, cities have been divided, residentially, commercially, and socially. The very word 'ghetto' has its origins in renaissance Venice, more than 500 years ago, where it designated an enclosed quarter restricted to Jews. In the eighteenth century, in both Paris and London, the west of the city was already clearly fashionable, and the east plebeian, perhaps because the prevailing wind blows from the west, perhaps because the courts of Versailles and Westminster had pushed fashion westward (Hohenberg and Hollen Lees 1995, 297). Some form of residential segregation, whether forced or voluntary, of minority groups (however defined) has been the rule in most large cities of North America and Western Europe since the beginnings of social-science research on cities. A minor social-science industry has grown up around the analysis and measurement of residential segregation in cities (Elizabeth Huttman [1991] provides an excellent recent compendium).

Many modern students of the city, including contributors to this volume, appear to sense, if only intuitively, the emergence of a new, more brutal, form of spatial polarization, often subsumed under the term 'exclusion.' 'Exclusion' has a much stronger connotation than 'residential segregation.' In chapter 1 we suggested that exclusion may be seen as the polar opposite of social sustainability. The modern city offers new possibilities for physically, politically, and socially isolating ('excluding') certain groups, if only because of the wonders of modern transportation technology (more on this below). Economic opportunity and social integration ('inclusion,' in other words) in the modern city are inextricably linked to access to 'spaces' that define one's participation in society: to land, living space, recreational space, workspace, localized institutions, and services. The walled city is certainly not a new phenomenon, but existed primarily for military reasons, not for reasons of social exclusion. The rise of gated communities for the wealthy, protected by guards, in Latin American, North American, and African cities, however, suggests that, under certain conditions, the strains of modern urban dynamics can lead to a breakdown in the collective will (or capacity) to live together harmoniously in a common urban polity. Those strains are visible in many of the case studies presented in this book. We may well ask: Is social exclusion a necessary outcome of the dynamics of the modern (or postmodern) city? Is the social sustainability of the modern city a utopian dream?

Learning from Each Other

Based on the ten case studies contained in this book, should one be optimistic or pessimistic? There certainly are grounds for pessimism. The plight of the American inner city, vividly portrayed in the Baltimore and Miami chapters, demonstrates that national economic progress and prosperity alone are not sufficient conditions to ensure the social sustainability of cities. The Geneva case study makes the same point. In short, one should not expect urban exclusion in São Paulo, Nairobi, Cape Town, or San Salvador (or, for that matter, in any other developing city) to magically disappear as their respective nations (one hopes) grow richer.

Is there something irreversible or universal in the dynamics of modern (or postmodern) society that threatens to undermine the roots of urban social sustainability? Residential polarization, often with decaying (battle) zones reserved de facto for the 'excluded,' is a sad reality in growing number of industrialized cities, not just the United States;[1] the roots of this condition seem to grow more intractable as cities evolve. In part, this may simply be a result of the sheer size and anonymity of the modern city, different from the more compact walking city of yesteryear.[2] Other factors have equally been suggested by contributors to this book, most notably deindustrialization and globalization, specifically in the cases of Rotterdam and Geneva, with their concomitant impacts on labour markets, immigration, and possible weakening of the welfare state.

Many trends underlying the dynamics of urban exclusion are almost irreversible: trends related to innovations in transport technology, rising incomes, and the physical expansion of the city (see Policy Choice no. 1, below). However, others are linked to policy choices that can differ from nation to nation, producing different results. We can usefully learn from the experiences of others, both successes and failures. The American urban experience, as noted earlier, is especially rich in this respect. Arguably, the United States has been the least successful of all major industrialized nations in producing safe, livable, and inclusive cities.[3] Crime rates in U.S. cities are systematically well above those for other industrialized cities, and often even above those for Latin American cities. Figures for 1990 show homicide rates in Greater Miami approximately three times higher than those in Buenos Aires or Caracas, and about ten times those for metropolitan Toronto and Montreal (Camp 1990). Not surprisingly, the issue of crime looms large in both American case studies (Baltimore and Miami), with Jonathan Simon (in chapter 4) going so far as to propose crime (or rather the fight against crime) as a paradigm for urban governance, a new euphemism for exclusionary policies to keep the 'nice' parts of the city safe and the 'others' out of sight. We shall often refer to the U.S. case, both because of this author's familiarity with the terrain,[4] and the usefulness of the American urban experience as a warning signal to Southern cities.

However, there is equally room for optimism. The American model is neither universal nor inevitable. European and Canadian contributors to this book are, on the whole, less pessimistic than their American counterparts. Perhaps most surprising, it is the Canadians (Toronto and Montreal case studies), *a priori* the closest in many ways to the United States, who are the most positive about their respective cities, in sharp contrast to the pessimism of the two American case studies. It is difficult to argue that differences between Canadian and American cities are explainable by fundamental differences in economic systems, levels of development, or the impact of (universal) factors such as deindustrialization and globalization. In other words, differences between Canadian and American cities (and perhaps also between European and American cities) are, it would appear, at least in part due to policy choices and different governance systems. It is these policy choices that interest us in this closing chapter.

In the following sections, seven policy choices are identified that can act upon 'exclusion' in an urban setting (negatively or positively). With the exception of the first, they largely follow from the six policy areas set out in chapter 1, although formulated differently. The emphasis is on learning from the experience (often mistakes) of the North. The cities of the South should be wary of blindly copying the urban models of the North. As in the preceding city case studies, we focus on *local* issues and policy choices, although reference to national policies is made where appropriate.

Policy Choice No. 1: Fluid Housing Markets and Residential Mobility

This first point is not really a policy *choice* in the sense of a set of avoidable policy options. Rather, the purpose here is to set the stage, stressing social and economic transformations that are essentially inevitable, the result of economic growth and technological change. Policymakers should be aware that certain modern trends, *a priori* positive, can have unintended effects and facilitate urban exclusion.

Let us begin with residential mobility. In simple terms, residential mobility refers to the urban resident's capacity to choose 'freely' in which neighbourhood he or she wishes to live. Thus, in principle, residential mobility should be seen as a good thing. The greater the urban resident's geographic scope of action, the more he or she has 'real' choices, and therefore greater mobility. The range of housing and neighbourhood choices will largely be a function of the available means of transport (effectiveness and cost); of the urban resident's income level; and, lastly, of the fluidity and efficiency of the housing market. Where housing markets are perfectly fluid (where it is easy to buy, rent, and sell housing units) and where the means of urban transport are extensive and affordable, the social and ethnic profile of neighbourhoods will be largely determined by the 'free' choices of the city's inhabitants.

Residential mobility will in general increase as a result of rising family incomes, coupled with the effects of improvements in the means of urban transport. Unlike in the pre-industrial city, residents are no longer constrained to reside close to their workplace. This transformation constitutes one of the principal factors underlying the physical expansion of cities, a universal trend, observable in the growth of suburbs located ever further away from the city-centre (see Policy Choice no. 7). Again, on the whole, this expansion of the urban perimeter may be seen as a good thing. Today, residents of most industrialized cities possess far more freedom of movement and are able to consume far more space than their grandparents, who often were born and died in the same small house or dwelling.[5] Surely, few would prefer a regime where people are forced, by legislative fiat or police command, to live in designated neighbourhoods against their will. The apartheid regime in South Africa was probably the most notable post–Second World War example of a policy restricting residential choice.

The introduction of 'free' and fluid urban housing markets is a fairly recent occurrence. The allocation of housing remained at least partially outside the framework of the market in most pre-industrial cities, most notably in Europe, even in societies already largely oriented towards market economies (Vance 1976). The emergence of a fluid housing market required not only a sustained increase in the level of income of the general population (property ownership was out of reach of the majority in most pre-industrial societies), but also the introduction of legal systems, with appropriate means of conflict resolution, defining property rights, contracts, and sanctions. The emergence of an efficiently regulated modern banking system, capable of sustaining the growing demand for housing mortgages, was equally a precondition. Such institutional reforms still often constitute the chief bottleneck impeding the emergence of a fluid housing market in developing cities. Here again we must speak of progress, certainly for the cities of western Europe and North America. Few would wish to return to a time when property was the exclusive privilege of a moneyed elite.

However, there is a negative side to this new freedom of movement within the city. Given the choice, human beings will generally show a tendency to prefer their own kind as neighbours. As noted earlier, residential differentiation by class or ethnic origin has become a universally observed phenomenon in modern cities. Precursor to the quantitative studies of segregation alluded to earlier, a new branch of social geography and urban sociology emerged during the first decades of the twentieth century, generally referred to as 'human ecology' or 'urban ecology,' but also known as the 'Chicago School' in honour of the city that was to be the object of analysis of its earliest pioneers (Burgess, Park, and McKenzie 1925). The term 'ecology' was well chosen, for, as do all animals and plants, the human ecology of the modern metropolis defines the rivalry between groups (or species) competing for the occupation of a given territory – urban space in this case. The occupation of space by one group means, by definition, the exclusion of another.

The 'exclusion' to which we are referring need not be the consequence of a conscious act of rejection or discrimination of 'others' (whoever the others may be). Exclusion within a fluid housing market is the necessary reciprocal of the 'natural' tendency of the various subcategories of the human species to congregate, to prefer certain neighbourhoods to others. Differences in wealth and power will necessarily mean that certain groups end up de facto excluding others, whether through the price mechanism or by other indirect means (see Policy Choice no. 5). The typical modern metropolis is made up of a myriad of neighbourhoods, each more or less defined by the social, and sometimes also by the ethnic, status of its residents. However, the degree of fragmentation (or its opposite, integration) is very sensitive to policy, a point to which we shall return. Unless policy choices are made to counter the 'natural' trend to fragmentation of urban space, the dynamics of residential mobility, rising incomes, and urban growth can result in the relegation of groups at the bottom of the social or racial ladder (the 'excluded') to designated less-desirable areas.

The message for Southern cities is clear, but also disquieting. The establishment of property rights and 'equitable' access to land and housing (issues stressed in the Nairobi and São Paulo case studies) are surely preconditions for inclusion and social sustainability, but they are not sufficient conditions. Flexible land and housing markets will facilitate the integration of marginal populations (often located in peripheral squatter settlements) into the urban fabric, but may in turn result in new forms of urban exclusion, which leads us into the six policy choices discussed below.

Policy Choice no. 2: Urban Highways and the Use of Cars in Urban Space

Modern means of urban transport are perhaps the most direct facilitator of the 'natural' tendency of human groups to distance themselves from those who are dissimilar. The motorization (increased car ownership) of urban populations is a universal trend. The first objective aspired to by many inhabitants of the developing world, once adequately nourished and lodged, is the purchase of a private car. Who can blame them? Here again, as with earlier references to increased residential mobility and freer housing markets, we must speak of progress.

However, the use of the automobile (as opposed to collective transport) in urban space can result in increased distance between social groups, as well as in reducing points of contact. The car, as a private means of transportation, allows its user to travel without any necessary direct contact with 'others.' If, in addition, the metropolis is streaked with elevated urban highways, as is the case in Miami, Los Angeles, and many other American urban areas, the driver can travel from one point in the city to another without ever observing neighbourhoods inhabited by other ethnic or social classes. Not only can urban highways act as effective physical barriers between the classes (or races), but their existence also literally allows car users to ignore the presence of other groups and lifestyles in urban space. A resident of Somerset West, a prosperous suburb of Cape Town, can drive into the centre of the city without having to come into contact with the (poor, mainly black) residents of the areas the highway crosses.

The car owner will also have a greater range of housing choices. Contrary to the user of public transport, the car user is not dependent upon the public transport network (bus, mini-bus, train, subway) for his or her choice of neighbourhood, but can choose to settle in zones accessible only by car – generally upscale suburban neighbourhoods (see also Policy Choice no. 7). The urban resident who cannot afford a car will very simply not have access to these areas. In many suburban neighbourhoods in the United States, shopping, school, work, and entertainment – in short, almost everything – is accomplished by means of the car, and it is not unusual for families to own two or three cars. Similar neigbourhoods are developing in many Latin American and African cities. It is not difficult to understand why one would rarely see the poor (or people of other races) in the shops and the streets of such car-centred suburban neighbourhoods.

Philip Langdon (1994) is particularly critical of the socially divisive effects of the car-oriented suburb, creating an isolated universe where the young seldom come into contact with 'others.' In such neighbourhoods, children who are too young to drive have to rely on their parents to get them around, thus reducing the complexity and diversity of their social space. But parents are often too busy driving to and from work (often over long distances) to act as chauffeurs for their children; no wonder so many children stay glued to their television sets.

The dominance of the car in American culture and in most American cities is not coincidental, but rather the result (perhaps unintended) of national policies. The price of gasoline (petrol) is markedly cheaper in the United States than it is in Europe, the result of much lower levels of taxation. Compared to some European nations (Italy, for example),

Figure 12.1 Petrol Consumption and Petrol Taxes, 1990

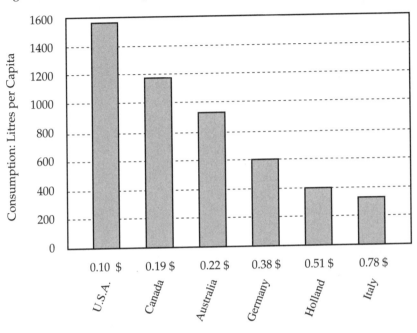

Taxes: Cents U.S. per Litre

Source: Drawn from *Le Devoir*, Montréal, 18 July 1995; based on IMF and
International Energy Agency Sources

taxes on gasoline are almost eight times lower in the United States. It is
not surprising that average kilometres driven and average petrol consumption are higher in the United States than in other industrialized
states (see figure 12.1).

More important, however, starting in the 1950s, coinciding with the
era of accelerated urban expansion, the federal government launched a
vast construction program of interstate toll-free highways, which now
criss-cross the United States. Two points need to be noted that distinguish American highway construction policy from many of its European counterparts. First, the network was and has remained largely toll-
free, constituting an implicit subsidy to car users. By some estimates,
taxes on motorists cover only 60 per cent of the real costs involved with
government-related road services (*The Economist* 1994). However, the

United States is not the only culprit in this respect. Highways remain largely toll-free in many industrialized states, including Canada.

Perhaps most important of all is the difference in the spatial configuration of highway systems. In Holland and Switzerland, as well as Germany and Italy (the latter three also impose heavy highway tolls), the national highway systems were largely designed to provide intercity road connections; that is, to provide transport links between urban areas, and not between neighbourhoods. Only rarely do highways in most European countries criss-cross urban areas, and are therefore of limited use for daily suburb–to–city-centre commuting. The American highway system, on the other hand, includes intracity highways, which allow motorists to move between city neighbourhoods. Greater Los Angeles, perhaps the extreme example, is cross-crossed by a complex web of appropriately named freeways (all toll-free) which constitute the main transport links between its spread-out patchwork of neighbourhoods.

In both Baltimore and Miami (our two American case studies), it is possible to drive directly into the centre of downtown using an urban highway. By contrast, no urban highways cross the centre of Geneva or Rotterdam, our two European cases. Architectural and heritage considerations aside, is it any wonder, then, that most European cities are still relatively compact, with lively, walkable, and socially mixed city-centres, while most American cities have long since expanded over wide areas, often leaving downtown in a state of semi-decline (see also Policy Choice no. 7)?

But, which road (pun intended) are Southern cities taking? The trends are not necessarily encouraging. The authors of the Cape Town and São Paulo case studies both deplore recent highway-oriented investment choices that favour car users. As both point out, these are implicitly subsidies to the rich (who own cars), the most telling example being the $1.3-billion investment in a highway tunnel in São Paulo reserved for cars, rather than in public transport (see chapter 8). Unfortunately, São Paulo and Cape Town are not exceptions in the developing world. The São Paulo story brings home the fact that all public expenditures necessarily involve policy choices, in this case between alternative modes of transport, which brings us to our next point.

Policy Choice no. 3: Intermodal Competition and Public Transport[6]

The various modes of transport in the city are necessarily in competition. If a resident chooses to take his or her car to go to work, this naturally means that he or she has opted not to take a bus, mini-bus, subway, or other means of collective transport. Both cannot be used at the same time. This means that any policy that facilitates the use of cars will necessarily weaken the demand for public transport. This lesson is especially crucial for developing cities. Intermodal competition is not always easy to recognize in the initial stages of urbanization and development. In most developing cities, the demand for public transportation remains vigorous, the majority not having the means to purchase a private vehicle. In Mexico City, where income and car ownership levels remain well below those for most industrialized cities,[7] the public-transport network is highly diversified, with a combination of *colectivos* (mini-buses), buses, and subway lines, the former two transport modes generally being delivered by private operators. Similar diversified systems, often with an impressive array of vehicles of different sizes, may be found in most Southern cities. This diversity reflects the continuing strong demand for public transport.

However, rising incomes threaten to weaken this demand. Car ownership and income growth go hand in hand. It is at this juncture in the development process, when demand for public transport is *still* strong, that policy choices are the most critical. It is when car ownership begins to rise sharply that the state, often without seeing the impending consequences of its actions, will choose to invest public funds in urban highways rather than in public transportation systems, often in answer to the calls of car owners stuck on increasingly congested streets.[8] Every public dollar invested in urban roads or highways will increase the relative attractiveness of automobile use.[9] If, in addition, as discussed earlier, private car users are not charged for the true costs of public infrastructures (roads in this case), and petrol taxes are kept low, the state will further increase the relative attractiveness of automobile use. The results can be anticipated. As car use increases, the demand for public transport declines. This is what has occurred in the majority of American cities after the Second World War (see figure 12.2).

Thus is often set in motion a vicious circle of decline (see figure 12.3): the quality of public transport services deteriorates as demand plummets; in turn, demand diminishes even further. At the same time, it becomes more and more costly to maintain the system as the number of users drops. Most mass transit is very sensitive to scale economies and to fixed costs. This in turn triggers price increases, which again will cause the number of users to fall further. Private operators (i.e.,

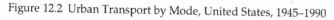

Figure 12.2 Urban Transport by Mode, United States, 1945–1990

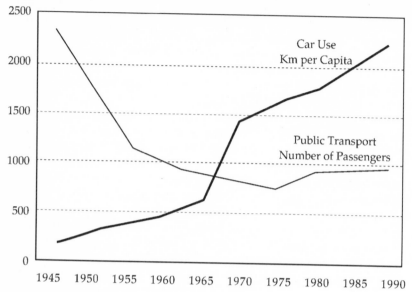

Source: Author's calculations on the basis of data in Mills and Hamilton 1994, Table 13.1.

colectivo or bus owners) will abandon the sector for other, more lucrative, business ventures. Most public transport systems in the developed world are today sustained by public subsidies.

Even public subsidies may not be sufficient to maintain the system, however, if the process has gone too far. In extreme cases, not unknown in the United States, the combined effect of rising motorization, car-oriented public policies, and land-extensive suburbanization (see Policy Choice no. 7) can mean the quasi-disappearance of public transport. In many American metropolitan areas, especially in the South and Southwest, public transport systems no longer exist, at least not in the sense normally understood by Europeans or Canadians.

The consequences for urban exclusion are major. First, what remains of the public transport system becomes the quasi-exclusive refuge of those without cars – the poor, minority populations, adolescents, and senior citizens (the 'excluded'). In short, two systems of urban transport coexist: one for the owners of cars, one for everybody else. As a general

Figure 12:3 Rising Incomes, Motorization, Public Transport, and
Urban Exclusion
Source: The author

1. City x, during the early stages of development, has an efficient collective transport system, much of it privately owned. Demand for collective transport is high because of low car ownership.

2. Incomes rise in City x. Car ownership increases. Demand for collective transport decreases as more residents switch to cars. Firms providing collective transport become less profitable.

3. Public investment in roads and highways (toll-free). Low fuel taxes and other taxes on car use. Car ownership and use increase further in City x. Demand for collective transport decreases further as incomes rise.

5. City x (now richer) is left with a two-tier transport system: (a) one for the 'included,' based on the car; (b) another for the 'excluded,' based on an inferior and subsidized public transit system, which will largely define where the 'excluded' can live.

4. Collective transport ceases to be profitable. Private firms leave the market or collapse. The quality of collective transport declines. Demand for collective transport decreases futher.

rule, the public system will be rudimentary. In a car-oriented society where the car is an indispensable tool for mobility, the geographic isolation of the less fortunate can be truly tragic. They are in essence denied access (or at least easy access) to the public and private institutions, recreational spaces, public services, and jobs located in the 'modern' city. Two cities coexist in the same metropolitan area: the 'modern' city nurtured on the car; the 'other' city dependent on other, more traditional, means of transport (including walking). The best hospitals, schools, and public recreational facilities will seldom be located in (or even close to) the 'other' city. This model of spatial separation, with local variations, is observable in the United States and Southern cities presented in this book, with the authors often using the expression 'dual city.'

The contrast with the European (and also Canadian) experience is significant. In most European cities, Geneva being a prime example, public investments in transit systems are a major element in the urban-planning and urban-governance process. Indeed, in the Geneva case, 'regional' cross-border institutions of governance are in part the result of the need to ensure the efficient management of public transport systems. Both Canadian case studies (Montreal and Toronto) establish a link between the creation of regional (metropolitan) governance systems and the need to finance public transport collectively. In all such cases, this implies public subsidies to mass transit, whether financed regionally or nationally, or by some mix of the two. The Canadian authors clearly think such subsidies to be justified. In both Canadian case studies, the maintenance of an affordable, hub-oriented, public transit system is deemed to be one of the chief elements explaining the apparent success of Toronto and Montreal in building socially sustainable environments. Both the European and Canadian experience underscore the importance not only of (competing) public-investment choices, but also of appropriate local-governance structures to finance collective goods, which brings us to our next point.

Policy Choice no. 4: Fiscal Decentralization versus Central Transfers

We refer here to the division of taxation powers and accompanying financial responsibilities between local governments (communes in Europe, municipalities in North America) and higher levels of government. Public services can be financed locally or via transfers from other levels of government, or by a combination of both. Fiscal decentralization empowers local communities and should make them more financially responsible and accountable. However, decentralization can contribute to urban exclusion where it is applied to municipalities *within the same metropolitan area*, specifically for the financing of basic social services. It is essential to distinguish between 'social' services, on the one hand, notably primary and secondary education, and health care, and, on the other hand, 'territorial' services, such as water, street maintenance, public security, parks and public spaces, and waste collection and disposal. The former are much more important than the latter for ensuring equality of opportunity and social mobility.

We shall concentrate here on primary education for simplicity's sake, but also because it is perhaps the principal public institution for ensuring the future social and economic integration of the young. In the majority of European nations, and also in most Canadian provinces, the financing of primary education is not the responsibility of municipalities. However, in most U.S. states, the financing of primary education is local, via local school boards that have the power to tax local residents. Most revenue is derived through local real-estate taxes. The income of school boards, and thus also the quality of local schools, is largely determined by the taxable wealth of their respective territories, which generally correspond to the boundaries of municipalities or similar entities.

In a metropolitan area divided into municipalities of differing social status, it is almost inevitable that the wealthy and the poor will attend different public schools, simply because of location. Such differences may be observed in the large cities of most nations. If, in addition, however, as in the United States, schools dispose of different financial resources, depending on the municipality's social status, then the incentive becomes even stronger for the wealthy to congregate in certain municipalities, thereby indirectly increasing the financial disparity between have and have-not municipalities. The differences between municipalities within the same metropolitan area in the United States can be impressive. Per-capita income in Baltimore city is only 64.3 per cent that of the suburbs (chapter 5). Metropolitan Chicago has more than 1,200 separate tax districts. In one jurisdiction, Harvey, a declining community, the local school board was able to raise $1,349 per primary school pupil in 1993, compared with $7,178 in wealthy Wilmette, also located in Metropolitan Chicago (*The Economist* 1994). Some financial redistribution may occur via the state to even things, depending on which United States state is involved, but the differences generally remain substantial.

Here a second vicious cycle is set in motion (see figure 12.4): as the wealthy residents (often whites in the case of the United States) of community x move to wealthier communities (municipality y in figure 12.4) with better-quality schools, the taxable wealth of community x declines. This in turn weakens the quality of local schools (or increases the taxpayers' local fiscal burden) and leads to the further flight of the wealthy towards community y. The final result: municipality x (often the central city in the United States) is left with an impoverished tax base, an increasingly deprived but also highly taxed population, and a poor school system. In the extreme case, where municipality x is chiefly composed of a single racial or ethnic 'minority' group, public schools can become veritable seedbeds of exclusion and violence. The grim picture which Marc Levine paints of inner-city Baltimore is by no means exceptional. Fear of crime, in turn, helps to accelerate the exodus of the white middle class to racially homogeneous suburbs. The percentage of metropolitan Baltimore's white population living in the central city went from 65 per cent in 1950 to 12.5 per cent in 1997 (chapter 5).

To understand the full exclusionary impact of fiscal decentralization, we need only extrapolate the reasoning just applied to primary education to other public services. In the extreme case where most public services are dependent on local taxation, their quality will depend on local wealth. In the absence of a regional system of equalization payments between wealthier and poorer municipalities of the metropolis, differences will often be compounded, following the pattern described in figure 12.4. Endowed with a solid tax base and a wealthy population, municipality y will have well-equipped parks, well-maintained streets and sidewalks, superior community services (swimming pools, libraries, and so on), efficient lighting and security services, hi-tech fire stations, and so the list can go on for other locally financed and managed public services. The portrait of community x will be quite different.

This is not the end of the story. Since community x disposes of a weaker per-capita tax base than its neighbour y, the residents of municipality x must support a proportionately higher fiscal burden in order to receive a comparable (if not totally analogous) level of services. In the end, the residents of x will pay relatively higher taxes than their wealthier neighbours. In addition, the lower quality of public services will equally affect the private sector and the cost of doing business. In neighbourhoods with less efficient fire-prevention and law-enforcement services, the cost of insurance (fire, theft, damage) will be proportionately higher. The risks of theft, bodily harm, and damage to

Figure 12:4 Fiscal Decentralization, the Quality of Public Schools, and
Residential Segregation
Source: The author

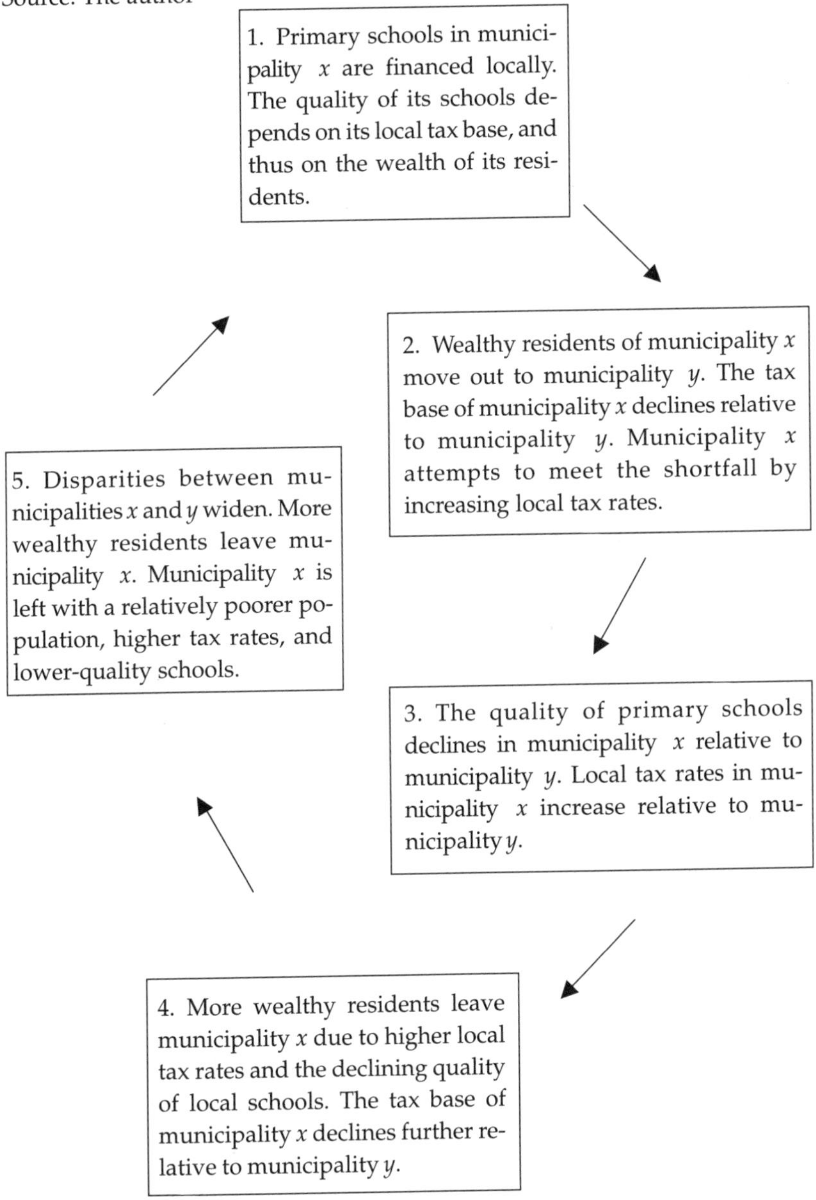

> 1. Primary schools in munici-
> pality x are financed locally.
> The quality of its schools de-
> pends on its local tax base, and
> thus on the wealth of its resi-
> dents.

> 2. Wealthy residents of municipality x
> move out to municipality y. The tax
> base of municipality x declines relative
> to municipality y. Municipality x
> attempts to meet the shortfall by
> increasing local tax rates.

> 5. Disparities between mu-
> nicipalities x and y widen. More
> wealthy residents leave mu-
> nicipality x. Municipality x is
> left with a relatively poorer po-
> pulation, higher tax rates, and
> lower-quality schools.

> 3. The quality of primary schools
> declines in municipality x relative to
> municipality y. Local tax rates in mu-
> nicipality x increase relative to mu-
> nicipality y.

> 4. More wealthy residents leave
> municipality x due to higher local
> tax rates and the declining quality
> of local schools. The tax base of
> municipality x declines further re-
> lative to municipality y.

property will similarly be higher. Finally, community x will undoubtedly find it more difficult to attract good teachers and good doctors to its neighbourhood institutions.

Here again, the contrast with the European and Canadian cases is significant. Although specific fiscal arrangements vary from nation to nation and province to province, the territorial equalization of social services is generally sought, with accompanying fiscal redistribution. Taking the Montreal case, primary education is centrally financed by the province on a per-pupil basis, with implicit redistribution. Thus, the quality of primary schooling is not linked to the local tax base. Health services, including hospitals, are equally centrally funded. In short, the quality of social services does not significantly vary according to neigbourhood. In the Toronto case, the current situation operates in a similar fashion. Note that we are referring to fiscal decentralization and not to the decentralization of decision making or management. It is entirely possible that local school boards, for example, enjoy an important degree of autonomy in the management of schools, even if they are centrally financed. This basically describes the Canadian model.

What lessons can be drawn for developing cities, besides the obvious conclusion of the need for redistributive mechanisms to finance social services? First, the current trend in favour of decentralization, promoted by agencies such as the World Bank, should be approached with caution. In many cases, centralization is preferable. Second, social sustainability at the local level requires appropriate national legislation, defining the roles and responsibilities of municipalities and/or regional governments. In short, national governments (or state/provincial in federations) must remain important actors at the local level. Regional urban governments will, for example, generally not come into being without central intervention, a point stressed in both the Toronto and Montreal case studies (see also next point). The Rotterdam chapter equally illustrates the essential link between national redistributive policies (in this case, for housing) and local social sustainability.

This, however, is not necessarily good news for Southern cities, precisely because of the weakness, not only of local government, but also of national governments. In all too many cases, primary social services (education, health, etc.) will be left to local actors, including NGOs, because the state cannot finance them, with similar socially divisive results to those described for United States cities. Many developing nations simply do not have the administrative apparatus or the political tradition of trust which are necessary preconditions for the efficient functioning of an equitable taxing system. It is a this vital juncture that the calls for full 'citizenship' and political inclusion, at the core of the Nairobi, São Paulo, and San Salvador case studies, take on their full meaning.

Policy Choice no. 5: Metropolitan Governance versus Local Autonomy

This policy choice is an extension of the previous point. However, as noted in the Baltimore chapter, the issue of metropolitan government (or its opposite, metropolitan fragmentation) is of sufficient importance to warrant separate treatment. The socially divisive effects of fiscal decentralization (see above) will be compounded in metropolitan areas that are subdivided into numerous autonomous local jurisdictions. David Rusk (1993) demonstrates, for the United States, that amalgamated metropolitan areas (with metropolitan-wide governments) are on average less segregated racially and show less dramatic income gaps between suburb and city than is the case with metropolitan areas that are highly fragmented. Thus, 1989 figures show that average income in the central city of Houston (part of an amalgamated metropolitan area) was 11 per cent below that in the suburbs; in comparison, in Detroit, a fragmented metropolis, incomes in the central city were on average 50 per cent lower than in the suburbs (Rusk 1993, 33). Both Rusk (1993) and Gregory Weiher (1991) argue that it is the fragmentation of United States metropolitan areas and attendant local autonomy and lack of redistributive measures that lie at the heart of the U.S. urban dilemma.[10] Along the same lines, Levine pleads in favour of what he calls 'socially just regionalism' as the only way out of Baltimore's urban morass.

It is not difficult to imagine the results of a regime where local autonomy is given primacy over redistribution. Mirroring the example of primary education presented earlier, the metropolis becomes a collection of 'unequal' socially and ethnically homogeneous municipalities. Municipal political boundaries become the equivalent of social and cultural boundaries, as indeed they are in many cities in the United States. In such a regime, citizens will vote with their feet, not only to choose the desired bundle of services and level of local taxation (to use the terms of Charles Tiebout's [1956] 'rational' economic model), but also to choose the desired racial and social group with which to live. Admittedly, this maximizes individual freedom of choice and local autonomy, but the long-term exclusionary consequences can be dramatic, as we seen.

Therein lies a powerful argument in favour of metropolitan governments or agencies encompassing the whole urban agglomeration (the metropolis), at least for the most socially significant and costly public services. By the same token, this is a powerful argument in favour of cost sharing of certain basic services. In the case of the Montreal Urban Community (MUC), which brings together two-thirds of the metropolitan population, police and public transit costs are the shared responsibility of the twenty-odd municipalities which make up the MUC. In the United States, highly diverse models of metropolitan cooperation exist, with varying degrees of success (see Weiher 1991; Rusk 1993). On the whole, however, American municipalities are more autonomous and less prone to cooperate (or be forced to cooperate) than their European or Canadian counterparts. In part, this can be traced back to the American political tradition of non-interference by senior governments (state or national) in local affairs,[11] very different from the European and Canadian model, where municipalities remain creatures of the central state, often jealously supervised from above. In addition, the social and racial fragmentation of the metropolis creates its own political logic. It is not surprising that the wealthiest communities (frequently also the 'whitest' ones) will often be fiercely opposed to projects of metropolitan integration or cost-sharing. Moving to South Africa, it is equally not surprising that the issue of metropolitan government is at the heart of the political debate around future forms of urban governance, as amply demonstrated in the Cape Town chapter. The old white municipalities of the apartheid era are understandably not overly eager to share their wealth with neighbouring black or so-called coloured communities.

In most nations, local autonomy generally implies the power to regulate land use and the built environment, which can be used as a weapon of exclusion under certain circumstances. Local governments can no longer openly deny residence to given population classes (blacks in the United States and South Africa, indigenous people in Latin America). However, even without openly practising discrimination, laws and regulations conceived with enough imagination can de facto achieve the same end. Local regulations governing architectural design and housing styles (frontage, height, green spaces) or construction standards may be so designed as to minimize the chance that certain categories of the population will move in. Local traffic control, parking regulations, and street design may work in the same direction. Finally, regulations to forbid certain undesirable land uses (heavy industry, dumps, and so on) can similarly be used as a means of conserving the 'exclusive' character of the municipality. Such prohibited land uses will thus be relegated to other municipalities whose political power to exclude is less or which simply cannot afford to exclude such land uses, given their weak fiscal base.

In developing cities, the fight by the 'excluded' for access to land and housing is often a fight against unjustly regulated, bureaucratic, and undemocratic local environments, dominated by local political bosses and patronage (see the Nairobi and São Paulo chapters). Here, again, we may ask if reform is possible without prior reform at the national level, or without central state intervention. The challenge of creating democratic metropolitan-wide governments, capable of regulating land use in a socially just manner, is compounded in developing nations by the rapid rates of urban expansion, with the expanding urban fringe often left to itself, the reserve of squatter settlements. In this case, exclusion is achieved, in essence, by keeping the 'others' outside the legal city, a Third World variant on the United States model of metropolitan fragmentation.

Policy Choice no. 6: The Spatial Distribution of Social Housing

The term 'social housing,' as used here, refers to housing financed, subsidized, or constructed by the state, generally targeted to the poor. We shall not concern ourselves here with the mechanisms for allocating such housing, but rather concentrate on the spatial dimensions. Social housing is not a major factor in most U.S. cities, and we shall thus not refer to the United States case under this heading. However, social housing, in various forms, is a major factor in many European cities, exemplified in this book by the Rotterdam case study. In the Dutch case, social housing accounts for approximately 50 per cent of the housing stock in cities such as Rotterdam and Amsterdam (chapter 7). The percentages are generally lower in most other European cities, with social housing more clearly targeted to the poor.

Social-housing policies are, by definition, founded on laudatory social objectives. Their initial intention is certainly not to promote social exclusion. As a general principle, social-housing programs seek to ensure adequate access to housing for low- and/or middle-income groups. In many cases, however, these policies have resulted in the de facto relegation of low-income groups to designated areas of the city. Since access to social housing is determined by income, social-housing estates run the risk of becoming socially homogeneous spatial units, avoided by other social classes. In cases where access is filtered through a political and bureaucratic process, entire social-housing estates may end up as the quasi-exclusive 'reserves' of identifiable groups; this is notably the case in France, where the groups are often of North Africans and Africans. In the Dutch case, such housing equally attracts high percentages of 'outsiders': Surinamese, Javanese, Turks, and Africans.

The exclusionary impact of social housing is very sensitive to the scale, architectural quality, and geography of the housing units produced. In this respect, the French experience, although not covered in this book, is particularly devastating. French social-housing estates are generally known by the acronym HLM, for *habitations à loyer modéré*. After the Second World War, the French government promoted the development of veritable HLM cities – massive housing towers covering many city blocks. Their generally low building costs resulted in estates that were often neither aesthetically pleasing nor particularly attractive as homes. As the French population as a whole grew wealthier, such housing corresponded less and less to the needs of lower- and lower-middle-class French people. They became occupied increasingly by poor immigrants, especially from the former French possessions in Africa. As the European French abandoned these estates, they have evolved over the years, in many instances, into true neighbourhoods of exclusion, comparable to the ghettos of U.S. inner cities. The levels of violence, fear, and resentment are often equally intolerable. Contrary to the U.S. model, however, HLM estates were generally built in the suburbs. Thus, urban exclusion is largely identified with the suburbs in France and not with the city-centre (Vieillard-Baron 1997).

The Dutch experience is far less dramatic than the French one, if only because the Dutch did not build the same massive apartment blocks. But, the spatial evolution of the population generally follows the same pattern, as native middle-class Dutch families move out of social housing into private owner-occupied dwellings, leaving the initial stock to immigrants and/or to the poor. Spatially, the Dutch model is closer to the American model in that social housing is largely concentrated in the central city (in chapter 7, the centre of Rotterdam).

What lessons can be drawn from the above? First, where the state wishes to subsidize social housing, it is essential not to concentrate units in a limited number of geographic areas. Second, the scale (height, number of units) should be kept small. Furthermore, in order to facilitate social diversity and the integration of social housing into the pre-existing fabric of a neighbourhood, it is important that such housing units do not 'stick out,' aesthetically or otherwise. The Montreal experience (chapter 2) is instructive in this respect. The authors of the Montreal case study note that the dispersal of social housing (generally small units) is one of the factors that explains the absence of ghettos in Montreal. The message for developing cities is clear. The subsidization of massive housing projects for the poor may answer a social need (see specifically the São Paulo chapter), but unless properly designed may later produce new forms of social exclusion.

Policy Choice no. 7: Should One Worry about Downtown,
Urban Density, and Urban Form?

This last policy choice relates to the presence (or absence) of metropolitan spatial planning as a socially integrating factor. The links with previous policy options are obvious, especially intermodal competition and metropolitan governance. The difference between the United States and most western European nations (and Canada) is major. The tradition of spatial urban planning (often from above), regulating land use, fixing densities, and designing regional transport systems is deeply entrenched in most of western Europe. The Geneva chapter is a good example. Most such planning exercises seek to regulate metropolitan urban form, generally designed around a strong and nodal city-centre. In both the Toronto and Montreal cases, metropolitan urban-planning and transport systems are explicitly core-oriented. Both metropolitan areas have very strong (socially mixed) downtown districts, with adjoining residential areas.

By contrast, land-use planning and controls are relatively lax if not entirely absent in many United States urban areas, as well as in the majority of large cities in Latin America. This laxity is particularly apparent at the expanding urban fringes, where city and countryside meet. Viewed in conjunction with the previous points (specifically metropolitan fragmentation and car-oriented development), the results are predictable: extensive modes of land use and more or less chaotic expressions of urban form. It is for example difficult to discern any 'order,' much less a planned order, in the development of the Miami or Los Angeles urban regions. A declining downtown, abandoned by the middle-class, is often a corollary.

In the United States, the lack of effective spatial planning has been compounded by metropolitan fragmentation and tax measures that promote the extensive use of urban land. The various incentives in the federal tax code, including the deductibility of mortgage payments, promote the overconsumption of housing and suburban land; taxpayers are also allowed to defer capital-gains taxes if they buy a new home of equal or greater value, which pushes buyers towards higher-priced houses, most of them on the edges of cities. On a strictly economic level, land-extensive and disordered models of metropolitan expansion compound the difficulty of profitably operating public transport systems, further accentuating dependence on the private car. Extensive and disordered models of land use increase the costs of providing public infrastructure in general (Blais 1995). The message for Southern cities is clear: extensive models of urban settlement are expensive.

It is the social consequences that most concern us here, however. Without any unifying metropolitan framework or incentives to consume space more rationally, the ultimate outcome will often be an urban agglomeration comprising a set of autonomous and separate communities, isolated from one another not only by social, but also by geographic, distance. Little may hold them together. Joel Garreau (1991) enthusiastically heralds the emergence of what he calls 'Edge Cities' at the periphery of major United States metropolitan areas. Garreau is referring to economically autonomous suburban communities with their own business centres, commercial areas, office towers, and cultural institutions. In short, Edge City residents no longer have any need to travel downtown. The four Southern cities examined in this volume all exhibit, in various degrees, similar tendencies towards the creation of spatially divided cities, with gated suburban communities as the ultimate modern manifestation.

Creating a Shared Vision of the City

In a spatially divided, suburban-dominated, culture the old central city (usually the historical core) can be abandoned and forgotten, left to the 'others.' In developing cities, the division is often between the suburbs (or rather, a suburban elite) and a downtown abandoned to informal street vendors and the poor. The circle is complete. There is no more need to have any contact with the 'others,' except perhaps as gardeners or domestics. Social life is restricted to activities by persons of the same neighbourhood and of the same social class. There are no more common public spaces; the city no longer has a centre. In fact, there no longer is a city in the sense of a public city, shared by all, with parks, squares, streets, and the symbols of a common urban destiny. Taken to the extreme, we see an *anti-city*: a hodgepodge of suburban villages jealous of their autonomy, bereft of a common centre and a spirit of shared existence. What remains of the downtown area is purely functional: a business centre defined by a line of office towers, where employees arrive at work at 9:00 am impatiently awaiting the 5:00 pm drive back home. Many downtown areas in the United States, but fortunately not all, have indeed been reduced to their most elemental 'functional' definition.[12]

The above is admittedly a caricature, but dangerously close to the truth in all too many cases. The danger signals, as noted earlier, are alarming for many African and Latin American cities, already deeply divided socially, now engaged in the triple process of suburbanization, motorization, and metropolitanization. The San Salvador chapter clearly demonstrates the precarious nature of the historical core in many developing cities. The symbolic and integrative role of the centre, as a shared space for all citizens, risks being lost without urban-planning and urban-design policies aimed at keeping the metropolis together. Civic identity and pride, and thus also the willingness to share, must rely on a minimal amount of shared social space. But how can such sentiments be nourished in the absence of shared public spaces, in the absence of social interaction?

The Baltimore chapter demonstrates the limits of pure spatial planning and investments in physical infrastructure in the absence of a common (metropolitan) vision of what the city should be. Let us quote Levine's concluding sentence in chapter 5: 'Without such a common vision, the centre cannot hold, and Baltimore's possibilities for socially just, sustainable development will be grim indeed.' This for a city heralded as one of the United States success stories of downtown renaissance. The message is unmistakable. Little can be achieved in the absence of a sense of common metropolitan citizenship. The need for political inclusion, of bringing 'others' into the system, runs through all the developing-city case studies in this book, a quasi precondition before anything else is possible. We have returned full circle to the issue of governance, of building a polity in which the excluded are included.

As the case studies in this book bear witness, building such a common polity at the metropolitan level is far from simple. Many modern trends point in the opposite direction. Cities are constantly changing and expanding. Once the wrong policy choices have been made (often unintentionally), their effects are often almost impossible to reverse: witness the continuing quagmire of the American Inner City. However, such policy failures carry useful lessons for the future. Let us at least attempt to learn from each other. As this first urban century draws to a close, we know now that some things work, and some things do not. Building socially sustainable cities is not a utopian dream, provided citizens and decision-makers are well informed and the political will exists.

Notes

Parts of this chapter are based on two earlier texts: 'Les sept péchés de l'exclusion urbaine: pourquoi des espaces d'exclusion surgissent-ils dans nos villes?' (1997) and 'Learning from Our Mistakes: Thoughts on the Dynamics of Residential Segregation and Urban Exclusion' (1999). The author wishes to thank Olivia Stren for her translation of the earlier French text.

1 The case of French social-housing estates (known by the acronym HLM) equally springs to mind (Veillard-Baron 1997). In recent years, these zones have often been witnesses to violent upheavals, with the police, in some cases, refusing to intervene (see also Policy Choice no. 6, below).
2 It is well known among researchers that so-called segregation indices are highly sensitive to city size. For an early example of the statistical analysis of residential segregation see O.D. Duncan and B. Duncan 1955.
3 Gregory Weiher (1991, 1) starts his book with the following sentence: 'I try to convince my students in ... Urban Politics that the United States is the most fragmented country in the world.' Weiher is referring chiefly to municipal fragmentation, but also to its social counterpart, points to which we shall return.
4 The author resided in the United States for seventeen years, specifically in New York, Philadelphia, and Los Angeles.
5 Comparing the average residents of industrialized and developing cities, those in Montreal or Toronto consume about twice as much housing space (rooms per person) as those in Cape Town or São Paulo, and about eight times as much as those in Bombay (Camp 1990).
6 By 'public transport' we do not necessarily mean publicly owned transport,

but any means of transport that is collectively used (buses, mini-buses, trams, and the like), whether the provider be in the private or the public sector. Thus we shall also employ the synonym 'collective transport.'

7 As a simple benchmark, GDP per capita in Mexico in 1994 was about one-fifth that of Canada, and car ownership per capita about one-seventh (1988 figures) that of Canada (*The Economist* 1990; World Bank 1996).

8 Of course, most politicians and high-level civil servants will themselves be car owners.

9 In some cases, however, investments in roads may also help public-transport modes; for example, the designation of reserved lanes for buses or *colectivos*. We shall not go into such details here.

10 Their argument is convincing, as many of the other policy choice areas, especially those linked to the use of the car (nos. 2 and 3), are also observable in Canadian cities.

11 Thus, Weiher (1991, 3) writes: 'The creation of units of local government [in the United States] is, for the most part, not supervised by any central government unit.'

12 The author can recall having searched, without success, for a restaurant open after 6:00 pm in downtown Dallas.

References

Blais, Pamela. 1995. *The Economics of Urban Form*. Report prepared for the Greater Toronto Area (GTA) Task Force. Toronto: Queen's Printer for Ontario.

Burgess, R.E, E.W. Park, and R. McKenzie. 1925. *The City*. Chicago: University of Chicago Press.

Camp, Sharon, ed. 1990. *Cities, Life in the World's 100 Largest Metropolitan Areas: Statistical Appendix*. New York: United Nations Population Crisis Committee.

Duncan, O.D., and B. Duncan. 1955. 'Residential Distribution and Occupational Stratification.' *American Journal of Sociology* 60: 493–503.

The Economist. 1990. *Book of Vital World Statistics*. New York: Times Books and Random House.

– 1994. 'Cities: Onwards and Outwards.' 15 October, p. 31.

Garreau, Joel. 1991. *Edge Cities*. New York: Doubleday.

Hohenberg, P., and L. Hollen Lees. 1995. *The Making of Urban Europe, 1000–1994*. Cambridge, MA: Harvard University Press.

Huttman, Elizabeth, ed. 1991. *Urban Housing Segregation of Minorities in Western Europe and the United States*. Durham, NC: Duke University Press.

Langdon, Philip. 1994. *A Better Place to Live: Reshaping the American Suburb.* Amherst: Massachusetts University Press.

Mills, E., and B. Hamilton. 1994. *Urban Economics.* New York: HarperCollins.

Polèse, Mario. 1997. 'Les sept péchés de l'exclusion urbaine: pourquoi des espaces d'exclusion surgissent-ils dans nos villes?' In *Terres d'exclusions, terres d'espérances,* ed. Antoine Bailly, 65–74. Paris: Economica.

– 1999. 'Learning from Our Mistakes: Thoughts on the Dynamics of Residential Segregation and Urban Exclusion.' Discussion Paper 99–01, *Villes et développppement.* Montreal, INRS-Urbanisation

Rusk, David. 1993. *Cities without Suburbs.* Baltimore: Johns Hopkins University Press for the Woodrow Wilson Center.

Tiebout, Charles. 1956. 'A Pure Theory of Local Expenditure.' *Journal of Political Economy* 82: 826–44.

Vance Jr, J.E. 1976. 'Institutional Forces that Shape the City.' In *Social Areas in Cities: Spatial Processes and Forms,* ed. D.T. Herbert and R.J Johnson, 81–109. New York: Wiley.

Vieillard-Baron, Hervé. 1997. 'Les banlieues françaises entre exclusion et intégration.' In *Terres d'exclusions, terres d'espérances,* ed. Antoine Bailly, 27–40. Paris: Economica.

Weiher, Gregory. 1991. *The Fragmented Metropolis.* Albany, State University of New York Press.

World Bank. 1996. *World Development Report and World Development Indicators.* Washington, DC: The World Bank.